# Santa Clara County Free Library

# INSTANT CITIES

# THE URBAN LIFE IN AMERICA SERIES

RICHARD C. WADE, GENERAL EDITOR

# INSTANT CITIES

## Urbanization and the
## Rise of
## San Francisco and Denver

GUNTHER BARTH

New York
OXFORD UNIVERSITY PRESS
1975

To Ellen

# Foreword

Nineteenth-century America was, as the novelist Harold Frederic observed, a "century of cities." The most obvious expression of this first "urban explosion" was the majestic rise of New York in the East and the miraculous quick presence of Chicago at the southwestern tip of the Great Lakes. But in the mountain areas beyond the Mississippi and further still along the Pacific slope, young towns sprang up in the most improbable places providing a focus for settlement and producing primitive urban economies among vast stretches of wilderness. These "instant communities" developed far in advance of the line of settlement, leading the report of the 1890 census to observe that it was no longer possible to draw an unbroken line through the West representing the thither edge of settlement. Rapid urbanization had ended the frontier era of the West. This volume deals with the crucial decades of that great transformation when urban centers sprouted in the unoccupied land beyond the farmers' frontier.

Moreover, in doing so Mr. Barth has placed the American phenomenon in an arrestingly broad setting. He finds the antecedents of far western urbanization in the ancient world where similar necessities produced frantic urban activity. Of course, the time span was greater and the numbers smaller; yet the process was strikingly similar. The "temple city" of Salt Lake had its analogue in many places and times; the mining town of Freiberg in the twelfth century foreshadowed the experience of Denver. And, of course, the commercial entrepôts of medieval and early modern times presaged the San Francisco of nineteenth-century America. The author thus produces a refreshingly new discussion of what is often considered to be a very modern development.

The author's interest is in the urbanization of the entire West—the vast stretch of plains, mountains, and valleys lying beyond the great Missouri. Here a primitive pattern of towns existed before the great sweep of the American people into the area. Santa Fe in New Mexico, Monterey in California, and Champoeg in Oregon represented the old, comfortable, and static urban life which was ultimately overwhelmed by the new forces. But, he concentrates most on San Francisco and Denver, the commanding metropolises of the West. These two were the premier "instant cities," rising in exotic settings and wielding immense influence over immense areas.

Though separated by nearly a thousand miles and the Rocky Mountains the two cities shared a single historical development. Both owed their early growth to the discovery of gold; both fed off the kinetic transiency of prospectors and speculators; both witnessed spectacular initial growth later fortified by the transportation revolution. Population figures were a measure of the swift change: San Francisco grew from a small town at midcentury to 56,000 in 1860; then to 150,000 a decade later, and to 300,000 by 1890. Denver's expansion was proportionately even greater. In 1870 the mountain mining center had less than 5,000 residents. Ten years later this figure jumped to 35,000; the 1890 census counted 106,000 people; and another 33,000 were added by the end of the century. In the twenty years between 1870 and 1890 Denver grew more rapidly than any other city in the country. And with a third of all Californians living in San Francisco in the 1870s and a quarter of Colorado's inhabitants residing in Denver, these two remote states were among the most urbanized in the nation.

Moreover, the internal development of the two cities bore a similar resemblance. Though San Francisco lived by maritime commerce and Denver by inland trade and travel, the social structure of each belied their locational differences. Each quickly produced its own economic and political élite. And they were proud of the fact, each publishing lists of the wealthy with estimated assets. Indeed, the sudden success of men from these new cities became part of the international social coinage—the *Frankfurt Gazette*, for example, declared John Mackay of San Francisco the richest man in the world, estimating his income at $25 a minute which exceeded that of Lionel Nathan de Rothschild and Tsar Alexander II by $5 a minute. But, the heights of power were always insecure. Only three San Franciscans remained in the top one hundred in their own town from 1851 to 1871.

If Denver and San Francisco shared success, they also shared the problem of growth. Young municipal institutions were too new and weak to handle the swelling population. Since many newcomers thought of the cities as bivouacs rather than communities, they resisted attempts to establish ordinary public controls or to pay for needed services. Municipal officials were unable even to maintain a tolerable order, hence almost coaxing vigilante movements, with their serious threat to civil liberties, into action. Only slowly did more stable forces assert themselves, and the rawness of young societies gave way to more settled and urbane constraints. John Jay had once observed in the early Republic that "it takes time to make citizens out of subjects"; Mr. Barth asserts that time was also necessary to produce what he calls "reluctant citizens" out of transient wealth-seekers.

It is this process that is the theme of this book. The "instant city" was in many ways unique, though the author finds analogues throughout European history. It owed its origins to a single factor; other elements encouraged growth; suddenly a city appeared with all the dynamism (and pathologies) of urban development. Even after the original rationale for its existence disappears—the end of the gold and silver boom in California and Colorado—the city's momentum is sustained by sheer numbers and new functions. The young metropolis spreads its power into the surrounding areas, ultimately bringing even remote places into its economic and cultural shed. As it does so, it ceases to be an "instant city" and becomes an "ordinary city," indistinguishable in most ways from older, more established urban centers in the East.

The fundamental agency of this change was the transportation revolution. The railroads tied the Far West with the old America, making it a part of a growingly comprehensive metropolitan system. Since Denver lacked water connections, its leaders were quick to appreciate the importance of transcontinental railroads. To be bypassed would have consigned the mountain capital to a permanent second-class status. With them, however, Denver would be the hub of a massive network of almost imperial proportions stretching over thousands of miles. San Francisco, at first complacent because of its historical orientations toward the Pacific, rapidly joined the scramble for rails thus adding an inland dimension to its economic empire.

Moreover, the internal aspect of the transportation revolution, mass transit, also related "instant cities" to their counterparts in the East. For both San Francisco and Denver began their population "take off" at the same time that the omnibus, horse-drawn railway, and cable car were introduced into older cities. This common heritage produced common characteristics. It laced the streets with tracks, encouraged the outward spread of the old downtown, created residential "suburbs" at the edge of the city, and developed the characteristic social geography of older metropolises. Social emulation accompanied physical likeness. The two western entrepôts even entered the booster sweepstakes by putting on extravagant international expositions. By 1890, a visiting Bostonian would have seen enough familiar urban objects and enjoyed enough urban society to feel quite at home in the "instant cities" at the foot of the Rockies or on the shore of the Pacific.

Other scholars have dealt previously with "boom cities." In this *Urban Life in America* series, for example, Roger Lotchin has looked intensively at the first decade of San Francisco, and Howard

Chudakoff has applied new quantitative techniques to examining Omaha's expansive years at the turn of the twentieth century. Yet, none has placed the analysis in such a broad context, nor attempted to compare such diverse urban experiences as Champoeg and San Francisco, Salt Lake City and Denver. Mr. Barth's arresting perspective, though lacking the intensity of other monographs, provides an important comparative dimension both in time and space. He sees the urbanization of the Far West as analogous to city building in earlier times as well as the common experience of a single generation of nineteenth-century Americans.

In constructing this thesis, the author has drawn on new and widely scattered materials rather than new techniques. It builds especially on a careful reading of newspapers, manuscripts, and public documents and, especially, on an extraordinary knowledge of the whole urbanization process from antique times. This book thus has unusual scope and is especially helpful to a generation afflicted with problems stemming from rapid, uncontrolled metropolitan growth. It is useful, if not wholly reassuring, to know that what is often thought to be new and contemporary is simply the most recent expression of an old process. Thus *Instant Cities*, like other volumes in this series, both brings new knowledge to an old historical problem while it furnishes a fresh perspective on contemporary issues.

Richard C. Wade

# Preface
## The Concept of the Book

Once upon a time, about one hundred years ago, the fog of the ocean and the haze of the prairies conjured up two magnificent cities called San Francisco and Denver. The aura of mystery evoked the cities' special character, their unique position in the United States, and their place among remarkable cities of the Occident. The following pages attempt to penetrate the surface of nineteenth-century San Francisco and Denver, in search of those special elements that combined to produce these two unusual urban developments.

In my attempts to assess the significance of San Francisco and Denver, I realized that what distinguished them from all other cities was the suddenness of their emergence and the speed with which they joined the ranks of cities that had taken centuries to evolve. Consequently, I began to call them "instant cities." By separating these two cities from other urban developments by the speed with which they moved from wilderness to full urban status I was able to come to grips with their development in the isolation of the wilderness of the Far West and to contrast them with earlier offshoots of far western urbanization. In particular, I dealt with three earlier types of settlement west of the great bend of the Missouri— the economic town, the colonial outpost, and the marketplace, and one variant of the instant city, the temple city of the Mormon Church at the Great Salt Lake.

The people who built San Francisco and Denver saved me from losing myself in abstractions. Their predicament ensured my awareness of the human foundations of cities. As I delved deeper and deeper into their search for riches and their struggle for survival, however, I discovered that their experiences were strikingly similar to that of the men and women in the Late Middle Ages who populated the new mining towns and trading centers of central Europe that emerged quickly in response to mining rushes and commercial expansion. Observations found in the fairy tales and chronicles of the Middle Ages touching on the problems of migration, the consequences of the destruction of the wilderness, the fickle nature of mining, the hazards of commerce, the routine of industry, and the building of cities paralleled those to be found in the accounts of early San Francisco and Denver. As I pursued my research further I found other examples of such instant cities as far back in Western civilization as the Hellenic Migration, about three thousand years ago. In our own day, Brasilia came to mind as a modern example. In each case, I was struck by the universality of the reactions of the individuals who fostered or were caught unawares in the throes of intensified urbanization and industrialization.

Obviously, there are still many differences between San Francisco and Denver, on the one hand, and earlier antecedents. Parallels between migrations, mining booms, commercial ventures, and city building in the thirteenth and nineteenth centuries ended abruptly in the face of the frenzy that accompanied the fulfillment of American manifest destiny and the modernization of all of the United States. But these distinctions further support my ultimate contention that San Francisco and Denver were not only unique exceptions to the American enactment of an age-long process that ultimately resulted in the concentration of the majority of people in cities but were unusual among instant cities also.

The concept of the instant city became an analytical tool that helped me investigate the effects of rapid urbanization on people. It also helped me gain a better grasp of some of the intricacies of writing urban history. The adjective "urban" is a convenient catchall for activities that do not fall readily into the many loosely drawn categories of historical enterprise. Frequently it is used to describe political, economic, social, and cultural affairs that seem to be as unrelated to a city as a meadowlark. Sometimes, there may be little harm in the careless designation. But elaborate definitions of sticky methodological problems arise from the indiscriminate use of the adjective. They demand the sifting of more material than most researchers can absorb or turn "urban" into nothing more than a label without a role in the analysis. Yet a definition of boundaries can only be drawn within the framework of a specific study. For that task, I have tested various events by their relation to and role in the development of instant cities, isolating those areas of endeavor that constituted the distinctly urban experience of San Franciscans and Denverites. As a result, I gained a different perspective on the nature of city life than I would have approaching the subject by a quantitative analysis.

A concept such as the instant city is, of course, an abstract construct. I point this out merely to express the necessary warning against allowing concepts to assume a reality of their own and block the meaningful analysis of sources. The concept allows me to bring out certain details of a complex development more fully, and thus to increase my ability to determine the significance of San Francisco and Denver to American growth.

In the perspective of strict analysis, one should not need to indicate that the instant city, from its beginning, accumulates general features until it becomes an ordinary city. However, the act of wrapping up an event is necessary because of history's obligation to tell a story. Whereas a good story has a beginning and an end, only the beginning of the instant city is clear-cut; the end is obscured as it becomes entwined in a new story.

In the same vein, the generation that lived during the birth and rise of the instant city is another abstraction, and it will be recognizable as such by the coming and going of people, thrown

hither and thither by the urban explosions. Populations are always in
flux, and that first generation is nothing but a device, not an actual
unit of people. It reveals the common experience of a diverse
multitude of men and women molded by the hectic rise of cities.

In essence, I am telling the story of people who rushed into the
unknown and built cities in their search for the good life. They
quickly brought about the inhuman conditions that then plagued
them and they did little to prolong the hopeful moments that kept
them going. They encountered obstacles bigger than themselves but
struggled on, resilient and alert, and survived as people through the
cities they sustained. I am struck by the universality of the ordinary
human qualities they preserved, in spite of their unique experience in
instant cities, but I have refrained from stressing that insight because
the study of history does not stimulate unguarded optimism.

My work has been made possible by assistance from various
quarters for which I am deeply grateful. I had the support of the
Committee on Research, the Humanities Research Fellowship Program, and the Department of History of the University of California
at Berkeley. A fellowship from the John Simon Guggenheim
Memorial Foundation and a grant from the American Philosophical
Society enabled me to begin formulating my research. A Fulbright
lectureship in Germany enhanced my perspectives on cities. In the
final stage of writing, a stipend from the American Council of
Learned Societies released me from academic obligations.

Help from the custodians of many libraries and archives aided my
research. In San Francisco I relied on the San Francisco Public
Library, the Sutro Library, the Society of California Pioneers, and
the California Historical Society. The California State Archives and
the California State Library at Sacramento and the Henry E.
Huntington Library and Art Gallery at San Marino made their
resources available. In Denver support came from the Denver Public
Library, the State Historical Society of Colorado, and the Colorado
State Archives. In Germany I am beholden to the libraries and
institutes at the University of Cologne and at the Free University in
Berlin.

I would like to acknowledge specifically my indebtedness to the librarians of the Bancroft Library and the General Library of the University of California at Berkeley, and of the Western History Department of the Denver Public Library. At the Bancroft, I was particularly fortunate in having the friendly assistance of a group of librarians devoted to their magnificent collection. I am especially grateful to John Barr Tompkins. Until his retirement in 1974, he always shared my interests, and I have benefited from his reading of drafts of the first four chapters. At the Western History Department of the Denver Public Library, Alys Freeze, Head of the division until her retirement in 1973, introduced me patiently to the rich holdings. She gave freely of her intimate knowledge of Denver and never failed to answer my inquiries, placing at my disposal the far-ranging knowledge of her splendid staff. Eleanor M. Gehres, the new Head, has continued that tradition.

My search for direction profited from conversations with my colleagues at Berkeley, particularly Hans Rosenberg and Woodrow Borah, and with my colleagues at large: Hunter Dupree, Brown University, Howard Lamar, Yale University, K. C. Liu, University of California at Davis, Arthur Mann, University of Chicago, and Richard Wade, City University of New York. My students contributed their interest and insights. At Cologne, I learned from discussions with Erich Angermann and the members of his Anglo-Amerikanische Abteilung des Historischen Instituts der Universität; in Berlin, I profited from the stimulating hospitality of Rudolf Braun, then Director of the Kennedy Institute and now at the University of Zurich. For several years, Sheldon Meyer of Oxford University Press has helped and encouraged me.

The manuscript improved as a result of assistance from Earl Pomeroy, University of Oregon, who carefully went through a draft of the first four chapters and provided detailed suggestions. My Berkeley colleague, Robert Middlekauff, also read that part of the manuscript. The last four chapters benefited from the critical comments of Rawson L. Wood whose incisive mind alerted me to faulty reasoning and poor logic. Marlene Keller, Catherine Scholten, and Michael Griffith tirelessly checked my quotes and citations. The Berkeley Institute of International Studies typed the manuscript, and for that friendly and inspiring gesture to errant scholarship I would like to thank Cleo C. Stoker and Bojana Ristich. William Bowen of the California State University, Northridge, combined his great talents as cartographer and historian and drew maps that capture the changing settings of the instant cities. In the final stage at Oxford University Press, the manuscript benefited immensely from the editing of Susan Rabiner and Ann Lindsay.

Two friends shared the work. Willis L. Winter, Jr., University of Oregon, sacrificed his time and paid attention to my sentences and paragraphs. He edited, and commented, and never lost his patience or wit, although at times I may have sorely tried both. My wife Ellen went with me through the instant city, after I had stumbled onto it, and came out of the adventure quoting poetry,

> Things are in the saddle,
> And ride mankind

and I dedicate the book to her.

G. B.

# Contents

# Introduction
## Living With Chance and Change

At mid-nineteenth century, San Francisco and Denver emerged in the wilderness of the American West. Within thirty years they became cities of 233,959 and 106,713 inhabitants, respectively. They swiftly adopted the life styles of great cities and determinedly extended their economic supremacy over vast areas. These accomplishments attest to their uniqueness even more strikingly than do the startling population figures. The rapid rise of San Francisco and Denver distinguished them from most other American cities, which matured from settlement to town over many decades and even centuries. In the Far West, the fierce tempo of life in these two cities set them apart from the calm pace of those towns that had earlier cut a few urban inroads into the wilderness; the casual disorder of San Francisco and Denver contrasted starkly with the planned urban experiment of the Mormon Church at the Great Salt Lake.

San Francisco and Denver were instant cities. They came into existence suddenly and flourished immediately. Magic seemed to account for their rise, but it was the discovery of gold that touched off the urban explosions that led to their development. The lure of easy riches attracted the masses of humanity who made the instant cities. The returns from commerce and manufacture sustained the momentum and made available even more capital which, in turn, fostered at these two sites the atmosphere and aspirations of urban centers. Ultimately, technological advancement overcame the physical limitations of the sites and the isolation of the wilderness, and pulled San Francisco and Denver steadily into the normal framework of American society and its national market economy.

In contrast to cities in general, instant cities came into existence Athena-like, full-blown and self-reliant. Some instant cities rose in response to the command of a ruler, the design of government, or the bidding of a faith. However, most emerged only when several conditions were met simultaneously. The presence of something valuable in or on the land, such as gold, silver, timber, trade, or people worth exploiting was one condition; the abrupt influx of people of diverse skills, motivated by personal gain, was another. Originally, the nature of the site was important, but with man's increasing ability to control his environment through technological advances, almost any locale could be made habitable.

All instant cities were transplants, but their roots were often widespread and diverse. They lacked traditions of their own and learned to adapt to their immediate needs the customs and components of the disparate life styles brought by the first settlers with them from distant lands. Thus the cities pieced together a mosaic of practices, largely borrowed from the past, but reflecting in their immediacy and usefulness the creativity of the new cities. The wealth or the power that launched the city, gold or despotism in the most extreme cases, supported sufficient order to keep the instant city viable as it developed into a mature society.

Instant cities, like the people who built them, differed from one another. No two were alike. But the differences among the varieties never obscured the distinctions that separated them, as a type, from cities in general. Ordinary cities resembled trees that grew haltingly, matured slowly, and decayed imperceptibly. They were integral parts of the widespread society that they served and, consequently, provided a focus for many aspects of life: seat of authority, center of culture, place of refuge, hub for transportation, communication, marketing, and industry.

In ordinary cities, custom and tradition reinforced the staid pattern of life, supported by time-honored laws upholding previous accomplishments. Unless precipitated by violence or disaster, commercial revolutions or industrial innovations, change came slowly and almost imperceptibly. The resulting transformation, stimulated by massive outside forces and not generated exclusively by the cities, affected the whole society. Urbanization and industrialization molded ordinary cities, too, but over a longer period of time and with less ferocity than in San Francisco and Denver.

These two cities stand apart as monuments to the ordeals of many diverse migrants who suddenly congregated in isolated spots and endeavored to find food, shelter, clothes, and happiness. The plight of the men and women who built these cities, almost overnight, was caused by processes so complex they were often rendered merely as abstractions: urbanization and industrialization. And yet these were ordinary people, and many aspects of their lives duplicated those of people in ordinary cities. Both lived through war and political conflict, cultural blight and depression, but the people of instant cities were affected less by the ups and downs of national fortunes than by the ups and downs of their immediate environment, whose quintessence was deterred by a receptivity and vulnerability to chance and change.

The residents of San Francisco and Denver were strangers to the wilderness they converted into cities and strangers to one another. Initially, they wanted to get rich quickly and to return home, not to build cities, but their very presence, in vast numbers, demanded the services that only cities could provide. They adapted to San Francisco and Denver as best they could the codes and customs of their former homes. Yet, they lived in a culture so totally different from the ones they had left that often the transition was almost unbearable. Almost everything they created was made to serve the moment and most of their early work disappeared or fell into disuse when the moment passed. Only when the wave of technology that they rode in overcoming isolation propelled their instant cities into the ranks of ordinary cities did San Francisco and Denver achieve permanence.

Fortune shaped the lives of the men and women who made San Francisco and Denver. Accidents reinforced the rule of change and heightened the reign of uncertainty. Without common traditions and customs, self-interest fostered social cohesion when the needs of property demanded organization. The concern for opportunity, stimulated by the dazzling promise and the blatant insecurity of the cities, curbed the effectiveness of government. In the absence of success, only the future mattered. It held out the promise of the completion of the cities as the ultimate source of personal prosperity. A past did not exist, and the present was continually rendered obsolete by change that sustained the development of the cities until the urban explosions spent themselves and the cities' uniqueness vanished.

Then the humdrum of routine replaced the chaos of chance and accident. Sudden change gave way to slow transformation. The dimensions of time claimed hold over the affairs of man. The residents came to recognize their history and, with it, their cities' past. The present shed its precarious position as a fleeting moment and gained stability. The future now ceased to be the capricious handmaiden of speculation that in the service of Fortuna warded off the cities' collapse with the casual promise of another morrow and another day. It held little more in store than ups and downs, mirroring the progress and decline of cities in general.

The struggle of the people of San Francisco and Denver amidst the concentrated throes of urbanization sheds light on the momentary intensity that forces generally stretching over decades and centuries can acquire when compressed into a generation. The residents of San Francisco and Denver tried to secure the social, political, economic, and cultural values that their counterparts in other cities found as a heritage of what appeared to be natural growth. The encounter produced shining cities. But the human suffering accompanying their rise also presaged the pessimistic assessment of city life as an agony leading to squalor and decay that defied rational solutions.

Like ships in the turbulent waters of the urban flood, the instant cities pointed a course, charted by audacity and imagination, to the hoped-for shore of urban tranquility and harmony. Tempered by conscience and reason, the people's audacity and imagination averted the cities' downfall and transformed imminent disaster into an ongoing struggle for survival. With the time to experiment and the will to endure the residents survived and slowly the cities' problems solved themselves by spawning new ones to consume the old. Despair kept alive the memory of people as the core of cities. Their essential humanity gave strength and hope for living with chance and change.

# INSTANT CITIES

# 1

## Variations of a City Type

Across the prairie flatness, the emigrant train toiled on a track stretched taut, horizon to horizon, like a "cue across a billiard-board." On either side of the laboring train, noted one of the passengers, "empty earth" faded into "empty sky." With each new hour, with each new day, the passengers saw nothing new, although they could see farther than they had ever seen before.

One of the travelers, homesick for the mountains of his native Scotland, recorded his disappointment. Crossing what appeared to be the endless plain of Nebraska he awaited the hills of Wyoming. But when the terrain did slowly rise, the grand emptiness of the plain merely gave way to "nothing but a contorted smallness." A night out of Laramie, he watched the sun rise, only to see it again "shine upon the same broken and unsightly quarter of the world." Through the seemingly endless hours, "down the long, sterile cañons," the clattering and steaming train became the "one spectacle fit to be observed in this paralysis of man and nature."

Despite his own quiet frustration with the sterile landscape, Robert Louis Stevenson, that emigrant train passenger, envisioned the process of track laying and railroad building and recognized that the completion of this railway had been the outstanding achievement of his age. "If it be romance, if it be contrast, if it be heroism that we require," he mused in August 1879, "what was Troy town to this?" [1]

The Transcontinental Railroad had actually been completed in 1869, ten years earlier. Yet it had taken the intervening decade for most to accept the reality of the change and to absorb the drama of railroad building itself. Two years before the joining of the tracks at Promontory Point, Utah, a commentator in the *North American Review* saw in the completion of the railroad little more than a technological accomplishment. In his view, the laying of tracks across the continent was an engineering problem that had been reduced to a routine task, a mere question of time, not involving any new principle of construction. He had missed altogether the dramatic impact of the railroad's ultimate triumph in America, the tying together in a complex physical and social relationship of two halves of a vast continent.[2]

Only later would Stevenson and others bring into focus those aspects of the achievement obscured by the preoccupation of an earlier generation with the technology of construction. Stevenson saw the laying of the tracks as part of a final clash between the Indian and white civilizations. He recognized the role of the gangs of laborers who provided faraway speculators a share in the spoils and in return made possible the passage of emigrant waves from the Atlantic to the Pacific. He sensed a new society emerging in the Far West, the first ground broken by ragged, polyglot railroad crews under the direction of men in frock coats.

But Stevenson's find of romance, contrast, and heroism along the railroad line deflected his view away from the rising cities that were sprouting in the West to rival the fabled Ilium.[3] For himself and for his contemporaries, towns would gain a life of their own, apart from their roles as stepping stones in the social and economic expansion of the United States, only in the distance of time. Yet, for all the towns that would take many decades to transform themselves from wilderness to city, there would be some that would telescope that process into the time span of a single generation. These few represented a unique type of settlement in the development of urban

America. Instant cities comes to mind as a name for this type of development. Although this term does not appear in the sources usually documenting the explosive rise of these towns, it rings more real than the "magic" or "fantastic" city used contemporaneously to distinguish instant cities from other rising towns.[4]

In the West, the second half of the nineteenth century was the age of city building. Inspired by the success of New York, Chicago, Philadelphia, St. Louis, Boston, Baltimore, Cleveland, Buffalo, Cincinnati, Pittsburgh, New Orleans, and Detroit as urban powers of the Atlantic seaboard, the Great Lakes, and the Mississippi Valley, many incipient communities of the West dreamed of future greatness. Numerous portly gentlemen, outside the pages of Mark Twain's and Charles Dudley Warner's novel, *The Gilded Age*, supported Colonel Beriah Seller's vision of an inland empire that would one day rival the East with flourishing cities crowning empty stretches. The frequent frustration of this vision by hard reality took place on countless bends along sluggish streams. The satire of the coming of the railroad to Stone's Landing and of the river boat to Goose Run revealed many of the delusions.

Still, the speed and complexity of American urban growth, even in those many small towns doomed never to achieve full urban stature, had been, frequently, surprising to foreign travelers. "Nothing earns our admiration as much as the rapid rise of towns in those parts of the American Union . . . twenty-five years ago . . . still inhabited by Indians," Count Adelbert Baudissin stressed in his Missouri immigrant guide of 1854. "We Germans," he confessed, ". . . are amazed at the progress of a town if, now and then, a few new houses are built, but we never see a new town in our fatherland arise as if through a stroke of magic." [5]

Although demographic, economic, and technological influences brought many a town into sudden being most of these towns never achieved the size and independence representative of the instant city as a type. Frontier settlements, outfitting posts, jumping-off places, transportation links, markets, and ports experienced a growth pattern far different from that of the instant cities. Many of these remained apart until the sudden wealth and population explosions spent themselves, and the equalizing trends of urbanization and industrialization drew them into the ranks of ordinary cities.

Although San Francisco and Denver were the distinct products of nineteenth-century American urban growth, the phenomenon of the instant city is as old as the process of urbanization in the Western world. At the time it was difficult for contemporary observers to recognize ancestors. Many eyewitnesses lacked sufficient concern, or knowledge, to see the process in a historical perspective. Some observers of the rising instant cities in the nineteenth century were so involved that they simply could not detach themselves sufficiently to analyze accurately what was happening around them. In 1860, the author of the first history of Denver attributed its swift development to American mastery of the practical arts, of which he thought none were better understood by his countrymen than that of town-making. He argued, illustrating his point with examples of western cities, that "this nation of town-builders" did in a few decades "what was formerly accomplished in centuries," and, now, the decades formerly required "are indeed becoming reduced to years." [7] In his vignette of rising San Francisco, the first governor of the State of California, Peter H. Burnett, recalled that he had "seen the events of several generations crowded into one." [8] Others were so preoccupied with recording their impressions that they did not strive for that felicity of expression and depth of analysis that enlivens descriptions of complex events. "But one short year since first these mines were known, behold, like magic, lo! a town is shown," a rhymester in the Meadow Lake *Morning Sun*, in Nevada County, California, marveled on June 9, 1866.[9]

A few bemused observers referred back to the classics or mythology to describe what they saw. A reporter of *Frank Leslie's Illustrated Newspaper* likened the growth of Leadville to a "Brobdingnagian mushroom," and the same urban boom inspired a correspondent of *Scribner's Monthly* to imagine that "the men who sprang from the stones Deucalion cast behind" would have built a close counterpart to Leadville had they "set themselves to make

America. Instant cities comes to mind as a name for this type of development. Although this term does not appear in the sources usually documenting the explosive rise of these towns, it rings more real than the "magic" or "fantastic" city used contemporaneously to distinguish instant cities from other rising towns.[4]

In the West, the second half of the nineteenth century was the age of city building. Inspired by the success of New York, Chicago, Philadelphia, St. Louis, Boston, Baltimore, Cleveland, Buffalo, Cincinnati, Pittsburgh, New Orleans, and Detroit as urban powers of the Atlantic seaboard, the Great Lakes, and the Mississippi Valley, many incipient communities of the West dreamed of future greatness. Numerous portly gentlemen, outside the pages of Mark Twain's and Charles Dudley Warner's novel, *The Gilded Age*, supported Colonel Beriah Seller's vision of an inland empire that would one day rival the East with flourishing cities crowning empty stretches. The frequent frustration of this vision by hard reality took place on countless bends along sluggish streams. The satire of the coming of the railroad to Stone's Landing and of the river boat to Goose Run revealed many of the delusions.

Still, the speed and complexity of American urban growth, even in those many small towns doomed never to achieve full urban stature, had been, frequently, surprising to foreign travelers. "Nothing earns our admiration as much as the rapid rise of towns in those parts of the American Union . . . twenty-five years ago . . . still inhabited by Indians," Count Adelbert Baudissin stressed in his Missouri immigrant guide of 1854. "We Germans," he confessed, ". . . are amazed at the progress of a town if, now and then, a few new houses are built, but we never see a new town in our fatherland arise as if through a stroke of magic." [5]

Although demographic, economic, and technological influences brought many a town into sudden being most of these towns never achieved the size and independence representative of the instant city as a type. Frontier settlements, outfitting posts, jumping-off places, transportation links, markets, and ports experienced a growth pattern far different from that of the instant cities. Many of these would-be Western metropolises enjoyed temporary success as people passed through on their way to some distant and more attractive goal. Most of these communities with early promise of becoming instant cities degenerated as urban centers when they failed to hold a permanent population capable of producing wealth. Others managed a meager existence until they were rescued from oblivion by tourism and nostalgia.

San Francisco and Denver, however, rising in isolation, far from their neighbors, gained significance so quickly that from the beginning they were ultimate destinations for migrants as well as bases for hinterlands. Whereas small groups of migrants had long moved down from the Appalachians along the Ohio River, drifted past the Great Lakes, and trickled across the Plains, tidal waves of immigrants flooded San Francisco and Denver, the immediate approaches to the riches of California and Colorado.

The rise of these two instant cities, special as they were, in the second half of the nineteenth century simply highlighted the emergence of urban society in the Far West. The quest of the Gilded Age for profitable ventures made symbiotic town building and the exploitation of natural resources. Mining, ultimately one of the most destructive of extractive industries, set loose a flood of wealth that drew thousands of people into western cities. Between 1860 and 1910, their enterprise contributed to an increase in the number of Americans living in communities of 2,500 inhabitants or more from 20 per cent of the population to 46, while the total urban population grew from 6 million to 42 million. Scores of new regional centers appeared as a result of intensified rivalry for control of hinterlands.[6]

The mining booms in the vicinity of Denver and San Francisco instantaneously produced an economic base for a population composed of a great variety of people of different origins and social positions. To pursue their goal of getting rich quickly these miners all needed tools and equipment, as well as food, clothing and shelter. The mere presence of great numbers of people in the gold fields stimulated the flow of commerce and the emergence of emporia—

supported by dues merchants paid for these new business opportunities—and turned mining towns into commercial centers, converting mineral riches into mercantile wealth.

In addition, gold and silver not only attracted diverse groups of people and spawned a style and tone of life imitative of that of large eastern cities but also produced an urban culture as well. Newcomers brought to the instant cities the various patterns of urban life they had known before moving west. Familiar with, and used to, the amenities of cities, they exerted pressures that hastened the maturing of urban societies characterized by burgeoning social, economic, and cultural services. This flowering of urban life stimulated by the sudden riches, coupled with a search for social cohesion and cultural identity, set the instant city apart from the score of other western towns developing rapidly during the second half of the nineteenth century as well as older cities that had grown quickly in earlier phases of American history.

Because their rise coincided with the industrialization and urbanization of the entire country, instant cities were, as well, thrown full force into the contemporary urban problems of their eastern equivalents. In San Francisco and Denver, the population problems plaguing these eastern American cities in the second half of the nineteenth century were particularized by the influx of formerly rural Americans who had not yet experienced industrial development. The plight of those newcomers, exposed to city life for the first time, gave urgency to the search for an intensified technology adequate to the demands of rapid urbanization. Their acute needs exposed the stresses and strains that accompanied the adaptation of the simple devices of rural democracy to the practical requirements of big-city politics. As these newcomers groped for a meaningful adjustment to urban life their unique experience led them beyond the mere imitation of eastern urban societies and produced a distinct instant city culture.

These factors set San Francisco and Denver apart from other towns in the history of urban growth in the United States. Both cities remained apart until the sudden wealth and population explosions spent themselves, and the equalizing trends of urbanization and industrialization drew them into the ranks of ordinary cities.

Although San Francisco and Denver were the distinct products of nineteenth-century American urban growth, the phenomenon of the instant city is as old as the process of urbanization in the Western world. At the time it was difficult for contemporary observers to recognize ancestors. Many eyewitnesses lacked sufficient concern, or knowledge, to see the process in a historical perspective. Some observers of the rising instant cities in the nineteenth century were so involved that they simply could not detach themselves sufficiently to analyze accurately what was happening around them. In 1860, the author of the first history of Denver attributed its swift development to American mastery of the practical arts, of which he thought none were better understood by his countrymen than that of town-making. He argued, illustrating his point with examples of western cities, that "this nation of town-builders" did in a few decades "what was formerly accomplished in centuries," and, now, the decades formerly required "are indeed becoming reduced to years." [7] In his vignette of rising San Francisco, the first governor of the State of California, Peter H. Burnett, recalled that he had "seen the events of several generations crowded into one." [8] Others were so preoccupied with recording their impressions that they did not strive for that felicity of expression and depth of analysis that enlivens descriptions of complex events. "But one short year since first these mines were known, behold, like magic, lo! a town is shown," a rhymester in the Meadow Lake *Morning Sun*, in Nevada County, California, marveled on June 9, 1866.[9]

A few bemused observers referred back to the classics or mythology to describe what they saw. A reporter of *Frank Leslie's Illustrated Newspaper* likened the growth of Leadville to a "Brobdingnagian mushroom," and the same urban boom inspired a correspondent of *Scribner's Monthly* to imagine that "the men who sprang from the stones Deucalion cast behind" would have built a close counterpart to Leadville had they "set themselves to make homes." [10] Unwittingly, this last correspondent reached back to an appropriate source when he alluded to the son of Prometheus who survived the deluge to become the ancestor of a renewed human race, because the earliest examples of instant cities are to be found in that phase of human development when Greek legends passed into the consciousness of history. The dawn of Western urban civilization produced one of the first variations of the instant city and furnished an early antecedent to the variant of the type that occurred in California and Colorado.

In contrast to the rise of instant cities in the nineteenth-century American West, the rise of these ancient counterparts was intimately linked to the power of a particular group or individual. Within the context of directed migrations, planned colonization, royal designs, and imperial visions, the voice of command took the place of mineral deposits and economic enterprises as the force that brought men together in a new setting. Authority secured the place, ordered and embellished its life, and produced that immediate level of culture associated with instant cities. Merchants expanded their operations to take advantage of these new markets until finally the power of merchants supplanted the command of empire builders in new colonization ventures. At that point the instant city as emporium emerged.

Both forms, the instant city as an instrument of imperial design and the instant city as emporium, direct attention to yet another ancient form, the instant mining town. Brought to life by the lure of sudden treasure, the instant city as mining town developed, unlike its predecessors, fully exposed to the free interplay of social, economic, and political forces. A discussion of these three variants and the long line of heirs they sired furnishes a strong historical background to an examination of the new variant epitomized in the United States by San Francisco and Denver, mining towns and emporia brought to life by the immediate wealth of mining booms and sustained through the steady need for supplies required by these mining operations.

Accelerated urban growth brought forth instant cities from Mycenaean times to the Hellenistic Age, when the Greeks ringed the

Mediterranean world with towns of colonists sent out from Greece and Asia Minor. As early as the fifth century, B.C. records of instant cities can be found, but tantalizingly little evidence illuminates their development. Most documented events, like treaties and interventions, represented exceptional conditions and not the daily life.[11] However, a glimpse at the history of Greek colonization provides a few generalizations concerning ancient instant cities.

Pressured by overpopulation and a need for land, primarily from the eighth century B.C. on, the Greeks, during their great migration, aimed at establishing "self-sufficient Greek *poleis*, with enough land to feed their population."[12] They achieved this end through territorial conquest, negotiations with the native population, or through a combination of these methods. Once planted, the colonies became full-fledged cities, attracting additional people through their own strength. They grew, "apart from the rapidity of the development," politically and socially more or less like their mother cities, with various degrees of autonomy.[13] The cultural life of the new cities flourished immediately. Normally the colonies continued the "cults, calendar, dialect, script, state offices and citizen divisions" of their mother cities.[14] During the great colonizing period of the seventh and sixth centuries B.C. both state and private enterprise sent out an estimated average of one colony per year.[15]

The development of the *apoikia*, the planted city of the great Hellenic migration, awakened statesmen and governments to the vast political potential of systematic colonization. On the eve of the Hellenistic Age, as the instant city as instrument of empire was developing, Plato reflected on what he saw as the political and social advantage to the mother society from this type of colonization. "When men who have nothing, and are in want of food, show a disposition to follow their leaders in an attack on the property of the rich," the philosopher mused, "these, who are the natural enemies of the State, are sent away by the statesman in as friendly a spirit as possible; and this dismissal of them is euphemistically called a colony."[16] The strategic importance of instant cities in statecraft and in warfare, their possible roles in commerce and in the exploitation of natural resources, continued to intrigue politicians and thinkers in the Greek world.

Alexander and his successors, examining the Greek prototype of the instant city as well as the insights of Isocrates and Aristotle, put this information to good use.[17] Alexander is said to have founded seventy cities—of these twenty-five are known for certain to be his creations. He initiated a vast scheme of colonization in the Near and Middle East that established him as the greatest city builder of all time. Interested in control and uniformity, he deliberately modified the *apoikia* of the Hellenic age to meet the requirements of his personal vision. He operated with mixed groups of settlers, among them Greek mercenaries and army veterans, from disparate areas, and relied no longer on people from a single mother city on the Mediterranean coast. Designed for strategic reasons and to advance the "fusion of Europe and Asia on the basis of Greek culture," Alexander's instant cities were cultural and political outposts ruled by colonial governors responsible to Alexander. The traditional autonomy of the Hellenic colonies was subordinated to insure the success of his imperial vision.[18]

A few of his creations, really new towns, represented the variant in its purest form. Although many settlements turned existing sites and royal residences into cities and others enlarged and hellenized old settlements, certain new towns, carrying Alexander's name from the Nile to the Indus, indeed, sprang into existence overnight. At Alexandria the Farthest, the present Chodjend in Turkestan, founded as a defense post against the Sogdianian nomads in 329 B.C., within twenty days the mud walls were finished and the city was occupied by veterans and disabled soldiers.[19] Among all of Alexander's cities, Alexandria on the Mediterranean in Egypt, his first great urban creation, was the model and inspiration for his own subsequent developments, as well as for the far-reaching urban designs of his successors.[20]

Within literary tradition, of course, there are many rivals to Alexandria. In fact, almost any city that inspired or captured the imagination of men has been associated with its emperor, king, or national hero. The muses singled out the Jerusalem of David, the Babylon of Nebuchadnezzar, and the Rome of Romulus. Some cities became so closely tied to the action or name of a ruler that their actual origins were ignored when these interfered with the more auspicious identification. Even when a political leader seized upon an existing settlement instead of finding a new site, the evolving conglomerate often came to be viewed as his creation, an instant city.

Succeeding generations quickly cashed in upon the tremendous political and personal power that attached itself to the founder of an instant imperial city. In 324 A.D., Emperor Constantine gained control over the Roman Empire and set out to build his own city, Constantinople. Although his original plans were for Naïssus or Nish, his birthplace, once he saw the city of Byzantium it became his choice. Fortifications were begun and in a few years his capital was complete. "New Rome which is Constantinople" remained the city's official name until the Turkish conquest in 1453. It symbolized the transformation of the Roman Empire into the Byzantine Empire.[21]

Likewise, Charlemagne created Aix-la-Chapelle as the symbol of the birth of the Occident. Contemporaries often called it the new Jerusalem and the second Rome.[22] The city was strategically located astride the Carolingian lines of communication, both as a base for the Saxon war and as the center of the Civitas Dei that Charles believed he had set up. At the same time its location emphasized the Frankish character of his empire. At a time when fully developed cities flourished in Western Europe, Charlemagne established a cultural and administrative center in the setting of a rustic world marked by an aversion to urban life.[23]

It was a group of cities in northern Italy, the Lombard League, that sponsored an instant imperial city to foil the ambitious flights of fancy of a latter-day Charlemagne, Frederick Barbarossa. In 1167, as a visible sign of its urban might, the Lombard League supported the unification movement of villages in the Po Valley and then helped build a city strong enough to withstand an expected siege by the emperor's army. When Rome closed its gates to Barbarossa's archenemy, Pope Alexander III, the League came to the pontiff's defense, offering him asylum. In defiance, it named this asylum Alessandria as a lasting reminder of the League's liberation from the tyrannical Barbarossa.[24]

St. Petersburg, an instant imperial city founded in a desolate location by Peter the Great, symbolized the opening of Russia to Western influences. Determined to modernize his country, Peter left a flourishing populous capital with numerous government buildings in favor of a wooded area on the banks of the Neva, amidst the Finnish moors. In 1703, when he transferred the imperial residence there from Moscow, the site lay in a province ruined by war and actually, in point of law, the property of his powerful Swedish enemy. Although the czar failed to establish on the Baltic a copy of his beloved Amsterdam, St. Petersburg successfully won out as the imperial center of Russia. Through the new city, elements of Western culture infiltrated Russian society and intensified the rapid changes that produced the new Russia of the Enlightenment.[25]

In comparison with Peter's urban experiment, the beginnings of Karlsruhe appeared like a bit of comic relief following a dramatic struggle. They accentuated the role of personal whim, which was subdued by the magnitude of the czar's herculean undertaking. In 1715, Margrave Charles William of Baden-Durlach, unhappy with the citizens of his residence and family town of Durlach, was inspired by the construction of a new hunting lodge in the lovely Hardtwald to lay out a rival city around it. Fanning out from the lodge, avenues were cut into the forest. When he moved his chancellery to the new site in 1718, Charles's Rest became not only the cultural center but also the administrative center of his principality.[26]

The transfer of offices and administrators to a newly laid out town site on the Potomac assured the success of the instant city as an instrument of statecraft in the United States. In 1800, the arrival of government records and the belongings of federal officials carried by boat from Philadelphia to Washington, D.C., gave meaning to the groups of buildings scattered over the four-mile expanse. The houses had been erected according to the federal commissioners' code in an area covered, a decade earlier, by woods, orchards, and fields.

The capital was an anomaly among the cities of the United States, since it did not grow on a commercial foundation. It represented the republican form of that great tradition in Western civilization that utilized instant cities for the purpose of empire. The founders of Washington, familiar with the great cities of antiquity and of Europe, envisioned their instant city on the Potomac not only as the useful and necessary seat of government and commerce, but also as the beautiful and dignified capital symbolic of the ideals of their young republic.[27]

These classic examples: the elevation of Constantinople to capital of the Roman world, the selection of Aix-la-Chapelle as center of the Carolingian Empire, the establishment of Alessandria by the Lombard League, the creation of St. Petersburg, the founding of Karlsruhe, and the building of Washington, D.C., all substantiate the value of the instant city in statecraft. The men who built these cities reflected a boldness in planning that forewent established sites and used unbroken urban ground if it advanced the political design. Constantinople, Aix-la-Chapelle, and Alessandria still relied on proven sites, but St. Petersburg, Karlsruhe, and Washington, D.C. flourished on new land. Together, these creations perpetuated the success of the instant city as instrument of imperial design up to the beginning of the nineteenth century, and Singapore, Hong Kong, Shanghai, New Delhi, Canberra, and Brasilia extended the phenomenon into our days.[28]

Other variations of the instant city began to appear within the context of the feudal world of the High and late Middle Ages. Two of these, the instant city as emporium and the instant city as mining town, foreshadowed some of the particular characteristics of urban life displayed centuries later by San Francisco and Denver. In fact, the so-called eras of feudalism and of capitalism contain many common elements, and a comparison of these elements enriches the historic dimension to the urban growth that took place in the American West.

The instant city as emporium or mining town appeared because of, and in response to, the population shift from Western Europe into central and Eastern Europe and ultimately into the New World.[29] In some instances, the activities of long-distance traders and the rush of miners following the discovery of gold and silver in the twelfth century created towns. Those who populated the newborn settlements came with the hope of finding a better life. Soon, king and bishop, as well as lesser territorial lords, competed with one another, and at times collaborated, to open up vast areas east of the Weser River that had barely known the plow.[30] Germans, Danes, and Poles sometimes chose to hide their specific goals in the guise of a religious crusade.[31]

The migrations stimulated thought and action, which, in turn, perfected the process of town-making. Ideas on the arrangement of the town as a physical grouping of people, as a commercial and manufacturing center, and as a way of life naturally accompanied the merchants, miners, and colonists on their ventures. These ideas facilitated and accentuated the rise of instant cities as emporia and mining camps.[32] "The oldest, most important and influential cities of our country," a historian of the Kingdom of Saxony concluded, "are without exception deliberately planned new towns." [33]

By the beginning of the twelfth century, the development of a prototype of *the* medieval city for transplantation was a prerequisite to further urban expansion. In the second half of the century the know-how had been formalized. The method for laying out the sequence of planted towns that extended eastward was created, and produced, consequently, commercial and industrial communities independent of agricultural settlements, frequently along the lines of the great continental trade routes. With royal blessing, ambitious territorial lords and enterprising merchants brought into being a scheme of urban planning. The privileges granted by the lords supported the burghers of the emerging cities, and the urban centers, in turn, increased the territorial control of the lords.[34]

Merchants, primarily from Westphalia, took over the projects of nobles and established Lübeck, at the extreme southeast corner of the Baltic, as the gateway to long-distance trade to northeastern Europe. A few years later, these merchants expanded their activities to Visby on Gotland, and, in 1201, to Riga in Latvia.[35] In the middle of the twelfth century, Vienna was thriving again, on the ruins of a Celtic settlement and a Roman garrison, with support from the commercially oriented Babenbergers. It served as a way station for merchants from Regensburg who followed the Danube through Hungary en route to Kiev.[36] Outside the realm of the Holy Roman Empire the year 1253 marked the inception of a period of large-scale urban planning by Polish princes, which quickly led to a flourishing urban life.[37]

Although colonists had begun to move east in Charlemagne's time, it was during the late High Middle Ages, from the twelfth century onward, that German settlers, advancing into central and northeastern Europe, capitalized on the urban components of their culture.[38] New urban communities flourished on the rapid transplantation of town laws, architectural forms, and the basics of city planning. As more towns sprang up, the accumulated experience quickly turned the raw cities into better places to live. And instant cities became instanter as well as better—generally speaking. In the twelfth century alone, there arose in central Europe in rapid succession new and relatively full-blown communities such as Chemnitz (1143), Lübeck (1143, 1158), Schwerin (1160), Leipzig and Brandenburg (before 1170), and Jüterbog (1174). Commonly, their respective populations stemmed from Old Germany; however, by the first half of the thirteenth century these towns were sending out colonies of their own.[39]

Feudalism, by its very nature, prevented both the older German towns and the rapidly growing new ones from acquiring that political and territorial might that Italian cities like Venice, Pisa, Milan, and Genoa had achieved on the eve of the First Crusade. The residents of the mother cities in Germany were not fully sovereign even within their own walls; and the instant cities that members of their merchant class had created in central and eastern Europe flourished only through the privileges granted by the German or Slavic princes.

Feudalism played a role analogous to the federalism of the United States that allowed the free-for-all ambiance that stimulated the urban explosion of the nineteenth century but bound the emerging towns as political dependents to states dominated by rural legislators.

Sanction for the founding of towns in the twelfth century resided with territorial lords, but with the burgeoning of mercantile centers in Old Germany the initiative frequently was taken by the upper stratum of merchants. Through their involvement in long-distance trade, these merchants realized that instant cities could enhance the eastward expansion of commerce.[40] The deliberate extension of a proven process of urban settlement as well answered the marketing needs of the German emigrant peasants. The farther away colonization advanced from its base in Old Germany and from the trading towns established in the initial phase of the migration, the more the peasants clamored for markets in which they could sell their goods and buy necessities. Towns were attracted to a region by these increasing demands from the countryside for urban services, particularly if the logistics of long-distance commerce had not touched the area with its trade routes.[41]

The process of urban expansion profoundly influenced German colonization in central and eastern Europe in conjunction with the activities of German and Slavic lords, and knights and monks, who used the new cities to their own advantage. The instant emporia cities created by merchants as centers of long-distance trade fused with the growing Slavic commercial centers that antedated them. The new towns became the foci of large mercantile transactions, and the old markets preserved their significance as legally recognized towns enjoying special privileges.[42]

A vigorous debate has taken place amongst scholars of the Middle Ages as to the impelling factors in the rise of instant cities. Some scholars cited the evolutionary growth of Slavic markets into towns, others defended the crucial role of the colonial towns founded by privileged German colonists, and yet others suggested that Slavic princes summoned German colonists, handed their markets over to newcomers who, in turn, built colonial towns where once had been

only "an empty market place and a small enclave of foreigners." [43] In
the 1920s, an American scholar expanded the controversy when he
saw parallels between the German eastward colonization and the
American westward migration.[44] Recently, the collective of authors
of a compendium about Slavs in Germany stressed that "the
beginnings of urbanization in the area of Slavic history is one of
the most contested problems in medieval history." [45]

The complexities of the historiographic debate resembled the
complexities of the instant trade center as a city of strangers. The
migration of people of many origins accompanied long-distance
commerce, and Jews, Syrians, and Latins were among the path-
finders of the traveling traders in northern Europe. They gave to the
new towns elements of their own respective cultures, which added a
measure of cosmopolitanism to what would otherwise have been a
mere extension of the culture of the mother city. All men were
strangers to each other in the instant city, and the inhabitants of
these instant cities were likewise strangers to the people from the
surrounding countryside. The new towns facilitated intercourse
between the groups of foreigners who circulated news about the
affairs of the world and gathered and passed on knowledge of their
own surroundings. Thus, these cities served as centers for the
exchange of information in a vast communications network and
spawned a distinct urban culture despite their small populations.

Cities did not depend on the number of their inhabitants or on the
size of their territories for their status, and when recorded, population figures were of doubtful value. Cities frequently considered it in
their interest to appear larger than they actually were. As well,
though the estimates of a chronicler may have been made with the
noblest intentions concerning accuracy, men were difficult to count,
particularly in a quickly growing city of people of diverse origin.
Until the rationalism of the eighteenth century elevated the public
use of figures to a cult, the population counts of many cities were
often kept secret.[46] Some of the statistics given were tailored in ages
when survival may have depended on the fabricated count of men
behind the walls. Even in the nineteenth century, local politicians

considered the compilation and publication of population figures their prerogative, as the decennial bickering between American cities and the United States Bureau of the Census over the official tally indicated.

The momentum for continued expansion of these commercial centers came from the same forces stimulating the general social, economic, political, and cultural expansion of older Europe. The liberation of manufacturing from the control of territorial lords and feudal rule was under way. Long-distance trade had become one of the driving forces of the emerging money-oriented exchange or market economy. The urban world was radiating its commercial success, political innovations, and cultural glory to the fringes of Western civilization in central Europe. The upsurge in economic and political affairs and the heightened cultural life stimulated new activities and invigorated old ones.

Among the effects was an intensification of the search for mineral wealth. It was hoped that gold and silver would provide assets more quickly than laborious statecraft, costly conquest, unpredictable commerce, cumbersome industry, and ascetic frugality. The preoccupation with easy riches was further fostered by the increased demands for treasure in the developing money economy and the specific need for gold, silver, iron, lead, copper, and tin in industrial, commercial, agricultural, and artistic enterprises. Speculation about new sources of wealth heightened curiosity concerning the mysteries of the material world and the hidden treasures of the subsoil.[47] It stimulated a series of mining rushes that produced many instant cities in the form of mining towns in various parts of central Europe.

The infectious fascination with precious metals touched many people. Traders and settlers turned into prospectors, everywhere seeking for ore containing gold or silver. They moved beyond their traditional experience and skill in working the large mines in the Siegerland from Merovingian times, in the Harz Mountains from the reign of Otto the Great (936–973), and in the Black Forest from the beginning of the eleventh century.[48]

The activities of the prospectors and the history of the mining booms in the Middle Ages, unlike their counterparts in the American West, were not preserved in travelogues, reminiscences, journals, diaries, or business papers. A few medieval tales and legends added color to the facts preserved in scattered documents.[49] Prospectors swarmed through valleys and canyons panning in river beds for the yellow metal, which, if lucky, they detected in increasing amounts as they neared the primary deposits. Agricola's treatise on mining of 1556 became the standard source of their activities.[50]

In Europe, and later in the nineteenth-century American West, the efforts of the gold hunter were sometimes rewarded with unexpected finds, such as silver or iron. Deposits were also accidentally uncovered by road builders. Even the mundane pursuits of tilling the soil, clearing the forest, or searching for salt sometimes revealed valuable minerals. Speculation about deposits was also inspired by the knowledge that some Slavic tribes, the Sorbs, Lutizes, and Obodrites, possessed large amounts of silver; it seemed likely that they had engaged in mining since the ninth and tenth centuries.[51]

Natural phenomena, floods, storms, and avalanches, probably exposed seams of ore even to those not seeking them, as when lightning splintered rocks and water eroded the sides of mountains, or storms uprooted trees and rushing torrents changed the course of rivers.[52] Necromancy played its role in detecting hidden treasures, as the commentaries of Albert the Great (Albertus Magnus) in his thirteenth-century writings on mineralogy indicated.[53] When systematically undertaken, prospecting resulted in more and more discoveries of mineral deposits in Saxony, Bohemia, Moravia, Slovakia, Silesia, and Hungary.[54] New strikes set new migrations into motion and in quick succession produced mining camps that attracted a constant influx of people, an essential ingredient in the creation of instant cities.

The rapidly rising mining towns formed a striking contrast to the gradually emerging centers of rural settlement in the process of agricultural colonization. These slower growing agricultural colonies responded only indirectly to the political, ecclesiastical, and commercial activities of kings, churchmen and lords, miners and merchants.[55] The settlers here patiently developed fields and meadows and their needs brought forth the small town serving the inhabitants of the surrounding network of villages.

Conversely, the instant city as mining camp responded quickly to riches and large new influxes of people and quickly achieved full-blown forms of urban life. The spectacular rise of Freiberg in the Erz Gebirge, a mountain range on the boundary between the present German Democratic Republic and Czechoslovakia, exemplified the link between the discovery of silver and the rapid advance of settlements in central Europe during the High Middle Ages. As at San Francisco and Denver many centuries later, the influx of miners and traders flooded the entire area with prospective residents. The high quality of the silver veins led to an unusual density of population and concentration of towns throughout the region of the Erz Mountains.[56]

Silver was a powerful magnet that attracted men from near and far, but mining, in general, lured people from home because it seemed to offer freedom from restraint. From many sections of Germany, men flocked to Freiberg, in particular, because, as its name stated, they were free to mine the mountain, and that they did, as early as 1168. Streams of experienced workers left for Freiberg from the Harz Mountains where Henry the Lion of Saxony had destroyed mines and smelters during his sieges of Goslar in 1168, and again in 1181.[57]

The arrival of these displaced miners expanded the Margrave of Meissen's plan for agricultural colonization into what became, essentially, a city-making enterprise.[58] Freiberg received town rights and walls between 1186 and 1190.[59] As is understandable in the face of such a startling phenomenon as the instant city, the measures of growth taken from Freiberg's legal history do not do justice to the pace of urban development. The eighteen years that elapsed between the discovery of silver and the formal establishment of the Erz Mountains mining camp as a town reflected the reluctance of the margrave to give up control over the most precious portions of his territory, in which, in fact, his men had just started clearing the heavy forest in 1160. Perhaps another reason for this delay was the margrave's disinclination to grant to rough migrant miners the rights of burghers.[60] The city's real rate of growth vividly reminded a Freiberg historian, in 1900, of the "rapid rise of American mining towns." [61]

The complex social and economic problems of Freiberg brought about a concurrent development of mining law and municipal law. Feudal practices reinforced the legal parallelism. Yet, it is almost a truism that in the relatively loose life of American mining camps, mining law preceded municipal law. Consequently, of those who observed the stampede of the polyglot adventurers looking for gold in California, many warned, some quite forcefully, of the potential threat posed by these waves of prospectors and miners to California's social and political development.[62] The instant city of the mining rushes of the High Middle Ages, however, had the tremendous advantage of the simultaneous development of mining law and municipal law. Jihlava (Iglau), in Moravia, and Banská Štiavnica (Schemnitz), in Slovakia, were two communities among many that so benefited.[63]

In 1871, a counselor in the German Imperial Chancery, in Berlin, unwittingly touched on the real limits of individual freedom and corporate liberties in the High Middle Ages when he saw in the rise of the cities in the mining regions of the American West a contemporary parallel to the mining rushes of the High Middle Ages. Stressing the disorder of American mining towns, he emphasized with obvious satisfaction that "in the relatively shortest period of time" orderly conditions appeared in the "suddenly emerging cities" in central Europe, thanks to the "energetic and open-minded regulation of the communal life as well as the organization of miners." [64]

In its ordered life, its splendor and magnificence, the rising Freiberg resembled more an independent republic than a town of the Margraves of Meissen.[65] Freiberg demonstrated the complexities of the instant city as mining town. But, the urban development of other sections of the Erz Mountains two centuries later produced yet another variant of this type. The new form incorporated the instant city as mining camp within the financial design of princes.

Feudal lords created "company" towns at desirable economic locations. In this specific field of town building, private corporations became a later counterpart of feudal lords, deriving special powers from a legislature, and receiving privileges reminiscent of the relationship between baron and king. However, the princes had been less knowledgeable in management and less powerful in economics than were the corporations of later centuries and so gave their towns the measure of freedom within which they flourished and without which the nineteenth- and twentieth-century company towns eventually stagnated.[66]

Several of the territorial lords, in the latter half of the fifteenth century and the early part of the sixteenth century, viewed mining with heightened interest as a way of easing their financial burdens. Their search for quick riches coincided with an infiltration of outside capital into silver production which stimulated an expansion or a revival of those mines that had declined for lack of funds to deal with the twin problems of depth and water. The activities of the competing princes extended into politics when the division of the ruling House of Wettin, the Dukes of Saxony, established two major branches whose interlocking territories produced the threat of rival authorities in the mining region.[67]

The princes' interest in mining, the availability of outside capital, and the rumors of the discovery of new silver deposits attracted ever greater numbers of people into established mining towns and new settlements. Eager to profit from the boom, the territorial lords utilized the potential of instant cities by asserting control over the establishment of towns.

The task of founding towns was placed in the hands of officials. During the 1460s, the city of Schneeberg was born of a silver rush and still could have been taken, simply, for a colony of nearby Zwickau.[68] However, in 1496, a commission of officials, guided by the humanist Ulrich Rülein von Calw, laid out Annaberg. House building commenced in the following spring. By the fall of 1497, the community received municipal privileges and, in 1499, its St. Anne's Church was commissioned by Duke Georg. Within ten years, the town had eight thousand inhabitants, more than either Dresden or Leipzig. In 1520, Duke Heinrich founded Marienberg on the site of a 1519 silver strike. Ulrich Rülein von Calw surveyed it, and Marienberg was given town rights in 1523. Scheibenberg, also a planned community, was granted town privileges in 1522.

The hectic building of towns had political repercussions. The founding of Oberwiesenthal, in 1527, by the Albertinian line of the House of Wettin, aroused the jealousy of their cousins in the Ernestinian line. The Ernestinians had previously been aggressive in erecting towns on the site of their own mining camps. They now sent two experts to Oberwiesenthal to wheedle their way into the mines on the pretense of seeking opportunities for investment. These early industrial spies conjectured that the major silver vein extended under territory in Ernestinian hands. The Ernestinians took immediate advantage of their report by building a mining town over the projected vein, in 1529, inappropriately called Gottesgab, God's Gift.[69]

While miners and princes established new mines and towns on the Saxonian slope of the Erz Mountains, some prospectors crossed the divide into Bohemia. In 1512, at a place later called Joachimsthal, and now Jachymov, two of them found silver but lacked the resources to work a mine. Count Stefan Schlick, whose great-uncle had received the territory from the Emperor Sigismund as security for a loan, together with business associates, took over the venture in 1516. He directed to the scene experienced administrators who had been connected with mining at Freiberg and Annaberg. His promotional activities helped attract miners to Joachimsthal, which by 1518 counted three thousand inhabitants.[70]

Thus far, instant cities have been dealt with in a general way, as a type of city arising out of such activities as empire building, commerce, and mining. Now, attention can be directed to an examination of the internal dynamics created by the concentration of masses of people who made the instant cities. Command or treasure, above or under ground, brought them to the scene. However, along with the specifics of a plan or the intricacies of commerce and mining as factors shaping the rising towns, was the particular chemistry of the concentration of inhabitants of a particularly heterogeneous heritage.

A survey of some characteristics of mining, as they appear in these three centuries, their effects on the people they brought together and on the interaction between mining and commerce, will underscore the parallels between Freiberg and Joachimsthal in the thirteenth and sixteenth centuries and San Francisco and Denver in the nineteenth century. Such an undertaking has obvious limitations. Any attempt to depict social conditions over three centuries encounters formidable difficulties. Questions concerning social stratification, highly complex in the late Middle Ages, are further complicated by an industry that produced immediately intimate links between so-called feudal and capitalistic economic practices. The fine line separating miners into owners, or shareholders, and laborers can be drawn only from case to case. The prevailing territorial and mining laws, the privileges of corporate and capitalistic bodies, the source of investment capital and the use of profits, the customs and the conditions of life and labor of the people—these, and other, factors need to be assessed.

Under such circumstances, any attempt to arrive at a meaningful synthesis reflects, on a minor scale, the dilemma of research, which Samuel Johnson described in the Preface of his *Dictionary*. He saw that

one enquiry only gave occasion to another, that book referred to book, that to search was not always to find, and to find was not always to be informed; and that thus to pursue perfection, was, like the first inhabitants of Arcadia, to chace the sun, which, when they reached the hill where he seemed to rest, was still beheld at the same distance from them.[71]

Without further disclaimer, inquiry into the social life of mining towns in the late Middle Ages seems justified, however, since it creates a perspective for understanding the rise of San Francisco and Denver as instant cities.

The dream of sudden wealth was as much an obsession in the late Middle Ages as it was in the nineteenth century. Most gold and silver hunters failed to improve their lot materially, but they persevered. It was only a lucky few who, during the first weeks of a mining rush, made their fortunes. But surface riches were soon exhausted, and when it became necessary to dig deep, to install pumps, and to form mining companies to get at the ever more elusive minerals, the financial returns of the miners fell off sharply. "If one man becomes rich," Paulus Niavis stated, describing the classic case during the late Middle Ages, "hundreds work for nothing. They sink gold and silver into their mines and they get stones and dirt in return. . . . Far more money has been put into the mountains than they have yielded as profit." [72]

Under the combined pressure of technology and finance many independent miners became hired hands. Yet, while they failed to get rich, they contributed their wages to the active commerce that stimulated the rapid development of the instant city. Knowing nothing but mining, they became, perforce, permanent residents in a community spawned by mines. Any new discovery leading to an extension of the mines brought new laborers into the area and increased the population. Even false rumors and shallow deposits contributed to the wealth and population growth of the town by inducing many people to come and others to invest their capital.

Those few enterprising miners who used mining as a springboard to trade and banking ventures were equally bound to the instant city. It became their base of operation and their center of communication. The often isolated locations of the new towns created a closed market, and the continuous demands of the mine operators for equipment enabled local capitalists to experiment with projects within the realm of their limited experience, funds, and privileges. Their businesses—blacksmith shops, forges, ropewalks, tanneries, and saw mills—employed workers who crowded the boardinghouses of the town. All these men, from the first capitalist to the last laborer, demanded food, shelter, and some measure of entertainment to make their lives tolerable.

The wage-earning miners populating the instant city as mining camp in the late Middle Ages became entitled to privileges based on a special class status. One may speculate that, in the absence of slaves in the feudal world of central Europe, there must have been hired laborers, pieceworkers, or wage earners in most mining ventures. By their very nature, knights, monks, merchants, and magistrates would not engage in the actual drudgery themselves. Before mining came to be divided into the activities of mine owners (capital) and wage-earning workers (manual labor), all miners held shares in so-called Gewerkschaften. These working partnerships had the character of legally protected associations, analogous to urban craft guilds, and created a special status for mine workers. Public interest and custom, as well as mining law, guaranteed the mine worker's right of mobility and residence as vital privileges of his profession.

In an age that mixed features of feudalism with those of early capitalism, mining booms were dependent upon this freedom of movement. The freely roving miner and the hectic industry complemented one another. Before the introduction of scientific methods of operation, the risky nature of the industry made mining another form of gambling. Especially with silver, where the extractive costs were high, limited capital could be quickly exhausted if a deposit did not yield an immediate return. Gross returns from silver mines were not large enough to compensate for the difficulties of accumulating great capital through silver mining, but it seems clear that some profits did flow as capital into other commercial channels.[73]

Owners of mines developed primitive forms of capitalistic organization, but they usually preferred, at that stage, to reinvest their gains in trading ventures. The mine owners thought of themselves primarily as merchants, traders, or money-lenders; they did not advance to the position of industrial capitalists but remained commercial capitalists. If they were noblemen, they frequently used ultimate profits from these other ventures to further their positions within the world of princes and dukes to which they aspired.[74]

Although the difficulty of accumulating riches shattered many dreams, its effect on the town was much less destructive. While the mine workers individually may have been discouraged, continued investments from wealthy burghers kept the mines growing. Money earned in trade and manufacturing, in the ore and money market, in real estate, or collected as rent or taxes, found its way into the glamorously speculative mining business and firmed up the base on which operations could be expanded and made more profitable. Trading privileges granted by the town to faraway merchants opened other sources of capital and thereby strengthened the pulse beat of the community. The upsurge increased the demand for hired hands, kept people working and brought new ones to the scene who identified with the instant city through their dependence on the mines.[75] The expansion also created a more stimulating social atmosphere, though it did not affect the life style of the individual laborer. He received other benefits.

All miners were burghers. Their profession gave them not only status as urbanites but also rights as citizens. Citizenship provided a protective armor for rich and poor miners in a world where riches, and lords, ruled. It enabled a few lucky men to enjoy their fortunes in the safety of a city, unmolested by a baron's inclination to participate in the earnings of former peasants. In their connection with the town, less successful men found a substitute for the riches that had bypassed them. Both rich and poor burghers were free and, in varying degrees, involved in the affairs of the municipality. Miners without property suffered little loss of identity as long as they identified with the rising instant city. Vicariously, they progressed, too, by identifying with the city's progress.

The direct involvement of many feudal lords, and the resultant dependence of these lords on the efficient operation of specialized and highly speculative ventures, led many to grant privileges through which the city council supervised mining. Control of the mines by its city council assured the near-autonomy of Freiberg.[76] Eventually the city councils of most mining towns seemed to have worked systematically to gain some ownership of the mines, as well as jurisdiction over them. In the town of Goslar, in the Harz Mountains, old knightly families controlled the operations initially, but during the middle of the thirteenth century, the patrician council endeavored to bring the mines into the hands of trusted burghers or under the jurisdiction of the council itself.[77]

The privileges granted by the territorial lords made the instant city as mining camp virtually a free, self-governing, town. These prerogatives set the burghers apart from German and Slavic peasants, inadvertently diminished the antagonisms among the ethnic groups of the rural population, and hastened the formation of a single estate of peasants.[78] The numerous privileges that the Margraves of Meissen gave to the citizens of Freiberg included free wood for building and for fuel, freedom of mobility within the realm, and freedom of commerce. They evolved into such vital components of urban independence as market right, self-administration, judicial autonomy, and election of officials. Freibergers did not pay taxes, did not know forced labor, and were not compelled to do armed service.

Mining camps, consequently, were exempt from many of the regular feudal regulations. This atmosphere of freedom attracted not only those legitimately part of the industry, such as smelter workers and charcoal burners, but also men who had gained their freedom from a craft or a farm and simply hoped to strike it rich. Together with runaways and drifters, all these migrants were attracted to some degree by the democratic air of a locale where a miner was automatically a burgher.

This avid search for wealth in an absence of traditional restraint produced secondary consequences that also were familiar by-products of the later American mining rushes in the nineteenth century. Mountain, forest, meadow, and field were destroyed. In 1910, a German commentator, struck by the destruction of the land that had been begun with the emergence of the mining town of Schneeberg in 1471, referred to the devastation as a "fascinating glimpse at the seemingly 'American' conditions surrounding the founding of a medieval German mining town." [79]

In the Middle Ages, as well as in later ages, personal wealth was the goal of all. If a lowly miner struck it rich, he was the equal of the lord of the manor. His prosperity stimulated a desire for luxury foods. With better food came an appreciation for the finer things in life. The increased market for goods from distant parts of Europe brought representatives of large commercial houses to the scene. With them came lawyers and doctors, ministers and teachers, scientists and artists to answer the clamor for their services. The influx of these professionals fostered a hybrid culture that reflected the down-to-earth foundation of the instant city as mining town.[80]

Their citizens wanted the good life and that craving increased chances that the mining town would become a center of trade. However, most mining camps did not develop into full-fledged emporia; their isolation worked against it and their hinterlands were restricted by many territorial boundaries that limited the spatial extent of the silver rushes. In contrast to the mining towns of the late Middle Ages, San Francisco and Denver combined the characteristics of mining town and emporium because new advances in technology and organization had linked them to major arteries of commerce. Their eminence could be sustained not only by mining but also by commerce. They flourished as entrepôts supplying vast hinterlands. Like the medieval mining towns, they rose in wilderness isolation, without the rivalry of nearby emporia, but, unlike their medieval counterparts, San Francisco and Denver thrived also as nineteenth-century versions of those commercial centers that rose along the medieval trade routes.

In the High Middle Ages, in central and eastern Europe, the instant city as emporium already looked back on several forerunners, among them the trading posts of the Vikings and Frisians, and the German emporia of the early Middle Ages. In the eighth and ninth centuries, the Vikings and Frisians linked northern Europe to the highways along the Rhine, Dnieper, and Volga. These entrepôts reached from Dorestad, in Friesland, over Haithabu, in Schleswig, and Jumne-Vineta, on the mouth of the Oder, to Birka, on the island of Björkö in the Mälar, the extension of the Baltic into southeastern Sweden.[81]

The Germanic emporia of the Early Middle Ages resembled commercial institutions of the ancient Mediterranean world. They were analogous to factories, trading posts operated by merchants and factors in foreign countries. An essential difference, however, separated the Germanic emporia and the ancient factory from the Greek *polis* and from its offshoot, the *apoikia*, the planted city of the Hellenic expansion. The *polis* lacked almost entirely commercial character. It was rather primarily agricultural in its roles as political and religious centers. The Hellenic colonization, during the eighth and seventh centuries B.C., had little to do with active trade but aimed instead at the establishment of agricultural settlements and fishing stations.[82]

During the High Middle Ages, the commercial factory and the planted city as an agricultural colony accompanied the expansion of West Europeans into central Europe. Along their trade routes, both water and land, the Hanseatic merchants used the factory in building their far-flung empire of commercial entrepôts.[83] Later, agricultural colonies (plantations) and trading factories (emporia) also facilitated the transatlantic migrations of Europeans and were the nuclei of many European settlements in America.

The emergence of towns during the colonization of America had an impact on that colonization and on some of the divergent strands to take hold in the urban heritage of Western man. Many composites of European culture took root in the New World, and among them were variants of the instant city. Spaniards brought across the Atlantic a concept of the town as part of Latin life and as a device of local government.[84] Their commitment to the town as a traditional aspect of daily life and political organization stimulated the rise of instant cities in Latin America. The crown encouraged the trend also as one way of curbing the political prerogatives of the Columbus family and granted privileges to the emerging municipalities that placed the towns directly under the supervision of royal officials.[85]

Spanish colonists who did not come from the urban centers of the kingdom also recognized town life as their way of life. They were accustomed to the agro-towns of the Mediterranean and its numerous inhabitants cultivating large fields held in *latifundia* ever since the Roman days.[86] When, as a result of the Reconquest, these lands fell into the hands of the nobility and the clergy,[87] tenantry, under one guise or another, predominated, and no mystical attitude toward the land helped to diminish the tenants' burden. These people did not regard the tilling of the soil as an ennobling experience; in our days, social anthropologists find the same outlook prevalent among Spanish peasants.[88]

The concentration of settlers in towns was also fostered by the need to protect small groups of aliens who were determined to live in the midst of, yet dominate, a large Indian population. The original instructions of September 16, 1501, to Frey Nicolás de Ovando, Governor of Española, stressed that "Christians . . . shall not live dispersed" about the country, and this rule "was observed more or less throughout Spanish America." [89] With the reign of Philip II the "standing royal regulations provided that Spanish settlement be in towns." [90] In the sphere of Spanish colonization the instant city thus arose in response to the security requirements of the settlers and as an instrument of royal policy.

English colonization, commercially sustained as well as rurally oriented, brought forth the instant city only in isolated cases when the visionary designs of individual founders and the sudden growth of a region, as a result of its economic development, spontaneously created the instant city. Early attempts failed to check geographic factors inhibiting urban growth.[91] In general, the settlements in the English colonies grew into cities only if these settlements were situated such as to promote the flow of goods.[92] In their intellectual baggage the English emigrants to America carried two concepts that directed their settlements away from instant cities and into towns that "just grew naturally." On the one hand, they viewed the town as an integral part of national life; on the other, they shared an age-old aversion to urban living.

This age-old aversion to urban living had come from their Saxon ancestry. In fact, the Saxon actually favored the solitary homestead as the center of his world. Each family unit shaped its own economic and social life, and only traces of urban life existed. Some forms of the old Roman urban system persisted in a number of cities that survived as military posts and trading places, and the general drift of peasant life from freedom toward servitude also tended to reduce a man's independence.[93] But Saxon towns did not emerge in Britain until long after the invaders had settled the country. Then, under pressure from Danish invasions, the Saxons, setting up defenses through the burghal system, contributed to a resurgence of urban life in England, which was greatly intensified with the arrival of the Normans.[94]

At first, the Normans diminished the gulf between town and country inadvertently through their affiliation with the merchant class and the consequent restriction of the privileges of feudal lords. The limitation of seignorial justice by the crown, and the resultant shrinking of baronial revenues, then forced the lords to look elsewhere for money. Their land dealings brought them into close contact with town merchants, who were drawn to opportunities for buying and selling in country and town. Complex commercial transactions did not stop at the gates of the town but finally pervaded all sections of the country, urban as well as rural.

Political developments also fostered the integration of the town into the national life. English feudalism had never completely destroyed the popular and legal support for the monarchy. At sessions of the county court, in the presence of royal justices, representatives of lords and clerics, town dwellers and country people would come together. Parliament was prefigured, so to speak, in the county court. There was only a limited need of the towns as distinct political entities. Later, Parliament created a union that, through the borough system, further integrated the towns into the political life of the country.[95]

The urban heritage of the English emigrants then was balanced by a tradition of rural living. In the new world, a continent that could supply space for everyone, this tradition was to be revitalized. Stories about the new American continent also fired the imagination of Englishmen. Men living in a state of nature suggested the possibility of a primitive egalitarian society. As part of their reaction to reports, often based on an all too limited understanding of America, Englishmen, in the seventeenth and eighteenth centuries, rediscovered a special significance in their Saxon past. Pamphleteers expressed the opinion that Saxon life had had a strong resemblance to the natural state of mankind, in which most Europeans imagined the people of the New World were living when Columbus found them. During the English Revolution even the Levellers succumbed to the myth, calling for the return of primitive Saxon freedom after centuries of Norman tyranny.[96]

Strong intellectual and economic influences supported the ideals of rural life. The industrialization of agriculture and the spread of the enclosure movement heightened the attractions of biblical images. They stimulated a fascination with the Golden Age of Mankind, the legendary world created by the timeless literary conventions in praise of rural life, agriculture, and animal husbandry; so much so, that on the eve of the Civil War the debate accompanying the division of England into court and country castigated the vices of the former and extolled the virtues of the latter.[97] In the mid-eighteenth century, the writings of the French physiocrats lent scientific sanction to the advocacy of rural life, propagating agriculture as the basis of economic life. Some time later, Adam Smith praised small farms and glorified country life. He combined both ideals with an aristocratic paternalism and an advancing technology into the cult of the farmer as protector of natural morality.[98]

Many Americans emphasized the value of country life in the eighteenth century. In 1705, one of the earliest products of American literature, Robert Beverley's *History and Present State of Virginia* regarded the conquest of primitive man by white civilization as a catastrophe.[99] Other Americans seemed to anticipate the romantic dictum that the English poet William Cowper expressed in his defamation of city life at the end of the century: "God made the country and man made the town." [100]

Americans willingly paid lip service to these arguments because the fertile soil of North America made it possible to realize the dream of a return to the natural life of the isolated farm. The great majority farmed, and that heightened the importance of the land. Whenever possible, colonists avoided settling together as a defense from Indian attacks. Most Indians of North America never abandoned their treasured individualism long enough to marshal forces in a concerted defense of their land against the invaders. The result was the settlement of the country through the establishment of isolated homesteads as much as towns.

Despite the emotional and material influences that supported the ideals of rural life, powerful social and economic factors eventually shaped the American westward migration in favor of towns. The trend was reinforced, at times, by religious groups. Pilgrims and Puritans recognized the advantages of political organization and regimented life. They considered the town, in addition to family and church, an instrument of social control. William Bradford's *History* shows the concern with which the colonists fought to keep Plymouth Plantation intact in the face of the constant lure of the land. Bradford regarded the settlement not merely as a bulwark against Indians, but as a guarantee of a strong communal life, insuring attendance at church and the suppression of sin. In June 1658, the *Plymouth Colony Records* reported that Joseph Ramsden, who "hath lived long in the woods, in an uncivil way," was ordered "to some neighbourhood" before October, "or that then his house be pulled down." [101]

In time, the challenges of North America itself brought town dwellers and farmers to the integration of town and country into a common life. The continent presented itself to them, with the exception of a few religious groups, as a wilderness. For generations, Americans considered it their task to civilize and to model this wilderness on a European image. Natural resources lured them deeper and deeper into the continent and the search for its treasures stimulated the settlement of North America. Colonization and exploitation produced commercially oriented towns as places of transit, collection points, and harbors, which focused the immigrants' affairs on an urban way of life.

The urban trend was reinforced through the implementation of ideas underlying the official policy of the British Empire. The doctrines of mercantilism suggested using the cities on the Atlantic coast, such as Boston, Newport, New York, Philadelphia, and Charleston, as instruments of politics, centers of civil organization, military strongholds, and bottlenecks of economic control. However, the cities did not serve solely the interests of the empire; they also answered the social, cultural, and economic needs of the immigrants and attracted steadily growing numbers of inhabitants. Philadelphia, which was founded in 1682, counted 24,000 inhabitants by 1760, and was second only to London in the British Empire.[102]

The expansion of the functions of the East Coast cities was crowned by the political independence of the colonies. Within a few decades, industrial cities came into being and helped to make the new country increasingly independent of England through the exploitation of natural resources, immigrants, and slaves. Technological innovations produced a transportation revolution and speeded up the opening of the continent. Railroad networks pulled the regional economies together into a national market and, in turn, oriented the various centers of production toward a national economy.

The development implemented the new American views about the integration of town and country into a national economy. In the nineteenth century, when industrialization threatened the importance of agriculture, Jeffersonianism singled out the family farm as the most desirable way of life, a sort of last stand against the stresses and strains of developing industrialization and urbanization. But, as a new political creed, Jeffersonianism was out of step with its time. It ignored the significant influence of the ideas of physiocratic federalism, which fostered the rise of large-scale agriculture and farmer-entrepreneurs to insure adequate production of foodstuff for an ever-expanding industrial urban population.[103]

An awareness of the pull and push to the city accompanying the colonization of North America could also come from the writings of Karl Marx and his followers. Marxists did not concern themselves specifically with the phenomenon of cities in North America, but their arguments cannot help but throw light on the urban trend in the development of the colonies. Their analyses of European expansion between the fifteenth and the seventeenth centuries emphasized that only in North America did conditions match the Marxian view of an overseas colony as a settlement. In these English colonies, at least initially, land seemed easily accessible, and that criterion for Marx defined a settlement colony as the only "real" colony. The individual Indian did not seem to desire land as private property, and the abundance of land attracted waves of settlers. The hopes of the mercantile sponsors of colonization faded when North American commodities proved to be of little value to England and tended to compete with her products on the world market. When the colonial bourgeoisie did not subordinate its aspirations to the commercial interests of the English metropolitan bourgeoisie, as mercantile theory expected, the activities of the colonial capitalists reinforced the growth of commercial centers along the Eastern seaboard.[104]

Most colonization movements developed a potential for instant cities, and so did the one in British North America. The process of colonization produced many building blocks required by instant cities; yet these last did not spring into existence for want of the necessary command, or people, or wealth. The first instant city rose when the political needs of the independent colonies gave birth to Washington, D.C. as capital of the United States. None followed because the struggle to protect the fruits of independence and to assure the expansion of the new nation strained the economy of the young republic.

The vast continent absorbed and dispersed the energies of the nation and diluted the concentration of human and material resources in the few places that might have seen the emergence of instant cities. However, the slowly growing towns furthered the technique of implanting offshoots in virgin soil to develop on established patterns. Their inhabitants, as true colonials, looked to England, and to the East Coast, for the legitimate expressions of their world, and this tendency was reinforced by the common experience of migration and settlement. The towns, by their nature as colonial establishments, were able to thrive on the transmitted set of social, economic, political, and cultural practices adapted to a new setting.[105] As settlements penetrated North America, these devices were woven into the fabric of national life and facilitated the spread of towns. With the passage of time and the appearance of new opportunities, more cities sprang up along the major lines of migration and reinforced the pattern.

In mid-nineteenth-century America, the repetitive process of settlement presented the components for the rise of instant cities without governmental decree. The discovery of gold in California and Colorado brought wealth and people, and produced San Francisco and Denver. The demands for goods and services sustained their rise. Their isolation and their role as supply centers for the mines turned them into emporia even before their function as mining camps gave way to a position as gateways; the wealth of the mines flowed through these cities into the world, and the products of the world passed through them into the mines. Their roles as mining towns and emporia made San Francisco and Denver unique variants of the instant city in the United States. They also exemplified an urban tradition of more than two thousand years that reached back to the planting of the first colony by a Hellenic city on the shores of the Mediterranean.

# 2

## Temple City

Almost simultaneous with the emergence of San Francisco and Denver in the mid-nineteenth century, an altogether different variant of the instant city appeared abruptly in the heart of the western mountains. It was a temple city laid out in July 1847, by Brigham Young and his Mormon followers as the center of their Great Basin Kingdom.[1] Young and his followers originally named the site "City of the Great Salt Lake;" in 1868, however, they officially deleted the adjective whose application had been to the nearby body of water rather than to their religious kingdom.[2]

Salt Lake City was the first instant city in the Far West. Yet, in contrast with the instant cities about to appear in California and Colorado, the Mormon Kingdom of God was not merely an urban capstone in the structure of an empire. Here these People of Israel would gather to execute the design of the most high: building a city of God, according to the revelations and instructions of their founder and prophet Joseph Smith.

"The temple city," as Lieutenant John Williams Gunnison of the Corps of Topographical Engineers first called the experiment at the Great Salt Lake in 1852, was designated to fulfill the double commission of initiating the gathering of latter-day Israel and of

sheltering the temple of their gospel ordinances.[3] Its rise coincided
for most Mormons of Brigham Young's day with the initiation of a
second phase of a religious progression outlined by Mormon
theologians in the doctrine of celestial marriage.[4] In this phase, the
Saints, walking on earth in their human bodies, struggled to achieve
spiritual dominance over their corporal bodies. Their temple city, as
an urban site, was equally exposed to the forces of a wicked world
conspiring to complicate the insecure present and to cut short the
glorious future, and was, therefore, also in jeopardy of being misused
for the purposes of Babylon.

For the builders of Salt Lake City, therefore, awesome responsibility lay in building a Zion able to withstand the tests of a secular
world. Their goal was the establishment of an ecclesiastical settlement isolated from the worldly aspects of urban growth and
governed within the framework of their special religious vision.
These goals set the Mormons apart from other sects and set the
temple city apart from other instant cities as well as from other
ordinary cities.

The linking of ecclesiastical and civil government was not
unknown in the American experience. Ralph Waldo Emerson viewed
the Mormon experiment as "an after-clap of Puritanism." [5] In some
aspects, it was. A little more than two hundred years prior to the
founding of the Mormon Church in upstate New York in 1830, John
Winthrop, one of the leaders of the Great Migration of Puritans to
New England, compared the building of a Puritan church in America
to the founding of Matthew's city upon a hill on which the eyes of
mankind were fixed.[6] But the Puritan vision had remained internal-
ized. Like most Christians since the days of St. Paul, they believed
that their Jerusalem was not of this world. The Puritans conceived
the Civitas Dei as an abstract commonwealth of believers. No place
was holier than another, Richard Mather warned his congregation of
Puritans, and he stressed that Canaan was special ground "only while
the Lord there appeared." [7]

Salt Lake City's position was most closely analogous to that of
Jerusalem's before the desecration and destruction of the shrine of

Yahweh by the Romans in 70 A.D. The chief city of the Jews had
sheltered a temple that had administered to the religious, ecclesiastical, and secular needs of a Chosen People in a Promised Land.[8] After
the destruction of Jerusalem, Mecca represented the closest parallel
to the Mormon temple city. About 610 A.D. Muhammed had elevated
Mecca from a tribal sanctuary to the center of Islam, and the sanctity
of the city and its Ka'bah rewarded with salvation every Muslim who
made the pilgrimage there.[9] Even more than pagan Rome, Delphi,
Assur, or Memphis, Mecca was a true temple city, like Salt Lake
City, fortified by a religion and a sanctum that marked it as the
center of the world.[10] The similarities of the religious roles of the two
cities were noted even in Brigham Young's day. Many non-Mormons
spoke of Salt Lake City as the "Mecca of the Mormons," Mormonism
as the "Islam of America," Joseph Smith as the "American Mohamet"; the analogies also encouraged speculation as to the degree
to which the planners of Salt Lake City had utilized the design of
Mecca.[11]

   In fact, only in a few cases did Christian reformers express a
doctrinal need for a temple city. One of these instances occurred in
1420. In that year, radical Hussites established the town of Tabor in
Bohemia in culmination of their adventism and in response to a
threat of annihilation. About fifty miles south of Prague, they
envisioned Tabor as the only place of refuge, believing that God
would destroy all mankind save the inhabitants of their new city.
Although Tabor was a religious necessity, Hussite theology did not
utilize the concept of a temple or, for that matter, of a city. The town
never seemed more than an encampment to weather His wrath or a
city state in an area of Taborite strength.[12]

   The Mormons, however, recognized sacred places and, in keeping
with Joseph Smith's revelations of the biblical command to build a
Kingdom of God, they strove diligently to fulfill their duty. They
incorporated a commitment to the erection of a temple into their
doctrine of the gathering of the faithful, and set out to implement
their beliefs through a threefold program of evangelism, emigration,
and colonization.[13] While other millenarians in the first half of the

nineteenth century set a time and waited for Christ's reign on earth, the Saints "appointed a place" and "rallied to a platform of achievement." [14] Although they were driven by their enemies from one place to another, they were "determined to build a city wherever their lot is cast," Wilford Woodruff, one of their leaders, noted in his journal.[15]

As the creation of the Mormon Church, Salt Lake City bore its special marks. It held to a concept of urban life defined by the Prophet Joseph Smith in his Plat of the City of Zion. The close-knit society of Mormon pioneers was to be governed by an overlapping of ecclesiastical and secular bodies. In contrast to the atomized groups of people who would settle in San Francisco and Denver and be shaped by the unrestrained interplay of social, political, economic, and cultural forces, Salt Lake City, from its inception, was to be a homogeneous and cohesive religious community whose members sought isolation from the hustle, bustle, and influence of Babylon.

With this idea always before them, the Mormons began the task as soon as their vanguard reached the Great Basin. "This is the place, drive on," Brigham Young is said to have told the members of the advance party on July 24, 1847, his pronouncement reflecting his determination not to be sidetracked from the great task even by the group's arrival at the actual site. Subsequently, he remarked that he had seen the valley in a vision and had heard a voice exclaiming, "This is the place where my people Israel shall pitch their tents." [16] His reluctance to provoke the Ute Indians living on the choice lands around Utah Lake may have been among other factors that influenced his selection of the site.[17]

Brigham Young's confidence in the place was not shaken despite the temporary misgivings of other members of the group. Exploring parties kept finding spots that seemed more inviting or better suited for settlement.[18] Elder Samuel Brannan, so impressed with the success of his group of Mormons on the West Coast, rode horseback from San Francisco to the Green River to meet the vanguard of the Mormon trek across the Plains and to lure them on to California. Brannan filled the camp with reports about the advantages of

California and especially of San Francisco, "the great Emporium of the Pacific and eventually of the world." [19] Some of the veterans of the Mormon Battalion who had seen California during their military service shared his view.[20]

But, despite talk of other places, Brigham Young never wavered in his conviction that the Lord had directed him to the best possible location, the isolated Great Basin. From the beginning, his certainty and industry erased any false impression that the vanguard had camped merely at another temporary rest stop. On July 28, 1847, in the afternoon of that Wednesday, Brigham Young, with seven other members of the Council of the Twelve Apostles, paced off a plot of ground between the two forks of what became City Creek, eleven miles east of Great Salt Lake, waved his hand and said, "Here is the place for the temple to be built." On the spot, the group passed upon a plan for the city that was approved unanimously at a town meeting that evening, as were decisions to build a temple on the chosen site and to make the Twelve a committee to superintend the design of the entire community.[21] These, and subsequent, events the Mormons recorded with their customary determination to fully document their affairs. They furnished an unusually detailed picture of the beginnings of a settlement, albeit a very special one.

On the first Sunday celebrated by the Mormon pioneers in the valley, Apostle Orson Pratt christened the Mormon camp with passages from the Hebrew prophets. God will, he said, "hide his people in the chambers of the mountains" and in these "last days" will "establish his house on the tops of the mountains, and exalt it above the hills." On the very next Sunday, August 1, he and Apostle Heber C. Kimball were the first to preach in the newly constructed bowery on the temple block. Apostle Pratt, in his discourse on the prophecies of Isaiah, again assured the assembly that the location of Zion in the mountains of Utah was the fulfillment of the biblical promises.[22]

Step by step many of the prophecies became reality. The town lots of the new community were laid out, the first of those squares that would eventually cover the earth, in fulfillment of the predictions of

Joseph Smith. The streets, eight rods wide, formed square blocks of ten acres each. The eight lots of each block measured one and a quarter acres. They maintained the spacious air of open country and a degree of privacy unusual in an urban setting. They also assured neighborliness through attempts to blend the best of urban and rural worlds. But the new community in the Great Basin was to become more than the first "Mormon Farm Village" in the Far West.[23] To be sure, the Plat of the City of Zion, the extraordinary group solidarity, and the favorable environment combined to bring about the prototype of *the* Mormon farm village. Other factors, however, immediately directed the development beyond the restricted framework and imagery of a village to that of a temple city. When the lots were ready for distribution, Brigham Young and the Twelve, given first choice, selected blocks adjacent to the temple square. Their response reflected the special role of the temple in Mormon society.[24]

The earliest Mormon communities—in Ohio, Missouri, and Illinois—reflected Mormon religious attitudes but were a far cry from temple cities. With the exception of the city of Nauvoo, the last town built by Mormons before the establishment of Salt Lake City, they all rose prior to that point in the development of Mormonism when eternal bliss became contingent upon the individual's participation in certain rites and ceremonies to be performed only at the temple. In addition, the Saints had not yet implemented their insight that in order to assure a determination strong enough to subordinate the worldly by-products of city growth to their religious beliefs and to protect the temple city they would have to extend their instruments of social control to urban planning. Still, during the wanderings of the Saints across the continent in the years 1830 to 1847, from the Burned-over District in upstate New York to the New Canaan in the West, these Mormons struggled incessantly to insure that their religious ideas manifested themselves as much as possible in the way they built camps and settlements along their route.

To be sure, every Zion that the Mormons built in their migration suffered the instability and insecurity that accompany urban growth, commercial transaction, and industrial development. Because of the small number of settlers, the proximity and hostility of Gentile neighbors, and the brief duration of those Mormon settlements at Kirtland, Ohio, Independence and Far West, Missouri, however, the compromises made with their religious goals were obscured.[25] But the experience at Nauvoo opened the eyes of the Mormons to the complex task of building a temple city in a Gentile world, exposed to the rough and tumble of competing and conflicting social, economic, political, and cultural forces. It was an arduous task but they learned from failure and gained confidence from success.

The Saints actually saw their city of Nauvoo rise within a few years out of a malaria-ridden swamp along the Mississippi River, and their attitude toward urban life was shaped, in particular, by the insights they gained from this experience. Under Mormon guidance and control, the town of Nauvoo in Hancock County, Illinois, grew between 1839 and 1844 from an insignificant Gentile village, called Commerce, to the largest city in the state, larger than Chicago, Alton, Springfield, Quincy, and Galena. Inevitably, Nauvoo towered over the nearby Gentile towns of Hancock County. By 1843, the earliest known map of the county attested to the sudden overwhelming size of the city.[26] Its lumber and brick yards, saw and grist mills, lime kilns and home industries, river landings and warehouses threatened the economies of neighboring Warsaw and Carthage. The rivalry between the towns deepened the gulf between Saints and Gentiles, formed by the divisive issues of religion, economics, and politics. Ultimately, Nauvoo's city charter, granted by the Illinois legislature, added to the suspicion and fear. The rights specified in the charter were similar, in many ways, to those accorded Gentile Chicago, Alton, Galena, Springfield, and Quincy, but unlike those cities Mormon Nauvoo appeared inclined to use its freedoms to create a sovereign religious state within Illinois.[27]

On a block where the river bottom rose to a hill, the Mormons erected a magnificent white limestone temple. The awe-inspiring building radiated an aura of its own that touched Mormon as well as Gentile. It was a wonderful, indescribable structure in the opinion of such a detached observer as the Bostonian Josiah Quincy, son of *the*

Josiah Quincy. In 1844, upon seeing it, he was certain that the temple could not be "compared to any ecclesiastical building which may be discerned by the natural eyesight." [28] In Mormon eyes, the temple was a direct, obvious testimony to the City Beautiful, their expression for the community's Hebrew name, Nauvoo, and a constant reminder of its heightened significance for the Church.

It was not until the latter part of those tumultuous years in Illinois, however, that the temple became the focal point of a power struggle within the Church for control of the theology and organization.[29] In what had been a period of relative lull in that incessant fight with Gentile detractors, between January and July 1843, Joseph Smith opened the debate by giving out instructions for the establishment of new temple rites and ceremonies. These innovations were largely ritual and doctrinal in nature. They had a profound impact on Mormonism, first because many of these special rites—the doctrine of celestial marriage, and the ordinances for the living and the dead, to cite but two—could be performed only in the temple to assure a Saint's eternal bliss. And second, because some of them seemed linked to Masonry and polygamy.[30]

Although the anti-Masonic tone of the *Book of Mormon* reflected Joseph Smith's response to the campaign against Masons in upstate New York and, specifically, to the Morgan hysteria of 1826, the Prophet had long since overcome his aversion to the Masonic ritual. By 1843, he had apparently become convinced that a fellowship of that order would shield the Saints from new sufferings and, in particular, from a repetition of their bitter Missouri experience. Furthermore, he also treasured his Solomon-like role as a temple builder, and to the Hebrew Solomon the legends of Masonry traced the origin of their order. Embracing it, he found in it inspirations for elaborate temple ceremonies that "transformed the Mormon Church into a mystery cult." [31] The introduction of these rites and the new connection with Masonry reopened old sources of division among the factions of the Church, and created new ones. Finally, some of the followers openly dissented to the rule of the Prophet when the new teachings also called for having several wives at the same time, a practice that Gentiles called polygamy although polygyny would have been the correct term.

The turmoil and trouble of the Mormons was water on the mill of their enemies. To the Gentile world of Hancock County, the establishment of the Masonic lodge at Nauvoo seemed to be another piece of tangible evidence that the Mormons, as a community of urban dwellers, had again outdone the inhabitants of the older towns, as they had previously, in the size of their city, the wealth of their business, the beauty of their buildings, and the style of their life. Even Gentile fellow-Masons contributed to the brewing storm in Hancock County. Threatened by the sudden addition of many Saints and the growing Mormon influence in the Masonic Order, they, too, turned on their Mormon fellows. Finally, when the press of a Nauvoo newspaper critical of Joseph Smith was wrecked, charges of riot and treason were brought against the Prophet. While incarcerated in the Carthage jail, he was murdered by a mob of Gentiles on June 27, 1844.[32]

The introduction of the temple rites hastened the end of Nauvoo as an experiment in city building, and burdened the Mormons for nearly fifty years with plural marriage until the Church's Manifesto of 1890 officially ended polygamy.[33] However, the doctrines also affirmed the increased importance of the temple that made the next Mormon urban experiment, Salt Lake City, unique in American history.

Although the Mormons' first large-scale urban experiment had failed, its ambitious size brought the problems of urbanization into focus and forced the Mormons to acknowledge their inexperience in dealing with the complexities of city life. The corrosive influences of urbanization had hastened the triumph of the Wicked Kingdom at Nauvoo. The growth of commerce and industry in Nauvoo had blurred Joseph Smith's vision of a "THEODEMOCRACY, where God and the people hold the power to conduct the affairs of men in righteousness." [34] Worldliness had thrived on speculation in land and buildings, and profanity had sprung from the concentration of increasing numbers and varieties of people in a limited locale.

Babylon steadily extended its degrading influences into the religious
core of a world of agrarian patriarchs faced with the mission of
building a city, determined to mold their lives in the image of the
Bible and supporting themselves through farming and animal
husbandry.

At Nauvoo, religious and worldly aspects of Mormonism had
become hopelessly ensnarled in the tangle of urban problems. The
accelerated growth of population tempted some Saints to tamper
with the concept of the village, set forth in the Plat of the City of
Zion, by building homes on the farmlands surrounding the town. The
animosities between the promoters of hill and flat triggered the
sequence of open hostilities that ultimately led to Prophet Joseph
Smith's death.[35]

The worldly success of Nauvoo produced other seeds of its
undoing. Thieving camp followers, who pillaged Saints as well as
Gentiles, darkened the Mormons' reputation in Illinois and undermined the Mormons' faith in their urban experiment. Nauvoo turned
into a burgeoning river town, and the advent of boatsmen brought a
relaxation of the prohibition on tobacco, coffee, tea, and alcohol that
had been enforced in the Church during the 1830s. Excursion boats
carried visitors to Nauvoo to see the sights and to enjoy the town.[36]
Worldliness raised its head in many forms and increased the turmoil.

In addition, Joseph Smith, founder of the Mormon Church and
also chief proprietor of Nauvoo, had been fundamentally ignorant of
the relationship between urban life, commercial development, and
industrial growth. He shared the rural background of most of his
followers. Inspired by the sights of New York, he went so far as to see
a city as the work of man resembling God's creation.[37] But his
attempts to intermingle the real life and the ideal life at Nauvoo
indicated his limited understanding of the intricacies of a city. "I
attended city council in the morning," Joseph Smith noted in his
journal on May 14, 1842, "and advocated strongly . . . some active
measures . . . to suppress houses and acts of infamy in the city."
After council, confident that his good intentions would clean up the

town, he worked in his garden, "walked out in the city, and borrowed two sovereigns to make a payment." [38]

Some of the difficulties encountered by his city had their roots in the nature of Joseph Smith's prophecies about the good and righteous life in the Kingdom of God. His instructions failed to meet the pressing need of the mushrooming Nauvoo for a functioning economic base.[39] Without guidance, the city's economy was wide open to hazy schemers and crafty manipulators. Once the rising value of real estate was accepted as a substitute for ordinary forms of making money, land constituted a major source of capital. It was as easy to mortgage the land as to buy land on credit. On the basis of the constant demand for city lots as well as farm tracts, credit was floated without banks. The bubble burst when the demands of weary and hardened creditors rudely shattered an economy based on faith.[40]

Real estate speculation as a monetary stopgap had been attractive to some Mormons in light of their experience with the first major community at Kirtland and with the bankruptcy of the Kirtland Safety Society Anti-Banking Company, in 1837. In that year of economic despair, many banks failed in the United States, but the Kirtland bank represented a special case since it was founded on divine revelation, had no charter, and expressed in its name opposition to its function. There was little in the Kirtland experience in general to prepare the Mormon city builders for the tasks at Nauvoo. The economy depended on the expanding Church for revenue. Temple building was the chief enterprise at Kirtland, from 1833 to 1836, and provided a temporary economic base in the absence of the sound operation of agriculture, commerce, and industry.[41]

At Nauvoo the search for an economic base brought about frenzied real estate speculation. The buying and selling of land titles produced monumental financial and legal tangles.[42] The confusion in the Church stemming from the introduction of polygamy, the tragedy of Joseph Smith's death, the subsequent contest for a new leader, the repeal of the Nauvoo city charter by the Illinois legislature, and the beginning of the Great Exodus in the winter of 1845 increased the agony. The extent of the suffering could still be sensed half a century later when Elder Brigham Henry Roberts, inspired by Longfellow's *Evangeline*, introduced his *Rise and Fall of Nauvoo* with an account of the Acadians' anguish facing the burning of "their lovely village." [43]

The Nauvoo of the Mormons never was an Acadian village. Any lofty dreams of bucolic life that Mormons preserved through the years of persecution in Missouri and brought with them to Illinois were shattered quickly by the worldly factors that were present in Nauvoo. Even as a "holy city," Nauvoo showed many of the ordinary characteristics of any rapidly growing urban center. Consequently, after the Mormons were forced to abandon Nauvoo the leaders of the Church were determined to protect the new temple city at the Great Salt Lake from these influences and so contributed to the uniqueness of the rising community.

The founding of Salt Lake City marked the full operation of a new phase of Mormon theology and of a novel departure in the Saints' response to urban problems. The New Mormonism, practiced at Salt Lake City, had been introduced in the Nauvoo Temple as an outgrowth of the Original Mormonism. In like manner, the Zion of the Mountain was an outgrowth of Nauvoo. The City Beautiful on the Mississippi served as a prototype for the Mormon community in the Great Basin. The outlines of Mormon society in the Far West were drawn in Nauvoo: the forms of social organization and control, the union of ecclesiastical and civil government, the notion of an independent Mormon nation-state within the Union, the plans to settle a new country with convert-immigrants, and the polygamous family system. In 1851, the charter of Salt Lake City was "almost a verbatim copy" of Nauvoo's, further attesting to the "important formative influence of Nauvoo on the political institutions of Utah." [44]

The similarities between Nauvoo and Salt Lake City were obscured by debates between splinter groups of Mormons and the main body of the Church over details of the Illinois experience. The fabric of romance woven around Nauvoo as a lost, though glorious, cause helped to enshrine that experience in Mormon culture as a heroic legend and to obscure the significance of the failure of the city as an urban settlement.[45] Gentile writers, on the other hand, were insensitive to the magnitude of the enterprise and the grandeur of the vision demonstrated in Nauvoo and thus bypassed an opportunity to observe people of the United States confronted with the problems of rapid urbanization.[46] As a Mormon experiment in urban living, the verdict on Nauvoo was ultimately suspended by the onslaught of the enemies of the Church who destroyed the city little more than one year after they had murdered its prophet.

But the experience at Nauvoo kept alive the Saints' heritage as children of the Jacksonian Era. Although they thought of themselves primarily as the Chosen Children of God, the Mormons, as men and women of the Age of Jackson, shared their generation's heady optimism about past and future national growth, along with a willingness to conduct social experiments.[47] Although sustained by revelation and inspired by prophecy, it was through a synthesis of American with Hebrew and Christian themes, that the Mormons "transformed and energized" the "myth of the common man." [48] Their belief in a literal, imminent fulfillment of biblical promises of the Kingdom of God was buttressed by the success of their practical endeavors—from Kirtland to Nauvoo—living proof that faith was rewarded. Those among them who descended from a line of tenacious frontier farmers may have felt doubly certain of the righteousness of their new ways because the tablets of their faith had been wrested from the earth instead of delivered from on high. The special appeal of the golden plates that Joseph Smith professed to have recovered from a hillside in upstate New York in the 1820s, more than half a century later, in Russia, impressed Leo Tolstoy who stressed in a conversation with the American minister to the czar the power of religious insights drawn from the soil.[49]

The murder of Joseph Smith and the end of Nauvoo contributed to the mental anguish and the physical hardships of the Exodus, but

these impediments added a new sense of urgency to the building of
Zion in the Great Basin. Thus, in practical terms, too, Nauvoo
influenced the course of events in Salt Lake City. Almost five
thousand converts from England had gathered in Nauvoo. Their
presence testified not only to the appeal of the Mormon missions in a
world struggling to adjust to population growth, industrialization,
and urbanization, but also to the reality of the Mormon faith. Having
been converted by missionaries under the direction of the Council of
the Twelve Apostles, these Englishmen helped to strengthen the
position of the Twelve within the Church. In Brigham Young, the
Twelve eventually recognized the successor to Joseph Smith. They
furnished the leadership that established the Mormon state of
Deseret in the Far West by transplanting the temple city of the
Kingdom of God from the Mississippi to the Great Basin.[50]

The lessons of Nauvoo taught the Saints to guard their temple city
near the Great Salt Lake against contamination. Their defenses did
not depend on the exalted role of the temple as part of the Nauvoo
heritage or the existence of a temple building as such. Even in
Nauvoo, the structure was not officially dedicated until the spring of
1846, some time after the Mormon Exodus in the previous winter.[51]
Although the Saints had vowed to build a temple upon their arrival
in the Great Basin and reaffirmed their obligation during the forty
years it took to complete that ambitious edifice, the Salt Lake
Temple was not dedicated until April 1893. By that time, the
Mormons had already erected five other temples of which three were
actually in service.[52] Under the circumstances, the actual state of the
physical structure was not important; significant was the Saints'
certainty that their flight from Illinois, during which they had relived
the experience of their oldest spiritual ancestors, the Israelites, would
enable them to build a city as adequate shelter for the temple.

The Exodus from Illinois gave Mormons the opportunity to erect a
temple city under the control of the Church. God "can guide us to
bring forth a better city," the Nauvoo *Neighbor* counseled them in its
last number, October 29, 1845, "an hundred fold of gathering, and
five times as good a temple, in five years, where demagogues will not

deceive us for our votes, and then connive at our extermination." [53]
Through the Exodus the Saints gained an economic base and a
political framework to usher in the earthly Kingdom of God.[54]

The isolation of the Great Basin encouraged the Mormons in the
belief that they could build an absolute church-state, far removed
from their enemies and distant from Mexican authorities who
actually governed the area, at least according to international law.
The progress of the Mexican War, which the Mormons shared
through the march of their battalion from Fort Leavenworth via
Santa Fe to San Diego, assured them that soon again they would be
living under the flag they cherished more than any other—as long as
its officials did not interfere with their way of life. Even after the
exchange of the ratifications of the Treaty of Guadalupe Hidalgo
incorporated the area into the United States in May 1848, it was
outside the jurisdiction of any organized state and territory. Far from
the influence of their adversaries, the Saints had found the no-man's-
land of American expansion that they had searched for in vain on the
Missouri and the Mississippi rivers.

After Nauvoo the Mormons left little of their urban experiment to
accident. Even the natural setting of their new world had to conform
to their vision. The hardship of the Exodus was expected, and so was
the isolation of the Great Basin. Toiling in their newly found
Promised Land, the Saints knew that only God's beneficent smile
upon his Chosen People would make "the desert 'blossom as the
rose.' " [55] Since they now faced a world far different from the
Mississippi Valley, their Apostles came to identify their land as a
desert, in line with biblical tradition. Orson Pratt, one of the first to
see the newly found Kingdom, had initially shouted with joy "the
moment this grand and lovely scenery" came into his view on July
21, 1847. Twenty years later in his Discourse, "Orson Pratt the First
to Stand on Temple Square," he saw it as a "dreary desolate land,"
relying on David's image from the 107th Psalm.[56]

The desert of official Mormon theology formed a striking contrast
to the paradise found by Father Francisco Atanasio Domínguez and
Father Silvestre Vélez de Escalante, fresh from arid New Mexico in

1776. Their reconnaissance had led them from Santa Fe north and west to Utah Valley.[57] Less than a year before the arrival of the Mormon vanguard in the Great Basin, a Swiss traveler on his way to California, Heinrich Lienhard, had been enchanted by "the clear, sky-blue surface of the lake, the warm, sunny atmosphere, the nearby high mountains, with the beautiful countryside at their base." And so were other travelers, explorers, and trappers, who crossed and recrossed the Great Basin before him. "All day long I felt like singing and whistling; and if there had been a single white family there," Lienhard confessed, "I would have stayed." [58]

Emigrant trains bound for California gave evidence of an intensified popular interest in the transmontane West, but they passed along the northern border of the Great Basin on a road pioneered by the Bartleson-Bidwell Party in 1841.[59] When the Mormon scouting parties infiltrated the northern reaches of the Mexican territory, the attractions of Oregon and California had already lured most emigrants on to the coast. The only people they found were Indians in Utah Valley and Miles Goodyear at Fort Buenaventura, whose farm and trading post in the Weber Valley was the beginning of Ogden.[60]

The absence of Gentiles in the Mormon settlement produced a population "almost all of one faith" and guaranteed the fusion of church and state.[61] For the first time in the history of the Church, the Saints were able to create a new social order according to their teachings, without interference from the outside. They lost little time building their religious commonwealth. Almost three decades after the establishment of territorial government in Utah, Apostle Franklin D. Richards still insisted: "Theoretically Church and State are one," and "if there were no Gentiles and no other Government, there would be no Civil Law." [62]

This land that other Americans had passed by on their way to Oregon and California fell into the hands of the Mormons. It was allotted by the leaders of the Church according to the need of the settlers. In contrast to the practice at Nauvoo, the city lots of Salt Lake City were neither bought from Gentiles nor sold to Saints but

apportioned to applicants, primarily through lotteries, according to
the law of stewardship. Real estate speculation was forbidden and
the right of property was subordinated to the common purpose;
emphasis was laid on self-sufficiency and cooperation as well as
isolation and independence.[63] The enforcement of these rules "made
the settlement of the city and the farming lands very compact, and
created a community of interest which could not have been felt
under other circumstances," Apostle George Q. Cannon recalled in
later years.[64] The lots of the original plat were all taken up within a
month, and a new plat was surveyed and additional lots provided for
latecomers. The city was divided into eighteen ecclesiastical wards
with a bishop in charge of each ward caring for the temporal and
spiritual needs of the residents.[65]

The struggling settlement quickly absorbed other Mormon pioneers who arrived on the heels of the advance party. Before the first
month was out there were almost as many women on the scene as
there were men, and that balance between the sexes continued to set
Mormon colonization apart from most other early settlements in the
Far West.[66] Almost seventeen hundred Saints spent the winter of
1847–48 in the Salt Lake Valley. Brigham Young, elected President
of the Church at Winter Quarters, Nebraska, in December 1847,
returned with many settlers in September 1848, which brought the
total Mormon population to 4,200.[67]

Hungry and destitute, poorly clothed and housed, lacking tools
and equipment, the Mormons saw their vision of a Great Basin
Kingdom severely tested until the gold discovery in California in
January 1848, lured a stream of travelers through the Great Basin,
leaving many benefits behind. The Gold Rush furnished them with
money and provided some of the means for immigration and
colonization projects essential to the building of the Kingdom.[68]
"Many wanted to unite Babylon and Zion," Brigham Young warned,
but the Mormons did not join the race to the mines although groups
of them were in California and the settlers in Utah were in a good
position to reach the gold fields early.[69] "We are gathered here," the
First Presidency said, reasserting the Saints' mission and cohesiveness

as a social body in 1854, "not to scatter around and go off to the mines or any other place, but to build up the Kingdom of God." [70]

Until the rapid growth of the community necessitated the establishment of the Provisional State of Deseret, Salt Lake City was a Stake of Zion, a territorial subdivision of the Church comprising several ecclesiastical wards, with "no secular functions in the common sense." [71] In the isolation of the Great Basin, the social controls, the result of the intertwined ecclesiastical and civil functions of the stake, appeared more fully than they did at Kirtland, Independence, and Nauvoo where the proximity of Gentiles had curtailed their flowering. The members of the High Council, the governing body of the stake combining religious and political authority with complete executive, legislative, and judicial powers, had been selected by the leaders of the Church before Brigham Young's return to Winter Quarters in August 1847. They were ratified by popular vote towards the end of the year. Under the supervision of the bishops, land was divided among the people, canals were dug, roads built, and bridges constructed, and society governed by the High Council. [72]

The first ordinances appeared in December 1847, dealing with vagrancy, disorderly conduct, disturbance of the peace, adultery, fornication, theft, arson, and drunkenness. During the second winter, in order to safeguard the survival of the settlement, the powerful Council of Fifty created the State of Deseret, the political counterpart of the Kingdom of God. However, the new organization foreshadowed the end of purely theocratic government in the Great Basin. The eighteen bishops soon became magistrates of the several city wards. Until the incorporation of Salt Lake City by the General Assembly of Deseret in January 1851, these wards functioned like municipal corporations. [73]

The people looked to the Church authorities for leadership and, of course, viewed the Church itself as the initial step in the realization of the Kingdom of God. [74] The plans for Salt Lake City represented a conscious effort to eliminate some of the difficulties that had endangered the urban experiment at Nauvoo, but the elders of the

Church were not able to wholly neutralize the effects of worldly growth on the lofty design of the temple city. Even if the Gold Rush had not directed a stream of Gentiles through the Great Basin, the ordinary growth of the city would have attracted outsiders and shattered its isolation. Some of the very functions of Zion within the Church would have brought the forces of the world to the scene.

Salt Lake City, as the gathering place of the Saints, was literally the center of the Kingdom and the nucleus of migration and commerce. Many newcomers from the East and immigrants from Europe, unprepared for the rigors of the arid region of the Great Basin, remained for a time in Salt Lake City while they learned to till the soil and to construct irrigation ditches under the guidance of experienced colonizers. During their period of adjustment, these new arrivals supported themselves through skills acquired in their earlier exposure to industrial society. They were able to earn a livelihood in the emerging workshops and petty factories. Their exposure to industrial discipline served the community well when the time came for the godly enterprise of building the temple. However, the industrial and commercial pursuits of these new arrivals also hastened the worldly growth of Salt Lake City and reinforced trends in other areas of life that moved the development of the city off its intended course. In particular, the high freight rates on imported manufactured goods, almost as much as their desire for independence from the Gentile world, stimulated the denizens of the new city to make their own products. These activities, supported by the authority of Brigham Young, contributed to the breakdown of those defenses that had previously sheltered the temple city from more temporal urban life.[75]

When circumstances required the establishment of a civil government superimposed over the ecclesiastical organization, the secular compromises further secularized the temple city. Official administrative functions were added to the city's religious and ecclesiastical, as well as commercial and industrial, roles. From 1849 to 1851, Salt Lake City was the capital of the State of Deseret, which appeared to be a free and independent state.[76] When Deseret gave way to the

Territory of Utah, the territorial government endorsed Brigham Young's idea "to force the pattern of core expansion into a particular direction" by locating the capital at Fillmore in the Pauvan Valley in central Utah.[77]

The removal of the capital 150 miles to the south, however, was not only one move in a system of demographic controls, but also one attempt to protect the temple city from the pernicious influences of the world. The move seemed to assure that unwanted federal appointees of the territorial government and their entourage of office seekers and lobbyists would operate at a safe distance from Salt Lake City. But the design overcompensated; the scheme failed because sparse settlement and tenuous communication at Fillmore made apparent rather quickly its total unsuitability. The legislature held only one complete session in Fillmore, the fifth, and in December 1856, by joint resolution, made Salt Lake City Utah's capital.[78]

As the new capital of Utah, Salt Lake City drew more and more outsiders to its folds. These alien influences, naturally, further threatened the purity of the temple city. In addition, the new political significance of Salt Lake City coincided with the peaking of westward migration. As it became apparent that there was a limit to the resources and spoils of the continent, Gentiles began to seek their opportunities in the Mormon country, too. Economic and industrial development flourished on the city's role as entrepôt of immigration, center of commerce, and communications link between the Missis-sippi and the Pacific. Worldliness collided with the ideals of the temple city, imposing a dual identity on this former sanctuary: Zion and Babylon, "holy City of the Far West" and bustling way station to the coast. On the eve of this secular onslaught two other instant cities, San Francisco and Denver,[79] were about to emerge.

The full weight of this onslaught, made more potent by new internal pressures within the temple city, had not yet been felt when San Francisco and Denver appeared on the scene. Nor had the complex definition of the struggle that pitted modern science against sacred beliefs, individual freedom against social cohesion, national-ism against separatism, and human instincts against godly designs made themselves manifest. However, it was obvious from the beginning that the builders of the temple city would not let this sanctuary suffer the fate of Nauvoo. They would battle incessantly against the corrosive influences of urbanization and industrialization, the logistics of geography and communication, the coercive force of national politics as well as the base aspects of man's nature. Despite the dichotomy of Zion and Babylon dividing their urban experiment, their determination assured Salt Lake City of both its survival and its uniqueness.

The subordination of the free interplay of social, political, economic, and cultural forces to a religious ideal set this instant temple city on the far western scene apart from the instant city as mining camp and emporium. On the scale, and in the isolation, of Salt Lake City, such a degree of practical community planning, through a fusion of ecclesiastical and secular affairs, had never before been achieved in the course of American urban growth. It made Salt Lake City and Mormons, "as ideas and realities . . . wholly inseparable." [80] Their successful application of a definite plan to urban development antedated, by half a century, the beginning of modern city planning that shaped the Chicago World's Fair of 1893. Their struggle provided a preview to the search for harmony between man and his constantly expanding urban environment.[81]

Salt Lake City enjoyed a unity of life to an unusual degree. Although the temple city emerged harmoniously "in the pristine American wilderness," some Americans added Salt Lake City to the "growing list of Mormon crimes against man and nature." [82] The other versions of instant cities in the Far West, San Francisco and Denver, which rose on the ruthless exploitation of nature by miners, were heralded as shining symbols of the American conquest of the wilderness. They emerged about the same time, in about the same isolation of the West, but San Francisco and Denver were as different from Salt Lake City in their interest and view of wild nature as in their open embrace of the ambitions and vices of the Gentile world.

Despite the distinctions between the temple city and San Fran-

cisco and Denver, Salt Lake City shared the explosive character of
all instant cities. Brought forth by the stern command of prophets,
the city emerged suddenly in the heart of wild mountains. Its appeal,
although directed at the religious fulfillment of a Chosen People and
not at the inquisitive instincts of vast multitudes, generated urban
enterprises on a scale that forced Mormons and Gentiles alike into its
ban. The "Jerusalem of the American desert displayed an animation
and life resembling the movement in the Eternal City during the
Carnival and Holy Week," two European scholars concluded when
they witnessed one of the biannual conferences in 1855 regulating
the affairs of the Church.[83]

The struggle for a glorious future shaped Salt Lake City as much as
it did San Francisco and Denver. The precise nature of that future
divided the builders of the three cities, but their mutual determination and drive brought a new pace to the farthest third of the
continent. The new dimensions of urban life their activities created
were defined by hectic change. Whether responding to divine or to
worldly inspirations, their vision and ambition formed a striking
contrast to the narrow and confined urban world of the Far West in
the middle of the nineteenth century, on the eve of the rise of instant
cities.

# 3

## Urban Experiences in the Far West

Between the rolling prairies of the Plains and the thundering breakers of the Pacific lay an area measuring more than a third of the continent. Yet, up to the middle of the nineteenth century urban civilization had touched only a small part of that wilderness, insignificantly dotting the miles and miles of virgin terrain. Some of the isolated communities had arisen before the land was part of the nation. A few owed their origin to the initiative of men driven by the lure of wealth and fame or the commands of kings. Other settlements appeared slowly and grew as accidentally as the straggling trees on the parched slopes of western hills.

Three of these early communities, Santa Fe, Monterey, and Champoeg (Champ-OO-eg), dominating New Mexico, California, and Oregon, were typical of the urban growth of the Far West before the emergence of San Francisco and Denver. In contrast to the dynamic character of the instant cities, the three earlier settlements reflected the static quality of the first far western towns. Santa Fe was the economic hub of the southern Rocky Mountains, Monterey the colonial outpost of Mexico on the Pacific, and Champoeg the marketplace of the wheat farmers of the Willamette Valley. As products of the Spanish-Mexican world of the Far

Southwest, and the Anglo-American world of the Pacific Northwest, they had come into existence in response to events dating as far back as the late 1590s, when Don Juan de Oñate founded New Mexico and planted the seeds of the Rio Grande settlements, and occurring as recently as the late 1830s, when the fur traders of the Hudson's Bay Company began buying the grain of the settlers of the Oregon Country.

The oldest of the three, Santa Fe, established in 1609, was transformed during the 1840s by American traders and soldiers into the economic center of the southern Rocky Mountains. The traders gave way to resident Santa Fe merchants who sold their imports to small farmers, and, in turn, bought and shipped east the produce of the farmers. Monterey, designated in 1775 by the king of Spain the capital of the most recent addition to his empire, became the administrative center of that area. It was a port of entry and through its all-important custom house moved goods serving the Spanish and Mexican settlements stretching from San Diego, in the south, to Sonoma, in the north. Despite subsequent political upheavals in Spain and Mexico it remained the administrative center and the port of entry for the territory until the American conquest destroyed the Californios' way of life and made archaic Monterey's former function.

If for no other reason than its obscurity, Champoeg appears out of place in the company of Santa Fe and Monterey, both famed by history and romance and well-known to travelers and tourists. Tucked away on a bend of the lower Willamette River, its attractions still do not entice many tourists to leave the freeway on their rush through the lovely Willamette Valley to or from Portland. In a different light, in a historical analysis of urbanization in the Far West, however, Champoeg clearly has earned a place in the company of Santa Fe and Monterey.

Champoeg was a marketplace, a type of settlement as crucial to the West during its early stages of urbanization as the economic town and the colonial outpost. As a marketplace where settlers bartered their produce for the necessities of life or sold them for money, Champoeg shared the fate of many similar marketplaces: it grew too quickly and died very quietly, a constant reminder that towns do not grow as naturally as trees. Nothing ever came of it, and no prosperous city currently bears its name. Unlike all the other market towns, however, its brief days were filled not only with a time for harvesting and a more prosaic period for bickering over prices but also with events that gave Champoeg a special moment in history when modernization and urbanization reached this marketplace unprepared for turbulent change.

Santa Fe, Monterey, and Champoeg, therefore, exemplify various forms of early urbanization in the Far West. They grew in the mountains, on the ocean, and in the forest, and the contrasts in geography account for some of the differences. Unlike Santa Fe and Monterey, Champoeg had no older culture to which it could adhere. Although it had grown on trapping and farming, activities predating recorded history, its traditions and culture did not look back beyond the founding of the United States.

Like Santa Fe and Monterey, Champoeg seldom allowed its quiet life style to be disrupted. These early towns had a special ability to absorb what elsewhere might have produced change and to restyle it to their pattern of life, so that only a modest compromise seemed to take place. Their ageless culture favored absorption over adsorption of the new and different, and their development stayed clear of that point of transition when quantitative accumulation produces qualitative change. Figuratively speaking, in towns like Santa Fe, Monterey, and Champoeg, men grew older and older but never died, water became colder and colder but never turned to ice, and days grew darker and darker but night never came. The allegiance of the residents of these towns reinforced their timelessness. Change was a stranger in these communities, and when it did come, it had to disguise itself as a relative of the old.

The responses of Santa Fe, Monterey, and Champoeg to the far-reaching events of the 1840s differed in each case, but all three struggled to absorb the forces of change into patterns and rates of growth acceptable to their static lives. Their potential to do this while maintaining the desired but precarious balance differed as widely as the three types of towns they represented. Santa Fe weathered the troubled years of the American conquest of the Far West on the strength of its role as economic center of the Southwest. The resilience and vitality of this ancient city deflected the impact of the change so much that the newly developing ways of life seemed to be merely extensions of the old ones. Monterey, however, lost its function as colonial outpost when Mexican rule in California collapsed; in an attempt to ignore this new political reality, the town retreated into its past. Champoeg, with no past of its own, faded into oblivion when other successful marketplaces replaced it in control of the new Northwest.

The confrontation of these stable societies with new ways of life began gradually but was intensified by military and diplomatic conquest. Although at first the encounter barely altered the appearance of the towns, the forces of change would finally leave marks that presaged the powerful effect that they would have in the dynamic settings of instant cities.

During the first half of the nineteenth century, Santa Fe had grown slowly, if at all; its population during the period, about five thousand, varied little from year to year.[1] Most citizens of old Santa Fe lived off the produce of their small parcels of irrigated land, which comprised over three-fourths of the town's total area, raising corn, wheat, beans, chilies, melons, and squashes. Only a few businessmen made a living in Santa Fe. In the 1830s and 1840s storekeepers began to attract farmers and ranchers to the town who were eager to trade on a year-round basis in shops stocked with goods brought in from the United States by merchant-adventurers. The community's wealth was divided among a few leading families whose peons tended large flocks of sheep and herds of cattle on haciendas in nearby valleys.[2]

At first sight during the 1850s, the modern city of Santa Fe hardly differed from the old. During that earlier period, the epic phase of the Santa Fe trade, the town reminded some American merchants of a large brick kiln or a fleet of flatboats, a dilapidated brickyard, or a colony of prairie dogs. It was to be the commercial conquest of New Mexico by these traders from Missouri that set in motion the transformation. Through the initiative of these adventurers, gambling on Santa Fe's great distance from sources of supply in Mexico, Santa Fe developed from a predominantly agricultural market, with most of its people making a living on small plots of irrigated land, into *the* economic town of the southern Rocky Mountains, where merchants competed for the trade all the way from Taos, New Mexico to El Paso, Texas. During the Mexican War, the conquest of the city by the Army of the West, under General Stephen Watts Kearny, brought the form of law and order most suited to the needs of business enterprises. Yet, neither the commercial nor the military changed Santa Fe's outward appearance. It was an ageless settlement, formed by the drab adobe fronts of single-storied, flat-roofed houses, with almost continuous walls lining lanes leading to the gardens and fields of a valley watered by the Santa Fe River and encircled by barren hills and the slopes of pine-covered mountains.[3]

Behind these ageless adobe walls the complex process that would shape the Santa Fe of the 1850s took place. With the commercial and military take-over, the slowly developing town was threatened by change. The activities of the merchants and the presence of the soldiers injected American concepts of business and law into the commercial life of the community. Merchants and soldiers began to rival politicians and priests as community leaders, despite the efforts of the former to reaffirm the position of Santa Fe as an administrative center, and the efforts of the latter to reaffirm the role of the church in the life of the community.[4]

The presence of soldiers and merchants was no unmitigated blessing for Santa Fe. The army, one of the instruments of change, was also an instrument of violence, which the permissive town had learned to neutralize in earlier days. The merchants, the other embodiment of change, too often cared only for the immediate material advantages they could garner and showed little concern for the ultimate effect of their activities on the community. Only when a second generation of merchants and new army officers, more responsive to the character of the city, made their influence felt, did Santa Fe manage to assimilate the new thrusts.

The rapprochement of the military with Santa Fe was complicated by soldiers who were at once conquerors, protectors, and lawmakers, but who in all these roles viewed themselves and were viewed as foreigners. Any good the army did could not compensate for the problems a body of men, far from home and loosely disciplined, invariably creates in a city. Civilians then, as now, were not tuned to the antics and riotous conduct of soldiers. Local confidence in the army was also weakened by the acts of officers who longed to play their role in the "real war" with Mexico and eagerly sought glory on the trails to San Diego and Los Angeles and the roads to Chihuahua and Monterrey in Mexico. These officers were abetted by volunteers who looked upon soldiering in the West as a great adventure and not as a military operation. However, while most officers managed to keep up a front, quite a number of the enlisted men, quickly losing their enthusiasm for the army, fell for the city.

Many of the soldiers fell in love with Santa Fe almost immediately. After the first unit of volunteers had trudged across the prairies, marching "873 miles in forty-nine days," the earthly tabernacles, Santa Fe's adobe houses, contained a sufficient number of mysteries for them, as well as for their comrades who followed, to satisfy their craving for adventures.[5] Ready for diversions, they were willing to forget their cultural bias. The tears of some of the Mexican women, who had expected "to be branded on the cheek with the letters 'U.S.' " by the conquerors, gave way, naturally and inevitably, to smiles.[6] The enviable role of the bloodless conqueror helped volunteers from midwestern farm communities find a friendly reception and adjust to the apparently ageless urban civilization of the second largest city west of the Mississippi.

Equally important, the town welcomed the demand for goods created by the army's presence. In the past it had depended on the annual caravans of Santa Fe traders from the United States to avoid the stagnation that threatened at the end of each trading season.

More customers, individual and corporate, meant more business. Army projects provided employment for civilians, and the construction of nearby Fort Marcy put additional coin into the pockets of volunteers who helped build it.[7] Money was then, "perhaps, more plentifully distributed in and about Santa Fe, than at any other time in its long history," a scion of one of the leading New Mexico families recalled.[8]

Eventually, however, familiarity bred contempt. The potent local liquor known as Taos Lightning and the common lack of understanding between New Mexicans and Americans as well as civilians and soldiers combined to erode the love affair between the army and the town. The officers found volunteers, fed up with drill and stimulated by the city, not merely undisciplined but insubordinate. In October 1846, Governor Charles Bent called on Colonel Alexander W. Doniphan, who had assumed command in Santa Fe after General Kearny continued his march to California, to "*compel* the soldiers to respect the rights of the inhabitants." [9] The tension increased when starvation threatened the overcrowded city. "Certainly in Santa Fe," the English traveler George Ruxton noted, the Americans "have not been very anxious to conciliate the people." [10]

The soldiers' affection for Santa Fe gave way to a "bullying and overbearing demeanor . . . by the dirtiest and rowdiest crew" roaming the streets.[11] Allowing their prejudices against the different life style of the conquered city to surface again, they tainted their relationships with all females by snide remarks about the dress and morals of New Mexican women.[12] "Crowds of drunken volunteers . . . brawling and boasting, but never fighting," raised hell. In retaliation the citizenry converted "every other house" into whiskey shops which continually disgorged "reeling drunken men, and everywhere filth and dirt reigned triumphant." [13] The army ignored the deteriorating relationship between soldiers and civilians until the residents struck back, using the guerilla tactics and techniques they had learned to employ against oppressive authority. Numerous graves near Fort Marcy "were filled by Americans found dead, beaten to death with rocks, no one knows by whom." [14]

The friction between soldiers and civilians reflected the days of real conflict after the quiet conquest. Until Congress set up a framework of government for the conquered land through the Compromise of 1850, power in New Mexico was in the hands of army commanders, civilian governors, and politicians. Each cooperated with one another only if it suited them. Some of the American politicians who had flocked to Santa Fe sought to provide a temporary government. Others hoped to establish, with the help of the army, their absolute rule in New Mexico.

That such anomalous government could arise and persist, even for a brief time, was due in large measure to the cultural diversity of the area and the mutual suspicions existing between New Mexicans, Americans, Pueblo Indians, and Indian nomads. The system added the arbitrary actions of politicians to the outrageous behavior of soldiers. What developed was a situation that reminded people of the rule of the last Mexican governor, General Manuel Armijo, who had governed New Mexico for many years for his own ends.[15]

The Compromise of 1850 provided for territorial government and seemed to offer a chance for orderly civilian authority. But, the threat of Indian raids still necessitated a strong military garrison that made the army more powerful than the government because the campaigns against the nomadic Indian tribes were so intimately connected with the profit motives of supply merchants and the economy of the entire territory. Colonel Edwin Vose Sumner, the first military commander of New Mexico officially told to cooperate with the territorial government, spelled out the relationship. The "only resource of this country is the government money," he explained, and "all classes depend on it, from the professional man and trader down to the beggar." [16] When problems of defense and economic welfare became combined, the army, naturally, became the stronger government.[17]

Santa Fe symbolized for Colonel Sumner the devil at his back. Here crossed the lifelines of the territory, here arrived the orders from Washington, and here soldiers, politicians, and merchants made their deals. He saw no way to keep the army out of the political and economic mess, but was determined, at least, to rescue his men from the corrosive influence of the city, "that Sink of vice and extravagance." [18] The colonel was backed by his superiors in Washington who endorsed the transfer of all garrisons from towns to frontier posts to restore morale and reduce expenses.[19]

On the day of his arrival in the city, July 19, 1851, Colonel Sumner ordered the removal of the headquarters of the Ninth Military Department to the Mora Valley, twenty-five miles northeast of Las Vegas, New Mexico, on the Santa Fe Trail. At "some holes of water in the prairie," as a newspaper correspondent, facetiously bemoaning the "plight of the abandoned city," described the locality, Colonel Sumner established Fort Union in the hope of rebuilding the morale of his troops in the clear country air.[20] The colonel's plan failed when Santa Fe women established themselves in the caves overlooking the post and in nearby shanties. While some of his men relived the fondly remembered city life in the caverns, Colonel Sumner moved to Albuquerque where he could keep at least one eye on the government. Primarily for political reasons he transferred the military headquarters back to Santa Fe, but the stubborn Bostonian continued to reside in Albuquerque until he ended his stretch of duty in New Mexico, hailed by a Santa Fe paper as "The Big Bug of Albuquerque." [21]

Colonel Sumner's experiment in clean living did little to change the army or Santa Fe. His successor, Brigadier General John Garland, regarded Albuquerque as "the dirtiest hole in New Mexico," and opted for Santa Fe as his residence, as well as his headquarters.[22] There he could continue his friendly relations with the territorial governor, with whom he had traveled the last leg of the long overland trail to his new post. He, at least, sensed what most New Mexicans took for granted. Santa Fe was their oldest and largest city and their capital. Nearly three centuries ago, Spanish colonists, who preferred towns to strictly rural living and avoided dispersal in a hostile land, had established the city to protect themselves against the hostile Indians, and, in time, the city had become a center of culture and trade. It was only fitting for the new civil and military chiefs to live and work there, and the town could again take pride in its restored hegemony over the Far Southwest.

With an appropriate grand gesture, the citizens of Santa Fe indicated their readiness to incorporate some of the new ways into their old city. In August 1853, they celebrated the safe arrival of their new officials, Governor David Meriwether and General Garland, in their parish church in true Spanish-Mexican tradition. Bishop John Baptist Lamy sang the Te Deum and for the "first time in my life . . . I . . . witnessed this imposing religious ceremony," Meriwether later wrote in his autobiography. In "calm and stately dignity" the procession of notables paraded through the streets, "alive with the moving throng or the anxious spectator," to the plaza where "thousands congregated to witness the formality of a public introduction." In front of the "old Mexican Palace," Governor Meriwether delivered his inaugural address. He was followed by General Garland, who graciously acknowledged the plaudits of the residents with "the politeness and civility which invariably marks the true American officer." [23]

Civil and military affairs properly launched, story has it that the roof of the old prison at the west end of the Palace of the Governors caved in. The fall squared an old score of the new territorial governor with the city because it destroyed the cell where he was confined in 1820. Meriwether, once a fur trader, was the last American to be imprisoned by Spanish authorities on New Mexican soil for his attempt to trade with Santa Fe.[24] The superstitious New Mexicans interpreted the destruction of his jail as a favorable omen, evidence that the past was forgiven and forgotten, and all could now comfortably move forward in harmony—Santa Fe style.[25]

Obligingly, the territorial legislature greeted the return of the army to Santa Fe with a law that utilized the city's traditional feast days for the punishment of offenders. The statute not only specified as pimps "those persons, male or female, whose business is to procure women for the purpose of lascivious connection with men" but also stipulated that they "shall . . . be publicly whipped, receiving thirty lashes, and . . . be carried upon a Jack Ass, upon some feast day, through the streets among the people . . . followed by a town-crier, who shall cry out not less than five times the cause of such punishment." [26] The law was quietly repealed during the next session in 1854.[27]

The period of peaceful coexistence between soldier and civilian that followed exposed the ludicrous dimensions of the short-lived statute in a city trying to integrate strange soldiers into its way of life. Sharing such elementary rewards of the new common national existence as the Fourth of July holiday worked more effectively than threats of absurd punishments. In July 1856, an army clerk of the Commissary Department described some of the results. He wrote to his relatives in South Carolina that Santa Fe had observed the Glorious Fourth in the "old fashioned style." In the morning "there was a Grand mass celebrated at the Cathedral, afterwards a procession," orations in English and Spanish, "a dinner, and in the Evening a Grand Fandango. Americans far from home," he added, apologetically, to his enumeration of events on what had become another Santa Fe feast day, "are more apt to feel patriotic than those who are surrounded by all the comforts of home." [28] Town and army had, in fact, learned to live together.

In contrast to the military, the merchants—the other instrument of change to help create the modern town—were saved from the agonies of a slow rapprochement with Santa Fe by the effects of a worldwide commercial revolution. Its repercussions reached Santa Fe in the wake of the American occupation and eliminated from the community the economic influences of the traveling merchant-adventurers of the old Santa Fe Trail. The transformation brought resident merchants to the scene who built permanent establishments and stocked their firms with goods not brought by accident but in response to their assessment of well-calculated risks.[29]

The old Santa Fe Trail traders had laid the groundwork for the new commercial enterprise, but the emerging order was not for them because they had a rather different disposition. Merchant-adventurers like James Josiah Webb, Alexander Majors, and James, Samuel, and William Magoffin were content to operate on the Santa

Fe Trail as long as Chihuahua, with its flourishing mines and a population twice the size of Santa Fe, was the principal market of the overland trade. With the annexation of Texas and the conquest of the Southwest, the new international boundary separated the trade south of El Paso from Santa Fe. As well, these daring speculators loved risk as an element of their roving life and one suited to their temperament and had little interest in establishing the necessary routine of a resident merchant or, for that matter, in remaining in one place permanently.[30]

The excitement that formerly accompanied the sporadic arrival of the traders' caravans gave way in the 1840s to the more enduring benefits of specific orders brought in by resident merchants on regular deliveries. Furthermore, the resident merchant would remain in the town to spend his profits. The customs duties levied on the goods sold by the roving traders did not benefit Santa Fe and the town had been seriously depleted of its wealth in former times by the profits these traders took back East with them. The new merchants would not depart with the town's wealth.

The one resident merchant predecessor to the new entrepreneurs was Manuel Alvarez, whose store, established in 1824, was devoted largely to a local trade with virtually no imports or exports.[31] The new resident merchants would conduct business differently. The basis of their operation would be the exchange of manufactured goods imported from the East for corn and beans. These merchants represented the spearhead, in the Far Southwest, of immigrant German Jews who had come to the New World seeking security as well as gain. They repeated in New Mexico the pattern established in the East two decades earlier where this wave of immigrants saw its opportunity in the merchandising field.[32] From the East Coast these patient entrepreneurs began to fan out as peddlers, petty retailers, and wholesalers until their growing influence was felt nearly everywhere. During the war with Mexico, some of them moved West with the army as sutlers or soldiers, or both.[33]

The trend toward resident merchants had been foreshadowed by the Leitsendorfers, in 1844, and the Goldstines, in 1847, brothers who ran general merchandise firms. In October, 1848, Solomon Jacob Spiegelberg founded his business, later known as the House of Spiegelberg Brothers. In the following year, Sigmund Seligman arrived in Santa Fe and, with Charles P. Clever, started a firm that became Seligman Brothers during the 1850s.[34]

These newcomers were men of enterprise as well as enterprising men, not merely satisfied to sell any goods that roving traders dumped in their laps. They methodically built their firms on the sale of their own imports and, in turn, bought and shipped to eastern markets the dried products of the growing number of small farms. Their business acumen and perseverence stimulated stagnant areas of the city's economy and their cosmopolitan blend of European and American culture freed them to deal with equal facility with Indians, Spaniards, Mexicans, and Americans. With legal safeguards protecting their investments guaranteed by the army, these resident merchants prospered. Eyes set on a distant future, they helped metamorphose Santa Fe from a commercial backwater along the Santa Fe Trail to a position of economic dominance of a large region.

The strangers—adventurers, traders, soldiers, and the permanent cadre of businessmen—who wrought change on Santa Fe were, in turn, themselves changed. Although propelled to the scene by swift conquest they persisted only on Santa Fe's terms and at its sufferance. Likewise, the new business activities they brought in, while giving birth to a new economy had to find their way into the cultural and social fabric of the old city, a fabric of tan adobes that would continue to maintain their old appearance for many years. In a speech celebrating the national centennial on July 4, 1876, one of the new residents of Santa Fe also celebrated the town's longevity: "Where we now stand in the city of Santa Fe," he proclaimed, "there was a town according to tradition and to records" long before the actual beginnings of our national history and from that Indian pueblo, "with its many thousand inhabitants," grew the Spanish city of Santa Fe, "the Oldest City in North America." [35]

During the crucial decade of the 1840s, a period in which the future of the Far West was recast through the extension of American rule to the Pacific, the commercial heartbeat of the emerging economic town infused new life into the ancient city and assured the timelessness of Santa Fe. In these same momentous years, Monterey and Champoeg fell by the wayside because they failed to abstract from the forces of change a new self-significance allowing the continuation of their roles as colonial outpost and marketplace.

In August 1775 the king of Spain designated Monterey the administrative center of the recent extension of his empire in America. Thereafter, Monterey functioned as a colonial outpost first for the disintegrating Spanish empire and then for the Mexican republic, a nation weakened by internal strife. Its harbor was the chief port of entry to that part of the West, stretching from San Diego, in the south, to Sonoma, in the north,[36] that had been colonized by Spain and then Mexico in the latter half of the eighteenth and the early part of the nineteenth century. Until the invasion of American troops upset the precarious relationship between necessity and usefulness, the duties collected at the custom house assured the continued significance of Monterey. At times foreign vessels could pay their duties only at its custom house.

The Monterey custom house produced the real income of California by extracting dues on merchandise amounting to about 100 per cent of the invoice prices. A considerable amount of the money came from an impost on goods that American and European traders bartered in exchange for hides and tallow derived from the herds of black cattle, the major source of commerce. The flourishing trade yielded enough revenue to place control of California in the hands of the men collecting the money. Some of them regarded themselves as Californios rather than as Mexicans. Control by the central government in Mexico was weak at best, and the lines of communication, long and hazardous, did not permit close supervision.[37] When factional strife or the whim of a governor induced some officials to abandon their territorial capital, the loss of the money collected in the Monterey custom house lured them back. Furthermore, on those occasions when the Californios replaced governors appointed in Mexico City with men of their own choosing, Monterey became, in effect, a sovereign capital. Thus, while the town remained small—only 700 people in 1845 as compared to Los Angeles's 1,600 and to Santa Barbara's 1,000—Monterey held sway over both.[38]

Neither history nor appearance favored Monterey. Formally founded in June 1770, the presidio and the mission of San Cárlos Borromeo de Monterey were one year younger than California's earliest presidio and mission at San Diego, established in May and July, 1769.[39] An *Ayuntamiento*, a town council, the mark of a purely civilian community, granted to California's two original pueblos at San Jose, founded in 1777, and Los Angeles, established in 1781, was given Monterey only after the growth of population in the late 1820s.[40]

Monterey's harbor and defenses were at best second-rate. Sir George Simpson, the Governor of the Hudson's Bay Company Territories in America, considered the harbor as "infinitely inferior" to San Francisco Bay and San Diego, after his visit in January 1842.[41] Monterey's pitiful fortifications were well known. The lack of defenses was par for California, however. Aside from the Russian Fort Ross, and later John Augustus Sutter's New Helvetia, and to a certain extent, Sonoma, which gained some renown as a frontier post,[42] fortifications worthy of the name were unnecessary and unknown.

Defenses, regardless of their utility, were just part of the scene, and for the first forty years of its existence, Monterey was a walled post with most of its residents dwelling inside the presidio stockade. However, in 1821, after Mexican independence, foreign trade developed and adobes sprang up along the shore of the bay and over the hillside. By the 1840s about a hundred houses and hovels dotted the gentle slope. The haphazard nature of their growth subsequently prevented town officials from laying out neatly arranged streets.[43] Sir George Simpson caustically commented about the quality of the houses. Of public buildings, he said, Monterey could, "with a stretch of charity, be allowed to possess four." In addition to the church, "part of which is going to decay, while another part is not yet finished," he criticized the fort, commanding town and anchorage, if "rusty . . . guns can be said to command anything," and the guardhouse, "a paltry mud hut without windows." Fourth "and last" he mentioned the custom house "which is, or rather promises to be, a small range of decent offices, for, though it has been building for five years, it is not yet finished." [44] Church, fort, and prison conventionally represented the religious, military, and civil controls of the community, but in noting the custom house, Sir George's administrative eye detected the real source of power, which made Monterey the salient colonial outpost on the California coast.

The California pattern of life and labor upheld Monterey's position in the province. There were no rivals; towns, per se, were of slight importance. The hacienda overshadowed village and town in a ranchero society based on the availability of land, while the presence of an Indian labor force curbed the growth of a peon class. Soldiers and their numerous children, lured away from the presidios by the reputation that went with landownership, moved to the country and contributed to the decay of the military settlements. Once the mission phase came to an end and the lands fell into the hands of rancheros, American and European supercargoes outfitted their ships as shops or dealt directly with the rancheros at home. Their freewheeling operations undercut the importance of trade centers.[45] The few pueblos of neophyte Indians were at best "feeble approximations" of the towns they were supposed to become under the original system.[46] Urban life was insignificant in early California in contrast to New Mexico where town and village life along the Rio Grande dominated a feudal society of *patrón* and peon and followed a pattern established by the sedentary Indians before the Spaniards.[47]

The social self-sufficiency and the economic autonomy of the California rancheros and their Indian servants stifled the development of the pueblos as social and economic centers. "I went to the town only occasionally . . . on some urgent business," Don José del Carmen Lugo recalled, and he returned to his hacienda "without loss of time." [48] A few of the wealthy landowners, such as Abel Stearns, resided in pueblos and employed overseers to manage their estates, but they were exceptions in a society where the home of the ranchero was the focus of the all-important family life.[49]

Californios did not care much for towns, but they needed Monterey for their official business. As the administrative center of the province, the town attracted rancheros who wanted to record their real estate transactions, including filing and confirmation of land grants essential to their way of life. Californios were content to cultivate a standard of manners far exceeding their standard of living and they cared little for the routine of business. Shipping was in the hands of Americans and Europeans who also looked to the custom house in Monterey, as the gauge of their fortunes.[50]

Administrators as well as foreign traders lived in Monterey, and their presence gave the colonial outpost a special touch. In April 1846, United States Consul Thomas O. Larkin, in the course of preparing confidential notes for the Secretary of State, listed a total of twenty-three eminent men as residents of Monterey alone; he noted eight in San Jose, seven each in Los Angeles, around San Francisco Bay, and in the Sacramento Valley, six in Santa Barbara, and four each in Sonoma and Yerba Buena. The remainder were scattered from San Diego to Bodega Bay or lived on board trading vessels. Larkin was struck by the relative steadfastness of Monterey administrators, who, unlike some of the local politicians, were not given to restlessness. Perhaps his own levelheaded disposition and purposefulness made him more acutely aware of like qualities in his fellow-residents.

Monterey bureaucrats and technocrats assured continuity and stability to social and economic affairs during a generation that witnessed successive political revolts. Men like Secretary Manuel Jimeno, "well versed in the tittle deeds of the country"; Collector Pablo de la Guerra and Treasurer José Abrigo, who had "never taken part in a Revolution"; the Captain of the Port and other officers of the custom house, "quiet and unobtrusive in their inclinations," represented a group of residents who kept Monterey functioning as a colonial outpost and assured its hegemony in California. Still another element that contributed to Monterey's administrative leadership was the number of naturalized Mexican citizens employed in the custom house and other administrative departments or holding office in the local government.[51]

Monterey's life style, largely set by administrators and foreign consuls, was in itself a cultural force in the province. In a society fond of *bailes* and fandangos, dancing parties of varying degrees of formality, the officials found time and pleasure in organizing such affairs for almost any pretext. Once a trading vessel had been cleared and the duties assessed, the large hall in the custom house was turned into a ballroom. There, and on the colonnade skirting the seaward side of the building, the ship's officers and traders met the ladies and dignitaries of the capital, among them the very officials with whom they had just finished arguing over import duties.[52]

Ordinary fandango music in California was provided by anyone who played a guitar, but in Monterey paid musicians were part of a festivity. Thomas O. Larkin, frugal merchant though he was, spent as much as twenty-five dollars for the music at one of his versions of the celebrated cascaron balls.[53] The residents of Monterey lived lavishly during the carnival season and festivals, but their daily life style, itself, contributed significantly to the culture of the country at large. There were only a few things in the port that impressed William H. Meyers, a gunner on board the U.S.S. *Cyane*, but a piano was one of them. He recorded in his diary after a Sunday's shore leave in May 1843, that he "saw the first piano of Monterey at the Capitanio del Puertos." [54]

Monterey brought forth a style of architecture that in later years became a symbol for the self-sufficient society governed by the colonial outpost. "Monterey Colonial" used adobe walls and added a wooden porch, which provided shelter and shade and an elevated veranda from which the occupants could watch the people below. The design is attributed to Thomas O. Larkin, who came to Monterey in 1832 and three years later began building the first two-storey residence in California, save for the log barracks constructed at Fort Ross in 1812. In his adaptation of Monterey adobe to the wooden porch of his native New England, he did what came naturally, especially in view of a temporary shortage of milled wood for siding. Some of his neighbors, including Governor Juan Alvarado, erected new homes or remodeled their old adobe houses in the new style. When Edward Vischer, a Bavarian commission merchant and artist, arrived in September 1842, he called the town "homelike." [55] The style quickly spread as far north as Petaluma, where it inspired the hipped roof and the veranda of the Vallejo Adobe, and as far south as Santa Barbara, where Edwin Bryant noted "some . . . Americanized" houses in December 1846.[56] Most Californios, however, ignored Larkin's innovation in favor of their single-storey adobe homes.[57]

Monterey Colonial, the style of architecture, was in the vanguard of a series of influences that exerted drastic changes in the hitherto stable California society and economy. From such gentle beginnings as one man shaping his own home, the impetus to make over the country fused eventually with a military conquest that remodeled the entire way of life in the American image.

When the Mexican War came, Monterey was left to its own devices mostly because it had previously effectively neutralized control by the Mexican central government. In addition, the mother country was paralyzed by the invasion of the United States Army. For its part, Monterey, accustomed to political and military upheaval, took this newest calamity calmly, perhaps in the belief that it, like previous nuisances, would pass.

Under the onslaught of American military force, Monterey remained unperturbed. Indifference to martial events, however, could not avert the consequences of the collapse or the self-sufficient, if not affluent, economy of Mexican California. Finally, when the American conquest made California the capstone of a political structure spanning the continent from the Atlantic to the Pacific, the custom house at Monterey was suddenly obsolete, and with it the colonial outpost that it had sustained.

Time stood still in the colonial outpost that had lost the land it governed through the American conquest. "Monterey is about the same," Thomas O. Larkin observed in November 1846, several

months after the conquest; "it will not increase fast. It will I think be
a good moral, gentle town for California, more so for five years than
any other on the coast. Yerba Buena and other places in and about
San Francisco will be the busy, bustling uproar of places," he
remarked briefly, before the threatening changes relegated the
colonial outpost to the romantic past.[58] Some of its citizens, afraid to
be overtaken by other places, deserted it for greener pastures,
swapping lots in San Francisco for those in Monterey. The capital
went to San Jose, the naval depot and the army barracks to the Bay
of San Francisco. At Monterey's centennial celebration in 1870, a
speaker recalling the explanation given many years earlier by the last
military governor of California, General Bennett Riley, pointed to
the frantic speculation stimulated by the American conquest that
had caused these quick blows. In 1870, however, the turbulent 1840s
were part of the past, and Monterey was safe from all change and
celebrated as the "ancient Capital," the "time-honored City," and
the "City with which there are grand recollections connected." [59]

The American conquest destroyed the world of the Californios
which sustained the colonial outpost. The Gold Rush spawned an
instant city at the Bay of San Francisco and furthered the decline of
Monterey. Conquest and Gold Rush assigned no new role to
Monterey. Unlike Santa Fe in New Mexico, Monterey failed to
absorb the changes of the 1840s and to find new significance in the
new California. As colonial outpost it went down with the political
system it served. Suddenly its timelessness was of little avail and the
town could see in only one direction—toward its past.

The events of the 1840s hurt Champoeg even more than they had
Monterey and Santa Fe. They deprived the marketplace of its future,
and Champoeg, without a past to retreat to, faded from the scene.
The complexities of a phase of urbanization swept aside the town's
claim to timelessness seemingly assured by nature itself. As an
agricultural market, Champoeg seemed part of an eternal cycle. It
participated in the growing process of nature through the lives of its
people. They knew well planting, ripening, and harvesting. Living
according to the age-old calling of mankind, sanctioned by heritage

and religion, they modified the analogy to birth, growth, and death and saw the harvest as part of the seasonal cycle that nurtured the steadily maturing present into the future in a manner that knew no beginning and no end. In their setting, abrupt change was unnatural, and yet the very growth of Champoeg helped to unleash the rapid changes that destroyed the town's timelessness.

The fur trade had brought the original settlers, mostly former Canadian employees of the British Hudson's Bay Company, into the Willamette Valley. There they lived with their Indian wives comfortably and without much effort, not too close to, and not too far from, company headquarters at Fort Vancouver on the Columbia River.[60] Their apparent happiness attracted other men to the settlement. Chief Factor John McLoughlin, head of the Columbia District, and the other officers of the company, uneasy about these drifters whose carefree life suggested an alternative to the routine of work and leisure specified by company regulations, regarded all free trappers as a troublesome lot, irrespective of where they found them. From time to time, they tried to get rid of them. Ultimately, they even tried to induce the motley group of settlers to relocate in the company's agricultural settlement in the Cowlitz Valley, north of Fort Vancouver and south of Puget Sound. Few went. Some disliked the company, others the Cowlitz Valley, and most felt reluctant to abandon their fertile fields along the Willamette.[61]

During the 1830s, new settlers added their homesteads and ranches to the growing number of farms. Chief Trader James Douglas, in command when McLoughlin was visiting England, explained in 1838 that they were "restless Americans." He found them "brooding over a thousand projects, for improving the navigation, building steam Boats, erecting machinery and other schemes that would excite a smile, if entertained by a less enterprising people, with the same slender means." [62] These newcomers confronted the officials at Fort Vancouver with the specter of an independent settlement near enough to the head of navigation for ocean-going vessels to allow the American traders to penetrate the British fur empire.

Furthermore, it was the policy of the company not to encourage agricultural and, perhaps, industrial settlement in the vulnerable region south of the Columbia, this attitude stemming more from a fear of the free life of settlements than from objections to farming per se. Any group of heterogeneous people spelled trouble for the officers who saw their authority challenged by enterprises and ideas outside their monopoly. In order to flourish, Chief Trader Douglas emphasized, emerging marketplaces needed the "protection of equal laws," the "influence of free trade," and the "accession of respectable inhabitants," three elements which threatened the company's dominance that had been built on the control of the fur trade.[63]

The right of newcomers, if they claimed to be Americans, to live and trade where they chose was guaranteed by the Convention of 1818, renewed in 1827. This agreement placed Englishmen and Americans on an equal basis in the Oregon Country. The company could continue to retire its own employees from the Indian Country to Canada or Europe, as it was, in fact, bound to do by its charter from the British government. However, it had no direct influence over the freemen, that mixed lot of former employees of John Jacob Astor's Pacific Fur Company and the Canadian Northwest Company, nor over the stragglers from across the Rocky Mountains. Nor had it authority to exclude the traders of other nations.[64] West of the Rocky Mountains, the Hudson's Bay Company enjoyed exclusive rights only over British trade.

Economic sanctions were usually attempted to keep outsiders in line. When it finally became obvious, however, that the attractions of the farms matched the prospective settlers' fear of the company, Chief Factor McLoughlin still hesitated to adopt a stronger policy that might turn the Willamette freemen into allies of American competitors. He also suspected that if he broke up the settlements, their inhabitants might disperse through the forest to live with the families of their Indian wives. In the dilemma, McLoughlin began to assist some of his discharged employees to relocate along the river. He kept their names on the company roster to spare their families the hardships that would have resulted from forcing the retiring men to return East as the regulations required. The Chief Factor supported their search in Canada in 1836 for a Catholic priest and welcomed the arrival of two priests, two years later, as one way to balance the influence of American missionaries. He also came to the aid of newcomers to the Willamette Valley, in the hope of having the area peopled with men beholden to the Hudson's Bay Company.[65]

Yet, agriculture and fur trade were not irreconcilable forces as long as the farmers were subservient to the traders. Stripped of its beaver population since the 1820s, the Willamette Valley did not threaten to disrupt the operation of the company. The wheat harvest gave the settlers an opportunity to square their accounts with the officials and it gave the company a chance to receive payment for the seed, animals, and equipment borrowed at Fort Vancouver by destitute newcomers. The wheat supplemented the food needed at the trading posts, and the feelings of the officers toward the settlements along the Willamette grew as mixed as the blessings the farms produced for Fort Vancouver.

With markets for grain within their reach, and the wheat along the Willamette so abundant, the company officials avoided fighting the farmers directly. Instead, they extended the practices of the fur trade into the wheat business. As with furs, they bought up the entire harvest and kept the entire supply of the Oregon Country out of the reach of competitors. In 1839, as a result of an agreement between Russian and British interests known as the Hamburg Agreement, grain trading became a regular business function of Fort Vancouver. In leasing the coastal strip of southwestern Alaska from the Russian American Company, the Hudson's Bay Company assumed the obligation to furnish the Russian establishments in North America with wheat and other supplies.[66] The company incorporated the harvest of the Willamette settlements into its scheme of continental diplomacy, and the development of a marketplace on the Willamette became a necessity. Champoeg's location suited that role perfectly.

At a warehouse on a boat landing in the forest, about twenty miles above the Falls of the Willamette on the right bank of the river, where one of the fingers of prairie actually touched the Willamette, the agents of the Hudson's Bay Company began buying the settlers' grain. Their voyageurs transported the wheat to the Falls, that landmark of the Oregon Country about thirty miles upstream from the confluence of the Willamette and the Columbia rivers. The grain was carried around the cascading waters and then moved, again by boat, to the granary at Fort Vancouver on the north bank of the Columbia, the company's district headquarters near the mouth of the Willamette. From here Chief Factor McLoughlin shipped the wheat to the Russian settlements in the north, to the Hawaiian Islands, and to South America.

The boat landing at Champoeg proved to be a desirable location for the farmers also. It was accessible by water and land. The Hudson's Bay Company warehouse was the head of river traffic.[67] The Willamette was navigable far beyond Champoeg, but the current became stronger and the frequent turns of the river immediately above the landing increased the distances by water so much that most travelers continued south on foot or horseback. The Champoeg landing was the only place between the Falls and the Methodist Mission, fifty miles upstream, where a trail "could be opened to the river without having to cut through a heavy body of timber." [68]

The warehouse and a general store, in addition to the trading post at Willamette Falls, helped meet the needs of the settlers, and testified to the increasing involvement of the company in the wheat harvest.[69] The growing marketplace soon brought rivals of the company to the scene. "I was a thorn in their flesh," one such competitor, Francis W. Pettygrove, recalled in later years. In 1844, he built a granary and warehouse at Champoeg, where he took the farmers' produce in trade.[70] Despite the competition, Champoeg lived up to the expectations of the Hudson's Bay Company. By 1844, Dr. McLoughlin anticipated that the settlers would sell him 20,000 bushels of wheat, and he hoped for "a great deal more next year." [71]

The settlers and the traders both benefited from the arrangement, but did not become friends. On one occasion Chief Factor McLough-

lin's mercurial temper erupted when he witnessed the gentle taps
with which a company buyer settled the dirty wheat in the
half-bushel measure to get full weight. The Chief Factor rang the
side of the copper measure with a sharp stroke, but his cane
produced just the opposite of the result he intended. It stirred the
grain up, expanding the bulk of the wheat instead of settling it.[72]

This incident, in itself comical, was important as a barometer of
the atmosphere. Champoeg was a growing marketplace where
independent-minded people and not "old hands . . . too well trained
to say much openly" congregated.[73] As well it was a growing town
and the growth of Champoeg was a constant source of trouble to
those who wished to maintain the company's economic system
without an emporium. The settlers for their part grew restless about
the omnipresent company and the way some officials made their
presence felt.

In addition to French Prairie settlers south of Champoeg, other
communities contributed to the significance of the shipping center.
American homesteaders on the Tualatin Plains, north of Champoeg,
began to share in the flow of goods. Ewing Young's post, at the
mouth of the Chehalem Creek above the landing, served as a
marketplace, store, bank, and factory. Young, a former mountain
man, briefly ran a distillery on his ranch until he decided to
cooperate with the Oregon Temperance Society and dismantled the
plant.[74] He was an important partner in the loose compact that
linked employees of the Hudson's Bay Company, Methodist missionaries, French Canadians, and American mountain men into the joint
business venture known as the Willamette Cattle Company.[75]

Indians loved the fertile prairies but did not hinder the development of the settlements. Their initial contact with white men had
brought into their communities the diseases that would contribute to
the destruction of their world. In 1837, after the epidemics of the
1820s and 1830s, about twelve hundred were left in the entire valley,
William A. Slacum, a purser in the United States Navy and a special
agent of President Andrew Jackson, estimated in his report to

Washington. He mentioned Indians living on the bank opposite the landing.[76] Some Indians, as wives or slaves, were an integral part of the young farms.[77]

Enterprising Americans recognized the importance of the Willamette settlements before Slacum reported that a large volume of wheat could be bought there and sold easily in the Hawaiian Islands, the Russian settlements, or Peru.[78] As early as September 1834, the New Englander Nathaniel J. Wyeth, and his men laid out a farm on the prairie at Champoeg. His trading post at the mouth of the Willamette thrived and failed under the mixture of aid and obstruction carefully doled out by Chief Factor McLoughlin. It was the first American commercial establishment in the Oregon Country since Astor's enterprise of an earlier generation at the mouth of the Columbia River.[79] The ranks of these venturesome traders and farmers were strengthened by men of God.

Methodist missionaries, under the leadership of the Reverend Jason Lee, came to Oregon with the help of Wyeth in 1834 and wielded moral as well as economic influence in the growing Willamette community. For a long time, the Mission to the Indians of the Willamette Valley, the first in the Pacific Northwest, was the only organized body of Americans in the country, and their establishment on the river above Champoeg automatically shared some of the civil authority Dr. McLoughlin exercised at Fort Vancouver as Chief Factor of the Hudson's Bay Company. Soon, however, their particular ecclesiastical oligarchy brought them into conflict with one another, as well as with the several other groups occupying the Willamette Valley, and their station did not become a serious rival for Champoeg.[80]

In fact, the conflict made Champoeg the neutral political ground for the diverse factions. The problem to be resolved was not the merits of an oligarchy, but who was to rule. The debate brought to the scene programs derived from natural law for forming compacts to protect life and property. These compacts were treated as heresy by the Hudson's Bay people but were taken quite seriously and were entered into by most men, save the employees of the company. In the first memorial of the Willamette settlers to the United States Congress, the missionaries found a way that brought the French Canadians closer to their American neighbors. They stressed their common interest in the protection of persons and property, and managed to attract former employees of the company to a government willing to grant them title to their land and to respect their improvements.[81]

The missionaries brought the Willamette settlers closer together, but at Champoeg, and not at the mission station. Unconcerned with the question of which settlement would benefit most in its urban growth they indirectly strengthened Champoeg in their attempts to strengthen their influence in the Willamette Valley. In addition to its original religious and humanitarian functions, their station immediately became the major link in the weak chain of communication between the Oregon Country and the United States, and for a time was the "largest single group of foreign mission workers anywhere in the world." [82] The role and importance of the station brought these missionaries into contact with many people who, under ordinary circumstances, would have bypassed most clergymen. The mission counted among its workers skilled artisans, and their competence attracted settlers who wanted to learn.[83] However, when these visitors had learned enough and now wanted good company and a drink, Champoeg answered their desires.

Champoeg provided also a real place of exile or refuge from the mission establishment for people who parted company with the Methodists like Margaret Jewett Bailey. She was a teacher disappointed with the mission, who followed her new husband, a physician, to his claim near Champoeg. There Commander Charles Wilkes dined at her table during his trip through the Willamette Valley, but long before she published her experiences and infuriated Oregonians so much that only a few copies of her book survived their wrath.[84]

The increased exposure of the settlers to newcomers from the East added social and political dimensions to the role of the marketplace. In a sense, the gathering of men interested in the Willamette Cattle

Company at Champoeg, in 1837, foreshadowed the future. Although Robert Newell, a former mountain man, did not formally lay out a town at the landing until 1844, the quick growth of the community and its widening importance made it the natural site for the events in the spring of 1843 that constituted Champoeg's fleeting moment of political prominence.[85]

In March, a public assemblage at the home of a French Canadian settler approved recommendations by the Methodists designed to curb the threats from wild animals. The group elected a committee of representatives of its various factions to consider as well additional measures for the civil and military protection of settlements. In a memorial to the United States Senate they asked for "immediate action" by Congress to enact "good and wholesome laws . . . for our Territory." [86] A few weeks later, in May, another meeting of settlers, aware of the need for greater civil control, called for the organization of a provisional government. However, this Oregon Provisional Government gravitated to the Falls of the Willamette, to Oregon City, as the cluster of houses at the western end of the Oregon Trail had come to be known. To that place overland emigrants were drawn who turned Oregon City into a bustling community.[87] There the first provisional legislature assembled in June 1844, and Champoeg faded from the scene.[88]

Inflated claims, based on the brief moment of political importance, did much to assign a false significance to Champoeg in the international contest for the possession of the Oregon Country. The "Champoeg Legend," which credited the meetings with bringing the Oregon Country into the Union, today yields to a more sophisticated assessment of the role of diplomacy, economics, and politics in Great Britain, as well as in the United States, in determining the American ownership of the area below the forty-ninth parallel.[89] The reassessment, however, in no way diminished the importance of Champoeg in bringing into focus an aspect in the process of western urbanization.

Champoeg's decline as a center of political life accompanied its decline as a marketplace. Its role as a supplier of wheat to the

Hudson's Bay Company, as well as its call for a provisional government, both helped to end the very presence of the company in the Pacific Northwest. Without the company's monopoly, the stable economy that guaranteed Champoeg's position vanished and the shipping place was exposed to the hazards of urbanization. Soon Champoeg found itself not the sole purveyor of wheat, but one of many wheat-shipping centers in Oregon because it failed to attract a steady stream of overland emigrants to sustain its economic and political life.

The thoughts of the newcomers concentrated on bigger stakes than profits made from tilling the prairie around Champoeg. They hoped for a free homestead as well as quick profits through speculation in town lots. They were, for the most part, imbued with the Jacksonian notions of family farming and townsite speculation. In anticipation of their demands and with shrewd assessment of the changing times, McLoughlin had laid out Oregon City on a portion of his two-square-mile claim at the Falls of the Willamette in 1842, but without the strength of the company behind him, he was just pushed aside by the feverish activities of the newcomers.[90]

Townsite speculation was infectious. One of the early American settlers at Champoeg moved downstream, close to the juncture of the Willamette and Columbia, where he built a cabin in the forest, about fifteen miles below the Falls. In 1845 Francis W. Pettygrove named this site Portland, after he and his business partner had cleared enough of their 640-acre claim to accommodate four streets and sixteen blocks, part of which had formerly been in possession of William P. Overton.[91] Late in 1843, Peter H. Burnett and a partner founded Linntown, now within the city of Portland, which Burnett advertised, in the New York *Herald*, as the point nearest to the head of navigation for large vessels in the Oregon Country.[92]

Interest in real estate was booming by 1844, the first Oregon Tax Roll showed. Town lots ($26,370) ranked third behind horses ($47,562) and cattle ($101,280) in the total tax evaluations. Farm lands, the greatest asset of the country, were initially exempted from taxation, but money was needed to insure the working of laws

safeguarding the private ownership of land—one of the prime
reasons for a provisional government. Of the 422 taxable persons in
the Willamette Valley, 44 were assessed for 100 or more town lots
each, nine of the landholders for 1,000 or more, and McLoughlin for
4,200.[93]

By 1844, speculation in townsites had spread so far afield as to
make contact with the beginnings of white settlement in the Oregon
Country. In that year Jesse Applegate platted the town of Astoria at
the fort established by John Jacob Astor's Pacific Fur Company, in
1811 near the mouth of the Columbia. In 1813, the post had fallen
into the hands of Astor's Canadian rivals and had performed an
ever-diminishing role until the end of the 1830s.[94] In the winter of
1812–13, the men of the Pacific Fur Company from old Astoria built
the Wallace House in the Willamette Valley as a trading post.[95] Now,
in 1844, the impulse to form settlements came from the Willamette
Valley, and one of the new settlements was the old Astoria. The new
Astoria joined St. Helens, Milton City, Canemah, Milwaukee, Linn
City, Butteville, and other townsites in the Willamette Valley; they
all longed to emulate Champoeg's short-lived eminence as *the*
market of the Oregon Country.[96]

Champoeg did not survive the changes sought by the settlers,
including its own, but the wheat that had made the town did. In
December 1845, the provisional legislature defined good wheat, in
addition to gold, silver, treasury drafts, and business orders,[97] as legal
tender when delivered at the customary places. The act acknowledged the continued significance of the grain that had once promised
to make Champoeg timeless. However, with the retreat of the
Hudson's Bay Company north of the forty-ninth parallel in anticipation of the eventual settlement of the Oregon question, the
marketplace for wheat could and did shift to whatever locale was
regarded as the most promising site. The end of the diplomatic
contest between Great Britain and the United States was in sight,
and the Oregon Country lay open to the changes invited by
Champoeg's call for a provisional government. With the changes,
Champoeg's role as marketplace ended.

Despite their differences as types of towns, as well as sites of settlement, the measured beat of life in Santa Fe, Monterey, and Champoeg linked these towns together and set them apart from the hectic rate of progress of instant cities. By 1850, however, after Americans had spanned the territory from the Plains to the ocean almost in a single leap and decade, even these settlements came to manifest the expansive urge of a westering nation sustained by industrialization and urbanization. With improved communication through advances in technology and organization, the military campaigns against Indians and Mexicans, as well as the Oregon Treaty and the California Gold Rush, the migration toward the West increased. The flow of people stimulated by the momentous events helped to swell existing towns and to establish new ones. It not only completed the American conquest but also changed the urban situation of the Far West. New men and new ideas brought change to a stable urban world. Although they shaped the fate of some of the towns decisively, their influences never produced the rapid development intensified by constant change that was to characterize San Francisco and Denver.

Unrelated to their surroundings, these two cities would rise on the brutal violation of nature produced by mining, the frantic rush of men driven by gold, and the spectacular flow of goods stimulated by commerce. They would forge new lines of communication forcing the movement of people and products to their sites. Men and women would come and go, drops in the human tide surging to find another opportunity around the next corner at the next moment. In both cities internal change would become an integral part of life, transforming today what had been just completed yesterday so that tomorrow could take its turn in the sequence of fall and rise. Although San Francisco and Denver would emerge in out-of-the-way places, they had not been part of the isolated settings. Their remote sites accentuated their spectacular rise; they were the antithesis of the wilderness.

# 4

## Wilderness

Most of the vast expanse west of the great bend of the Missouri was wilderness at the middle of the nineteenth century, but it was crossed and recrossed by lines of communication linking urban islands to one another and to distant centers of authority, population, commerce, industry, and culture. Red and white men left traces in trails and river crossings, trading posts and military forts, as well as rendezvous sites and burial grounds, depots, and landings.

Explorers, traders, fur trappers, hide merchants, mountain men, soldiers, and Indians were the vanguard of an intruding civilization bent on exploiting the resources and reducing the wilds to fields and gardens. Their ventures stimulated a contest of exploration, trade, colonization, diplomacy, and warfare for the spoils. Before the struggle brought about possession of most of the coveted area by the United States, the rivalry had carried into the farthest West administrative, commercial, and industrial practices, each of which prepared the ground for the sudden rise of instant cities.

The initial waves of newcomers built no cities themselves, and few of their fur-trading posts and rendezvous sites became towns.[1] But, although they bypassed the familiar stage of occupation by homesteaders in a region generally considered unsuited to agriculture, these "Jacksonian Men," venturesome entrepreneurs and expectant capitalists, extended features of urban enterprises into remote areas.² Their response to the economic potential of the wilderness flourished on a scientific curiosity that would unveil many mysteries of the far continent.

The most momentous of a long line of explorations, the Lewis and Clark expedition, had inaugurated a trend of scientific exploration at the dawn of the nineteenth century. Their reports on the apparently boundless supply of fur-bearing animals had encouraged the mountain men to seek their share of the spoils.³ The lure of natural resources, the urge of commerce, the design of empire, and the reality of war enlarged the need for knowledge. They stimulated the systematic collection of an ever-increasing body of scientific information. The thirteen volumes of the Pacific Railroad Survey, published between 1855 and 1861 in response to the national debate about a transcontinental railway, reflected both the amount of available facts and the national interest in data of all kinds. As a result of that work, in 1858, Lieutenant Gouverneur K. Warren, of the Corps of Topographical Engineers, completed his "Map of the Territory of the United States from the Mississippi to the Pacific Ocean," on a scale of 1:300,000,000, or about fifty miles to an inch. His compilation of an accurate land form illustrated the state of geographic knowledge as a basic indicator of the penetration of the continent.⁴

The collecting of scientific data helped to spread knowledge of the wilderness without destroying that wilderness as yet. The explorers, and those who followed in the footsteps of the explorers, did little to bring the Far West into the context of white civilization or the everyday life of people. Yet, an awareness of the existence of a remote wilderness attested to the presence of some white men and their culture in the wilds of the continent. Without their presence, there would have been no wilderness because the use of this label for those parts of the continent not yet made over in the images of white civilization made as little sense to the Indians, who considered that very wilderness their home, as the white men's insistence to pursue their goal and, in the pursuit, destroy the Indians' land. But, the transformation of the wilderness culminated in the rapid changes that gave rise to instant cities and provided stunning evidence that urban civilization, the epitome of the white world, conquered the wilds of the continent.

The contrast that existed between wilderness and city added drama to the emergence of San Francisco and Denver. At both the San Francisco Peninsula and the South Platte Valley, wilderness stretched between the instant cities about to emerge at these two sites and the older centers of urban life in the East as well as the slowly developing towns of the West. San Francisco and Denver appeared outside the framework of gradually growing markets and industries. Neither an urban nor a rural frontier gave birth to them. Their rise was unrelated to the design of distant planners, the logistics of long-distance commerce, the colonial policy of faraway governments, the needs of farmers for markets, or the exalted visions of prophets. Sudden wealth propelled San Francisco and Denver into their independent development, sustained by the riches of mining and commerce.

Gold in the foothills of the Sierra Nevada and the Rocky Mountains was the magnet that attracted droves of men from around the globe. They rushed into a wilderness setting that provided space, support, and an outlet for their energies. Little stood in their way, and whatever did fell before them. They had it all their way, and, if not, their numbers, drive, and wealth eventually saw to it that they did. Only at the Bay of San Francisco did they find rudiments of urban growth, but they eradicated that Spanish-Mexican tradition of settlement as another variant of a wilderness that they were making over in the image of the urban life they knew in the East. At the South Platte, wilderness and city life collided head on.

Denver's unspoiled, natural setting differed from the sandy windblown peninsula on which San Francisco arose. In addition, two isolated outposts—a mission house and a presidio—approximately ten miles apart on the tip of the peninsula hinted of a past attempt at white civilization in San Francisco. Indeed, they had represented the beginning of Spanish-Mexican settlement on the northernmost part of the land that is now the site of the modern city. But the settlement had never materialized into a fully developed pueblo and when Americans reached the peninsula the eerie desolation of the site was reinforced by the sight of the crumbling remnants of these two buildings. Subsequent waves of gold seekers completed the break with the ecclesiastical and military heritage that the Spanish-Mexican settlement represented and assured San Francisco's independent beginning at the site of a village called Yerba Buena on a cove of the bay, roughly halfway between mission and presidio.

The topography at the extreme end of that barren peninsula, the southern shore of the gateway to the continent separating the Bay of San Francisco from the Pacific Ocean underlined the peculiarities of that wilderness. As part of the western rim of the continent, this neck marked the end of a world. The entrance to San Francisco Bay, the strait now known as the Golden Gate, interrupts the straight extension of the coastline to the north into what is now called Marin County. Although this tip of land also promised to be the beginning of another world—as a potential stop on a maritime highway that ships from many harbors might travel—the frequent fogs and nearly constant winds sweeping over the sandy hills and dipping into the brush-filled draws absorbed the attention of American newcomers. Largely barren, a "desert Wilderness," they complained, for the area resembled to some of them true deserts they had crossed on their way to California.[5]

Truly bewildering was an abandoned military outpost and a secularized mission—each, in its alien way, another dimension of wilderness. Most American newcomers were struck by the disintegration, but few newcomers knew of the circumstances that had given rise to mission and presidio, about life at the Mission San Francisco de Asís during its flowering, or the role of the Presidio de San Francisco in the international diplomacy of Spain, Great Britain, and Russia. Most failed to fathom the significance of these frontier institutions in the context of Spanish-Mexican colonization. Flushed

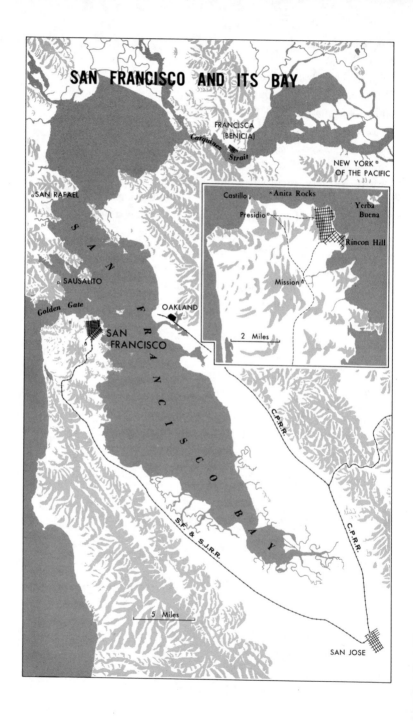

# SAN FRANCISCO AND ITS BAY

FRANCISCA
(BENICIA)

Carquinez
Strait

NEW YORK
OF THE PACIFIC

□ SAN RAFAEL

S A N

□ SAUSALITO

Golden Gate

OAKLAND

SAN
FRANCISCO

F R A N C I S C O    B A Y

C.P.R.R.

S.F. & S.J.R.R.

C.P.R.R.

5 Miles

SAN JOSE

Castillo

*Anita Rocks

Presidio □

Yerba
Buena

Rincon Hill

Mission □

2 Miles

with the glow of conquest, Americans saw in the crumbling ruins of the mission and the obsolete fortifications of the presidio relics of a world that they felt destined to overcome.

Through their encounter with disintegrating Spanish and Mexican institutions some of these American interlopers developed a rationale for the conquest of California. They convinced themselves that the strange Mexican system had not developed the country and that it was, therefore, their obligation to open up the country to the initiative of free men. The failure of the Mexicans to take advantage of the natural sites of the bay and the peninsula simply confirmed the general American suspicions of sloth, neglect, and incompetence. The newcomers were prepared to find a wilderness, or accustomed to leave one behind, but they were startled facing a wilderness perpetuated by the neglect of white men. They did not realize that the indifference had already freed Californios from some features of that feudal oppression from which Americans hoped to liberate them.

The mission, with its dependence upon, and concern for, the Indian, constituted the outcome of an attempt to form a relationship between two races wholly foreign to the newcomers. Incorporating the Indian into the social and economic system of Spaniards and Mexicans and converting him to Catholicism was seen by most Protestant Americans as a subterfuge used to tap the human potential, as well as the natural resources, of the New World. Thus, they argued, religion served only in the deliberate social and economic subjugation of the Indian.[6] As far as their own actions went, most Americans felt that they were merely exploiting material resources; they ignored the fact that they destroyed a way of life and sealed the fate of other human beings.

The classic epitaph of the Mission San Francisco de Asís, popularly known as Mission Dolores, came from the sharp pen of Sir George Simpson, the Governor of the Hudson's Bay Company Territories in America, during his trip around the world in 1841. The "wilderness of ruins presented nothing to blend the promise of the future with the story of the past," and the "scene of desolation had not even the charm of antiquity to grace it." The oldest building of the mission, established in 1776, "that now crumbled before us had not equaled the span of human life," Sir George argued, "and yet, when compared with the stubborn piles which elsewhere perish so gradually as to exhibit no perceptible change to a single generation of men, these ruins had attained a state of decay which would have done credit to the wind and weather of centuries." [7]

After the secularization, Indian neophytes lived at the mission for a few years, survivors of the San Francisco Costanoans whom the Spaniards had gathered there with members of nearby Wintun and Miwok tribes. In 1835, the California legislature officially designated the place as the Pueblo de Dolores, but here, as well as at other former missions, no Indian pueblo ever did develop. The mission property fell into the hands of the Californios, and the Indians moved away.[8] In January 1845, the residents petitioned for recognition of their occupancy because they constituted a "frontier" town against Yerba Buena "which is formed entirely of foreigners." [9]

What little communal life existed came to a standstill with the Mexican War and the arrival of American troops in July 1846. The pastor, whose parish included San Rafael and Sonoma, took the coming of the American troops as his signal to leave.[10] American newcomers quickly filled the void. In September 1846, the buildings adjacent to the church housed Mormon families from the *Brooklyn*, which had sailed into Yerba Buena cove at the end of July, three weeks after Captain John B. Montgomery of the *Portsmouth* had raised the American flag on the Yerba Buena Plaza.[11] "All the Californians living about the Mission except two have gone off," a resident of Yerba Buena wrote in December 1846.[12] "Nobody thought much of the Mission then," an Argonaut recalled in later days, and less of the "very old, rickety adobe building," with "a wilderness of scrubby oaks around." [13]

The presidio had fared no better than the mission; summer fog and winter storm had spared neither. None of its residents were around when a reconnaissance party from the *Portsmouth* examined its fortifications in July 1846.[14] The Castillo de San Joaquin, below the

presidio at the actual entrance of the bay, was an even more
foresaken place, its round shot covered with rust, its "gun carriages
partially decayed," and its guns lately spiked by Captain John C.
Frémont who arrived at the fort with his group of conquerors first.[15]
The scene brought Byron's "My own good hall is desolate" to the
mind of a naval surgeon whose account captured the romance
surrounding the decaying post.[16]

The dilapidated presidio commanded no respect from people
conscious of the role of arms in their history. In its better days it had
contributed the setting for California's "famous" love story, the
romance between Doña Concepción Argüello, daughter of the
comandante, and Count Nikolai Petrovich Rezanov of the Russian
American Fur Company.[17] As a military establishment, the presidio
reflected the fate of all posts in the territory. "In Alta California
there is no presidio," Governor José María Echeandía warned the
Mexican Minister of War bluntly in 1829, there were "mere squares
of adobe huts, in ruins." [18] The year 1820 had been the peak of
military manpower, with the four presidial companies at San Diego,
Monterey, San Francisco, and Santa Barbara up to their regular
strength of 410 officers and men.[19] After that, dedicated officers tried
to stave off the steady disintegration of fortifications and armaments,
but wind and rain wreaked havoc on the quickly deteriorating adobe
defenses.

Men, money, and incentive were lacking to keep up the constant
struggle with the elements. With no external or internal threats, the
decline of the San Francisco presidio was well advanced even before
the Russians abandoned Fort Ross in 1841 where their southward
thrust had stalled about fifty miles north of the entrance to the Bay
of San Francisco as a result of disease, the aftermath of the
Napoleonic invasion of the homeland, overextended lines of communication, and the depletion of the sea otter.[20] The condition of the
San Francisco presidio reflected the peaceful ways of the country,
contempt for military discipline, appreciation of the joy of living, and
almost complete indifference toward intruders and neighbors.

The Presidio de San Francisco never stimulated settlement,

although one sea captain compared it to Monterey in May 1825, and reported that it had a church, about 120 houses, and 500 inhabitants. More correctly, his records stressed the lack of agricultural produce and the dependence on the mission for all supplies.[21] Governor José Figueroa founded a presidial pueblo in November 1834, with jurisdiction over the entire area north of the Pueblo de San Jose, but it lacked a civilian community from which to form the nucleus for a settlement. The election of councilmen, and the meetings of the council, the *ayuntamiento,* were held at the presidio, yet when the Mexican Constitution of 1836, as supplemented by the law of March 20, 1837, came into full operation in California, *ayuntamiento* status was withdrawn because the pueblo had not been designated as such prior to 1808 and was neither a departmental capital nor had over 4,000 inhabitants.[22] The populace drifted away, and after the transfer of the garrison to Sonoma at the end of the 1830s, the records of the presidial pueblo were sent to the mission and then to Yerba Buena.[23]

American newcomers to the Bay of San Francisco assumed that negligence accounted for the wilderness of ruins on the peninsula. The bewildering scene struck them as strange as the wilderness areas of the continent that they bypassed on their westward migration because nothing stirred their desire or commanded their attention. Their own neglect, however, assured the continued existence of these pockets of virtually unspoiled nature.

One such area, at the confluence of Cherry Creek and the South Platte River, with the Front Range of the Rocky Mountains towering in the west, was practically untouched by white men, even in the middle of the nineteenth century. The main trail of traders and migrants swung around the barrier of its mountains, and it was not until gold was discovered there that the setting was named Denver, in 1858, after a governor of Kansas Territory to which it technically belonged. Two hundred miles to the south, and five hundred miles to the east and to the west, were the nearest sites of urban life, the towns of New Mexico, the farming communities of Kansas, and the Mormon settlements of the Great Basin. In the north, two hundred miles away, stood Old Fort Laramie between the North Platte River and the Black Hills, center of Indian trade, supply depot on the Oregon Trail, and army post. Vast plains and mountain ranges ensured the isolation of the South Platte Valley until its gold drove white men into the wilderness.

In 1858, gold seekers rushed to this unknown site at the end of the Great Plains first, on the strength of rumors that had reached Missouri of gold discoveries in the northwest corner of Kansas territory, a few miles south of the border of Nebraska territory. Then, Kansas newspapers began to publish detailed accounts. Most editors called the rush to the mouth of Cherry Creek the "Pike's Peak Gold Rush," after the mountain seventy miles to the south. In the 1850s, Pikes Peak was probably the best known landmark of the region and its short and alliterative name was the extent of most people's knowledge of the western end of the plains.[24] The actual silhouette of the distant peak inspired men during their stampede for gold.[25]

Western Kansas Territory, South Platte Rocky Mountains, and other designations were also used in reference to the gold region, but they were as nebulous to the potential gold miner in the East as Arapaho hunting grounds and Cheyenne country. In June 1859, one Vermonter founded in Denver the "United States of America, Pike's Peak, Platte River, Great American Desert Gold Company," and in March and July 1860, he still used "Denver City, Pike's Peak, Jefferson Territory" and "Pike's Peak, Denver City," in letters to the editor of the Bennington *Banner* to make sure that his friends in Vermont would know where he was.[26]

The wilderness made it difficult to define the location of the gold field for the people "back home." Before the Pikes Peak Gold Rush of 1858–59, the South Platte Valley was in the undisturbed possession of Indians. In the 1850s, it was the special homeland of the Arapaho who were closely allied with the Cheyenne. According to their traditions, they, and the Blackfeet, were the "ancient occupants" of the foothills of the Rockies, living in settled communities based on agriculture and hunting. When Spanish horses came north in the seventeenth and eighteenth centuries, the Arapaho took up a nomadic life and shared the Plains culture in which hunted buffalo furnished most necessities of life. Cheyenne and Sioux also came to the valley and Crow, Pawnee, Shoshoni, and Blackfeet made occasional visits. For generations, the Arapaho, with help from Cheyenne and Sioux, fought the Ute, the inhabitants of the mountains who raided the valley.[27]

From time to time, the region attracted white men who lived for a short time under the sufferance of the Indians, but they left few traces behind. When the fur trade changed drastically in the 1830s, the foothills along the South Platte, as well as the greater portion of the High Plains and Rockies, no longer attracted trappers. Farmers advancing from the humid lands along the Mississippi River viewed the High Plains with suspicion. The country was a barren, parched region without natural waterways by which to move farm produce to market. It was merely one more obstacle in the paths of emigrants bound for the greener pastures of Oregon and California, and of traders moving up the Arkansas River in search of the riches of Santa Fe and Chihuahua.

In the late 1830s, when the economic base of the South Platte Valley shifted from beaver pelts to buffalo robes, four trading posts developed along the river to handle the trade in robes made by the Indians and to accommodate independent trappers who continued to roam the mountains for beaver pelts. Within the few years of their existence, Forts Lupton, Jackson, Vasquez, and St. Vrain were links in a chain of communication from the Arkansas River to the northernmost outpost of the white man's world on the Great Plains, Old Fort Laramie. A few travelers along the South Platte route later recorded stopping at these four posts. Among them was Francis Parkman. In 1846, he saw some of the abandoned forts "fast tumbling into ruins," one day before he camped at the spot where the trail left the South Platte and crossed to Cherry Creek.[28]

In 1857, eleven years after Parkman's visit to the future site of Denver, a company of soldiers under the command of Major John Sedgwick bivouacked there in a "howling wilderness." Shortly, they came across prospectors from Missouri who had found gold in the foothills between the river and Pikes Peak before they were driven

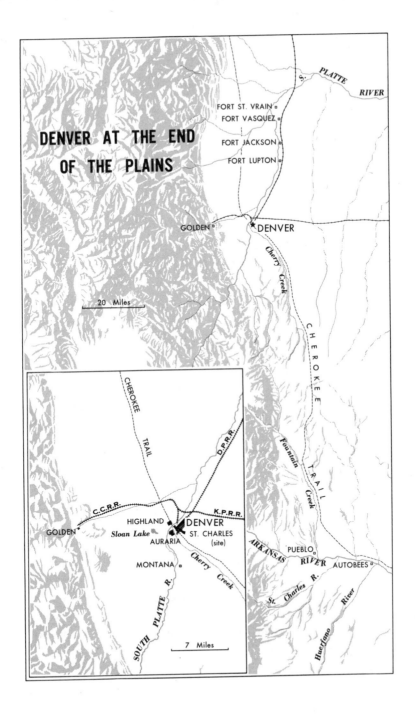

# DENVER AT THE END
## OF THE PLAINS

FORT ST. VRAIN
FORT VASQUEZ
FORT JACKSON
FORT LUPTON

S. PLATTE RIVER

GOLDEN
★ DENVER

Cherry Creek

CHEROKEE

20 Miles

CHEROKEE TRAIL

D.P.R.R.

C.C.R.R.
K.P.R.R.

GOLDEN
HIGHLAND
Sloan Lake
AURARIA
DENVER
ST. CHARLES
(site)

Fountain Creek

TRAIL

MONTANA

Cherry Creek

ARKANSAS RIVER

PUEBLO
AUTOBEES

SOUTH PLATTE R.

St. Charles R.

Huerfano River

7 Miles

off by Indians. Sedgwick's troops, under orders to join an expedition against a band of Cheyenne marauding in the vicinity of Fort Laramie, had come up the Arkansas and had followed the Cherokee Trail over the divide to the South Platte River.[29]

On their route along the north bank of the Arkansas they had passed some of the remnants of abandoned white settlements once nearest to the juncture of the South Platte River and Cherry Creek. The trail, past the ruins of Bent's Old Fort, built in 1833 and abandoned in 1852, was "so dim that it could hardly be followed." Thirty-five miles below the old fort, Bent's New Fort kept alive the memory of the famous way station of the Southwest. Further up the Arkansas, on the west side of the Huerfano, two miles above its juncture, a few farmers, traders, hunters, and trappers supported themselves on a farm that Charles Autobees began working in 1853.[30]

All other white settlements on the Upper Arkansas had been abandoned as a result of Indian raids. No longer did whites live at Pueblo, at the Fountain Creek and the Arkansas, seventy miles above Bent's Old Fort. The news of the massacre at Pueblo, in December 1854, as well as subsequent attacks on other villages, scattered most of the inhabitants of the settlement of St. Charles, a few miles below Pueblo.[31] The raiders struck, in addition, the Huerfano village that Dick Wootton, or his men, had built some time after October 1853, on the south side of the Arkansas, a mile above the mouth of the Huerfano, twenty-five miles downstream from Pueblo. In the vicinity had once been located "the largest white settlement" near the South Platte Valley prior to the Pikes Peak gold rush—a camp of 275 Latter-day Saints. This group of Mormons, en route to the Great Basin, had wintered here in 1846–47, along with disabled members of the Mormon Battalion sent to the Upper Arkansas to recuperate.[32]

In these villages of the Upper Arkansas, the white people had made the necessary accommodations to the wilderness and to Indians. There were only a few settlers in all, and because they were totally separated from the aids of communication and technology, they had a sharpened sense of awareness that they depended for

their survival on the establishment of a modus vivendi with the land
and the Indians. Although the centers of authority and culture were
distant, most of these settlers did not miss laws and social conventions. They had discarded them long ago or learned to live without
them. Once they managed to eke out a living, they no longer devoted
their time to the single-minded pursuit of wealth that characterized
the builders of the instant cities who readily subordinated man and
nature to the stubborn pursuit of their goal as long as they
themselves were not part of the sacrifice. The residents of the villages
of the Upper Arkansas were drifters who knew no tide strong enough
to pull them in a definite direction. Although they came and went,
straws in the wind that swept the prairies, during their brief years on
the Upper Arkansas, they found conditions suited to their temperaments and thus to their adjustment to the wilderness.

The river itself facilitated the temporary modus vivendi. The
Arkansas, an old frontier separating people, also linked many
different people together. It divided two hostile groups of Plains
Indians, but the Great Peace of 1840 reconciled Cheyenne and
Arapaho with Kiowa, Comanche, and Prairie Apache.[33] The south
shore was Mexican territory until 1848, and the international border
attracted smugglers and outlaws to the vast, ineffectively governed
area. Although the army was charged with controlling the liquor
traffic, and especially with preventing the sale of liquor to Indians,
the distances were so great and the dragoons so few that there was
not much control of anything. If a man still got into a jam, there was
always the Mexican bank of the river.

The Intercourse Act, passed by Congress in 1834, reserved as
Indian country all lands west of the Mississippi not included in the
states of Louisiana and Missouri, or the Territory of Arkansas, and
prohibited settlement on land set aside for Indian tribes and trade
without a license from the local Indian agent. The Compromise of
1850, creating the Territories of New Mexico and Utah, and the
Kansas-Nebraska Act of 1854 superseded the Intercourse Act, but
Congress extended the regulations of the Indian trade to these new
territories in order to maintain its Indian policy.[34]

The well-intentioned federal laws meant nothing to the men who saw Indian-white relations differently. The drifters frequently lived on Indian land and bartered with their Indian neighbors to stay alive. At times they huddled together in a plaza, a square of adobes built around a central patio into which they drove their animals for protection from the Indians. Commercial and marital ties kept whites and Indians from killing one another. At Pueblo and Hardscrabble, the residents traded wheat, corn, and vegetables to the Indians in exchange for robes and skins. They exchanged the hides in Santa Fe and Taos for flour and whiskey, which they peddled in the mountains for pelts and on the plains for buffalo robes. Their trading was anathema to Indian agent and licensed trader alike. It interfered with so many interests that the few commentators were automatically interested observers and generally at a loss to say anything good about the "mongrel crew of Americans, French, Mexicans and half-breeds," who were "unable to procure employment on account of past misconduct," in the view of one Indian agent.[35] Another described about sixty "Americans, Missouri French, Canadians, and Mexicans" at Pueblo and Hardscrabble, "nearly all having wives, and some . . . two," from "various Indian tribes, . . . Mexicans and Americans." [36]

In the villages, the settlers' mutual interdependence sustained an orderly anarchy. Respectable merchants mingled with smugglers, whiskey peddlers with trappers, ex-soldiers with deserters, and hunters with farmers, while renegades, desperados, and loafers were thrown in for good measure. At times, overland emigrants and Mormons, on their way to the Great Basin, left families behind. Although travelers along the Arkansas moved from east to west, most of the outposts oriented themselves along a north-south axis. They depended on the towns and villages of New Mexico for their social support and economic welfare, above all on Taos for their whiskey, a commodity of great importance in general and for the Indian trade in particular. Comancheros, the roving New Mexican traders on the plains who ventured as far north as the Platte River, supplied the villages.[37] Other links with New Mexico resulted from the particular legal status of parts of the area. Much of the territory below the Upper Arkansas fell within enormous Mexican land grants. Their owners, citizens of Taos, made some effort to attract settlers, who, in turn, reinforced the dependence of the area on New Mexico. The situation was analogous to that of the San Luis Valley. Separated from the Upper Arkansas by the Sangre de Cristo range, it was also settled by people from Taos. In that valley, in the summer of 1852, the United States Army built Fort Massachusetts at the northern base of the Sangre de Cristo Mountains, the first military post on what was to become Colorado soil, to protect these settlements against raiding bands of Ute.[38]

The modus vivendi between Indians and whites practiced at the Upper Arkansas failed to reach the South Platte Valley. In addition to Indian raids, economic and political changes undermined the role of the villages and lured the settlers to greener pastures. When the market for beaver pelts collapsed, the trade in buffalo hides superseded trapping, but by this time the buffalo had left the Upper Arkansas, roaming east and north. The American conquest of the Southwest opened opportunities in New Mexico, erased the international boundary, and brought about a closer control of the Indian trade. With outlets in New Mexico and the attractions of California enhanced by the discovery of gold, most settlers and traders drifted to more enticing scenes to the south and west.[39] In the North, the wilderness of the South Platte Valley offered nothing to lure men beyond the remnants of the settlements along the Upper Arkansas.

East of the South Platte Valley, the Territory of Kansas had been established, in 1854, more as a result of the sectional conflict over the extension of slavery and the construction of a railroad to the Pacific than for the sake of colonization and development. However, landseekers found good farmlands there and their success led to an extension of settlements. They tilled the fertile soil and turned the prairie into fields, but they kept their eyes on the political struggle for the future of Kansas. Since no one was certain of that future, rapid expansion did not occur in the face of such an additional obstacle as the Great Plains.

In 1857, when Major Sedgwick's Cheyenne expedition left Fort Leavenworth on the Missouri, the patchwork of their counties covered nearly all the 170 miles of the Kansas River and reached almost to the junction of its parents, the Republican River and the Smoky Hill River, but that was the extent of settlement.[40] After the soldiers passed Council Crove, where the Santa Fe Trail crossed the Neosho River, about five hundred miles east of the mouth of Cherry Creek, one of them felt he had left "the farthest western settlement on the Santa Fe Trail in Kansas," except for a few ranches and trading posts.[41] In June 1859, Horace Greeley was asked in Denver what he thought about the future of Kansas along the South Platte, which legally was part of Kansas territory, and he replied emphatically, "Good Heavens, Kansas stopped 500 miles east of this." [42]

At both the South Platte Valley and the San Francisco Peninsula earlier societies were still in existence. At the South Platte, Indians roamed the valley. They occupied the land that offered the gold, and their way of life clashed with that of the instant city rising on their hunting ground. At the Bay of San Francisco, Yerba Buena grew in the context of the Spanish-Mexican tradition of settlement and occupied the cove that would shelter the ships of the Argonauts. Yet Yerba Buena was not destroyed in the confrontation like the Indian world along the South Platte but simply swallowed by the instant city that rose on its site. In its protracted growth, Yerba Buena was sufficiently exposed to influences that assured its convenient disintegration before the tidal wave of urbanization inundated the peninsula.

Foremost among these influences were people and geography. The activities of some of the interlopers to Mexican California and the dictates of a site suited for little but shipping combined to produce a small, but relatively independent, anchorage on the Bay of San Francisco, on the peninsula roughly halfway between the mission and the presidio. The young village did not depend on the church or the army, though, in their respective ways, they contributed to its rise. Its site showed nothing more than slopes covered with sagebrush and lupine, and wild mint grew in such profusion that the fragrant herb gave the place its name.[43] Yerba Buena grew because it featured a sheltered cove that offered protection for ships and made possible ever increasing traffic between people of the land and people from the sea. In a country dominated economically by the agricultural pursuits of the ranchero society, Yerba Buena was the first settlement depending entirely on commerce. Although a pitiful sight as a commercial center, the few houses and shacks represented a decisive break with the traditional settlement pattern based on pueblo, presidio, or mission.

The shortcomings of the original Spanish anchorage off the presidio contributed to the rise of Yerba Buena. Traditional respect for office, more than the ignorance of landlubbers, located the old anchorage conveniently close to the *comandante's* residence at the presidio, the seat of authority on the bay. Shipmasters learned quickly that the open roadstead at the edge of Presidio Shoal, between the Castillo (Fort Point) and Anita Rocks, was unsuitable. They used it, however, until the great storm of 1824 forced the selection of a new anchorage, this time from the point of view of a navigator.[44] The new site was Yerba Buena cove, where ships, news, goods, and people drew other Californios from the peninsula. On shore, the young village of Yerba Buena accentuated the forlornness of the presidio and the deterioration of the mission.

Anglo-Americans were prominent in the development of the village.[45] William A. Richardson, an English seaman, reached San Francisco Bay aboard a whaler in 1822, and later married the daughter of the *comandante* of the presidio. Richardson educated himself about the tides, currents, and channels of the bay; he sketched the cove for Governor José Figueroa. When Richardson himself took up residence there in "a shanty of rough boards," in June 1835, Yerba Buena had its real beginning.[46] He laid out the settlement's first road along the trail from mission to presidio. In July 1836, his family was joined by an American merchant, Jacob Primer Leese, who underscored his arrival with a Fourth of July party at which the residents of the countryside feasted under the Mexican

Eagle and the Stars and Stripes.[47] When Leese moved to Sonoma
near his brother-in-law, Mariano G. Vallejo, he sold his property to
the Hudson's Bay Company, and John McLoughlin, the Chief Factor
at Fort Vancouver, dispatched his son-in-law, William Glen Rae, to
manage the company store in 1841.[48]

Despite its growing significance as a settlement nucleus on the
peninsula, Yerba Buena showed few traits of a future city. In
December 1841, Sir George Simpson wrote of the "pretty little bay
of Yerba Buena, whose shores are doubtless destined, under better
auspices, to be the site of a flourishing town." [49] In almost the same
breath, he criticized Chief Factor McLoughlin for locating the
company store "at the wretched place of Yerba Buena, which of all
others is the least adapted in point of situation & climate" for a
trading post.[50] In 1841, Captain Richardson moved to Sausalito, on
the north peninsula, which he thought had greater potential.[51] In
August 1843, William Glen Rae, the resident agent of the Hudson's
Bay Company, wrote to London that business was bad. Eventually,
the small, isolated place became so unbearable for him that he took
his life in January 1845.[52]

By the time of the American conquest of California, Yerba Buena
had 51 inhabitants more than the Mission; 152 persons lived at Yerba
Buena, 101 at Mission Dolores, and 28 at the Presidio de San
Francisco, according to William Heath Davis's final version of "The
First San Francisco Directory." [53] The Padrón of December 31, 1842,
listing the names, birth places, occupations, and ages of all residents
on the entire peninsula gave 196 names, including 47 neophytes,
Indians, and Kanakas; at Yerba Buena itself there probably lived 17
men, 4 women, and 5 children.[54] The increase in population was at
Yerba Buena where the ships anchored, but it was never as large as
the attorney for the city of San Francisco seemed to have believed in
1852 when he stated to the U.S. Commission for Ascertaining and
Settling Private Land Claims in California that on July 7, 1846, two
days before the American takeover, Yerba Buena "was a town of the
population of about one thousand inhabitants." Nevertheless, the 152

people who actually lived there reflected the magnetism of the cove over the former mission and presidio.[55]

Yerba Buena's special role on the Bay of San Francisco was acknowledged by the American conquerors who gave the well-known name originally designating the bay to the village. The new name was selected by Alcalde Washington Bartlett, a Spanish-speaking Lieutenant of the *Portsmouth*, the highest municipal officer under the new regime. Bartlett shared his generation's notion that urban growth was the result of successful town promotion and real estate speculation. He asked Civil Engineer Jasper O'Farrell to survey the town again and to correct Jean Jacques Vioget's "ragged, irregular delineation" of 1839 to facilitate speculation in town lots.[56] He topped his schemes when he forestalled the use of the familiar geographic name by town builders who were promoting rival harbors around the bay. He had no authority to confirm the new name; he simply published a proclamation in the *California Star* on January 23 and 30, 1847, and ordered the official use of "San Francisco," but the military governor who had the authority made the name change official several weeks later.[57] That Bartlett may also have been sensitive to the Spanish past of the site is a probability pleasant to contemplate. The town could easily have been called New Boston, New Philadelphia, or New New York. Yerba Buena, the only settlement that had grown recently *in,* but not *of* California, also inspired an awareness that a change of name was important under the new management. Yerba Buena Island, a short distance away, now preserves the name.

The American occupation of Yerba Buena in July 1846, and the change of the name to San Francisco in January 1847, were the significant steps which severed the links to Richardson's Yerba Buena and completed the break with the tradition of Mexican settlement. The conquest of California incorporated the foothills of the Sierra Nevada, which Spaniards and Mexicans had not colonized, into the white man's world of exploitation. It led to a communications system that assured worldwide attention for James W. Marshall's discovery of gold in contrast to the limited response which greeted earlier discoveries.[58] The conquest brought the excitement of commercial speculation into the static, pastoral economy and generated a significant demand for land which, in Mexican days, was not regarded as a marketable commodity. It opened the gate for the speculation in real estate essential to the startling development of San Francisco.[59]

Nothing prepared the ground for the rise of Denver. Instant city and wilderness clashed directly in the South Platte Valley. Neither the advancing agricultural frontier nor the Mexican and American settlements of the Upper Arkansas reached Cherry Creek. The Great Plains and the struggle for Kansas stalled the one, organizational weakness and Indian raids halted the thrust of the other. As a result, the influences of three disparate groups met at the mouth of Cherry Creek: the gold seekers with their agrarian-urban tradition of townsite booming and family farming, the fur traders, and the Indians.

Of these three, only the gold seekers shaped the character of rising Denver, together with the merchant as adjunct of their world. "Making governments and building towns" were the "natural employment" of these men.[60] They immediately strove for order before the establishment of properly constituted government and formed Claim Clubs, Citizens' Courts, and Vigilante Committees, and tried and punished offenders.[61] They sent out deputies to track down wrongdoers and bring them to justice, if not before the law. Their solutions to crime were weighted in favor of the white over the Indian and the resident over the stranger. Memory of the legal apparatus of the East was strong, and, through clever adherence to the technicalities of the law, they destroyed the wilderness and its people.

Their goal of quick wealth demanded legal and personal security. They were, in the main, sophisticated enough to know that the orderly anarchy of a struggling frontier village would not serve them. To achieve their mutual aim, they pressed for the passage of one of the first acts of their self-made territorial legislature in December 1859, which gave legal status to the decisions of Miners' Courts and Meetings, in order to perfect their claims against the paramount title of the government.[62] The claims of Indians to the land meant even less to them; they had no use for Indians. Their gold brought the necessities of life into the wilderness, their search for more gold ate up the Indians' hunting ground, and their farmers converted fertile land to their use. Their steadily increasing numbers drove the Indians from the South Platte Valley.

For a brief period, however, the villages of the Indians and the instant city of the gold seekers stood side by side. Thousands of Indians were encamped on the eve of their annual buffalo hunt in May 1859—bands of Arapaho, Cheyenne, Apache, and Comanche, Henry Villard reported to the Cincinnati *Daily Commercial*.[63] In the same spot, the attractions of a large Arapaho village of 160 lodges had captivated John C. Frémont many years earlier, in 1843, when the broad valley of the Platte, shaded by huge cottonwoods, provided him with a spectacular view, enhanced by hundreds of horses and mules grazing miles above and below the village.[64]

In the early summer of 1859, nearly three hundred Arapaho lodges stood in or around Denver. Fifty miles west, in the mountains, an equal number of Ute assembled in preparation for one of their periodic encounters with the Arapaho, their traditional enemies. In July, the Ute retreated before an Arapaho war party which had left their squaws and children behind in Denver "under the protection the presence of white men would afford them." [65]

In the light of their experience with mountain men and settlers on the Arkansas, the Arapaho's idea of fitting the white men into their affairs was not farfetched. However, the Indians also realized that the instant city clashed with their way of life because these whites did not depend on them for their survival and made it abundantly clear that they were not willing to tolerate the wilderness and its people. In the face of the gold seekers' dependence on the instant city for their life, nothing could protect Arapaho and Cheyenne from the threat that this urban civilization posed for their very existence. Nothing did, and the treaties which seemed to attest to the Indians' right to the land proved to be worthless.

The legal technicalities of the Treaty of Fort Laramie intensified the Indians' plight by clouding their title to the land on which Denver stood. Concluded in September 1851, the treaty recognized the right of the Arapaho and Cheyenne to the use of the South Platte Valley, but not their title. Furthermore, the United States Senate did not consent to the treaty as signed but proposed an amendment, and it took two years to get the acquiescence of some of the Indian signators to the changed document. Although Congress carried out the provisions for annuities, the hope quickly vanished that the treaty would solve the problem of peace on the plains.[66] The Kansas-Nebraska bill of 1854 placed the area under the jurisdiction of the Territory of Kansas, but the South Platte Valley seemed expressly exempted from the bill as "territory which, by treaty with an Indian tribe, is not, without the consent of said tribe, to be included within the territorial limits or jurisdiction of any State or Territory." [67]

At best, whatever legal claims the Indians had to the land were based on their previous occupancy and, in part at least, on the Fort Laramie treaty, which many white men seemed to have considered binding—as long as the South Platte Valley was useless.[68] The gold immediately exposed the gulf between the ritual of treaty-making and reality. In the Treaty of Fort Wise in February 1861, Arapaho and Cheyenne were forced to relinquish all rights, except for a reservation along the Arkansas.[69] They were now up against white men who cared more for possession of the land than peace on the plains and who used the treaty as an appeal to Washington on behalf of their city, when Congress was just on the point of establishing legitimate territorial government for Colorado.

With revealing emphasis on Denver's position and with total disregard of the Indians, "in consideration of the kind treatment received by the citizens," Arapaho and Cheyenne were compelled to request in Article 11 of the Fort Wise treaty that the proprietors of Denver "be permitted by the United States government to enter a sufficient quantity of land to include said city and adjacent towns, at the minimum price of one dollar and twenty-five cents per acre."[70] Prior to consenting to the treaty in August 1861, the Senate eliminated this article, but the entire treaty became obsolete when some of the mistreated and starving Indians reached the breaking point and open warfare erupted on the Great Plains in the early 1860s.

The Indians' verbal response to the rise of the instant city and to the sudden loss of a place to live remained a matter of speculation. James P. Beckwourth, a black mountain man and a Crow chief, probably came closest to expressing, in white concepts, the Indian reaction when he felt "like prosecuting the settlers, who are encroaching, and building cities on his old hunting grounds."[71] Beckwourth, who had taken charge of a Denver store in March 1860, received frequent visits from his Cheyenne friends delighted to see him after his return from California and irritated to find him in a city among white men who violated all rules of wilderness conduct.[72] "In passing through our hunting grounds," one Indian argued with Beckwourth, "many a pale face has been lost, but never has one come to a Cheyenne lodge without getting plenty to eat, and being set on the right road to his people."[73] All these Indians felt lost in the city, but one of them did so in particular because no white man had asked him to eat since his arrival.[74]

Jim Beckwourth, who owned city lots and a nearby ranch, was abundantly aware of some dimensions of the problem through the responses of whites to the color of his skin.[75] His experience as the "famous mulatto of the plains," a distinguished black man among whites, undoubtedly sharpened his perception of the fine and gross distinctions among various cultures, ethnic and racial groups.[76] His mixed parentage made him a man of two races; his life in the mountains and in Denver a man of two worlds. In his person, nature and white civilization seemed to have obliterated the dichotomy between wilderness and instant city.

His unique position between white and red men, between city and wilderness, was poignantly underscored by the last years of his life.

In November 1864, he accompanied the soldiers to Sand Creek who annihilated a camp of his Indian friends in retaliation for raids on farms and supply trains. In October 1866, he died in a Crow village on the Upper Missouri while serving as an army scout. One story has it that Beckwourth was poisoned by his Crow friends when he refused to remain and to lead them again as their chief, because they felt he would make better medicine for them dead than alive and in Denver.[77]

Beckwourth's death among his Indian friends brought out the irreconcilable differences between instant city and wilderness. Presumably he died of natural causes. When he felt his end coming on, he hastened to the Crow village to die, as he had once hoped, among his trusted braves; his action answered the question whether he was white, black, or red, a question once raised but ruled out of order in a Congressional inquiry.[78] The story of his death by poison suggested that many white men, preoccupied with securing the foundations of urban life, were unable to understand the simple human ties which drew him back into his Indian world. One trooper, however, sensed the closing cycle in the life of this mulatto who had lived among Indians and who, though exposed to a taste of urban living in Denver, preferred to die in one of their villages. To the soldier it seemed only strange that Beckwourth actually managed to "die among the Indians with whom he spent the better part of his life." [79]

The mountain man frequently intervened with the citizens of Denver on behalf of Indians who suffered in town specifically from the lack of white hospitality as well as the abundance of fiendish ruffians. "The Indians are as keenly sensible to acts of injustice as they are tenacious of revenge," he stressed in a letter to the *Rocky Mountain News*, "and it is more humiliating to them to be recipients of such treatment *upon their own lands,* which they have been deprived of, their game driven off, and they made to suffer by hunger, and when they pay us a visit, abused more than dogs." [80] Beckwourth remonstrated against a "lot of *drunken devils* and 'bummers,'" who raped women and looted the lodges of visiting

Cheyenne and Apache, in April 1860.[81] In response to his exhortations, a public meeting unanimously "condemned the outrages lately perpetrated upon our Indian brethren" and resolved that "the citizens of Denver entertain the Indians hospitably upon their visits . . . for the purpose of trade." [82]

The Indians suffered from the crimes of ruffians and the callousness of residents without redress because the century-old confrontation between Indian and white cultures was re-enacted in Denver. The struggle was intensified but also shortened by the rapidly emerging urban society. It repeated what was a familiar pattern in the wilderness where only a few people saw it. In the novel setting of the instant city anyone could see it, but only a few cared to look. The new urban experience curtailed the mountain man's and the Indian trader's traditional roles as links between the twelve to fifteen hundred Arapaho and Cheyenne, on their favorite campgrounds, and the thousand whites who wintered in Denver and Auraria in 1859–60. Most white residents of the growing city were preoccupied with their first year of real prosperity. The promises of progress were real and seemed to justify viewing the shameful outrages against the Indian as just another version of the age-old clash between civilization and barbarism.[83]

An eloquent, however fatuous, expression of this rationale appeared in the observations of a newcomer from Chicago, made in June 1860, after crossing the plains. "The city . . . presented a very neat appearance, and was far more extensive than we had conceived it to be," he thought after viewing the few brick buildings, the many frame houses and log cabins, and the numerous tents and wagon camps. "Before us were the abodes of civilization," he rejoiced,

while to the right were the smoky wigwams of the Aborigines, amid which could be seen . . . stalwart Indians, filthy squaws and naked children, lazily basking in the warm sun-light. . . . Here were the rude huts of barbarism, there the elegant abodes of civilization; here the wild untutored savage, and there the refined and educated white man. Surely the true extremes had met . . . in a region . . . which a few years since was unknown and uncoveted but is now the home of "a hundred thousand active, working men, bearing aloft the torch of progress." [84]

In Denver, rhetoric compensated for the small number of citizens and eloquence accentuated the contrast between wilderness and city. That extreme contrast San Francisco lacked as a result of the Yerba Buena interlude, but it experienced the excitement of a spectacular rush of men and ships to the bay in response to the news of gold. The sheer number of newcomers obliterated any lingering influences of mission and presidio which remained almost separate entities until the spread of the city eventually engulfed them.

Before the influx of the Argonauts, there occurred a series of regional rushes. One of them emptied San Francisco of its old residents and cleared the ground, so to speak, for the people of the instant city. The first began at Sutter's Fort in March and April 1848. Sonoma and San Francisco stirred in May, and San Jose, Santa Cruz, and Monterey reacted late in May and June to the gold fever. By midsummer, before the polyglot invasion from the corners of the world had actually begun, urban life in California almost stood still.[85]

The first newspaper report of the discovery, which appeared in the San Francisco *Californian* on March 15, 1848, added confusion to what had been only indifference on the part of the town's nine hundred inhabitants, including the one hundred Indians, Kanakas, Negroes, and Chinese.[86] The journalistic scoop of its rival, as well as the vagueness of its report, impelled the editor of the *California Star* to inspect himself, in the company of John A. Sutter, the gold fields. One glimpse of Sutter brought the prospectors, most of whom were his employees, temporarily back to his sawmill, and without their guidance the visitors did not find more than a few grains of gold. On his return, the editor still had little enthusiasm for the discovery, but San Francisco was rife with prodigious tales of gold, and these had their predictable effect: the believers led the exodus with the doubters quickly following. The evacuation was hastened by Samuel Brannan, the owner of the *Star*, who waved aloft a bottle of gold dust in Portsmouth Plaza and shouted, "Gold! Gold! Gold from the American River," after he had stocked his stores in the foothills with goods and equipment that the miners would need, an early demonstration of the close relationship between gold rush and commercial development that sustained the instant city.[87]

Amidst the spreading gold fever, the *Californian* suspended publication on May 29. "The majority of our subscribers and many of our advertising patrons have closed their doors and places of business, and left town," the editor explained. "The whole country, from San Francisco to Los Angeles, and from the sea shore to the base of the Sierra Nevada," his last editorial lamented, "resounds with the sordid cry of 'gold! Gold!! GOLD!!!' " The *Star* followed suit on June 14 since the paper "could not be made by magic." The few remaining inhabitants celebrated the Fourth of July as spiritedly as they could manage. The city council did not meet for two months; its members, with other officials, had all gone to the diggings. Once again desolation ruled the peninsula; San Francisco looked "like a place where the plague reigns, forsaken by its old inhabitants, a melancholy solitude." [88]

In the brief interval between the local rushes and *the* Gold Rush, San Francisco gave every indication of becoming moribund. Its streets were deserted and its houses empty. All able-bodied men, and some totally unfit for the rigors of mining, turned their faces east—to El Dorado. In these months, the city cast off its tenuous links to the past. The discovery of gold eradicated the old character of Yerba Buena-become-San Francisco and insured the rise of the instant city in a new world. The exodus completed the trend initiated by the conquest, the new survey, and the new name.

The hunt for sudden wealth shook the foundations of whatever society existed before the rush. Constantly moving men recast the social molds. The heavy rains and the cold weather that gripped the gold country in the fall of 1848 drove many miners, no longer able to work and to live in the hills, back to San Francisco. Not all returned, however; eight hundred remained at the Dry Diggings alone, and a large number on the Yuba, "working most of the time." [89] Their obsession quieted the last doubters; no one questioned any longer that there were rich deposits of gold in the foothills. All accepted their existence, but now they faced the problem of how to live with the temptation of possible sudden wealth. The glittering dust made poor men rich and ugly men beautiful, rich men poor and beautiful men ugly; gold made wrong right and right wrong, and within the wide range of these generalizations men came to see themselves and one another in a different light.

Lieutenant William T. Sherman observed some of these changes from the perspective of an adjutant-general. He often noticed General Persifer F. Smith with a can of meat in his hand on the way to his quarters, and when he asked his commanding officer why he took off his hat greeting Negroes, the general explained that they were the only real gentlemen in California. "I confess," Sherman admitted, that the fidelity of black servants "at a time when every white man laughed at promises as something to be broken, has given me a kindly feeling of respect for the negroes." [90]

Gold was not yet all powerful; the magic was still too new. It neither broke all bonds of fidelity and bondage nor erased all restrictions of custom and law on the freedom of blacks which kept them from sharing the diggings. For some time, gold dust ranked below currency; it sold for nine dollars per ounce in May 1848, for silver dollars, and very few of these were in circulation. Most luxuries required coin and not even gamblers were willing to play for gold dust. Men needing coin were obliged to sell low, and if the traders were short of cash the miner received even less. To most miners and businessmen, gold came from fields and was like any commodity harvested from the soil. They saw daily the gold pouring into the city and they assumed that the supply would depreciate its value. Gold was merchandise, but cash was money, and since most miners did not know differently, or were not able to wait for the gold dust to gain parity with coin, or badly wanted to share in the good life of the town, they sold their pokes to the merchants often for as little as four to eight dollars an ounce in the fall and winter of 1848. Traders were afraid to hold on to the dust and passed it on at a rate of ten to twelve dollars, and no one cared because gold seemed to have been found so easily that they all assumed the next summer would bring more.[91]

Gold quickly overcame most obstacles to its supremacy. It was more plentiful and lured more people to San Francisco than ever imagined. Gold was the driving force that "changed a comparative wilderness" into "the great commercial metropolis of the Pacific," one adventurer concluded during the early months of the Gold Rush.[92] It assured the rise of the instant city and gave reality to the vision of an independent beginning symbolized by Engineer O'Farrell's new survey and Alcalde Bartlett's new name of the settlement. It completed the break with Yerba Buena's past. When the shiploads of newcomers arrived they could maintain that they came to a place where there was nothing but gold and men. "There was no San Francisco," one of the Argonauts emphasized, "there were sand-hills, tents, huts, and some muddy places which were called streets," but "there were men," he recalled, "ready to build, to lay out streets, to pave them, to level hills hundreds of feet high, to make a San Francisco." [93]

On the San Francisco Peninsula, Indians were not among the obstacles of nature standing between the gold seekers and their instant city. Eliminated by earlier invaders, their absence spared San Francisco the racial conflict that shook Denver when Indians and whites met on the streets of the city. The struggle between Indians and whites in the South Platte Valley was aggravated by the frequent Indian raids on outlying ranches. Increased assaults also destroyed wagon trains with freight crucial to the city's population.[94]

The restlessness arising out of territorial politics, the Civil War, the fear of secessionist cabals, and the threat of a Confederate invasion from Texas only added to the frustration.[95] Natural and man-made disasters, floods, vigilante activities, false alarms, and rumors intensified the confusion and suffering.[96] White responsibility for any unrest was often blamed on the Indians. On the eve of the Civil War, Major John Sedgwick indicated the trend when he confided to his sister that "half of the murders that are committed on the plains, and laid to the Indians, are committed by white men." [97]

The Indian difficulties also were closely linked to interrelated political, economic, and military issues, but the fear of raids overshadowed all other considerations. "Is all quiet on the road? Did you see many Indians?" were the anxious questions which greeted Nathaniel P. Hill upon his arrival in Denver in June 1864. The citizenry, in order to assure that all whites were aware of the Indian threat to their survival, made public displays of their fellowmen who had fallen to fire arrow, war club, and scalping knife. On the day of Hill's arrival the "horribly mutilated . . . bodies" of a family "were . . . exposed in the streets . . . to convince the incredulous of the . . . murder. . . . So fond are these Westerners of excitement," said Hill, a thirty-two-year-old Professor of Chemistry at Brown University, who inspected the gold region on behalf of Eastern investors, "that all the people of the town with a few honorable exceptions went to see them." [98]

Fear spread like wildfire over the plains when war parties of Cheyenne, Arapaho, Sioux, Comanche, and Kiowa burned nearly all the ranches along the Platte and the Upper Arkansas. Though Denver was protected by block houses and pickets, these defenses could not deter the disruption of shipping into the city. Indian raids on wagon trains severely depleted supplies. Soaring prices led to concern that there might be a return to the exorbitantly fluctuating prices of the summer of 1859. Inflation increased the threat of famine, with flour up to $45 per sack in 1864, three times what it had sold for in 1859 and ten times its lowest price in 1861. Only stocks of flour and other provisions hoarded by speculators helped to quiet the hunger produced by distant Indian attacks on supply shipments inbound to the city. [99]

Fifty residents were killed by Indians in 1862, and 173 in 1863. At times false rumors about Indians massing to sack the town drove men, women, and children into the business district where they barricaded themselves in stockades on Blake Street. A proclamation by the governor directed all stores to close at 6:30 P.M. and ordered all men for daily weapon drills on the corner of Larimer and Fourteenth streets. [100] "It was deemed advisable in these earlier years," a woman remembered, "for all women living on this frontier to know how to load and use both revolver and rifle. Target practice was one of the amusements . . . , and many women became very expert markswomen." [101]

From the fall of 1863 to the fall of 1864, Denver resembled an armed camp more than the peaceful city of white people that its residents yearned for. The display of militancy produced its problems. Nathaniel Hill did not enjoy living in an area where "every man you meet thinks it safe to carry a loaded pistol." When he spotted the governor with a revolver in his belt and asked him if he thought it necessary to be armed in broad daylight, John Evans replied he considered it "the duty of every man to be able to defend himself at all times." [102]

In the summer of 1864, with Indians raiding the plains, the days of 1860 were forgotten when an Arapaho village stood near the busy walks of Blake Street. The growing excitement over Indian depredations along the Platte and atrocities on the Upper Arkansas compounded all other troubles that white men faced who struggled to assure a future to their instant city in the wilderness. Their doubts about their city were intensified by their doubts about their territory, and all uncertainties were magnified by the dismal sight of their country divided by civil war. The chastisement of the Indian raiders which the editor of the *Rocky Mountain News* advocated in the summer of 1864 appeared as the solution to many problems, that decisive action cherished by active men who felt stifled by many stalemates.[103]

Press and public alike hailed as a great victory over marauding Indians the news from Sand Creek, about 140 miles as the crow flies east-southeast of Denver. There Colorado volunteers and a handful of regulars, under the command of Colonel John M. Chivington, attacked a camp of sleeping Cheyenne and Arapaho on November 29, 1864, and killed many of them in a wanton slaughter.[104] On December 7, the *News* published its first exuberant report of the "Big Indian Fight" and the residents of Denver celebrated what it called a "needed whipping." [105] The attack was called a massacre when word of an impending Congressional investigation was received.

Although some citizens abhorred the method of Colonel Chivington, few went so far as to condemn the results of his action. Only in the safety of the mountains, the Montana Literary Society in Central City echoed the cry of horror that went up in the East when the details became known and "*Resolved* that indiscriminate massacre of all Indians, without reference to age or sex, is contrary to humanity, religion and common sense." [106] If Denverites felt differently, they did not say so, but many years later, the annual meeting of the Colorado Pioneers in September 1883, greeted Colonel Chivington "with a perfect thunder of cheers." "Men threw up their hats, women waved their handkerchiefs, and all huzzaed at the top of their voices." [107] When Chivington at the end of his apologia was still prepared to say, "I stand by Sand Creek," many whites who recalled the difficult summer and fall of 1864 saw eye to eye with him.[108]

Any pangs of conscience experienced by Denverites after Sand Creek were submerged by the clamor of self-righteous politicians who exploited the massacre for their own ends. In the face of the complete mismanagement of Indian affairs, few people were genuinely concerned about the welfare of the Indian.[109] After all, whites had been killing Indians for years, at great expense, one of them argued who thought that of all the game and wild beasts native to the South Platte Valley "the Indian is the most prominent, useless, pernicious, and costly to hunt." [110] Peace on the plains on the white man's terms was essential to Denver's lines of communication and crucial for physical survival and material progress. The desire to see Denver streets quiet and free of armed men appeared excuse enough for Chivington, his volunteers, and their mission of extermination.[111]

While Denverites were aware of the gross distinction between Governor Evans's plea for preparedness and Colonel Chivington's massacre, the attitudes they showed toward Sand Creek minimized any chance the Indian might have had to contribute his culture to the rising city. Their actions wiped out or corrupted most remnants of Indian life. In 1873, an administrator of a Ute agency in Denver which served briefly as a way station to hunting grounds on the Great Plains scotched plans by a group of whites to stage a Ute scalp dance in the city, but he failed to halt a similar ceremony in the next year, at Sloan Lake just outside the town, to which "lots of ladies, prominent in church and society circles, straining for a sight of the reeking scalps," were driven by their escorts in elegant carriages.[112] Denver society always accepted the brutal aspects of the wilderness —on its terms—but now the city actually was "the commercial emporium of the Pike's Peak Gold Regions," as the title of the first directory already boasted in 1859, and some citizens took the leisure to look at the wilderness.[113]

Almost nothing was left of the wilderness. The land was still there but cut up into city lots; the Indians were gone. The destructive swath of the instant city reflected a cultural tradition which restricted to a fleeting moment the peculiar mixture of urban life and wilderness in the streets of Denver. The American attitudes to nature and to urban growth demanded the destruction of the wilderness. The eyes of Americans, Alexis de Tocqueville observed a generation earlier, "are fixed upon . . . the . . . march across the wilds, draining swamps, turning the course of rivers, peopling solitudes and subduing nature." [114] The natural riches of the continent which lured men into the wilderness made possible the rise of instant cities in the Far West. The amenities of new cities spurred on men in their pursuit of wealth through the exploitation of the land, and any people standing in their way were pushed aside without second thought.

Along the South Platte, the love-hatred of Americans toward the wilderness was never the subject of dispassionate debate. A few dissenting voices came from men on the borderline of the new social respectability introduced by the city. Jim Bridger, the famous mountain man, reportedly extended his repugnance for St. Louis to Denver, as well.[115] Richens L. Wootton, another mountain man better known as Uncle Dick, in 1862 left Denver for good because the fluctuation of population got on his nerves; he did not like to "wear fine clothes" or to be "jostled about on the streets," and he abhorred the lack of "breathing space" and "the noise and dust of the city." [116]

The flourishing city had little use for these human reminders of the wilderness either. Two mountain men, John S. Smith and William McGaa were taken in as partners by the first town company of Denver, and McGaa mediated between Indians and whites and stayed in the city. He even had a street named after him, but in the early 1860s the city was anxious to have Ben Holladay's overland stages routed through Denver and, toward that end, changed McGaa Street to Holladay Street after people suddenly noticed that the former mountain man had taken to drink. The city wilderness caught up quickly with what Denver had made out of McGaa's wilderness when the street became infamous for its parlor houses and red light cribs, and since even the name Holladay could not survive such a reputation, the city named the street more accurately Market Street.[117]

Mountain men and seafaring traders belonged to the cutting wedges of white civilization, but they were an integral part of the wilderness and used to gradual development as their way of life, and these experiences kept them aloof from the abrupt changes generated by the instant cities. They implanted ideas of commerce and industry in remote areas and their activities softened the ground for the planting of settlements, but these settlements outgrew their modes of adjustment to the wilds and the Indians, after more and more white people responded to the lure of the continent. When the tidal waves of gold seekers and the rising instant cities swept aside the last vestiges of their modus vivendi, most of them turned their backs on the new order built on an absolute commitment to an urban way of life.

On the San Francisco Peninsula and in the South Platte Valley, the new way of life stamped the instant city as antithesis of the wilderness. Their builders, men and women seeking sudden riches, destroyed whatever stood in their way and assured the independent beginnings of San Francisco and Denver. Their single-minded pursuit of their goal produced cities in isolated settings which magnified the hectic pulse of urban life. The heritage of their reckless and tenacious chase of gold marked the cities, and these, in turn, shaped their people.

# 5

## Reluctant Citizens

The great numbers of people drawn by the discovery of gold in the West inadvertently created instant cities. They came out to take advantage of the chance of a lifetime, their only common goal a share of the hidden riches. All things considered, they behaved as people have under similar circumstances: they pursued their own interests and destroyed in the process whatever stood in the way of their returning home quickly with a fortune. Yet, because of their obsession and despite their avowed self-interest both San Francisco and Denver emerged as instant cities.

The men and women who built these two cities were individuals tempered by a unique experience: they raced through the entire process of American city building, "crowding a century into a generation." [1] Of course, only a few stayed to see the process through to completion. It was extremely unlikely, for instance, that a man who pitched his tent on Market Street in 1849 moved into San Francisco's Palace Hotel in 1875, or that a woman who lived under the canvas top of a prairie schooner on Larimer Street in 1859 resided in Denver's Windsor Hotel in 1880. [2] Brought here by the opportunity for personal gain, many left when opportunity passed them by. Some who witnessed the dawn of these instant cities stayed on through all the hectic changes that brought about urban greatness, but most came in late, or dropped out early, or ran only a few laps of the race. Their individual involvements were as varied as their lives were common in the context of mid-nineteenth-century America, but their collective experience provides an extraordinary and fascinating picture of the dynamics of explosive urbanization in the American West.

The multitudes who made the instant cities did not make instant citizens. Although their personal daring prepared them for the task of building cities in the wilderness, they started with no interest in this challenge. Most took for granted the need for controls to prevent anarchy, to facilitate individual attempts to get ahead, or to protect commercial and political ties, but that was the extent of their commitment to the developing urban society. Here for gold, they set their sights and talents on the gold fields and came to view the cities as depositories of wealth, to be mined as rigorously as placers and veins only after the gold fields fell short of their great expectations.

Frustrated gold seekers, determined to become rich, if not in the mines then at least because of them, created the instant cities of San Francisco and Denver. They had overcome inertia and endured the hardship of the move in the hope of bettering their lots and they clung to the cities after defeat in the fields because they were still bound to the creed of getting ahead in life. Some stayed to try to live off the business their own needs had generated and off the movement of money through their cities to and from the mines. Fatigue, poverty, or pride kept others from returning as failures to homes that now appeared restrictive in comparison with the opportunities of the West. A lucky few actually found the pouch of gold they all vied for and some others eventually made their fortunes in the cities. But most worked or sought work, schemed or speculated, fought on or resigned, their migration yielding little more than an identification with the struggle.

Although so many found themselves in much the same financial situation from which they started, their participation in the thriving cities gave even the losers in the free-for-all a vicarious victory. For their own aborted dreams they substituted the cities' spectacular achievements, and as they gained novel identities as San Franciscans and Denverites they began to mark the successes of their cities as their own.

Life in San Francisco and Denver demanded a knack for improvisation, and the men and women who made the cities used the cities creatively in the pursuit of big and small goals. Although the rapid rate of urbanization taxed their ingenuity, they loved chance and shunned routine. The burgeoning cities exposed them to the hectic pace of living with frequent change but the settlers favored abrupt solutions to their problems over solutions produced by steady attention to everyday tasks. They had a flair for the drama of adventure, and the stark contrast between the rising cities and the natural setting heightened the magic and unreality of the scene. In their single-minded pursuit of riches, these settlers, who seemed bent on destruction, came up with dynamic urban environments and were themselves turned into citizens.

The struggle of men and women of diverse origins with the turbulent world of instant cities compounded the complexities of American urban growth throughout the country. The second half of the nineteenth century was a period of extensive internal migration and immigration as well as ethnic and racial struggles. The search for economic and social mobility added to the ordinary difficulties even of those who were settled in old cities; so did attempts to incorporate technological advances into the fabric of life, to apply a rural democracy to the city, and to develop an urban culture. The plight of the inhabitants of established cities and old towns, shaken by the impact of industrialization and urbanization, was brought into focus by the intensive exposure to rapid urbanization experienced by San Franciscans and Denverites.

Much of the urban experience of Americans prior to the birth of instant cities consisted of variations on a basic theme; migration to new townsites, or to established cities, and adjustment to new neighbors. Along the way, these urbanites struggled to adapt political and social institutions, technology, economics, and culture to the emerging common needs. The differences within communities were differences of degree dependent upon such factors as the locale, the homogeneity of the population, and the particular characteristics that distinguish the city. But the number and complexity of the situations that the residents of instant cities encountered in the number of years it took instant cities to move from tent to town suggests a unique experience.

Nothing sheltered the residents of instant cities from the stresses and strains of the urban explosion they triggered or eased their adjustment to urban existence as a way of life. The steady flow of newcomers, on the lookout for the opportunity of a lifetime, increased the number of people waiting for fate to touch their lives with riches. Although this growth sustained the rising cities, it increased their instability.[3] In the 1880s, a quarter of the people of Colorado lived in Denver; five hundred a day entered the state, and nine-tenths of them passed through the city.[4] In the 1870s, one-third of California's population crowded within a few square miles of San Francisco sand dunes while thousands of square miles of fertile land furnished homes "only for the squirrel or the jackass rabbit." [5] The stream of people kept in flux the population of the cities, which contained among their residents few who were born in them.

Living in instant cities that were spawned by accident and sustained by change amounted to living in one time horizon—the future. Men and women carried in their heads a set of accomplishments that they hoped to see in their lifetime, the firsts of practically everything, sidewalks and street lights, trains and trolleys, restaurants and hotels, schools and churches, all fused into their image of new cities, better ones than those they left behind. On her arrival in the drab Denver of 1860, after a fifteen-day trip from Council Bluffs, for instance, a woman was assured that she would "live to see the streets . . . lined with marble palaces," and when a Denver journalist published a few of her letters, in 1893, he commented, in the spirit of the initial promise, that she had lived to see Denver "possessing the finest school buildings, and finest street-car system without exception, of any city in the world," and a "greater proportion of fine churches, fine theatres, fine hotels and fine private residences than any other city of its age and population." [6]

Unlike Bostonians, New Yorkers, and Philadelphians, the residents of San Francisco and Denver could not rely on their cities' momentum to produce progress through steady population growth, commercial and industrial development. They shared no traditions like those that shielded the citizens of Santa Fe and Monterey from changes wrought by outside forces in a timeless world. In the development of instant cities, nothing resembled the kind of organic growth that had brought Champoeg into existence. Like the builders of another instant city on the shore of Great Salt Lake, the residents of San Francisco and Denver lived on hope. It gave direction to a chaotic present, but the future, unlike the certain future of the Saints' temple city, lay exposed to the swift intercession of chance.

Chance governed the rise of San Francisco and Denver and affected all phases of their development. It drew people to sites that lacked the standard prerequisites for urban greatness, and the cities thrived primarily on the concentration of many people in limited locales. Conversely, ordinary towns grew in various settings and attracted residents primarily on the basis of their geographic advantages, the strength and value of which affected their maturation to cities over decades and centuries. The success of such laborious development corresponded to the potential of the sites and protected the towns from the kind of spectacular collapse that threatened San Francisco and Denver. Fulfillment stretched beyond a single generation and was blurred by the ups and downs of the protracted growth. But in instant cities the perpetual rush of new gold seekers compressed this complex process of city growth into a single generation. Overnight they built cities on sites that had not demonstrated an ability to attract and sustain a population of urban density. The problems arising from the haphazard choice of locations threatened San Francisco and Denver with doom in the event that they failed to continue to attract newcomers.

The inhabitants of San Francisco and Denver ignored this threat to their dreams. Once entangled in the urban scene, they chased fortune there as stubbornly as they had in the mountains, intrigued by the instant cities' hidden opportunities, which resembled quartz veins that divided and disappeared but might be found again with pluck and luck. Men and women, who never saw the gold fields but heard so much about them, took the opportunities of the cities as substitutes for the missed opportunities of the diggings. With the conviction of seasoned gamblers, the fortune hunters believed that luck would come their way and they hesitated to leave the urban gamble until they had seen the last card. They were ever ready to follow the lure of gold and to stampede to new diggings at the first rumor, yet they ignored paper schemes promoting rival city sites that had all the prerequisites of urban greatness but one—people.

Because of the spectacular success of their cities, the residents argued that their existence was free from such petty encumbrances to urban development as a city's favorable location, level land and transportation links, wood and water.[7] Inspired by the collective accomplishment they paid little attention to men who attempted to exploit concern about expansion space and communication lines through the promotion of rival towns. Fate determined the sites of their cities, and with their respect for the rule of chance, they left the hassle over the best site in the area to the few who took it up for their own good. This indifference, or restraint, left to a handful of people the task of safeguarding the cities' future from potential disasters, ranging from the inauspicious sites to the stranglehold of railroads. Belief in chance, formidable among people fascinated by luck, ultimately relegated political affairs to vigilantes or bosses and cultural activities to nouveaux riches or impresarios.

The habit of staying clear of the cities' affairs took root in San Francisco and Denver after a few men easily defended these mediocre localities against the bungling schemes of half-hearted rivals. Most residents felt secure because San Francisco dominated life around the bay despite crucial space and access problems and Denver regulated the commerce of plains and mountains although its location, at the confluence of an insignificant creek and a river unsuited for transportation, was no more favorable than half a dozen other places nearby. With the eyes of most inhabitants fixed on their personal dreams, indifference insured that chance would continue to determine the course of development. They correctly assumed that their numbers would make the difference between city and wasteland.

Undaunted by promising townsites around the bay, notably Francisca-Benicia, on the Straits of Carquinez, and the City of New York of the Pacific, at the juncture of the Sacramento and San Joaquin rivers, San Franciscans took for granted the actions of Lieutenant Washington A. Bartlett, who ordered the use of the well-known name San Francisco, and of Captain Joseph L. Folsom, who picked the city as the depot for his quartermaster department.[8] Most assumed that the personal interests of these officers, whose decisions ensured the continuation of the city's development, also lay in San Francisco, and in this spirit they faced the opposition, a group of prominent advocates of Benicia's superior site.[9] With their eyes on ships and men, San Franciscans knew the direction of the human tide even before 1850, when it became obvious that San Francisco had taken the vast commerce and Benicia the miniscule agricultural trade, and "Gotham-on-the-Pacific" had lost out entirely.[10]

Rhetoric about the ideal townsite never swayed San Franciscans, neither at the peak of the townsite fever nor in later years. General William T. Sherman, who as a young officer had been unimpressed by San Francisco's location, still insisted in 1875 that Benicia was "the best natural site for a commercial city" and would have become a "city of palaces" had it received "half of the money and half of the labor since bestowed upon San Francisco." [11] A decade later, Hubert Howe Bancroft condemned San Francisco's location which imposed "endless expense, inconvenience, discomfort, and disease upon millions of men for probably thousands of years." [12]

While they thrived on chance, the residents needed plenty of stamina, a virtue abundant in Denver according to their first historian. Pluck came naturally since the great majority were "most desperate and reckless adventurers" who alone were capable of crossing the plains, searching for gold, and keeping the Indians at bay.[13] They endured the uncertainties of a topography that barely distinguished between camp site and townsite. Town-founding fever struck them along the South Platte ford of the Cherokee Trail at the mouth of Cherry Creek. However, the development of townsites went on only during lulls in the raging gold fever.[14] In the late fall of 1858, Auraria, on the left bank of Cherry Creek, and Denver, on the right, began competing for control as the central gathering place of the gold seekers.[15] In 1859, town building had to wait as a new mining boom drove people to washings up and down the South Platte and into the mountains. When hard times followed the collapse of the boom, the few determined people who had stayed called for the merger of Auraria and Denver and the end of the petty rivalry.[16] During the first four years of the ebb and flow of fortune and population at the mouth of Cherry Creek, residents persevered and most kept their urban tempers under better control than did Uncle Dick Wootton, hardy mountain man though he was, who in 1862 made up his mind that hectic Denver was a good place to get away from.[17]

The population fluctuations, as well as the lean and prosperous years chasing one another, constantly taxed the residents of instant cities who craved assurances provided by numbers, the most direct indicator of success. Census after census, they questioned the correctness of the official count.[18] Invariably, they considered the figures too low, although San Francisco rose quickly, from 56,802 inhabitants in 1860 to 149,473 in 1870, 233,959 in 1880, 298,997 in 1890, and 342,782 in 1900, according to the census. Within two and one-half decades, the city acquired over a third of a million people; Boston had required two and one-half centuries to reach this population figure. While Denverites griped about the differences between various counts, they had reason for their obsession with numbers. During the stagnation of Colorado mining during the 1860s, the population remained static according to the census. It recorded 4,759 inhabitants in 1870, just ten more than ten years earlier, but the official figures reached 35,629 in 1880; 106,713 in 1890; and 133,859 in 1900. Between 1870 and 1890, the population of Denver increased about twentyfold, a rate faster than that of any other city in the country.[19]

Bewildered, the inhabitants of San Francisco and Denver watched these numbers that never fully acknowledged what seemed to them to be obvious. Their running battle with the official figures drew them closer to their cities because their own experiences indicated that their cities' resilience would sustain them when all else seemed to fail, even mining and commerce, grit and luck. However, a generation eager to be vindicated by statistics as they floundered between excessive optimism and a haunting fear that their cities would never offer that avenue to quick riches, they felt the need for the kind of certainty provided by the presumed objectivity of numbers.[20]

"Serene, indifferent to fate," a poet eulogized San Francisco and a traveler lauded Denver's "solidity and permanence," but in order to evoke these impressions their residents frantically spun lofty images of urban greatness to cover their cities, and their intensity convinced Rudyard Kipling, during his visit in 1889, that "neither serenity nor indifference" were found in San Francisco.[21] They "build recklessly" and "boast in proportion," the rector of an Episcopal church and headmaster of a boys' school in a prosperous suburb of London noticed during his first visit to Denver in 1872, seven years before he came back to take charge of Saint John's Church in the Wilderness.[22] The outsiders' critical assessments brought the residents to the defense of their cities. In cities that substituted the gambler's heart for the stable power of diligence, the contrast between the cities the residents saw and the cities they wanted to see was obscured with imagination and magic. The gray fog of the bay and the spectacular mountains encircling Denver were used to buttress visions of urban grandeur.

When wilderness and isolation that once had enhanced the mystique of their city vanished, San Franciscans relied on the fog to perpetuate the dream of a special city that would make them rich. What meteorologists describe as low stratus clouds influenced the pattern of settlements, and the parallels between maintaining the myth of the great city and defending the weather of the bay drove home the significance of the fog to the developing image of San Francisco.[23] The residents' difficulties with the caustic comments of visitors about the climate were analogous to their difficulties with the stern count of the census. The steady breeze blowing sand, fog, or rain was not really much to boast about, and only blind loyalty and consistent bragging seemed to protect San Franciscans. Yet the fog helped to embellish meager urban accomplishments with dramatic rays of sunshine.[24] Newcomers encountered a "city of expensive ideas" but cheap reality, hidden behind a natural shroud; yet every time the veil lifted, the radiant sun presented the "large beginning, confident promise, but rather mean performance" of San Francisco as a spectacular success.[25] To the fortunate observer of the spectacle, the vanishing clouds seemed to reveal charms which the city could no longer conceal behind the gray mist, and the elevation of the fog to the topic of an erudite panegyric indicated its significance for San Franciscans, even outside the circle of realtors and rhymesters.[26]

While the frequent spectacle of drifting clouds attuned San Franciscans to the constant changes to which the rising cities were subjected, the western horizon of Denver, "the grandest stretch of mountain scenery on earth," [27] attested to the permanence of this city. With city and setting combining in a timeless sight, "a gem on the side of the largest mountains in the world," Denverites ignored the gap between the young settlement and the old mountains and immersed themselves in Denver's natural scene.[28] Instead of "the great braggart city," which an Englishwoman saw in 1873, "brown and treeless, upon the brown and treeless plain," they preferred the images evoked by the vivid imaginations of their local newspaper reporters.[29]

In a city where boasts about the climate were contradicted with references to 48-degree drops in temperature in an hour, the reporters' accounts ran the gamut from clichés about nature's wonders to stereotypes of men's reactions.[30] The outline of the mountains was visible, some of the stories went, yet the haze of the range robbed the peaks of their rugged harshness. When hidden by a cloud, the sun provided the brilliance of the typical silver lining. Pikes Peak often seemed almost lost in fleecy clouds, but was still discernible, enveloped in white.[31] " 'How beautiful,' came involuntarily from many an observer." [32]

Travelers who caught their first glimpse of the city from the window of their railroad car often noted how the scene was "like a revelation," after twenty-four hours on the prairie.[33] Coming from the opposite direction and descending the foothills, others found the first view of the distant city with the plains stretching to the horizon "even grander" than the reversed image with the Rocky Mountains in the background. It was "more suggestive of human life and death, of enterprise, of struggle, of suffering," and that range of experiences one traveler saw symbolized by the "Young Empress of the Plains, to whom the old kingly mountains pay tribute from their hidden treasure chests—fair desert child of this wondrous golden age, with her stirring yet pathetic legend, strange and wild and tragic." [34] The laborious interpretations of the majestic scene, and the contest sponsored in later years by the Denver Real Estate Exchange, "Why Denver Should Be the Summer Capital" of the United States, reflected the strain to enhance the city's prestige.[35] They also indicated the degree to which the Denverites had become the captives of their own magic.

In the pursuit of their dreams of success, San Franciscans and Denverites backed their flights of imagination with speculations of a sort different from those that motivated people in ordinary urban settings. Whenever possible, they liked work that provided excitement: extensive treasure hunts on ocean, prairie, or in the mountains. They shunned the small, steady returns of patient industry, and that mentality made them, in some degree, unfit for the routine and discipline of manufacturing industries. Their attitude surprised a Frenchman during his visit to Denver in the late 1880s who marveled how "this population of 200,000 managed to live" on nothing but four smelters and two or three packing houses as permanent industry; "Denver is too young a city to be a great manufacturing point," its Board of Trade had stated bluntly a few years earlier.[36] As westering people, the residents of instant cities were given to adventures involving considerable risk but offering the chance of large gain. The atmosphere of their cities, saturated with accident and change, kept this spirit alive. Living in settings shaped by the hazards of rapid urbanization amounted to an exciting continuation of their adventures, and the residents willingly speculated on their uncertain projects because they had been originally intrigued by the fickle nature of their cities' major enterprises, mining and commerce.

Commerce and mining heightened the proclivity for speculation, and speculation, in turn, bound the residents to the instant cities. When mining came to be restricted to the mountains, daring men quickly expanded commercial enterprises, banking on the cities' strength to harness the needs of town and country for supplies. In ports, located on an ocean of water or a sea of grass, they gambled on the potential of San Francisco and Denver as points of transshipment. Isolated from the centers of production and the sources of capital, they hoped to profit on the fluctuations of supply and demand and for months waited anxiously for cargo ordered at a time when it was impossible to predict accurately the behavior of the market at the moment of delivery. They saw fortunes within their reach, only to see them vanish again with the sudden appearance of a competitor's clipper ship or prairie schooner on the horizon. Their great game ended in the 1860s when telegraph and railroad bound the cities to the national market.

Actually, only a handful of the residents of San Francisco and Denver experienced directly the capricious nature of mining, then the pursuit of a bonanza by poor men. Only a few searched the mountains, sank prospect holes, staked out a claim, mined a placer or a vein, and then, having been lucky on every count, were forced to realize that it took a mine to run a mine. Many came to California or Colorado seeking gold but when they saw San Francisco or Denver concluded that riches could also be found there. For those unable to raise capital and engineer men and machinery, mining offered nothing but employment as wageworkers tied to small towns in the mountains. The fortune hunters quickly turned their backs on the deadly routine of backbreaking labor, substituting a mania for speculation in mining stock as their first, last, and only avenue to quick riches.

Different experiences with mining in San Francisco and Denver influenced the direction of speculative interests. Although they lived in an emporium, San Franciscans took to speculation in mining stock because the city clung emotionally to the adventurous world of the prospector-miner, the proverbial "honest miner" of the Gold Rush, even after that world disappeared with the emergence of mining as an industry rather than as a one-man gambling game. The romance of the brief years lived on and kept the minds of San Franciscans on colorful, distant scenes. The story developed an existence of its own and flourished on a yearning to perpetuate the city's youthful image, a characteristic of any rapidly maturing society plagued by urbanization and industrialization. San Franciscans, whose city had never been threatened with extinction by the irregularities of mining, regarded the enterprise as an integral part of their city's image and, only then, as the economic base of their welfare. As early as November, 1850, circulars advertised to the East the operations of California quartz mines and presaged the trend of subsequent decades that made San Franciscans middlemen between the mines and the distant sources of investment capital and turned so many of them into speculators in mining stock.[37]

The emotional links expanded beyond California gold to Nevada silver. Using economic ties, San Franciscans made Virginia City, the center of Nevada mining, a suburb of their city, and as a suburb it relived San Francisco's sudden rise without hope for a future of its own. Its residents went to the bay, in fact and fiction, whenever they could.[38] The impact of the Comstock Lode on San Francisco's development was comparable to the effect of Leadville silver on Denver's Great Boom of the late 1870s, but until Leadville's silver magnates gravitated to Denver, Denverites kept this potential rival apart from their own world.[39] Residents of Denver held this entire new industry at arm's length until the decline of the market value of silver in the 1880s baptized the newcomers and a new gold bonanza made up for the economic consequences.[40] Then, they did show that affection for the mining industry that they had been unwilling and perhaps unable to give during the 1860s while the fluctuations of mining still seemed capable of making or breaking their city and tantalizing their citizenry.[41] In general, they left the relationship to a handful of bankers, mining kings, engineers, scientists, and politicians who combined mining in the mountains with smelting in Denver to the city's advantage.[42] That restraint was sorely tested in the 1860s, which saw people attracted to bonanzas in Nevada, Idaho, and Montana, frightened by the Civil War and Indian raids on the Plains, disheartened by the Union Pacific favoring the transcontinental railroad through Wyoming, and enraged by President Andrew Johnson's refusal to approve statehood for Colorado.[43]

While some adventurers followed the ever elusive gold into the mountains, discovered silver, and extended their search to timberline with that singlemindedness that kept H. A. W. Tabor going for eighteen years, Denverites looked for excitement and romance to their city's role as supply center of the Colorado mines and to their geography as outlet for their speculative urge.[44] To the chagrin of the promoters of mining stock, Denverites speculated wholeheartedly in real estate. In contrast to the situation back east in Kansas City, Omaha, Minneapolis, and St. Paul, promoters stressed that real estate steadily increased in value between 1885 and 1890, and Denverites facilitated their pastime through the founding of the Real Estate and Stock Exchange Board in 1887. The residents leaped at the development and improvement of subdivisions, laid out suburbs on the prairie, on paper only, and asked fancy prices and, at times, paid them.[45] Few natural obstacles stood in their way; unlike San Francisco, where the complicated terrain made real estate speculation a rather exclusive affair, Denver could expand in any direction.[46] When the design of a venture limited the number of participants, Denver's small speculators—who in San Francisco were the mainstay of the mining exchanges—sought the best accommodation they could, within large schemes, or speculated in street railways, water ditches, lotteries, or even turned to cattle where speculation bordered on being an act of faith; but Denverites refused to get involved in mining stock.[47]

A mining journal lamented in the 1880s that the "taint given mining thirty years ago, by faint-hearted fellows, who lacked the stamina to become true pioneers," accounted for the general contempt in Denver, and men who made and were making fortunes in mining "have been so cowed with public opinion that they dare not openly avow their obligation to this industry." [48] From September 1862, mining stock exchanges simplified speculation in San Francisco, but in July 1889, Denverites were still debating the establishment of a stock market. This led to the incorporation of the Colorado Mining Stock Exchange. All previous attempts had failed because they seemed to confirm the suspicion of people who once detected the rascally associates of the defunct Colorado Stock and Exchange Board during its brief operation of 1875–76 and during another try in 1879.[49]

San Franciscans compounded the mining gamble with the exchange hazard because they did not know better or did not care. The speculative fever gripped many so strongly that they were unable to see how much the odds favored manipulators of stock with inside knowledge of mining operations. They were hooked and continued to play the market even after the "great business of 1874–1875." That was the "greatest, grandest, most profitable year" in the history of the San Francisco Stock and Exchange Board, but ended with the collapse of the Bank of California and the Panic of 1875.[50] This led to the period of wildest speculation in the Comstock that climaxed in 1876. "There was hardly an individual who was not gambling," and during the business hours of the exchange no one walked, most ran, and the general greeting was, "How's Stocks?" [51]

San Franciscans viewed their stupendous losses on the market as much with pride as with regret. The blows wrecked speculators, small and large, with "thousands of families in our midst who are irretrievably ruined." [52] The extent of their folly was lost in scarce or conflicting evidence. In 1876, the volume of stock transactions was placed at $525 million, but much of that sum may have been just so many pieces of paper because the losses of the small speculators were said to have reduced the deposits in savings banks from $75 million to $25 million between 1875 and 1879 and to have burdened 20,000 owners of real estate with $100 million in mortgages.[53] The few facts that came to light did not unduly depress people who viewed their stock gambles as one way to keep in step with their successful fellow men. In that light, speculation in mining stock, although unsuccessful, seemed a laudable undertaking.

The familiarity of the losers with the few who grew rich also lightened the losses. The names of the archvillains in a novel on stock gambling, Highwater and Obrian, pointed a thinly disguised finger at the outstanding operators of the market from the bonanza firm of Flood, Fair, Mackay, and O'Brien.[54] Ruined speculators tried to overcome swiftly the roadblocks to fortune with the help of "scientific inquiry" and "undeniable lessons of statistical information." Failures were further impersonalized by dividing performance analyses of about 150 mining stocks over four years into first-, second-, third-, and fourth-class gambles, and by providing those eager to test their refreshed hopes with daily records of the highest and lowest quotations for six months.[55]

Whenever a bubble of speculation burst in San Francisco or Denver, it appeared as if the instant cities sheltered more fools per square mile than any other part of the globe, as one mining journal suggested in regard to San Francisco in 1879.[56] Other characteristics of the residents negated that assumption, a Denver newspaper stressed in 1882, because fools "rarely ever get this far from home." [57] Most of the people who flocked into the instant cities to live by their wits had the genuine article. They were desperate, however, to catch up with the more successful men with whom they had set out in the race for riches years before. Thus, they plunged into speculative ventures and became easy prey for the sharks of the market. As energies diminished and opportunities faded their losses bound them to the instant cities.

In cities of strangers, men clung to the memories of their common beginnings and, in cities of fortune hunters, to enterprises everyone could follow, like the activities of the miner-prospector and the merchant-speculator of old. When new prerequisites for success, special knowledge of business affairs and market conditions, rational calculations, and well-organized operations obviated the egalitarian beginnings of the cities, only speculation remained as a link to those bygone days in which all men were on the same footing. In a way, the residents' failures strengthened their ties to the cities. The fates of the unsuccessful speculators evoked the past because each shared misfortune with a community of losers and lightheartedly associated his lot with that of the carefree losers of the gold rush. "Our system of stock-gambling," the San Francisco *Chronicle* commented facetiously in 1878, "has made us wonderfully democratic." Never since the fall of Adam, the paper explained, has there been "such a tumbling to low levels" and mixing of "starched linen and blue jeans." [58]

The frequent setbacks on the road to success kept society open and encouraged amicability toward strangers in instant cities. Their residents' friendliness overshadowed even the helpfulness of other westerners. Perhaps, the openness was more evident because it contrasted with the reserved attitude and a conservative viewpoint that usually characterizes those who have succeeded. Both characteristics might have been less noticeable in emergent urban societies were they not a reaction of people who had made success by the skin of their teeth in cities which impoverished today those who became rich only yesterday so that others might be wealthy tomorrow. The freewheeling and the straitlaced attitudes, surging into the future and backing the status quo, prevailed side by side because they were not so much the opposite characteristics of two groups as the ends of the social seesaw that all residents rode, going up and down according to the way fortune shifted the balance.

Many persons in San Francisco and Denver embraced gambling to capture that aura of success which the daily run of affairs never quite produced. They maintained the rationale that had contributed to their initial resolve to try their luck out West, where the hazards of mining and commerce legitimized a gambling predilection as a proper element in the makeup of ambitious men. They discovered a vein by sheer luck, or they bet daringly on a favorable future market. They looked on gambling simultaneously as moral Puritans and cultural Latins and responded to urban conditions that neutralized the dominance of religious views in manners and customs. Because it was sinful to get something for nothing, they knew that gambling was a vice—their Puritan heritage spoke clearly on that point—but their urban experience justified viewing the issue with the Latin mind, which told them that men could get much from God, and nature, absolutely free. Their cities appeared as such gifts, and strictures against gambling became of small consequence in the great gamble of their lives.[59]

Gambling was a mania in San Francisco, one exposé of life on the bay stated in 1876, outdone only by an account of gambling in Denver which depicted "brick-layers, carpenters, plasterers, and day laborers of all classes. . . . with their dinner buckets in their hands, crowding and jostling around the different games apparently wild over the hope of winning a few dollars." [60] Most men at the bottom of the social ladder gambled less melodramatically, running games on the output of their work or raffling off their small possessions, a ring or a watch, in the company of their acquaintances.[61] The strangest in these cities of strangers, the Chinese, combined in their games a maximum of thrill to dilute the harsh routine of hard work with the exhilarating chance of sudden gain. Their cultural belief in chance, intensified by the strains of their sojourn, corresponded with the mentality of most residents of the instant cities, although in other ways they were a world apart from the society that surrounded their teeming quarters. If someone were to destroy their fan-tan counters or pie-gow blocks they would likely bet on the number of seeds in an uncut orange, not unlike iron molders who placed bets on the weight of a flywheel or a plunger that they were making.[62] The spirit of gambling, for a fleeting moment, bridged the gulf between immigrants and native Americans, particularly in San Francisco, which counted 104,244 immigrants and 129,715 native Americans in 1880, in contrast to the smaller number of foreign-born residents, 8,705 to 26,924, in Denver.[63]

People who surrendered desperately, or naïvely, to the human desire to receive something for nothing were sitting ducks for the tricks of confidence men. When their greed interfered with their common sense, they put their trust in honorless men. Confidence men helped turn San Francisco and Denver from cities once thought to be shrines of the golden fleece into havens for golden fleecers. Their success was due partially to the attitude of the residents. Living in cities that rose apparently from nothing, the settlers tended to view these men, who made money out of nothing, as kindred spirits. In fact, on the occasion of Oscar Wilde's lecture tour in 1882, Denverites prided themselves that their confidence man could outdo the English poet when it came to talking. They credited Charles L. Bagg with having sold worthless metal as gold bricks supposedly coming from stage coach robberies for $10,000, a fifty per cent discount, and they marveled at the audacity with which he urged purchasers to take sample filings that he surreptitiously replaced with genuine gold that passed the assay test. They were impressed by Doc Bagg's ability to sell three bricks for $20,000 to an out-of-town banker, cunningly advising him to hold onto the bricks until the robbery was forgotten.[64]

When it came to the matter of their cities' potential for quick riches, the residents' gullibility knew no bounds because their faith gave meaning to their urban plight. The inhabitants of San Francisco and Denver seemed to provoke the Great Diamond Hoax of 1872. They took it for granted that their mountains would yield precious stones, after reports about diamond fields in South Africa stirred their imaginations. Wearied by their futile chase after gold and silver, they were grateful for another thrill, even at their own expense. After two prospectors who had salted a mesa in the remote northwestern corner of Colorado with diamonds and rubies were exposed a San Francisco newspaper pointed out that anybody could steal, tamper with stocks, rob a bank, or salt an ordinary mine, "but to plant diamonds . . . in the desert . . . and make them . . . blossom . . . —this, to our mind, is the highest evidence of business capacity." [65]

Many men leaped at the diamond craze as a last opportunity to free them from the bondage of the cities. They wanted a part in the new bonanza and were encouraged by such men as the banker William Ralston and ex-Senator Milton S. Latham, who formed the New York and San Francisco Mining and Commercial Company, and by William N. Byers, editor of the *Rocky Mountain News*, and Samuel H. Elbert, son-in-law of Colorado's second territorial governor, who were members of the Denver Diamond Company. They derived additional confidence from the lectures on the "Diamond Regions of Colorado and New Mexico" of William Gilpin, first territorial governor and an ardent believer in Colorado as the "center of the wealth of the world." [66] The craze spread and produced twenty-five different companies with a total capitalization of about $250 million. At the last minute, thousands of adventurers were saved from another disaster by Clarence King, and other geologists, who exposed the fraud, blocked the transfer of worthless stock, and kept men from rushing into nowhere at the outset of winter. [67] With the lost opportunity weighing as heavily as any other loss, the residents searched the cities desperately for quick riches.

The acquisitive instinct and the speculative temper fed on the craving of the inhabitants for a hold on the most illusive of all winnings, a better future. With a cockeyed optimism, the residents kept their thoughts on a tomorrow that might yet bring a fortune. Even after the wane of the national rage of spiritualism in the late 1850s, they searched for clues in precognitions of especially gifted people. To the magic of fog and mountains, they added "the vision of the seer," which supposedly flourished on a "powerful charge of human magnetism" created by the "wonderful transparency of the atmosphere," the "mineral magnetism" of the gold deposits, and the strong passions of the Argonauts. [68] Skeptics succumbed to the demonstrable female charms of well-known San Francisco mediums of the 1860s or to the so-called radicalism of women politicians of the

1870s, most of whom, a newspaper claimed, were spiritualists.[69] This "wild cat religion," according to Samuel Clemens, did not produce more fanaticism than that which normally occurs among earnest Presbyterians.[70] That spiritualism was a serious business in instant cities was indicated by the frequency of the listings of clairvoyants in city directories.[71] In the spring of 1875, Denver spiritualists appointed a committee to protect the citizens against dishonest mediums like the couple who had hurriedly left town after the discovery of a passage through which one of them had crawled into the séance room from an outside cabinet.[72]

Men and women who lost out on the promises of the instant cities chose to relate their misfortune to the consequences of a bad medium, a weak stock, or a wrong card. Liquor served to ease the reality of failure and relieve the tensions of instant city life. In young societies of rootless people, alcohol also served as a convenient mechanism of social integration extending the search for companionship into the saloons.[73] Those who made up the instant cities were outstandingly excessive drinkers even in an age of hard drinkers, partially because their societies recognized no social pressure to restrain alcohol consumption. Middle-class rules on liquor found few supporters in cities that had arisen independent of small capitalists fostering town growth. For those who might have been uneasy about drinking, the climate of San Francisco and Denver prevented "any apparent evil" consequences, and even moderate drinkers, fearing the chills of weather, believed that without some liquor they could not last, while with it, they might have a chance.[74]

Hectic drinking reflected the frenetic pace of the instant cities. Only men with the firmest resolutions against alcohol could resist the temptation to partake of the free hot lunches in local taverns that offered company and liquor as well as food as part of their daily fare. They paid a standard charge for any kind of drink, dividing the bars into two-bit, bit, and five-cent saloons, and gained a lunch that for variety and quality seemed better than the ones they found at home, in restaurants or at hotels. At the corner grocery, they also encountered liquor linked to food. At many intersections throughout the cities, these stores sold family supplies. But they also had a rear section, shielded from view by a wooden partition, where workers gathered in the evening for a simple buffet enjoyed around a plain table, while talking and playing cards for drinks. Two entrances, one through the store, and the other at the rear marked "Sample Room," allowed men to slip in for their morning appetizers if they did not care to be seen drinking at that hour by their families.[75]

Drinking was an accepted antidote to the accelerated pace of developing urban life in instant cities and temperance societies had little effect. The Sons of Temperance appeared in San Francisco in September 1850, but their proposed state liquor law was defeated in 1855. In the early spring of 1859, the first "Dashaway Association" founded by volunteer firemen persuaded a number of the settlers to dash away the bottle for six months.[76] The Independent Order of Good Templars, pledged to abstinence and the abolition of the saloon, appeared in Denver in 1864 and, in the summer of 1877, the Murphy, or Blue Ribbon, Movement had its full share of Denver.[77] However, in instant cities, temperance societies were not "very popular organizations" because they interfered too much with business.[78]

Drinking simply was big business in cities where many people drank heavily; San Francisco counted over two thousand saloons, or one saloon for every 117 residents. In the 1880s, as Denver's population grew, the number of saloons increased from 97 in 1880 to 322 in 1890.[79] However, drinking was always more a response to the cities than the business of the cities, despite allusions to the political pull of saloon keepers and liquor dealers.

Despite other effects, liquor did not really dull the discontent of those residents who had failed to make their fortunes. They lived through the sum total of changes that produced the flourishing cities, and after a bewildering period of adjustment to the hectic life, they grew old with the maturing cities. Individual successes rewarded only a few rich men. Most were ignored. Those who had been passed by found themselves on the same step of the social ladder that they had occupied before their migration. But now their lack of accomplishment was accentuated by their familiarity with those who had reaped the promises of the instant cities. Once the hope of rising to a higher station in life was shattered, those who stayed felt intensely the stresses and strains of the urban explosion.

One by one, each change needed for the cities' development further restricted some residents' chances to succeed. Technological innovations and economic advances brought organization and industry and provided access to capital for factories, a labor pool, and raw materials but diminished the importance of mining and commerce. In the 1860s, manufacturing had played a minor role because capitalists could still obtain quicker returns on their money in other investments. Laborers, too, earned more in other endeavors, and producers suffered from the high costs of raw materials. A decade later, industry was on the scene, through the sudden reversal in the costs of the factors of production as a result of the diminishing isolation, the diversification of California's and Colorado's economy, the completion of railroads, the Comstock and Leadville bonanzas, and the heightened demands of mines and farms for the products of foundry and machine shops.[80]

The social costs of the rapid development became visible, too, bringing into sharp focus the toll demanded by the instant cities. Unlike laborers in remote mines, or sailors in distant ships, factory workers were on the scene viewing the luxurious lives enjoyed by mining magnates, merchant princes, and railroad barons not as indicators of the promise of their cities but as mocking reminders of their inability to keep pace. The gap between individual and collective achievements intensified the sting of poverty, and their personal conditions exposed the discrepancy between dream and reality.

San Franciscans and Denverites responded to their vanishing dreams with heightened violence and disorder. These responses were considered characteristic of turbulent cities, even of those under far less trying circumstances, as a result of "the greater facility with which intrigue and ambition can there operate on ignorance and want." [81] The growing attitude made working men synonymous with struggling men; it lay at the roots of the Kearneyite movement in San Francisco, of the legions of drifters in Denver, and of the anti-Chinese riots in both cities. Independent of the specific circumstances triggering particular conflicts, mounting social pressure produced strife and this strife could no longer be absorbed or disguised by the excitement accompanying the rapid rise of the cities.[82] The confrontation between American workers and corporation presidents was further compounded by the availability of docile Chinese laborers. These violent outbreaks were desperate attempts by large numbers of people to press, once more, their claim to a share in the abundance. The specific implications of their particular charges were often blurred in the general unrest that accompanied the adjustment of American society to industrialization and urbanization in the 1870s and 1880s. Simultaneous acts of individual violence, however, brought out the particular nature of the unrest in San Francisco and Denver and reflected the linkage between the instant cities and the struggle of their residents for common rewards.

Men with insatiable ambition resorted to individual acts of violence in the hope of shaping society in their favor before social flux hardened into final molds. The atmosphere of the instant cities deprived them of the stable environment that might have imposed restraint. Stifled in their search for the free life in the West, they particularly resented the self-restraint demanded by these societies in fermentation.[83] They literally fought their way out of this situation in order to turn the wheel of fortune in their favor.

The feuds between the proprietors of the *Chronicle* and other prominent San Franciscans, between 1879 and 1884, culminated in the shooting of the Reverend Isaac S. Kalloch by Charles de Young, then the killing of the latter by the former's son, and the subsequent shooting of M. H. de Young, the dead man's brother, by Adolph B. Spreckels, a son of the sugar magnate, Claus Spreckels.[84] The events, another newspaper commented, were "fostered by certain social, political, and physical conditions" of young societies and by the

extension of the frontier spirit into an urban setting.[85] Frequently
finding right and virtue on the side of stronger fists and faster guns,
unruly men in unstable societies maltreated anyone who seemed to
be weak. In cities where destruction of one thing sometimes
amounted to the creation of another they adhered to a code of honor
that required the assassin to attempt, through one lucky shot, to
destroy the economic, political, or social antagonist whom neither
careful scheming nor serious plotting could graze.

The opposite mentality chose self-destruction, instead of the
destruction of others, as its escape from the pressures of the instant
cities. "In no part of the world," a comment on the high rate of
suicide in San Francisco ran, "is fortune so fickle" or "invites that
depression of spirit that so often precedes the act of self-destruction." [86] San Franciscans and Denverites recognized the strain that
living in instant cities entailed, but they shielded their lack of
genuine sympathy for those who broke under the pressure behind
their tolerant acceptance of town characters. An outstanding example was Joshua A. Norton, who ruled San Francisco as Emperor of
the United States and Protector of Mexico after he lost his fortune
and mind speculating in grain.[87]

The hazards of making a living in San Francisco and Denver
increased the dimensions of failure born of chance, constant change,
and illusive success. The struggle for riches left everyone behind
except for a handful of men who kept in step with the rapidly rising
cities through their enormous wealth. The functional interdependence forged by the accelerated urban development undermined the
independence of the rootless residents and the opportunities for
sudden riches diminished as technology and communication turned
the instant cities into ordinary ones. The hardening division into
haves and have-nots weakened the only bond once recognized, the
mutual pursuit of a fortune, and exposed what had formerly been
disguised by the opportunities of the instant cities—the cleavage
between individuals of divergent backgrounds. As the urban bonanzas diminished, the less fortunate men and women, measured against
the lucky few, substituted identification with San Francisco and

Denver for the chase of their dream. They became successful only as citizens of successful cities.

Their treasure hunts had lured them into the urban adventure and then bound them to the cities. But instead of being sources for their riches, San Francisco and Denver emerged as sources of their identity. With their dreams having vanished, the residents mellowed. They sublimated their determined chase for wealth with resolute devotion to San Francisco and Denver. Footloose men and women, Easterners, Europeans, Latin Americans, and Asians, without bonds to their surroundings in California or Colorado, turned into citizens of San Francisco or Denver and took pride in being San Franciscans or Denverites as their last opportunity to get close to success. Bound to the tensions of the instant cities, they endured the physical and social flux with a flexible state of mind, a keen eye for opportunity, and a callous heart for anything but themselves.

As the people who made possible the rise of San Francisco or Denver, the first residents of the instant cities showed a remarkable indifference to most aspects of urban life that did not directly affect their pursuit of wealth. Their belated identification with San Francisco or Denver, after their dreams of making a fortune in these cities had vanished, reflected an aversion to urban life and a lack of concern about the quality of city life characteristic of much of nineteenth-century America. Condensing the disappointments of several generations into the agony of one generation, their concentrated urban experience revealed the nature of the country's general indifference to the city as a way of life.

Unlike Europeans who created towns for political and social as well as economic reasons, Americans founded their cities primarily as sources of commercial opportunities and economic ventures. When their hopes did not materialize, they learned to adjust to their urban existence as Bostonians, New Yorkers, Philadelphians, or however they called themselves as residents of specific places. Most became resigned to starting and ending their lives on the same rung of the ladder, but the shattered illusions nurtured their aversion to the city. Their disenchantment kept these citizens of various cities from becoming metropolitans, men and women committed to the city as a way of life. The slow process of urban growth over centuries absorbed their predicament until it was exposed by the intensified experience of San Franciscans and Denverites as the instant cities' not so instant citizens.

# 6

## A Minimum of Order

San Franciscans and Denverites were out to make themselves rich, not to build cities. Yet, their rapidly multiplying numbers precluded the deliberate and natural evolution of societies rooted in primitive frontier environments. These residents hurriedly adapted transplanted social and political practices to deal with basic organizational problems. Drawn from diverse backgrounds by a common call to financial success, these newcomers bound themselves together not to create a city, but to ensure the continuation of their own bonanzas. They recognized that man must and can make his society over but were not primarily committed to the task of cultivating cities, and frequently abandoned the activity in the turmoil of urban conflict and in the pursuit of personal aims. They cared most for ways and means to expedite the realization of personal dreams.

Although most San Franciscans and Denverites shunned city-building, the search for and protection of their new fortunes often entangled them in the process. The need for some sort of regularized contacts with others within social and political rules loomed large among men separated from family, friends, and old alliances. The search for organizational frameworks of society brought solitary people one to another and thereby provided identities for discrete individuals who had been lost in the multitudes. Whereas pursuit of wealth bound the settlers to the locale of the instant cities, the development of political and social groups linked them to each other.

In the formative years of San Francisco and Denver, the egalitarian atmosphere stimulated the proliferation of these associations, illustrating one of Alexis de Tocqueville's laws of human societies, formulated in the 1830s after his visit to the United States: "If men are to remain civilized or to become civilized, the art of association must develop and improve among them at the same speed as equality of conditions spreads." [1]

The newly created groups tackled many of the residents' basic organizational problems. They were also the embryonic stage of later municipal governments and shortened the period of turbulence that preceded the foundation of legal frameworks of society in San Francisco and Denver. They produced the modicum of stability and order needed to ensure the continued expansion of the instant cities, and guaranteed the continued growth of San Francisco and Denver as cities open to newcomers. By uniting footloose individuals and providing them with a forum in which to express themselves, they furnished ways to distinguish between men in amorphous masses. They united individuals in groups, and the groups separated the multitude of people into identifiable and expressive sections. Organizations fostered cohesion, differentiated among the residents, and maintained the egalitarian air of the instant cities. Thus, they produced functioning political entities in the wilderness of the Far West for widely different people with a minimum of coercion.

Although the tendency to form associations pervaded all spheres of life, cultural and economic groups responded less directly to the basic problems of organizing the vast masses of residents than did political and social associations.[2] This was due, in part, to the distinct problems of the instant cities. The sudden concentration of heterogeneous individuals required the development of social groups to make possible both social cohesion and social differentiation to cope with the twin problems of rapid urbanization: the atomization of society and the anonymity of life. The overriding concern to keep alive the goose that laid the golden egg required the formation of those types of political organizations that best assure stability and order and most effectively reduce the influence of men advocating minimal government and rugged individualism.

Many of these early groups originated in the Old Country or back East, in a distant port, aboard a vessel, in a jumping-off place for overlanders, or on the trail. They came into existence in response to the understandable desire of their members to lighten the hardships of migration by sharing these hardships with fellow travelers. If these groups survived the ordeals of Cape Horn, the Isthmus of Panama, the Plains, or the mountains, they gained added significance as symbols of daring and success among people who placed a premium on these attributes.

In California and Colorado these groups continued to provide the migrant with a forum for discussing common trouble in hard times but in addition became the clearing house for news of new opportunities, joint ventures and, as times became better, the social club of those who had become permanent residents. Members of Jonathan D. Stevenson's disbanded Regiment of New York Volunteers, raised to participate in the military conquest of California, for instance, continued to march together—in parades through the streets of San Francisco. They joined each other in real estate ventures, became a force in municipal politics, and contributed to the development of California, one historian of the regiment concluding, "as military colonists in the tradition of the Roman Legion." [3] Passengers of the *Panama*, who reached San Francisco with the first run of the steamer in June 1849, annually celebrated the anniversaries of their arrival, and their banquets provided a neutral meeting ground for successful, as well as unsuccessful, politicians and financiers among them.[4]

The members of the Lawrence Party, which left the Kansas town in May 1858 for the gold fields of the Pikes Peak region, did not part company when they finally reached the South Platte River. They remained together during their gold-seeking ventures. When winter neared, they organized a town company and laid out "Montana," the first white settlement and the first surveyed townsite within the present boundaries of Denver. The inauspicious site and a steady stream of newcomers always eager to be in on a good thing stimulated the formation of rival town companies. Established in quick succession were St. Charles, Denver City, and Auraria. Some men belonged to a company because they came with it across the plains, others seceded from their companies to join more promising ones, but all responded quickly to any opportunity to establish some kind of order through their associations.[5]

Yet, some of the groups that developed in the infant years of San Francisco and Denver were no more than social clubs, from the start established by individuals who simply wanted to preserve their style of life in a strange world. The companions of a lord, European sportsmen who hunted in Colorado during the 1870s, formed the exclusive Corkscrew Club in Denver with an atmosphere "less like that of Denver than London, or Cairo or Bombay."[6] Similar associations had appeared in connection with other great population movements of the nineteenth century to, and within, the United States. Migrants from abroad and those within banded together to reproduce in new places familiar social and political patterns, or to adapt those old patterns to new scenes.[7] They utilized ethnic clubs, first-aid centers, burial societies, and mutual-benefit associations to cope with the vicissitudes of adjustment or to deal with the institutions of established settlers. Still others had their antecedents in those American cities that preceded San Francisco and Denver. Their members had united initially to provide for level, clean, and lighted streets, for the fair distribution of water, or for protection from the threat of fire, and had remained available for future joint action.

From outward appearances in the rising cities, the importance of these associations to the development of social and political structures seemed small. At a glance, the residents of San Francisco and Denver were masses of individuals held together only by their common craving for spoils in raw and primitive cities.[8] The "inhabitants of the Dorado," the first Denver *City Directory* emphasized in 1859, showed no "steadiness of purpose and fixedness of residence" because searching for gold determined "the principal impulses of human action." [9] To Frank Soulé, John H. Gihon, and James Nisbet, the compilers of the 1855 edition of the *Annals of San Francisco*, the craving of early San Franciscans for quick riches severed the "feebler ties of affection and duty" and their single-minded pursuit of wealth turned them into rugged individuals, each out for himself.[10] They accurately detailed the general social context of their city's accomplishments but also spoke glowingly of the "undoubted talent, shrewdness, capacity for hard, practical work" of these "unruly spirits." Many casual observers saw life merely as a conglomerate of individual accomplishments.[11]

As well, the role of these organizations in the development of San Francisco and Denver was played down because it competed with a more charismatic identification, that of the self-reliant pioneer. This larger than life hero represented for generations of fascinated Americans the resourceful protagonist of westward migration. As empire builder, he dominated the historical record, if not the actual scene, and appeared to have laid single-handedly the foundation for the construction of a new society. In January 1881, at the immensely successful first annual reunion of the Colorado Pioneers, the principal speaker told the assembly in the splendor of Denver's newly opened Windsor Hotel: "The Roman Caesar conquered Britain, but you, gentlemen, the advance guard of the great Western pioneer column, you, the uncrowned Napoleons of the West, have conquered, by your indomitable perseverance and energy, an empire greater than that of the imperial Caesar." [12] Only when Americans noticed that the conquest of the continent also involved the adaptation of an old society to novel settings rather than merely the formation of a new society, did they recognize the individual pioneer's participation in social groups, the benefits he reaped from the sharing of collective experiences, and his use of transplanted practices to sustain himself in his endeavors.

Like other Americans moving West, San Franciscans and Denverites even enjoyed the reputation of being "natural" city builders and, at times, were called just that.[13] But the expression, generally, was not meant to convey the impression that here were devoted men and women who worked patiently or enjoyed a special talent for organizing masses of people into an urban society for the common benefit. The words paid tribute primarily to the entrepreneurial skills of those ingenious individuals who quickly grasped the economic potential of emerging towns and utilized this potential for personal advancement. All the inhabitants of new settlements were in some way entrepreneurs banking their hopes on the business opportunities a rising town stimulated, and it was recognized and accepted that if the townsites did not flourish they would take off for greener urban pastures.[14] The towns, therefore, viewed favorably the determination of these individuals to open up for themselves the best opportunities, recognizing that others would thrive on the additional opportunities provided by these proliferating enterprises. This individualistic approach to urban development was accepted as the way of city democracy.

Although some of the migrants to San Francisco and Denver experienced enough on their gold rush journeys to make them rather skeptical of human nature few isolated themselves entirely from their fellow men. An exceptional case was that of James Lick. This lonely Pennsylvania Dutchman by way of Lima, Peru, came to San Francisco on the eve of the gold discovery with $30,000. Single-handed, he acquired town lots, and parcels of land in other parts of California, and when he died, twenty-eight years later, he was worth $4 million. In his will, the recluse bachelor bypassed his illegitimate son and deeded his fortune to the public.[15] But even in self-imposed isolation, Lick was a considerable social force during his lifetime. He supported the Society of California Pioneers which strengthened the bonds among people who had come to California before 1850, and the Lick House, to mention one of his business enterprises, brought men and women together in the magnificence of San Francisco's first palatial hotel.[16]

Many newcomers to the instant cities carried in their cultural baggage loyalties that stimulated the rapid establishment of churches and fraternal lodges. These groups performed the same social services they had performed in earlier stages and in other settings of the westward migration. The Masons held their first meeting within ten days after the group's arrival at the Cherry Creek diggings, in November 1858. They immediately laid the foundation for that "grand Masonic building which now overlooks both mountain and plain," one of them noted in his reminiscences.[17] Two months later, about twenty-six members of the order lived in the settlements and their presence quickly attracted other members to the site. On the night of his arrival in Denver on horseback, in April 1859, William N. Byers, future editor of the city's first newspaper, sat in on a meeting of the lodge attended by forty members.[18]

The proliferation of associations helped to sustain the residents' determination to establish public power and control in municipal governments as quickly as possible. This determination was founded upon their recognition of the relationship between a stable society and that society's ability to attract more people, new capital, commerce, and industry. They recognized that their success depended on the establishment of a legal framework strong enough to guarantee undisturbed access to the promises of the accelerated urban development and to assure an extension of their control over vast hinterlands while the mining camps were still preoccupied with ascertaining the extent of the new riches.

Yet, the frantic climate of the instant cities and the heterogeneity of the population often hindered the development of meaningful authority. These two factors encouraged the residents in the illusion that genuine exertions toward the development of local governments would bring immediate redress from the uncertainties of life in instant cities. Once established, these governments would forever free the residents from those problems interfering with their pursuit of personal wealth. Consequently, once these residents of instant cities set their minds on the establishment of local governments they demanded instant governments, and set about to institute them at any immediate cost.

Despite obstacles posed by the survival of remnants of Mexican rule at Yerba Buena and the difficulty of isolating a legitimate source of municipal power in the Cherry Creek diggings, the residents of San Francisco and Denver were able to forge the rudiments of urban government within a few years. Commentators observed that it was "difficult to find a briefer history of the establishment of a government" than the one in San Francisco, and that municipal government in Denver "entered upon its career with a spirit and briskness that promised well." [19]

The eclectic influence in San Francisco's municipal affairs resulted, in part, from the enormously complicated legal status of California. As a city in conquered U.S. territory, San Francisco was subject to U.S. military law until Congress decided the future of the territory. However, a combination of democratic American practices and Mexican administrative procedures served during the interim in place of formally established and recognized government. The confusion increased further when a few inquisitive spirits began debating whether it would be more relevant to urban interest to have English common law with its rural heritage or Mexican civil law, which if not in conflict with the U.S. Constitution was to be continued until changed by "competent authority." [20] This makeshift arrangement was clearly unsatisfactory. San Franciscans hoped to extricate themselves from legal and administrative dilemma once and for all in March 1849, and established a legislature with supreme authority. The military governor, however, suspicious of the move that also threatened the authority of Congress, restored to power a makeshift city council, an *ayuntamiento* combining Mexican and American practices, in June 1849. Although "thoroughly acquainted with conditions in San Francisco," the governor explained he was more concerned with upholding "competent authority" than tackling the problems of the rising city.[21]

The impasse vexed the ambitious and impatient San Franciscans, who had intended not only to form a legislative assembly but also to strengthen the legal system and create a code of general law, to block the circumvention of laws by the military governor, and to curb the misuse of authority by the alcalde, their highest municipal officer.[22]

They recognized that the military governor's decree tied the city to a weak *ayuntamiento* and the one-man rule of the alcalde, without giving them a chance to make San Francisco, in regard to law and authority, "what it must shortly be in wealth and importance"—a well-ordered, flourishing city.[23] The residents' concern for their government coalesced with San Francisco's pressing need for social organization. In the absence of the familiar structure of territorial or state governments, the residents regarded their isolated city as a city-state. Since they linked the welfare of the residents to the rise of the city, some were ready to expand the customary powers of a municipal government. Searching for revenues, they advocated taxing businesses as well as real estate. They regarded licensing and operating gambling tables and billiard tables under the supervision of the police as "less injurious to the interests and morals of the community" than allowing such activities to be conducted in defiance of the law.[24]

These discussions and proposals for extending the purviews of local government seemed to give public support to the individual fortune hunt. However, in instant cities, formed by incongruous mixtures of people, these ideas suggested the potentially insidious situation of effective municipal government being formed on the conviction of one group that its kind of people have the right and, consequently, the obligation to organize government. Unable, or unwilling, to resolve the practical problem of how to express fairly in an urban democracy a multitude of individual goals while achieving common objectives, most residents fell back on the plodding, but officially sanctioned attempts to recreate a traditional framework of authority. After an initially negative response, they then accepted, expediently, a call for a convention by the same military governor who himself had no congressional authority for such a move and who had just crushed their illegitimate attempt to govern San Francisco. At the Monterey convention the representatives from San Francisco played a crucial role. Through their determination to see that California framed a constitution before Congress reached a decision about the conquered land, San Franciscans received their first charter from the legislative department of the convention, in April 1850.[25]

The multilateral cross conflicts between military law, congressional authority, Mexican usages, popular democracy, and entrepreneurial expedience complicated the establishment of municipal order in San Francisco; but, the absence of all authority in the Cherry Creek diggings made the formation of city government in Denver equally difficult. The need for organization was also as clearly felt, but no military governor played the role of a benevolent despot, no territorial or state government served the South Platte Valley, no vestiges of Mexican practices existed in the vicinity, and no international treaty necessitated Congressional debate over the area.[26] The Kansas legislature was responsible for the area, technically, but in 1855, handicapped by its own troubles and the intervening five hundred miles of prairie, it had merely created one gigantic county extending to the summit of the Rocky Mountains and then entrusted its administration to another county.[27] This stopgap device drove Denverites to an experiment with independence that substituted their own creation, Jefferson Territory, for the ineffective jurisdiction of distant Kansas authorities.

Independence did not alter the substance of government. The establishment of Jefferson Territory in the spring of 1859 set into operation a familiar municipal machinery, which took the place of the nominal government derived from the town companies. The change seemed momentous and led the *Rocky Mountain News* to believe that "the ball now started will continue to roll on until the most brilliant state in the Union will be fully inaugurated." [28] Although little came of the prediction, or of Jefferson Territory for that matter, Denver gained immeasurably. The halting operations of the new and independent state quickly made apparent the need for unification of the several Cherry Creek settlements. A town called Highlands existed on paper only, but the citizens of Denver and Auraria discussed and voted on the issue, and between December 26, 1859, and April 3, 1860, the settlements became Denver.[29] Jefferson Territory itself did not stand until it could "boast a million people and look upon a city of a hundred thousand souls." [30] It soon existed in name only because collecting taxes proved to be impossible and "the idea of . . . governing on *credit* for any considerable length" of time struck one observer as preposterous.[31] The charter of Denver from the Jefferson legislature steadily lost value, but the new urban entity survived.

Most Pikes Peakers recognized Denver as the center of their world but widely disagreed on which authority deserved their loyalty. Some supported Jefferson Territory, others respected Kansas officials, a third group stuck to people's and miners' courts, and finally there were those who argued that none of these governments had any say since they were in Indian territory.[32] After the experiment in independence, Denver's rueful return to Kansas seemed out of the question. The old town companies, the first associations to have organized Denver, came into play again, and Denverites worked through the board of the directors of the Denver Town Company to ensure congressional support for the establishment of legitimate government. The initiative of these men in Washington, in February 1861, helped to bring the Territory of Colorado into existence. Nine months later, in one of the most important acts of the first territorial legislature, Denver received a legal charter establishing municipal government.[33]

Bound more tightly than San Francisco to the ups and downs of a moving mining frontier, Denver's search for municipal organization was overshadowed by a more pressing struggle with individuals who took the law into their own hands.[34] As the major mining camp of the Pikes Peak gold region, Denver attracted only a handful of permanent residents who thought in terms of establishing legitimate government. Most drifters, preoccupied with the hazards of mining, supported people's courts and vigilance committees as a direct way to control individual outbreaks of disorder, but "the entire summer of 1860 was marked by trails of blood." [35] Many visitors commented upon the unique status of Denver as a settlement that possessed many of the normal features of organized society but also served as a haven for desperadoes.[36] Municipal order seemed restricted to the most primitive function of keeping "one man's fingers off another man's throat." [37] Territorial courts, people's courts, vigilance committees, the Denver Guards, and the Jefferson Rangers, constables and policemen, were some of the temporary forces used to bridge the gap between the few who favored legitimate government and the many who favored taking the law into their own hands.[38] Their disparate legal status and their self-help attitude toward justice obscured their roles as elementary instruments of order tightening the formal relationships among the residents of Denver.

The establishment of legitimate political frameworks gave San Francisco and Denver their first municipal governments, but the peculiar makeup of instant cities kept the residents from making extensive use of these governments. Their still-strong view of the cities as economic gold mines did little to induce them either to shoulder the burden of government or to compromise their personal goals for the abstract notion of blind justice. Most city officials were treated with salutary indifference because of their limited ability to stabilize the community and were judged only in terms of their usefulness to the individual in his pursuit of wealth.

Although there were venal men among them, too, judges, however, were the most notable exceptions to the disdain in which most public men were held. Pledged to uphold laws that represented, at times, the only bonds among the residents, they enjoyed some public esteem. Mammon and Gammon were the revealing nicknames of two venal, money-grabbing and gambling San Francisco magistrates during the 1850s, and, although William T. Sherman refused to believe that "in an American city" a judge could be the vigilantes' captive until he saw differently,[39] still the Vigilance Committee of 1856 both imprisoned one and—treated him with grudging respect. In 1895, a Denver grand jury praising a judge spelled out some of the qualities that distinguished him from other officeholders: "a man of sterling integrity, an able jurist, an honorable and just judge, patient, conscientious, humane, and fearless." [40] The pace, or the temptations, of the rising cities stripped many other officials of these qualities.

The rapid development of the city and its continuously changing relationships created problems of magnitude and urgency and left little room or time for the deliberate operation of democratic machinery. The confusion encouraged the natural tendency of men to divide along the lines of background and economic status, intensified the residents' deep loyalties to their associations, and drove even new wedges among the various groups. In the absence of tested and established methods of resolving conflicts deriving from economic and ethnic diversity, only apathy restrained government from misusing its power to create uniformity among the heterogeneous residents. With the spectrum of alternative forms of social and political organization before their eyes, the residents tended towards the orderly anarchy of frontier settlements in preference to the stern control suggested by the planned Mormon communities. In the final analysis, democratic government only barely managed to keep going in the turmoil that was the instantly arising city.

The strained period that developed consequently in San Francisco and Denver between the formation of municipal structures and the building of effective municipal governments was not, however, solely related to the nature of the instant city or to the rapidity of its rise. This impasse occurred in many nineteenth-century cities in the United States as efficient municipal government, social integration, and urban planning often were thought about only by imposing the will of a few over the entire city. When groups of residents of the instant cities finally chose to empower strong governments, as they did in the name of vigilance, they went about forcing their ways on others and suppressing those groups that lacked, as a consequence of their being very different, the committed protection of society.[41] When disorder heightened, the vigilance committees disrupted the benevolent reign of political inertia and organized confusion, interpreted the tasks of ordering society and policing cities in their own manner, and supplanted ineffective government with the rule of force. Confusion and inertia left a "Doomed City" to the "pitiless storm of treason and fanaticism," an eloquent opponent of vigilantism charged.[42] Many residents were effectively driven into silence by the vigilante outbursts; one of them vowed never to forget his lesson: "to mind my own business in all time to come." [43]

Depending on the degree of outside support, the vigilance committees demanded secrecy from their members or actively sought publicity in their actions. These two approaches pointed at the distinctly social role of political organizations in instant cities and the defining of political camps for the purpose of structuring society. In Denver, the small number of participants made secrecy expedient and the code of silence actually widened the range of people presumed to be involved. Vigilante justice made orderly men, while not members of a vigilance committee or a people's court, reluctant to correct general impressions that occassionally linked them to vigilance groups. Inquiries into the actual identity of the members, a historian of Denver emphasized, were "sharply understood to be a forbidden topic, and no one cared to disregard that understanding." [44] On the other hand, in San Francisco the strength and number of the supporters allowed them to surface and stimulated an extensive publicity campaign that culminated in a grand parade. Elaborate membership certificates testified to and honored position with the ruling group.[45] Although in these cities opposite approaches prevailed, the real and psychologically enhanced power of these groups contributed to dividing the residents on the basis of political and moral criteria.

In cities created by the search for riches, economic status overshadowed the traditional classifications of people according to birth, politics, morals, creeds, education, interest, and nationality. The first ranking of San Francisco's residents, which appeared as a pamphlet in 1851, quickly applied money, the moving force behind the instant cities, as the criterion for status.[46] The money criterion established an acceptable yardstick of achievement in a city committed to the quest for fortunes. With names rapidly changing on the lists, the roster of rich men also depicted individual accomplishments. A review of succeeding lists chronologs the collective success of the city in distinct stages. This ordering of society ultimately affected not only people but the history of the cities itself, as periods became known as the San Francisco of William Ralston or Leland Stanford and the Denver of John Evans or of H. A. W. Tabor.[47]

New names appearing on the lists of wealthy men attested to the continuing struggle for success and the constant presence of the threat of failure that characterized life in instant cities. The accomplishments of these newcomers accentuated specific forms of urban development and the presence or absence of specific activities defined phases in the city's rise. Dividing the anonymous accomplishments of the city into segments, the changing names on the rosters identified the factors speeding the accumulation of new fortunes and the destruction of old ones as a result of the intensified urban development. The lists revealed the role of gold, silver, and other natural resources, and drew attention to the competition for markets in the hinterland, the speculative nature of mining, the manipulation of real estate in the face of the coming railroad, the depression following its arrival, and the hazards of commerce and industry.

In San Francisco, within the twenty years between 1851 and 1871, real estate speculators, railroad kings, and silver moguls replaced lucky miners, daring importers, and—each other. Among the names of the 120 wealthy residents published by a San Francisco newspaper in 1871, three names only of the 509 rich men listed in the pamphlet of 1851 reappeared. James Lick, who two decades earlier headed the roster with $750,000, now was sixth with $3 million. The two others were real estate men, too, who had turned to banking. John Parrott, in 1851 twenty-third with $60,000, was fourth with $4 million, and James Phelan, formerly thirtieth with $25,000, ranked eighth with $2,500,000. Transportation magnates headed the 1871 tally, compiled two years after the completion of the Pacific Railroad.[48] Six years later, in 1877, the Big Four of the Central Pacific Railroad yielded the summit to the four Silver Kings of the Comstock Lode. This change in the top echelon of San Francisco's wealthy men was noticed around the globe, and the German Frankfort *Gazette* proclaimed John Mackay of San Francisco the richest man in the world, computing his income of $25 per minute to exceed by $5 that of Lionel Nathan de Rothschild and Tsar Alexander II.[49]

With time, several refinements in the procedures for determining the personal wealth of potential candidates changed these lists from simple economic rankings to sophisticated social and economic registers. In drawing up the earliest rosters, those responsible had relied on the enlightened guesses of publishers and newspaper reporters. Later on, more sound information was available in the annual tax rolls of the city and county assessors, and in place of news reporters, society page editors published the most heeded information. By continuously taking in new men and women who had used their wealth to enhance their position and prestige in the society, these lists, now called the rosters of "Our Solid Men and Women," reflected the leveling power of money over blood in the dynamic society of instant cities.

The "carefully prepared" rosters of "Our Solid Men and Women," published by the Denver *Tribune* during the 1870s and 1880s reflected the trend. In August 1872, the roster listed 66 taxpayers who had been assessed $10,000 or more.[50] Eleven years later, it spelled out 1,650 names with amounts ranging "all the way from $2,500 to $471,000." [51] Money classified people quickly and efficiently in instant cities long before Mrs. Crawford Hill attempted to draw the ultimate lines, in 1908, when she selected Denver's "Sacred Thirty-six" in her social guidebook.[52]

The sheer size of the sudden fortunes reinforced the role of money in the organizational structure of instant cities and the newly rich searched for an appropriate way to reflect their new status as wealthy citizens. The rapid influx of people made the flamboyant acquisition of land economically difficult, and as the nouveaux riches devised substitutes for land ownership as symbols of eminence their hunt for distinction bypassed the high political offices within easy reach of successful men. Most considered the returns too small, the positions too burdensome, and the exposure to the public too hazardous. The method they finally chose satisfied both the requirements of the wealthy for recognition and those of the city for cosmopolitanism: around the city the nouveaux riches erected libraries, art galleries, theaters, opera houses, and private mansions,

monuments to the magnitude of their accomplishments, yet acceptable and useful additions to their developing cities. In the raw
settings, the art of displaying distinctions required daily practice.
Among others in San Francisco, the McAllister family from Savannah
was involved in the task of differentiating between people, and the
lesson stood Ward McAllister in good stead when he organized New
York's "Four Hundred" in the early 1890s.[53]

Yet, early San Francisco and Denver Society—those who "belonged" as opposed to those who did not—could be entered by
various routes that were open to those with distinctions other than
material wealth. The diversified ways of ordering multitudes and of
identifying individuals who might get lost in the crowd included a
range of criteria, such as professional accomplishments and cultural
achievements. These ultimately provided an entré into society for
many other citizens and reaffirmed the initial egalitarianism of the
instant cities.

One of these other assets was simply the place of origin of the
citizen. These ties of common roots were particularly influential in
the determination of "good" company because men and women
shielded their emotional attachments to the old home and to the
memories of shared hardships from the corrosive influences of living
in instant cities and of experiencing sudden wealth.[54] Social graces
and personal attraction, less tangible factors than professional
standing and cultural distinction, were also among the criteria that
opened the doors of Society.

William Stone Botts was one of the most prominent men in San
Francisco Society during the 1850s, and its best dancer. Homely and
impoverished, on the strength of his good Virginian name he was
given a sinecure in the "Virginia Poor House," as the San Francisco
Custom House was known during that decade because of the many
gentlemen from Virginia among its clerks. The presence of the
diminutive man, with his bald head, huge red mustache, and hoarse
voice, insured the success of any ball or party. Billy Botts's social
graces were his chief and, one socialite remembered, his only
distinction.[55]

One of the most notable events in the annual social cycle of Denver Society was Mrs. Margaret Evans's "At Home" reception. For the year 1881, her list of guests featured the political friends and business associates of her husband John, who, in the 1860s, was Colorado's second territorial governor. It also included a wide range of people invited to the festive gathering because of good family names, or proper breeding. Membership in the Methodist Church, or work in cultural or charitable organizations, qualified others for Mrs. Evans's distinguished world.[56]

Yet, the egalitarianism of the instant cities seemed to fall by the wayside when Society members evaluated men's backgrounds and present positions. Although acknowledging the possibility that all men were created equal, the criteria reflected the urge to consider some more equal than others. Differences and distinctions were studiously cultivated through reliance on such credentials as mutual experiences, party affiliations, appointment to federal office, reputations in courts of law, or church membership. However, despite the various elaborations of the process that blossomed in the young societies eager to display the niceties of etiquette and to convey the impression of solidity, social standing in the instant cities was more a matter of subjective acceptance on one's merits rather than the result of a formal system of selection.[57] It was a bonus offered freely to those men and women who dared to throw in their lot with the instant cities where constant changes regularly opened new room at the top. In San Francisco and Denver, it was possible to scale the heights of Society much faster than in the older cities of the East.

The needs of the cities influenced Society's flexible entrance requirements. San Francisco and Denver depended on a steady stream of newcomers for their continued development. They thrived on the eagerness of fresh recruits, young men in whom the taste of disappointment had not yet destroyed faith in their own abilities. Every additional obstacle that kept these new arrivals from their full share in the promise of the instant cities deliberately cut off one of the instant cities' lifelines. Since the application of the criteria for membership did not assure exclusiveness, the methods of selection governing the admission of men and women into Society received little attention beyond the gossip and speculation that they stimulated. One insider admitted in his memoirs that it would serve no purpose to tell people who did not belong why they did not, while those who did belong knew why.[58] With a clearly understood dependence by the cities on a steady stream of newcomers, most residents wasted little time attempting to fathom the inner workings of Society, which had to remain open despite all pretensions of exclusiveness.

Although the organizations linking the residents of instant cities were only adaptations of older models, each one began a new life in the new environment of instant cities. In that narrow sense, all the transplants were untested, and this situation gave the men first on the scene special opportunities, which, in turn, magnified the openness of early San Francisco and Denver. In those years, the empty heights of Society were occupied by men and women, regardless of background or creed, who were there early enough and were fortunate enough to become rich.[59] Society in San Francisco and Denver, outwardly Anglo-Saxon and Protestant, consequently contained a noticeable admixture of immigrants, Catholics, Jews, and blacks. Clara Brown, "Aunt Clara," one of the first blacks in the Cherry Creek diggings, attended the banquet of the first annual Pioneer reunion in the Windsor Hotel, because she had succeeded to rise with a rising Denver.[60] Others, with lesser handicaps to overcome than this former slave, demonstrated that they, too, could make money quickly in mining, speculation, railroading, commerce, and industry. Their success also helped keep the ranks of Society open. Furthermore, the sheer size of new fortunes commanded respect. Their magnitude undermined any possible resistance of entrenched factions against the waves of nouveaux riches flooding the instant cities.

Ultimately, it was money that assured open societies in instant cities.[61] The top layers of the social pyramids of San Francisco and Denver were composed of men and women whose credentials consisted of the simple facts that they were present and successful.

Riches seemed within the reach of everyone, and with fortunes being made—or lost—overnight, wealth constituted a democratizing force. The frequency of sudden drastic changes from wealth to poverty, and from poverty to wealth, fostered an inclination to help old acquaintances down on their luck. As the natural link between men seeking riches and locations turned into cities by gold rushes, money was an important measure of all residents and, where social cohesion was concerned, a greater divider of people than ethnicity. A San Francisco weekly assured its Eastern and European readers that a lithograph of 299 eminent San Franciscans did not stretch facts

when the Bishop of the orthodox Episcopal Church is seen in pleasant *tête-à-tête* with the unorthodox divine of the Unitarians, or when the covenanting Presbyter is observed in happy contiguity with the Jewish Rabbi, and when all together are met in the auditorium of a first-class theater, where nature and human nature, and not schisms or creeds, are represented.[62]

In time, however, as the Society drew closer and closer to the point of being able to sustain itself without the steady flow of newcomers, the leveling power of money diminished. Many who saw the initial equality of conditions fading away became disillusioned with the rewards of living in San Francisco and Denver. Occasionally, some of the demographic characteristics of the instant cities continued to uphold the precarious equilibrium between rich and poor. Particularly the elementary divisions of urban dwellers into men and women, single and married folk, and light and dark faces showed a marked imbalance of the sexes, a preponderance of solitary men, and a mixture of people of different ethnic and racial backgrounds. These imbalances favored certain minorities and gave them a special status that created the impression as if the mold of the instant cities was still in flux curbing some of the prejudices of American society.

Women, families, and blacks, minorities who had not yet gained numerical significance, reaffirmed some of the cities' egalitarianism. In the evening, women promenaded past the finest stores of San

Francisco. Expensively dressed, cheerful, and self-assertive, they set the tone of a street life that leveled "all distinctions of rank as impartially as the grave." [63] Meanwhile, families living in their own homes rather than boardinghouses, apartments, or tenements gave Denver the appearance of a business center surrounded by many uniform clusters of well-arranged cottages on the plains.[64] In both San Francisco and Denver, the appearance of small numbers of blacks dispersed throughout the cities strengthened their images as wide-open cities.[65]

Because of their status as a minority, women in particular kept alive the memory of the initial egalitarianism. In cities where a great number of single men competed for spouses, the humiliation of one of the forms of nineteenth-century female bondage, marriage, was lessened, at least initially, because women had a wide choice of husbands. The ratio of women to men was high in San Francisco, 5 to 7 in 1880.[66] This obviously enhanced one's chance of finding a husband wealthy enough to provide an escape from the daily drudgery of housework. Sudden riches, divorce, and the chance of a good second marriage also represented potential escapes from domestic routine.[67] A friend of the writer of a "Lady's Diary," published in a San Francisco newspaper in the early 1870s, admitted that she had no money before she was married but complained that afterwards, when she had a little, the storekeepers insisted that she take too many things.[68]

Although for women life in San Francisco and Denver was less confining than in the settled cities of the East, the restrictions of American society and the conservative temperaments of westering migrants quickly made themselves felt. In the 1880s women received 25 to 50 per cent lower wages than did men in ordinary western industries.[69] Only a few were able to take advantage of the democratic atmosphere and to find work in areas other than teaching school, styling cloth, or keeping boardinghouses. In the early 1880s, one of them edited in San Francisco "the first paper published in the United States, by a woman, for the *industrial* education of women," and ran as an independent candidate for governor of California.[70]

Most women found at least some measure of equality in the context of the instant cities which presaged a "golden dawn of a new era for women." [71] They stood out as individuals and influenced the tone of San Francisco and Denver.[72] From time to time, some women shook off the aura of quiet submission to convention and created sensations as femmes fatales of their days.[73] In the 1880s, Denver's ladies of dubious virtue ridiculed a city ordinance which required every prostitute to wear a yellow ribbon. They promenaded through the streets, dressed in yellow from head to foot, until the ordinance was repealed since it appeared as though they were the only women in Denver.[74]

In addition to the general prejudices of American society against women, the apparent equality of the instant cities stifled attempts to back up that appearance by law. In Denver, politically concerned women worked for suffrage in the hope that Colorado territory would grant suffrage or would write the rights of women into its constitution when admitted to statehood. From early efforts in 1869 to the state constitutional convention in 1876, they argued the case. But they failed in the convention and in their subsequent drive for an amendment and only gained the right to vote in school district elections.[75] However, because of their position as a minority in the instant cities, women still enjoyed a measure of identity that was neither abrogated by a male-oriented world nor destroyed by the turmoil of accelerated urbanization.

In 1882, at the Denver Mining and Industrial Exposition unescorted women outnumbered men, at times, in a ratio of three to one.[76] They came without chaperones and returned to the city in the evening in the lively crowd of "young people of both sexes." [77] Through their jobs on exhibits and displays, in the restaurant and the concessions, some women indicated their independence from a male-oriented society dominated by female guardians of public morality. They encountered the criticism of "certain visitors of the feminine persuasion" who saw "fit to elevate their noses at angles which are certainly unbecoming, and must have been painful, as they passed the clerks." [78] Others became the talk of the town when they raced horses on the exposition track "with the skill of a jockey." [79]

The disorder of the constantly changing cities erased the old identity that many residents had carried with them into the novel settings. Chaos intensified the struggle to gain a new identity in the social maelstrom that reduced most people to anonymity. Women, blacks, and successful men stood out in the multitude simply because of their status as minorities. When most of the residents failed to make their marks despite the promise of the rising cities, they were steadily absorbed into the mass of nameless poor. They attracted notice only as population statistics. With their shattered dreams, the losers in the race for riches found it almost impossible to gain new identities in urban societies based on the supreme rule of their cities' exponent—money.

As long as hope balanced disillusionment, religious groups and fraternal orders, which were based on principles of association other than material distinctions, furnished common grounds for the discrete human components of the instant cities. Although some churches and lodges made efforts to concern themselves with the intangible needs of unsuccessful people, their mode of operation reflected the success orientation of wealthy supporters and left many poor men dissatisfied. Churches recognized the emotional problems accentuated by the mad life of the instant cities. While they helped with food, shelter, and spiritual guidance, their doctrines prevented any effort by their organizations to help in the search for identities, since faithful adherence to their teachings presupposed an everlasting identity.

Churches were utilized to alleviate the human problems of the instant cities, as exemplified by German Catholics in San Francisco in the 1880s. Only five hundred of the ten thousand German Catholics attended mass regularly, the archbishop reported to Rome, but as a group they supported three benevolent societies, two schools, a fraternal order, and an altar society.[80] Most clergymen could not satisfy all of the intense craving of the poor for a measure of human dignity, but, unlike urban politicians, they did not exploit the unsuccessful for their own ends.

Politicians built powerful urban machines on the losers' search for identity. The poor owned their persons, and that property, in the realm of democratic politics, translated immediately—or, in the case of most immigrants, ultimately—into votes. Some politicians understood the value of these votes in the control of cities, and they went out of their way to try to provide any voter with the measure of human dignity he craved as long as his vote paid for the service.[81] The symbiotic relationship between impoverished voters and scheming politicians is as old as the history of cities governed by democracies. However, the links between the poor and the bosses of the instant cities were strengthened by the heightened need of identity and by the general indifference toward effective urban government that made municipal politics an open field for the astute manipulators of the masses of voters. These conditions exaggerated the social functions of urban machines that characterized American city politics in the nineteenth century.

The poor balanced their failures with memberships in political groups that worked to adapt democratic processes, initially designed for the face-to-face contact of rural settings, to the anonymity of urban politics. Down-and-outers relied on ward clubs and precinct organizations to bring to their daily lives some of the meaning and importance that society at large bestowed freely on successful men.[82] They rotated through a profusion of offices and served on numerous committees; they marched in parades and waited in delegations; and through their exposure to other men in search of identities, they found their own. Small cogs in large machines, their activities were insignificant as far as the actual operations of municipal government were concerned, but when they identified with the ruling political machine, and, especially, when they turned out to cast their votes on election day, they vicariously experienced the sense of power of the truly powerful.

The political organizations of instant cities increasingly brought successful and unsuccessful men into partnerships as the growing gap between rich and poor upset an urban democracy based on equal hope of eventual wealth. The machines' influence over legislation affected many areas of urban life and attracted businessmen searching for ways to exploit the economic opportunities of the burgeoning cities. The party bosses and their cronies provided businessmen with shortcuts through the administrative jungles.[83] Their control of masses of loyal voters assured favorable legislation to all who gave support. Drawing upon men of various shades of success, the political machines forged hidden bonds between groups of residents.[84]

Only the alliance between bosses and businessmen survived the development of San Francisco and Denver as instant cities and carried over into the twentieth century. By then, the masses of residents had found their identity as citizens of San Francisco and Denver. The bosses let them drift away from the alliance because they found it more convenient to rule without bothering about the members of the district clubs. Their control of the district organizations produced the willing delegates who endorsed their nominations; all the bosses needed was "the appearance of votes," and the actual voter no longer mattered.[85] In contrast to their forerunners, the machines of Abraham Ruef and Robert Speer thrived on new needs produced by the changed urban environment. They capitalized on the concern of urban boosters and eager businessmen for efficient municipal government.[86]

The loyalty of the poor to a political system that furnished them with a measure of human dignity allowed unscrupulous politicians to plunder the cities. In 1890, the rupture of the Republican machine in Denver, which accompanied the indictment of a Republican mayor for blatant corruption, provided a glimpse of that city's political morass.[87] The "Gang" and the "Gang Smashers" vied for control of the Republican county committee. No faction was inspired "by any higher motive" for their activities "than the natural desire to be on top." [88] The removal of the mayor shook the foundations of existing municipal corruption, and the ward heelers of Denver, rising to the opportunity, battled for control in the subsequent primary. Open fraud marked the election, and no faction showed the slightest consideration for their party in their grim determination to beat their

opponents at any cost.[89] The collapse of the makeshift framework of
power and control seemed to turn the municipal operation of Denver
back to its beginnings. Everyone was out for himself, and the city
was again only a tool facilitating that simple act of self-fulfillment: to
acquire—now power as much as money.

The network of organizations in early San Francisco and Denver,
like the cities themselves, had served the residents' goal to get rich
quickly. The welfare of the cities themselves was neither a public
matter nor a private concern. The residents swiftly extended
familiar, old social and political associations into the new settings and
hastily adapted them to meet their unique needs. They produced
structures flexible enough to absorb the ups and downs of the rapidly
developing cities. They stimulated some cohesion among the masses
of heterogeneous people and offered identity to individuals lost in the
crowd. They were motivated by their hunt for fortunes and regarded
riches as the standard of their societies. As long as the cities
depended on the influx of newcomers for their continued development, the wealth which sustained San Francisco and Denver
facilitated the openness of their societies.

Weak and corrupt government left each of the residents free to
exploit the egalitarian premise of the instant city to his own ends.
They permitted divided people to avoid the forms of social control
and urban planning that would have amounted to superimposing a
ruling group's concept of order on all other groups. In the absence of
sound practices to protect the different ways of different people, the
inefficiency of municipal government allowed a beneficent lack of
order that gave multitudes of disparate people a chance to develop
into citizens of San Francisco and Denver with a minimum of
bloodshed and coercion.

In cities that were exorbitant and immoderate by their very
natures, the residents managed to maintain an equilibrium between a
minimum of organization that assured the pursuit of their personal
goals, and a degree of chaos that did not destroy all hopes of realizing
their dreams. The race for riches and the turmoil of the instant cities
distracted them from organizational tasks. Their abilities to master

the art of organization declined with the steady corrosion of the cities' initial egalitarianism. Their associations strengthened their numerical cohesion but they weakened also the ethical outlook of individuals who, on account of their goals, were not inclined to join together. When the significance of their spontaneous associations diminished, their freedom from organizational confines lost even the few traces of deliberate design it once had.

The complexities of the instant cities, perpetuated by change and compounded by strangers, converted the residents' freedom into apathy which preserved governments without plans or goals. The dilemma was the consequence of the interaction of forces larger than the residents themselves and incomprehensible to most of them, and they paid for it in blatant corruption and the opprobrium of posterity. In the face of great obstacles, great cities were cultivated —cities that achieved a minimum of order with a minimum of coercion. Their formula of organization provided most residents with a degree of freedom to utilize the promises of the instant cities for their own ends.

# 7

## Culture for the Moment

In 1859, a visitor to San Francisco returning to the site for the first time since 1835 could scarcely keep his "hold on reality" as he looked over the city "with its storehouses, towers, and steeples; its court-houses, theatres, and hospitals; its daily journals; its well-filled learned professions; its fortresses and light-houses; its wharves and harbor." [1] Yet, for those who had not once beached boats or grazed horses where hotels now stood, San Francisco and Denver appeared to be only a few steps removed from the wilderness. Both cities were stark mixtures of camps and towns. Empty sand lots, disrupting pretentious rows of houses, were almost as well known as city buildings. Poorly graded and atrociously paved streets ran aimlessly into sand dunes or emptied into prairies. Bold façades hid humble beginnings, and brick structures of more than four stories were landmarks. Wooden shanties flanked wooden mansions, and both fronted desolation.

On windy days, when clouds of dust filled streets and enveloped houses, even these few accomplishments seemed to vanish. Yet the residents insisted that these sites were cities, and, indeed, they soon were. In the interim, as residents waiting for their fortunes to be made and their cities to be perfected they sought out those amenities of urban life that characterized cities of the East Coast and of Europe. In the amorphous settings of instant cities—one part still phantom, the other real—the imported elements of eastern culture gave practical substance to the immediate illusions of urban civilization.

Unlike its effect on centers of population on the Atlantic seaboard where élite culture and popular culture separated the inhabitants, eastern cosmopolitanism thrived in the instant cities of the West without the need for particular cliques to adopt it as their own and use it to distinguish themselves from all others. Life styles in San Francisco and Denver were taken as accomplishments of the cities, not specific classes. Without the wealth and steady flow of new people furnished by the cities, cultural life would have been merely a faint reminder of distant scenes.

Once transplanted, the offshoots of eastern American society spawned rapidly in the favorable environment of the instant cities a setting that both required and stimulated the emergence of new life styles. In fact, unlike many other societies, the citizens of the instant cities sought answers to the problems of urban development testing each of the transplanted components of the larger American civilization but retaining only those that were viable in the new environment. Of necessity, the cities bred a state of mind that worshiped the useful and elevated the practical to a culture. Fortunately, the task of finding just those elements that contributed toward the building of modern urban life was expedited by a general trend toward a synthetic city culture in Western Europe and the Eastern United States, fostered by the rationality and technology of a new phase of urbanization.

In the industrially advanced countries, urbanization and industrialization stimulated cultural decomposition and played a role similar to that of migration and colonization in the civilization of the Far West. Change distilled inherited forms of city life into their constituent parts and freed the individual for new responses to the altered problems of city dwellers. Pointing to urban life as the way of the future, innovations abounded. Some became landmarks of a distinct urban culture when the fusion of architecture with engineering, theater with entertainment, and straight news with idle gossip produced high-rising buildings, vaudeville, and yellow journalism.

During the second half of the nineteenth century, world fairs helped advertise the ferment that was fomenting the explosive life styles of San Francisco and Denver and to overcome old styles and dated ways throughout the western world. Beginning with the London Exposition of 1851, they furnished previews of emerging solutions to the new interactions of industrialization and urbanization. In London, a new imagination conceived the plan of a building in prefabricated parts, and with the use of serial production the Crystal Palace, four times more spacious than St. Peter's in Rome, the largest European edifice, was assembled within six months.[2] Mechanization stimulated ways of life as well as processes of production, and a gigantic steam engine was the core of the Philadelphia Centennial Exposition of 1876.[3] The machine represented the "mightiest cultural factor" involved in the integration of steel and iron into the fabric of society.[4] The fusion of architecture and engineering assured unity, magnitude, and illusion in a "triumph of *ensemble*" at the Chicago World's Fair in 1893.[5] This formula of a new cultural synthesis provided an answer to the impact of steam and steel on society.

The recasting of old cultural elements into new forms placed San Francisco and Denver on an analogous footing with the leading cities of the industrial nations, in terms of assembling life styles. In the colonial transplants as well as in the established centers, people rearranged cultural fragments to give meaning to their existence in the face of teeming cities, noisy factories, and changed ways of life. The common features of their activities almost overshadowed the distinctive requirements that characterized the search in San Francisco and Denver for a culture suitable to the unique conditions of instant cities.

The original elements of eastern culture brought cross-country to San Francisco and Denver were those customs and traditions that, for decades and centuries, had allowed migrants to survive in the

East. Despite the fact that they were in a society marked by chance and change, the most recent migrants determinedly clung to these familiar tools. They relied on the familiar and only when the familiar failed did they seek modifications. Concerned about function and unconcerned about appearance, they had eyes only for the pragmatic and paid little attention to other considerations. They transplanted cultural institutions indiscriminately—hotels and theaters, churches and schools, fairs and libraries—whenever their means allowed. Often, their culture was more a state of mind than a set of distinct attainments. It produced an attitude that demanded spontaneous solutions to the needs of the instant cities and accepted the most primitive substitutes as the real thing.

In February 1859, Charles H. Blake's new house in Denver was immediately considered "a good theater building" by William Larimer who three months earlier had just put the settlement on the map.[6] The floor was packed dirt, and canvas tenting served as the roof. The first theatrical performance actually took place in October 1859, on the second floor of a two-storey structure that the Barney Brothers had built during the summer. Apollo Hall, "complete with floors and roof," had a balcony but still lacked a "false front" to disguise the pitch roof.[7] The ground floor served as saloon, tavern, gambling hall, and billiard parlor. After the opening night, Libeus Barney wrote home to Vermont: "A large, though not very remarkably *select* audience. Admittance, one dollar; comfortable accommodations for three hundred and fifty; receipts, $400, which tells well for the patronage, if not the appreciation, of art in this semi-barbarous region." [8] Not to be left behind, the settlement on the left bank of Cherry Creek called Auraria opened on the same evening with the "Cibola Minstrels" at Cibola Hall, or Reed's Theater, a dance hall built from logs.[9]

Instant city culture was in steady flux. The peculiar conditions of San Francisco and Denver shortcircuited most attempts to search for new expressions. Original achievements disappeared in the flood of made-to-order imitations of eastern and European models that served the daily needs much more readily than did genuine creations that consumed time. "Nothing original or striking, nothing grand or magnificent," a Denverite characterized his city's architecture, "remarkable for its pretentiousness and gilt-edge design." [10] Although the accomplishments rightfully belonged to the instant cities, they appeared as oddities in the ordinary context of daily life. Their limitations made it painfully obvious how difficult it was to reproduce Athens and Boston, London and Philadelphia, Paris and New York in the wilderness, with limited means and expertise. However, considering the cities' rapid rise and extreme isolation, the imitation of distant centers of urban life constituted genuine beginnings. The transplants did not only recreate models of behavior but also produced overnight the appearance of urban centers that made possible the subsequent flowering of an indigenous culture.

San Franciscans and Denverites lacked know-how and resources and that, together with their conservative temper as colonials, limited experimentation and improvisation. The buildings that dominated their cities reflected conformity and indicated an unwillingness to innovate beyond the limits drawn by tradition. However, exaggerated playful designs compensated for the reduction in size and material that accompanied the adaptation of eastern models to the limited resources of the instant cities. The result was a composite of extremes, a gaudy-conventional hodgepodge, christened with various stylish names. [11]

The Denver architects who built the Exposition Hall of 1882 were virtuosos of the gaudy-conventional style. [12] They reduced the gigantic rectangle of the Main Building of the Philadelphia Centennial Exposition to a Grecian Cross, which local workmen were able to build within a few months. Instead of wrought iron columns supporting wrought iron roof trusses, they used local brick for the pillars and wooden beams to support the three acres of tin roofing. As compensation for the lost dimension of the impressive Philadelphia model, they doubled the four towers, and to these eight towers, gracing the extremities of the cross, they added four that flanked the rotunda of the eighty-foot dome. [13]

The long row of windows in the brick arches was called "Modern

Renaissance" in the exposition edition of a Denver newspaper, but the windows were more Renaissance than nineteenth-century modern.[14] Although the North Italian Renaissance Revival appeared in the United States in the middle of the nineteenth century, three decades later Denver's strained technology still adhered to the original sixteenth-century formula of arched openings between columns and entablature executed in local brick, instead of the modern cast iron.[15]

On other occasions, the imaginative recreations of distant models also produced outstanding monuments of instant city culture. In the early 1880s, the inadequate Oakland Long Wharf gave way to the Oakland Mole, a solid causeway extending more than a mile into San Francisco Bay and widened at the end to provide enough space for twelve railroad tracks. For decades, this facility linked San Francisco by means of ferries to the rail network of the country.[16] The wood architecture of the large passenger depot and train shed rivaled in appearance and size eastern models constructed of iron and steel. The five thousand people who attended the grand opening in January 1882, were attracted by the novelty of an entire terminal equipped with steam heat and lighted by electricity, the lights set into the high wooden overhead arches of the wide roof. By the standards of the time it was "a depot equal, as far as convenience and comfort is concerned, to any in the United States."[17]

These and a few other inspired examples of the gaudy-conventional style turned makeshift into improvisation, substitution into innovation, and imitation into re-creation. "Contemporary architecture," a San Franciscan emphasized in 1872, "is original only in the adaptation of mixed styles to the uses of modern society."[18]

Originality, at times, stemmed also from a fortuitous mixture of the ingredients. Instant city culture existed side by side, or in conjunction with, transplanted components of colonial culture and immigrant culture. The French proprietor of Denver's fashionable "Delmonico of the West" saw to it that his restaurant came straight out of Paris, with a stopover in New York.[19] The San Francisco Palace Hotel extended Vienna's Ringstrasse to the corner of Market and New Montgomery, but it was as much a part of San Francisco as the fog and the wind. The Denver Windsor Hotel brought a touch of Windsor Castle in England to the intersection of Larimer and Eighteenth, by way of the Windsor Hotel in Montreal, Canada, and became as much a Colorado legend as H. A. W. Tabor's "Matchless Mine." [20]

Within the general context of life in San Francisco and Denver, only those European practices that served the particular needs of specific groups and that also managed to conform outwardly to the dominant strain of Anglo-Saxon culture survived. They were quickly reduced to stereotypes. The Denver correspondent of a New York paper described "daily life" in the following clichés: "English lords sun themselves in front of hotels. . . . French madames . . . show you the latest Parisian modes. Blonde Germans stand in saloon doors. . . . The Yankee and his notions are prominent." [21] Chauvinism tended to credit elegance to French residents, physical vigor to German turners, and pride to Spaniards and Mexicans.

The cultural life of San Francisco and Denver was at once an inspired extension and a slovenly imitation of the customs and manners of eastern metropolitan centers. Transplanted institutions ran the whole gamut from elegant churches to dilapidated meeting houses, from illustrated magazines to handbills. Splendid academies faced one-room schools, and magnificent theaters fronted sordid peep shows. Beer parlors and crib houses loomed over state saloons and plush palaces of pleasure. The hospitality associated with the hotels of both cities competed with the notoriety of the dives and dens. Belles-lettres contrasted with the hesitant beginnings of scholarship in the raw cities.

The residents' devotion to the practical limited the originality of their achievements as much as did the absence of facilities and talents. The power of convention reinforced the lack of technological know-how because conformism and parochialism shielded San Franciscans and Denverites from the hectic tempo of city life. Confronted with the social costs of rapid urbanization, they sought security in sentimental clichés and solace in stilted allegories. Since their urban condition kept them out of touch with real nature, their isolation conveniently allowed for experimentation with a studied harmony of art and nature as a vision of unity between men, man-made nature, and technology.

The San Francisco Midwinter Fair of 1894 erected cultural buffers against the trauma of living with chance and change. Located in Golden Gate Park, its man-made nature attempted to soften the discord among the residents that had been exacerbated by the depression of 1893. In the midst of winter, a quickly fabricated environment of blossoms and flowers, green lawns, shrubs, and trees greeted the spectator in a "City of Palms." The terrace of the Grand Court lined the exposition halls with allegorical statues and fountains, among them, as inspiration, Gustave Doré's thirteen-foot high and seven-foot wide bronze vase, "The Poem of the Vine," which extolled man's successful struggle with nature.[22] The fair's oriental theme intensified the suggested illusion of tranquility and order.

Adherence to an architectural theme gave unity and magnitude to the Midwinter Fair, as it had to the Chicago Exposition of 1893. But San Francisco's colorful Oriental motifs did more than merely compensate for the reduced scale. A rich conglomeration of building styles, Moorish, East Indian, Egyptian, Siamese, and Central Indian, as well as Spanish-Mission-Romanesque, took the place of the initially planned beaux-arts exposition architecture and of the ready-made drawings which the promoters' European advisors had brought from Chicago. Their novelty helped to foster dreams more effectively than had the neoclassical architecture of the Chicago World's Fair, designed after Greek and Roman examples. The change of theme also mollified local architects who, as practitioners of instant city culture, specialized in re-creations and were waiting to demonstrate their talents in a novel field.[23]

The exotic theme created an illusion of cultural harmony that momentarily bridged the divisions of the instant city. In line with the mirages produced by landscape gardening, allegorical statues and fountains, a special director of color on the fair's executive committee saw to it that the paint washes of the façades effectively enlivened the stucco of the buildings.[24] The vivid sights clashed with the bleak wintertime appearance of downtown. A powerful search-light on a 272-foot high Electric Tower and more than three thousand incandescent lamps framing this *Tour d'Eiffel en miniature* formed spectacular color patterns, or were kept blinking by an interrupter, while chains of bulbs accentuated the contours of the halls.[25] Technology assured the continued didactic tinting of the cultural environment and guaranteed that the lesson was not interrupted by the limited reach of the metaphors or the change from day to night.

Sentiment without feeling characterized instant city culture. In 1882, the favorite picture of the Denver Exposition was a life-size genre painting of a seamstress by Constant Mayer, a French-born painter working in the United States better known for his technical competence than for his creative power. It was called "Song of the Shirt," after Thomas Hood's ballad, which appeared in *Punch* in 1843.[26] The fabulous success of the poem made it "one of the genuine songs of the people." It was reprinted and dramatized.[27] When Richard Redgrave's illustration, "The Sempstress," pioneered what became in the 1850s an immensely popular type of painting, the sentimental scenes inspired by the poem were confused with compassion for the sufferings of people in distress.[28]

Denver newspapers began to quote from the ballad of the seamstress. "In poverty, hunger and dirt," she sang with "a voice of dolorous pitch . . . the song of the shirt." However, any concern for the afflicted and poor ended there. The sentimentality contrasted strikingly with the quick condemnation by the general public of the waiters of leading Denver hotels who struck for higher wages on the opening day of the exposition. One newspaper noted approvingly that they received very little sympathy and were "bounced summa-rily," and reported with glee that their places were filled easily with strikebreakers within a few hours.[29] In San Francisco, in the winter of 1893, the Midwinter Fair failed to provide a much-discussed relief for the unemployed beyond the distribution of box lunches.[30]

Human misery failed to move the social conscience of instant city culture. Any judgment concerning the quality of life was suspended by incorporating hardships into daily reality. At the Midwinter Fair, an ironic accident of design tipped the empty scales of Justice, dangling from a 300-foot crossbeam in the hand of a 150-foot tall Justitia.[31] Suffering was the expected lot of those who failed to amass fortunes in the instant city and sympathy only seemed to interfere with the race of getting ahead in life.

The pages of romances depicting poverty in San Francisco and Denver overflowed with platitudes that avoided the real problems. Poems and short stories fabricated emotions and ignored the misery.[32] Only the cities' "yellow press" reported in lurid exposés the ills of society and these newspapers, represented by William Randolph Hearst's *Examiner*, M. H. de Young's *Chronicle*, and Frederick G. Bonfils's and Harry H. Tammen's Denver *Post*, did so to increase their circulations.[33]

The banalities and trivialities that smothered social consciousness also served as buffers between the residents and their chaotic environments. Clichés assured the culture's viability in difficult urban conditions that left little room for genuine feelings or startling innovations. With platitudes, San Franciscans and Denverites braced themselves for their quick maturity. During the San Francisco visit of the emperor of Brazil in 1876, a newspaper assessed Dom Pedro II as "one of the men, who, in our time, have given respectability to the trade of king." [34] Stereotypes shielded the residents' emotions from the impact of the harsh realities of their hectic lives.

The clichés flourished amid a peculiar brand of parochialism that viewed life from the narrow perspective of people who often had little to be proud of other than their pride. A Denver journal informed its readers that their city "had the most brilliant architects to be found in any State" and hailed Denver as "the cap-stone of the continent for beautiful buildings." [35] The limited local accomplishments complicated attempts to be chauvinistic, and since cosmopolitan aspirations often proved to be unattainable, or were not appreciated, the parochial and cosmopolitan features blended to a provincialism. The isolation of the city strengthened its provincialism and shaped the level of its taste.[36]

Provincialism assured a cultural compromise at the Denver Exposition of 1882. The "classical grind" played by the exposition orchestra—the "German Military Band"—left no room on the program for popular tunes. A visitors' petition to the orchestra and hints from newspapers which found the neglect of "music which falls pleasantly upon the American ear" by foreign musicians hard to understand since "American dollars paid them" brought the desired relief from daily selections of Offenbach, Gounot, Bizet, Auber, Sullivan, Wagner, Strauss, and Suppé.[37] The resulting blend of musical selections made the conductor's cornet solo of "The Star Spangled Banner," "Yankee Doodle," and "Dixie" the musical highpoints of the day and turned an often-played medley called "Berlin Laughed and Cried" into an exposition hallmark.[38]

The insularity of instant city culture slowed the implementation of innovative approaches and directed them into conventional channels. Only after a San Francisco woman attorney returned with "an idea from Chicago," were she and her friends able to organize the San Francisco Council of Women in 1893 because newspapers were then more receptive to the advocacy of women's rights.[39] Inspired by the position taken by leading American feminists in support of the Chicago World's Fair, these women overcame the indifference that was San Francisco's initial response to such a project.

The accommodation to convention worked both ways, but in the end tended to reinforce the cultural status quo. With the positions changed, the women rightists altered their vocabulary and presented their plan for an exposition as an attempt to awaken "a spirit of intellectual activity and enterprise to the permanent material and mental prosperity" of San Francisco.[40] A hard-working Women's Auxiliary Committee won the influential Mechanics' Institute over to the idea and came up with the successful name, Midwinter Fair, but it was Mrs. M. H. de Young, the wife of the fair's director-general, who pressed the electric button at the opening ceremony.[41] Under the influence of a Committee of Two Hundred Prominent Women, most of the opponents of the exposition recanted, yet during the groundbreaking ceremony "a native daughter and highly accomplished author and elocutionist" who had been invited to participate by the executive committee declaimed: "Look at the men now before you, by whose genius this deed has been done." [42]

As true colonials, San Franciscans and Denverites always invited comparisons with the distant sources of their culture. They especially loved to talk about what they yet hoped to accomplish, as many travelers wearily acknowledged, and they leaped at any opportunity to exercise their obsession on a grand scale. In 1873, Denverites believed that their city would "become one of the most beautiful cities on the continent." [43] Before the architecture of their exposition hall suggested parallels with the Philadelphia Centennial, Denverites compared their new business blocks with Chicago models. In 1879, Denverites considered the Tabor Building superior to all other structures, a worthy symbol of Denver's great boom stimulated by Leadville silver pouring into the city. [44]

When a dearth of indigenous artists made favorable comparisons with outsiders difficult, as was the case at times in the field of art, local ownership of famous art pieces substituted for the absence of local talent, generating pride in those young cities that valued and sheltered celebrated art treasures. San Franciscans discussed those paintings of the giants of nineteenth-century European art academies owned in their city in an atmosphere that easily absorbed all proffered culture. [45] The milieu was assiduously cultivated by relating local painters to visiting masters and regarding both groups as products of the city. The landscape painter Albert Bierstadt was identified with Denver through his favorite sketching place on Cherry Creek and his tours from Denver into the Rocky Mountains. [46] When any artist who had so much as touched the cities gained national reputation, San Franciscans and Denverites claimed him as their contribution to national culture. Examples are Samuel Clemens and Eugene Field.

In acquisitive cities, constantly absorbing new cultural distinctions, boosterism blossomed. The residents' exuberance of speech, expressed in San Francisco's popular greeting of 1857, "Hello Johnny! How's your dog?," contributed to its flowering.[47] As part of the official local language, boosterism infected the language of onlookers. A Denver newspaper announced the launching of the Exposition of 1882 with the headline, "All Nations of the Globe to be Represented in the National Affair." [48] In a preview, *Harper's Weekly* stressed that the "entire world" had been invited to participate in a fair intended to link mining and the other great industries of the land.[49] The Kansas City *Review of Science and Industry* gushed that Denver "will not merely conceive the idea of a National Mining and Industrial Exposition, but put it into such execution that one will blush with pardonable pleasure." [50] The Denver paper closed the cycle of strained prognostications with the prediction that the Exposition Building would "remain a monument to its founders when each and all of them . . . shall have passed to pathetic dust, and for years hence will exemplify the spirit of an age when the race was with the swift and the battle with the strong." [51] The plethora of words generated more words. "No country with an equal population has, during the last ten years, been the subject of so many books," a San Francisco editor noted in 1860.[52]

Exaggeration heightened the preoccupation with the opportunities of the cities. The residents came to believe in the wild prophecies and kept their money ready to exploit any chance to make more. Words, they knew, were cheap, but money mattered, and that consideration dominated finances and dictated, in particular, a reticence to support enterprises for the sake of culture. Making money left "no time or taste for studying anything save the news of the day and perhaps an occasional work of broad humor." [53] Denver struck one traveler as "embodiment and manifestation of the new life of an enterprising people who pay more attention to money-getting than aesthetics." [54]

An unwillingness to spend money on public projects did not interfere with attempts to profit from cultural activities. Although the Denver Exposition of 1882 was staged "not for the purpose of

making money but for the posterity of Denver," the planners hoped
to do at least as well as the promoters of the Atlanta Cotton
Exposition of 1881, who evidently did well in the eyes of distant
observers.[55] Visionaries favored a pavilion "exclusively of iron and
glass," in the tradition of the original Crystal Palace or of the New
York version of 1853, but shrewd economists extolled the virtues of
the plain building of a current Cincinnati exposition that did not put
stockholders "to any expense at all." [56]

At times, tightfisted men came around. Despite the prosperous
times, the recently incorporated Board of Trade shunned direct
involvement in the Denver Exposition of 1882, although the board's
president predicted a population increase from 50,000 to 150,000
Denver inhabitants within five years.[57] In the face of the nationwide
depression of 1893, San Francisco moneyed men spoke out automatically against the impracticable scheme of a midwinter fair, and the
banking world followed suit because investors felt uncertain about
support from press and people in troubled times.[58] Both projects did
materialize, but on a reduced scale.

One of the characteristics of instant cities reinforced the residents'
reluctance to provide general support for cultural projects: most
were out for themselves and many familiar with the nature of culture
saw it only as a means to personal ends. In settings but a few steps
removed from the wilderness, certain men and women considered it
to their advantage to inaugurate and maintain a style of life
characteristic of great cities. This "metropolism" reflected the
tendency to retain an urban outlook and to aspire to city life
undeterred by the vast expanse of country separating their new
homes from their old ones in Boston, New York, Charleston,
Chicago, or New Orleans.[59] As a phenomenon of cultural expansion,
metropolism contributed to the flowering of urban culture in all the
migrations of Western man from the beginnings of Greek colonization to the movement of Europeans across their Atlantic boundaries.
In 1862, Denver's John Evans was part of that great tradition when
he laid the foundation of the University of Denver within six months
of his arrival. He did so in the same spirit that had prompted him

earlier in Illinois to found Northwestern University at Evanston, the city named after him, but many other men and women supported culture merely for private ends.[60]

Collecting books and paintings, establishing libraries and art galleries, or supporting theaters and opera houses brought immediate gain through heightened personal prestige. The acquisition and importation of old masters, precious manuscripts, and volumes by fashionable authors were also recognized as image-building activities. In 1893, a few San Franciscans captured a segment of the Chicago World's Fair and brought it West as a capsulated display of the cultural norm. In the following year they placed it, and themselves, on exhibit in the Midwinter Fair to demonstrate to the country their accomplishment and to the city their elevated position.[61] In Denver, fourteen years earlier, H. A. W. Tabor had shown a similar but more candid spirit when, as the story goes, he substituted his likeness for that of Shakespeare just before the opening of his opera house.[62]

Inasmuch as the cultural life, as all else in the instant cities, was continuously exploited by clever men for personal ends, the residents came to suspect most advocates of public undertakings. They had learned from experience that they footed the bill for artistic extravagances designed to improve the quality of life. The history of expositions in the United States reinforced the suspicion. Since 1853, when the promoter of America's first world fair withdrew from the project and sold his backers, for $10,000, the five-year lease to a site which he had obtained from the New York Common Council for one dollar a year, many people assumed that planners used public support to line their pockets.[63] Denverites instinctively adopted the attitude. Despite numerous statements that the managers were "gentlemen of large means and undoubted integrity," they only accepted the project after they were assured repeatedly that the exposition promoted the prosperity of Denver.[64]

Prosperity was a natural objective of instant city culture. Denver's success was the earliest publicized aim of the Exposition of 1882. Fortunately, it coalesced in the minds of the residents with the private aims of the promoters. The personality of H. A. W. Tabor, the rich figurehead of the exposition managers, made the identity plausible. A vain man, he regarded public acclaim as sufficient reward for his financial support. In one instance, when he verbalized his feelings concerning the relationship between himself, Denverites, and the fair, Tabor showed an understanding of human nature. He joked about the Exposition Association as a "mutual adoration society" and pointed out the affinity between prosperity and instant city culture: Denverites loved him for his ability to finance the fair, and he loved their adoration of his money.[65]

Instant city culture worshipped fortuitous achievement. In daily affairs it amounted to an affection for men who went from rags to riches. A reserve, at times bordering on animosity, greeted wealth amassed methodically through the careful manipulation of opportunities as opposed to wealth gained effortlessly through the bold exploitation of a stroke of luck. Denverites cheered Tabor's support of the Exposition of 1882 because they knew it came to him as spontaneously as other extravagant acts with which he tested the size of an enormous fortune made suddenly in Leadville silver. Conversely, many San Franciscans criticized the promoter of their Midwinter Fair, M. H. de Young, because they saw the project as another link in his intricate chain of economic, political, and social schemes.[66]

For two decades, de Young's manipulation of San Francisco created animosity which exposed him, as director-general of the exposition, to considerable abuse. In 1892, the owner and editor-in-chief of the *Chronicle* failed to succeed George Hearst in the Senate. His call for an exposition antedated by a few weeks his campaign for the other Senate seat vacated by Leland Stanford's death in June 1893, and led some people to believe that his mind was only on the Senate. The reputations and actions of some of his European associates whom he used to attract foreign exhibitors to the fair made him vulnerable to the charge that he profited from contracts and concessions.[67] Most detractors eventually stood grudgingly in awe of the outburst of public energy which he generated and that may have given de Young at least the satisfaction of the public recognition that he craved.

The respect for success and the concern for the useful corresponded with didactic interests. San Franciscans and Denverites accepted cultural imports as object lessons in new ways to cope with changed ideas of life. Strangers in the cities they built, they sought all possible help in coming to terms with their urban problems. An exposition was a "school at which thousands are learning," and this attitude characterized their naïve faith in innovation which would increase their mastery of the complexities of city life.[68] Denverites took it for granted that the light of electric lamps which illuminated the Exposition of 1882 would make possible the evening concerts and promenades which, they were told, were the marks of large cities. They waited patiently for a month until technicians improved the system enough so that the lights burned steadily.[69]

Their isolation from the centers of technological advance was so great and their collective experience as urban dwellers so small that they looked for help, too, from innovations already dated by further progress. In 1882, they watched for several weeks as mechanics completed assembling a hydraulic elevator to carry passengers to the four conservatories flanking the dome of the exposition building. Electricity was the marvel of the fair, and electric elevators were the trend of the future, but Denverites accepted the dated hydraulic elevator because that was what they had and since they felt compelled to make use of the available. In this particular lesson some did not learn much. When the valve of the storage tank above the elevator accidentally opened, the downpour of water soaked the passengers.[70]

In San Francisco a useful element of design, the bay window providing view and collecting sunlight, dominated the many traditional styles which the city attracted.[71] In Denver, brick characterized the scene after the Great Fire of 1863 had led to a ban on new wooden buildings in the business district. This was reinforced in 1876 by a city ordinance against frame structures everywhere, made possible by a proliferation of brick yards, one of Denver's major industries.[72] The ostentatious mansions which both cities produced seemed to be the epitome of waste, but they were immensely practical because they immediately and continuously testified to the prestige of their builders.[73]

Outsiders often identified the pragmatic attitude as crass materialism. The residents of instant cities seemed to be preoccupied with material problems because they seemed to lie at the root of a multitude of their difficulties—from the lack of houses to live in to the absence of material to build with and the lack of money to buy with. However, the urge of San Franciscans and Denverites to respond effectively to changing cities was a robust offshoot of the technological imagination of the age that saw in the steam engine the cultural complement to democracy.[74] Their solutions were at times primitive, and more often appeared crude, and neither characteristic helped dispel the lable of materialism that clung to them.

The materialistic ring reverberated the distinctly urban tone of life in San Francisco and Denver. The flowering culture underlined the instant cities' role as antithesis of the wilderness. Patterns of climate, labor, and land ownership magnified the cultural isolation of San Franciscans and Denverites from nature, heightened their distinctly urban existence, and attracted many newcomers to California and Colorado in the two cities. Fully half of the white people of California live in towns, the American Social Science Association learned in 1871, "a quarter of all in one town, and this quarter pays more than half of the taxes of all." [75] Few San Franciscans "leave their remarkable city until they are driven from it by the fogs and winds of midsummer," the editor of the city's leading magazine argued, "and then they love not Nature the more, but possibly San Francisco the less." One of his contributors compared California to ancient Greece with its low level of rural people and its high level of city dwellers.[76]

The pace of urbanization that widened the gulf separating San Franciscans and Denverites from nature also deepened their commitment to the purely urban ways of life. In the 1860s, a landscape architect could not find a single "full grown tree of beautiful proportions in San Francisco." [77] The dry summer months limited the use of gardens and the rising value of real estate did the rest. Cottonwood and maple abounded in Denver, but many residents who liked well-shaded streets "neither saw nor appreciated the necessity, value or utility of parks," and in the early 1880s only a much-reduced project for City Park became reality, "destitute of every park-like aspect." [78] In 1882, an elaborate garden surrounded the large hall of the Denver Exposition, but the sun burned the grass, and the lack of care turned it into a lawn of weeds.[79] In San Francisco nothing came of a far-flung proposal for metropolitan parks in 1866. Most people considered an urban amusement park called Woodward's Garden their city park. Every man, woman, and child in San Francisco, and more than two-thirds of the residents of California, had visited it often more than once, by the end of the 1870s.[80] In the same spirit, Denverites amused themselves in Elitch's Garden in the 1890s, with a summer theater "conducted upon a high plane" and a *"grand* Zoo." [81]

The contrast between wilderness and instant city never struck San Franciscans and Denverites as a cultural conflict. Their culture was strictly urban, without need for nature in the form of parks. In 1873, the project of San Francisco's Golden Gate Park, which dated back to 1870, struck a Santa Rosa newspaper as the biggest white elephant the city ever owned.[82] Only in the 1890s did a compromise between natural and urban existence begin to take shape with the staging of the Midwinter Fair in the undeveloped wasteland of Golden Gate Park[83] It utilized the park as a solution for a newly recognized urban need. Converting one thousand acres of shifting sand dunes to a concept of social harmony, the fusion of design and nature suggested the implementation of a novel vision: the intelligent manipulation of human environment.

From time to time, a few voices urged a great retreat to nature as an alternative to a meaningless race for riches in the city.[84] Generally, their appeal fell on deaf ears among people who indeed had just wrung their homes from the wilderness. Men with fortunes built suburban mansions, mostly to enrich the dimensions of their urban existence.[85] Nature came to loom large only in the 1890s when San Francisco and Denver began their metamorphosis from instant cities to ordinary cities. By then improved communication and transportation had lifted the isolation and reduced the gap between nature and cities. Less strain and more leisure drew some residents to the mountains. Others hoped to escape the urban wilderness that they had created. In any case, when San Franciscans and Denverites belatedly took a look at their surroundings, the wilderness was gone, either tamed or destroyed, but in the opening decades of the twentieth century Denver still managed to build up a system of distant mountain parks as one of the city's special features.[86]

The rejection of nature reflected the same psychology that reduced the original inhabitants of the wilderness to ciphers. When a special occasion brought a group of Indians into the cities, they were viewed as nothing but stereotypes: eloquent orators, taciturn medicine men, expert horsemen, and fabulous long-distance runners.[87] Only if they did not evoke the past were they tolerated. Some Southern Ute visited the Denver Exposition of 1882, but the Arapaho and Cheyenne, on whose land Denver stood, stayed away and did not test the sordid bit of humor that the Governor's Guard would be turned loose upon them afterwards.[88] In the most approved style, the sprawling camp and daily war dances of the Ute satisfied the curiosity of those Denverites who had never seen Indians before.[89] When the Southern Ute departed, some of the underlying feeling erupted in a comment that the popular song, "Old Towner's Dead," was the Indians' favorite tune, and that most Denverites wished the Indians were as dead as old man Towner.[90]

The appearance of Indians, blacks, and Mexican-Americans at expositions reflected no awareness of their part in either city's complex past or a concern for their contemporary plight. Rather, the residents viewed these exhibited people as curiosities much like the tightrope walkers and fire-eaters of the fairs' midways. Seeing them as "primitives" in specially constructed "villages" and "camps" assured San Franciscans and Denverites of the progress man had made in the urban settings and of the cultural distance separating their cities from the wilderness.

Among the Indians at the Denver Exposition was a black, born a slave in Kentucky, who had served in the Union Army, received his discharge in Texas, and lived with the Navajo before marrying into the Southern Ute.[91] John Taylor's adventures and his preference for Indian life did not remind any newspaper editor of James P. Beckwourth, "the famous mulatto of the plains," friend of the Cheyenne, adopted chief of the Crow, and resident of Denver during the early 1860s who gave up city life to die among Indians.[92] At the San Francisco Midwinter Fair of 1894, the presence of Wovoka, the Nevada ghost dance prophet, who "created the greatest religious ferment" known to his Indian generation, went unnoticed, save for a mention in a study of the ghost dance. Unnoticed, too, was the spiritual stamina of the survivors of the California and Nevada Indian population Wovoka embodied.[93]

Instant city culture bypassed the rich but controversial human heritage of San Francisco and Denver. Serving cities living in the future, it acknowledged no past but a narrow record of accomplishments. Toward the end of San Francisco's and Denver's existence as instant cities, their culture's restricted perspective acquired romantic vistas. The San Francisco Midwinter Fair of 1894 was "the natural product of the last hundred years of California's existence," the *Official Guide* of the exposition emphasized.[94]

In 1894, the Midwinter Fair used local color, the made-to-order landscape of Golden Gate Park enveloping a hideous canvas panorama of Mount Shasta, to integrate a Forty-niner camp into San Francisco's past. A special publication, the weekly *Midwinter Appeal and Journal of Forty-nine*, circulated nostalgia in twenty-six issues.[95] "Spanish señoritas" mingled with "honest miners" and represented the Spanish-Mexican heritage which San Franciscans had once striven to eradicate. When mining towns made up the back country, San Franciscans had also insisted that their city existence set them apart from all camps.[96] Now they proudly displayed two cabins, once the possessions of Silver King John Mackay and Senator George

C. Perkins, and camouflaged the incongruities of places and men with romantic tales.[97] Yet, their newfound willingness to display these tacky structures also suggested a lingering self-consciousness regarding origins of the city's wealth which they sought to eliminate by demonstrating how far they had advanced beyond their rough beginnings. At the fair, these cabins contrasted tellingly with the latest technological advances of urban living.

Many men who had seen the rise of the instant cities were still around in the flesh to serve as historical figures. They glossed over the general historical relevance of their common past, and stayed with individual reminiscences and chronicles. So many events had been packed into their lives that the remarkable longevity of some of them seemed even greater than it actually was. California's last Mexican governor, Pio Pico, was thought to be ninety-four years old when he refused indignantly to visit the Chicago World's Fair of 1893 because he feared to be turned into an exhibit by "those gringos." [98]

Most of the cities' living pioneers had left their marks on the cities they helped to build and, understandably, preferred their versions of the past over the assessments of others. That past, in the persons of founders who were also contemporaries, was scarcely more distant than yesterday. In 1878, the author of *A History of the City of San Francisco* felt that "no record . . . could ever be accepted as satisfactory . . . unless based on the authority of the actors themselves." [99] Two years later, in 1880, the publishers of the *History of the City of Denver* thought it "better to present the prominent points in the lives of a larger number than fulsome eulogies of a few." [100]

In the fall of 1893, William T. Coleman and Edward McGowan died within a few weeks of one another.[101] They were two of the many diverse personalities San Franciscans rallied around, particularly in 1856 when Coleman headed the largest vigilance committee in the city's experience and McGowan personified the law-and-order faction. They seem to have respected one another personally, and in their old age Coleman helped the destitute McGowan, but through-

out their long lives they retold their versions of the events in which
they played starring roles. An attempt to assess historically San
Francisco's past, Hubert Howe Bancroft's *History of California*,
promptly produced a libel suit by McGowan during the 1880s.[102]
Shortly before he died, Coleman once more stated his position in
print, while one opponent's rebuttal came, so to speak, from the
grave, in the form of letters by another "old San Franciscan,"
William T. Sherman, published after the general's death.[103]

The Denver Exposition of 1882, with events of the previous two
decades in the forefront of men's minds, pointed exclusively to the
future. In a culture without history, even the opening and closing
ceremonies of the fair ignored the past.[104] However, a visit by
General James W. Denver, whose brief term as governor of Kansas
territory had provided the Cherry Creek settlement with a name,
evoked a few reminiscences. One newspaper printed an old,
unflattering story and stirred political controversy, but was immediately censured by another paper for libeling an old-time fellow
Democrat. A long interview with "Denver's Godfather" dealt with
prophecies about the city's bright future and in the exposition hall,
although the band saluted General Denver, most people paid no
attention to him, despite his name.[105]

Men more intimately connected with Denver's past also received
only slight attention. William Gilpin, prophet of an inland metropolis
since 1846, first governor of Colorado territory, and safely removed
from daily politics, lived in Denver.[106] In 1882, his enthusiastic visits
to the fair should have been occasion for reflection because he had
envisioned some of the developments which made the exposition
possible long before others flocked to Denver and capitalized on the
realization of his dreams.[107] However, Denverites looked for more
tangible contributions to their city's success than a prophet's
eloquence. No one linked his presence to the displayed accomplishments, although Gilpin kept writing, and talking, about Denver as
the "focal point of impregnable power in the topographical configu-
ration of the continent." [108] Even the reporters' jokes about his tours
of the exhibits touched on the future and the large number of

children who accompanied Gilpin as result of his marriage to a widow with four children and the subsequent birth of three more.[109]

The culture without historical memory was itself quickly forgotten. Preoccupied with the future, the residents built life styles which served the moment and few achievements survived their days. Most of them vanished with the changing scenes. San Franciscans and Denverites, eager to stay one step ahead of the next change, kept remaking the settings, "tearing down and building up," a Denver paper called it in 1872.[110] Their modifications of the environment destroyed most of the unique cultural accomplishments that had characterized instant cities. The reports stimulated by such extraordinary affairs as expositions preserved some expressions of the fluid culture for posterity. They provided clues to the complex attitudes at the roots of the flowering life styles. They identified some of the features lost in the turmoil or overshadowed by those achievements that survived because they copied ostentatiously distant models of culture.

Like other expressions of instant city culture, expositions were affairs of the moment. Although they did not wholly escape the schemes of real estate speculators who profited from the rising value of land in the vicinity, the expositions were a no-man's-land in the contest for riches and checkpoints in the drive toward constant change.[111] Staged on ground especially acquired for the purpose, they were shielded from the corrosive impact of intensified urbanization. They were simply forgotten, when their time was up, since the general preoccupation with the future provided no incentive to maintain them. The illusion of cultural harmony they evoked did linger on, supported by the clichés of a culture that buffered San Franciscans and Denverites against the impact of the future they rushed to meet.

Adherence to the convention of the moment strengthened the protective mechanism. The colonials' respect for transmitted forms kept experimentation with new ways within the range of transmitted stereotypes. Their intellectual heritage provided no clues for solving the problems of instant cities and inspired no methodical search that could have produced a conscious clash with the dictates of their cultural models. Spontaneity, versatility, and imagination, stimulated by the cities' hectic pace of daily life, accounted for the independent accomplishments of San Francisco and Denver. A high degree of impulsive improvisation, in contrast to deliberate experimentation, enhanced the impromptu character of instant city culture.

Most achievements faded quickly. Inspired by the moment, they gave way when changing needs required other solutions. The pace of the instant cities steadily rearranged the components and precluded the formation of lasting expressions in a process that assured a modicum of stability and a maximum of development. Eclectic in nature and composite in form, the hybrids lacked purity of expression. The overall drift in situations which glorified the practical reinforced the amorphous nature of instant city culture.

On rare occasions, original accomplishments which fused architecture and engineering stood out in the general flux that inundated stage and press. These inspired solutions fused the components of transmitted culture so imaginatively that the originality of the new product defied definition in terms of conventional concepts and styles. Like the halls of the Denver Exposition or the San Francisco Midwinter Fair, they came into existence abruptly. They quickly shed all association with the names of their architects or builders and became properties as common as popular tunes which desert their composers. Unlike hotels and churches, theaters and mansions, they had no parallels on the local scene. Like the Oakland Mole, they were immensely practical solutions to problems of the moment and served as much the common good as the private interests which built them. Through their public functions, they retained some of the rising cities' spontaneity.

The adaptation and recreation of distant models reinforced the cultural cement that bound masses of people "made up of the odds and ends of creation" in instant cities.[112] The results were variations stimulated by scarcity, and not mere copies produced by convention, and they added a special pitch to the tone of life or gave a distinct touch to a few buildings. In turn, the instant cities accentuated their uniqueness. Such stark structures, as Selby's Shot Tower in San Francisco or Denver's Old Mint, received as much distinction from the cities as they gave character to the skylines.[113] The recreations radiated a special air and highlighted the adaptation of transmitted segments of American culture to living with intensified urbanization.

A sea of imitations engulfed the original accomplishments. The relentless urge to apply cultural transplants to the needs of the moment, to provide shelter, safety, and comfort, assured the domination of the stereotypes. The single-mindedness thrived on a practical outlook that utilized the transmitted culture directly to improve the quality of life with little thought for originality or aesthetics. The attitude, presaging a more general concern for function, scaled styles down to practical forms and indiscriminately embraced anything serving the residents' needs. The determined pursuit of the useful accounted for the forced flowering of urban life in the wilderness.

# 8

## Technology Stimulates Transition

Urban technology facilitated the rise of the instant cities, contributed to the practical orientation of residents, and even determined the physical outlines of San Francisco and Denver. It rapidly converted wilderness into city and earned San Francisco and Denver the sobriquets of wonder city, miracle city, and magic city. The details were less significant than the overall results. The editor of the *Overland Monthly* quipped in 1872: "Considered as a curious collection of boarding-houses, San Francisco is decidedly a success." [1]

Yet, ultimately, technology stripped the instant cities of their most distinctive natures. By broadening their economic bases, it saved them from the ever-threatening fate of becoming oversized ghost towns, but did so only by tying them into the national centers of population and manufacture. In time, these new ties turned the instant cities into regular cities and the residents of instant cities into settled Americans.

The double edge of the technological development affected the residents in many ways. The gridirons of streets and the blocks of houses pushed people closer together physically, yet caused them to resent the forced closeness. The coming of the telephone not only intensified the anonymity of the few who could use the new mode of communication but also separated, through forests of poles and webs of wires, the moving throngs in the streets from the familiar urban landscape. Technological advances cut the residents off from the physical images of what had been their instant cities, but linked them to the ultimate results of the urban explosions, San Francisco and Denver, which constituted the new sources of their identities.

At first, the railroads, streetcars, cable cars, and ferry boats seemed to represent forces that would draw people together, strengthening the social cohesion, and tightening the human weave of the instant cities. But once it was recognized that these new innovations made possible the separation of the home of the individual from his place of work, the real decentralizing impact of technology became apparent. Residents of the instant cities now became suburbanites, and San Francisco and Denver became like other cities in the United States.

In part, the technological take-over came as a consequence of the natural development of the areas, in part was shaped by the particular topography of the areas. In the early stages of the gold rushes, most miners wintered in San Francisco or Denver. As recognized centers of exchange in California and Colorado, these two sites were regular stops on the itineraries of mariners and freighters. The miners' constant requirement for equipment, know-how, money, and diversion strengthened the initial reputations of San Francisco and Denver as hubs of trade and eventually made them cores of communications networks through which investment capital, knowledge, and personnel moved into the mountains and dividends, experience, and information about the West returned to the East.

Economic forces and technological refinements finally merged and stimulated industrial ventures that went beyond small factories milling flour, lumber, and wool. Innovation brought large-scale plants, manufacturing machinery, and operating smelters, and widened the economic bases of the instant cities.[2] In their wake came railroads that pulled San Francisco and Denver into the national

economy and ended the isolation of the two cities. The industrial
milestones followed. In July 1888, the San Francisco Union Iron
Works launched the Cruiser *Charleston*, the first modern man-of-war
built on the Pacific Coast; a Denver journal stated laconically in
1889: "Our smelter business has no parallel in any other state." [3]

Nature itself assured the powerful sway of technology in the
instant cities. It favored San Francisco with an advantageous site
along established lines of maritime commerce, although it withheld
level land so essential to a flourishing city. Acreage abounded in
Denver, but its position in the no-man's-land between the Oregon
Trail and the Santa Fe Trail isolated the inhabitants from even the
few arteries of trade extending into the heart of the continent. In
both cases, the limitations of the settings necessitated the application
of technology to the problems. The characteristics of the cities'
topography, that gave the one what the other lacked and withheld
from the first what the second had plentifully, provided different
twists to the impact of technology on San Francisco and Denver.

Wedded to maritime trade, residents of San Francisco spotted a
cure for their site problems in the wharves reaching into Yerba
Buena Cove. Like "the first slender lines of ice before the water
hardens into a solid mass," the piers provided thoroughfares that
stretched for almost two miles over the waters of the bay.[4] By 1850,
some had become streets and the space between them was filled with
sand, debris, and beached ships. Steam paddies excavated dunes and
hills, which blocked the normal expansion from the shore to the heart
of the peninsula, and horse carts and railway lorries moved the sand
to the Bay and cast it into the deep. The filling of these water lots
created a new beachhead and on the newly filled land "half of the
city in front of Montgomery Street" was built, the old shore line
becoming the heart of the new business district.[5]

The wresting of new land from the ever-encroaching sea was a
distinctive feature of San Francisco's development, its earliest
chroniclers concluded, despite the fact that "plank-covered streets"
crisscrossed the business district and tidal water surged beneath the
pile-founded buildings. San Franciscans considered their city akin to

Venice and Amsterdam, "those other queens of the sea." [6] Another
analogy could have been made had San Franciscans been more
wordly. St. Petersburg, the instant city in Russia, had wrung its site
from the marshes of the Neva a century and a half earlier at the
Czar's command. In 1853, an Austrian woman, on her way around
the globe, stopped in San Francisco and noted the similarity. "San
Francisco is unanimously declared the City of Wonders," she
observed, and only two forces are "capable of effecting such
wonders—gold and despotism." [7]

Gold did the trick in San Francisco, yet increasingly, it was not the
yellow metal found in the mountains but the money produced by the
opportunities available in instant cities. A new breed of land
speculators, responsive to the hectic pulse of the expanding city,
invested in the newly expanded water front. Confident of San
Francisco's future, they were not afraid to wait a while for their
acquisitions to yield a rich return. They outdistanced the land grant
jugglers of the city's dawn who were content to sell at market price a
lot they had just obtained for a nominal grant fee.[8] In fact, so
sensitive were these investors to the long-range potential of those
parcels of land along the wharves that some of them tried to get
control of the expansion into the bay through the lawmakers in
Sacramento. Stung by the skyrocketing value of the first water lots,
auctioned off by the Alcalde back in 1847, they pushed a bill through
the legislature that would turn control of the wharves over to them in
return for the construction of a seawall to protect the shoreline.
Fortunately, in 1860, the governor vetoed their Bulkhead Bill, which
would have given the waterfront to a few monopolists.[9]

In 1863, the State of California, now in control of San Francisco's
waterfront, blocked further encroachment into the bay. By this time,
however, the residents had created a town site that, at least, partially
answered their need for level space to accommodate houses, offices,
and factories. Upon their unpromising hills the builders of San
Francisco superimposed a gridiron of streets, facilitating the sale and
resale of lots in advance of actual settlement, and thus assuring them
the benefits of real estate speculation for the promotion of undevel-

oped districts. In the absence of resources and talents, they stressed
practical and inexpensive solutions, and the simple consideration that
right angles were the easiest for a surveyor to measure strengthened
their faith in the usefulness of the time-tested rectangular plan. The
countless transfers of real estate and the divisions of lots, made easier
by the geometry of the gridiron system, strengthened the economic
heart of their young city.[10]

San Franciscans paid, it seemed to them, a small price for an
environment that made possible the continued rise of their city. As
they filled in the protected anchorage of the cove, they damaged the
harbor and exposed ships to occasional strong tides and gales, but
they considered seawalls and bulkheads a low price for level land.
They ignored the possibility that the violence done to nature could
produce physical and social blight. Their singlemindedness baffled
apostles of organic urban growth whose countrylike city streets
would have followed the contours of the forty-two elevations that
came to make up what Robert Louis Stevenson called San Francisco's "citied hills." [11] Their generation resolutely tackled obstacles
placed by nature in the path of progress and measured their success
in terms of the number of new people and industries attracted to
their city. Determined to live up to, and profit from, their exalted
dreams for the future, these San Franciscans embraced the rationality of technology as a welcome ally in their struggle with an
environment hostile to their visions.

San Franciscans who lacked the space for a city, in effect,
simultaneously built their city and created the additional room its
growth required. To them, their startling accomplishment seemed
almost commonplace. Change was the essence of the instant city,
and they readily responded to it. This attitude built up its own
momentum and carried over into their city building activities. The
city's image remained in flux until the completion of the Palace Hotel
in 1875. Only the expanse of the bay, a hill, or the distant Golden
Gate furnished familiar frames of reference on the changing skyline
of San Francisco.

Denver's skyline, unlike that of San Francisco, seemed to be frozen against the snow-capped peaks of the Rocky Mountains, during the 1860s. Because of its isolation, the city stood still during the years of San Francisco's dynamic development. The topography favored expansion in several directions. A bluff along the west bank of the South Platte and a hilly range running from north to south toward Cherry Creek did not limit the spread of houses and factories, and the impact of an occasional disastrous flood was quickly overcome.[12] However, the inadequacy of trade routes or navigable rivers blocked Denver's development and checked its effectiveness as a center of transportation.

The city's stagnation sensitized Denverites to the potential of technological innovation as a way to break their isolation. In January 1862, William Gilpin, the governor of the Colorado territory, recommended to the Secretary of State, William Seward, that the Pacific Railway be built through central Colorado. He had spoken earlier of Denver as the natural focus of the territory between the Mississippi Valley and the Rocky Mountains and continued to insist that Denver would become the nation's next metropolis thriving on mines and railroads.[13] In May 1862, on his first evening in Denver, John Evans, the new territorial governor, assured residents assembled in front of his hotel that the Pacific Railway would become "the great commercial auxiliary" of the city.[14] Denverites waited anxiously for the railroad to finally reach their town.

Before a fraction of these visions materialized, the latest techniques of overland travel, ox team, stage, and railroad, were utilized to direct through Denver the travel of men and goods moving from the Missouri to the Rockies. During this period, the operation of Ben Holladay's Overland Stage Company marked the final phase of a competition between several stage lines for passengers and mail.[15] By 1865, however, the demise of the stage was in sight, with schedules and terminals constantly shifting to adjust to the westward advance of the railroad terminals. The anticipation of better connections by rail quickly turned the "magnificent Concord coach" into the "terrible rattling stage." [16] Wagon freighting, which managed, with luck, two round trips from Omaha to Denver in a season, declined also once the railroad became part of the tenuous transportation system in 1866. The Western Transportation Company claimed that wagons would now move from the steadily advancing western terminal of the Union Pacific to Denver, and from there to the gold fields of the Rocky Mountains.[17]

As residents of a landlocked town, limited to stage and wagon in their contact with the eastern centers of population and industry, Denverites took to proposed innovations in land transportations more eagerly than did the residents of a seaport, linked by steam and sail to the harbors of the world and a vast hinterland. The future of Denver hinged on an efficient transportation system with rail connections to both coasts. The city and the railroad complemented each other. Rivals of the Union Pacific, attempting to penetrate the Great Plains, looked to the city as the future site of a distribution center at the edge of the central Rocky Mountain mining district. Their work gained a sense of purpose from the existence of Denver. It was the focal point of a region where gangs of laborers could lay track anywhere without reaching anything but "the western border of the great plains which extend uninterruptedly from the Mississippi and Missouri Rivers." [18]

The business calculations of the Union Pacific shattered Denver's snug confidence in its destiny as the rail center of the continent. The railroad executives shunned the cost of building tracks across the Colorado mountains. They ran the transcontinental railroad through Wyoming, across the Laramie Range and westward, explaining to disappointed Denverites the engineering difficulties of constructing a railroad across the Central Range of the Rockies.[19] Only the resolute response of some of Denver's leading men, represented by John Evans, Walter S. Cheesman, and David H. Moffat, saved the city from oblivion. They built the Denver Pacific to the tracks of the Union Pacific at Cheyenne and managed to run the first train into the city in June 1870. Their dealings with the Kansas Pacific, which was building a line through Kansas parallel to the Union Pacific, ensured the arrival of the second railroad in August 1870. The success of the

Denver entrepreneurs brought the Colorado Central to terms. Its principals had attempted to bypass Denver and to link the mining districts directly to the Union Pacific, but in September 1870, they connected Denver with Golden, a gateway to the mines about fifteen miles west of the city.[20]

These lines removed Denver's handicap. In 1870, the city had overcome its isolation and secured the links of communication necessary for realizing the old Jacksonian dream of a commercial empire in the heart of the continent. Denver had acquired the three prerequisites for urban greatness and wealth set forth by Jacksonian men of enterprise: control of trade routes, flourishing commerce, and gold.[21] Although the total length of the roads built in Colorado during the initial stage of railroad construction was just under three hundred miles, the city had achieved connections to both coasts.[22]

In subsequent years, when powerful transcontinental companies competed for the lion's share of the Colorado traffic and the control of the territory in the north and the south, Denver felt the power of the railroads.[23] The competing giants blocked the construction of an independent rail outlet for Colorado that might have diverted commerce from the established East-West lines. As tight as their stranglehold was, they assured Denver's position as a center of communication in an intricate network of rails. The Colorado Central, the only line that continued to threaten the hegemony by attempting to tap the traffic to the mines directly, ultimately lost out in January 1880. The Union Pacific consolidated the Kansas Pacific and the Denver Pacific into one system and deprived the Colorado Central of an outlet to a major transcontinental line.[24]

The rail lines strengthened Denver's trade links with an expanding hinterland of mining camps. It enabled the city to find new markets when the gold excitement played havoc with the old ones. The rails carried bullion and ore, as well as new millionaires to the city after the discovery of silver at Leadville shook Colorado mining out of its stagnation, in the late 1870s. They contributed to the "Great Boom" in Denver history that widened the economic base from commerce to industry and increased the annual output of the city's manufacturers from $250,000 in 1870 to $50,000,000 in 1899. Trains changed the operation of the burgeoning farming and cattle industries, although cattle continued to follow the trails to market.[25]

Roughly a decade elapsed between the coming of the railroad and the beginnings of industrialization in Denver. Without the railroad industrialization would not have occurred, but with the railroad and with industrialization, Denver changed from instant to ordinary city. The railroad became the natural partner of commercial interests and fitted harmoniously into the context of an emporium. Yet, the prolonged crisis in Colorado mining, the hectic laying of tracks, the intense struggle between rival railroads, and the shifting alliances of the competing companies delayed the immediate identification of the railroad with industrialization. Only near the close of the 1870s, when new mineral wealth from Leadville poured into Denver, did such industries of mining as smelters and refineries gravitate with the help of the railroad to the city.

Smelters led the way. Coming just before and after the first great miners' strike in Colorado history, they relocated close to a source of laborers and shortened the expensive haul of coal and coke into the mountains. The first to come was the Black Hawk plant of the Boston and Colorado Smelting Company, which began operating in January 1879, on a tract of land two miles northeast of the city. In 1882, the consolidated Omaha and Grant Smelting Company erected its new plant in Denver after a fire had destroyed the entire works of the Grant Smelter in Leadville, described as "one of the greatest industrial institutions that has yet been founded at any point between the Missouri River and San Francisco." [26] Other industries came, including railroad shops, iron works, and planing mills, and turned Denver, in the language of the times, into

the diamond center around which the machinery of the whole state moves—the fulcrum on which the Archimedean progress of the day places its lever to raise into the full view of Christendom the most rapidly developed mineral wealth and attending gigantic enterprises that have ever had existence outside the realms of romance and fairy land.[27]

Measured against Denver's intimate involvement in the railroad age, San Francisco remained indifferent to the potential of new modes of transportation. The port flourished on maritime trade, and there seemed little incentive to court the railroad. The busy wharves established the city as the transit point between maritime commerce and river traffic. They facilitated the transfer of supplies and people from ocean vessels to river craft, light-draft steamboats and sailboats. The piers serviced the river system that fanned out from the bay into the Great Central Valley of California and penetrated the mining districts of the foothills via the tributaries of the Sacramento and the San Joaquin rivers. They accommodated most travelers to the towns around the shore of the bay and the interior ports of Marysville, Sacramento, and Stockton, save for overlanders from the Great Plains, Oregon, and Mexico.

When the extension of the tracks across the continent guaranteed the future of the projected Pacific Railway, San Franciscans intensified their search for industrial sites and housing in expectation of future economic booms and incoming multitudes, despite the fact the land lay on the tip of a peninsula where ship and train could meet only with difficulty. Doubts remained concerning San Francisco's potential as a terminus of the road, but the railway attracted the attention of many residents, not only the small circle of financiers and speculators. Politicians argued over how to adjust to the anticipated masses of newcomers and artists fell under the spell of an innovation that would bring closer the eastern centers of culture.[28]

Convinced that the railroad of the Sacramento entrepreneurs would be operating within a few years, San Franciscans took drastic measures to catch up with the development. They cut a wagon road through Rincon Hill, the elegant core of their urban world, and gained access to South Beach and the inlets and swamps south of that obstacle to intracity freighting. There they created, by fills and drainage, the level space suitable for railroad yards, machine shops, passenger stations, and housing. The area provided the only access for tracks into the city, and after the San Francisco and San Jose Railroad managed to enter the city there, entrepreneurs pressed for the development of this newly created space as industrial parks. Projected train ferries to Oakland held out the possibility of direct connection with the East Bay. Speculation about the location of the western terminus of the Pacific Railway ended when the Central Pacific built its station for the line that was working from Omaha to San Jose by September 1869, south of Rincon Hill.[29]

The logistics of transportation also finally pulled the railroad into San Francisco. The tribute the city paid for capturing the new advance in transportation seemed small. Rincon Hill was destroyed as the city's fashionable center. For the few who called the grading an act of vandalism, hundreds of others felt that the reckless attempt to accommodate the coming railroad marked them as advocates of progress.[30] The fundamental space problem of their city, intensified by the industrialism of the railroad age, determined the outlook of most San Franciscans. They considered it more meaningful to sacrifice a style of life and another hill than to pass up a unique opportunity to assure the city's future.[31]

The future, of course, meant San Francisco's existence as a regular city. The destruction, in the name of progress, of the Rincon Hill enclave presaged the reduction of San Francisco to an ordinary city under the influence of railroad and industry. The residents had seen water giving way to land, sand dunes to streets, and hills to space for houses and factories. Although they had made sacrifices regularly they now saw the new course mapped, and sanctioned, by the actions of the inhabitants of older cities in the East who were taking similar steps in attempts to capitalize on technological advancement.[32]

The railroad as reality contrasted sharply with the railroad as vision. The Central Pacific and, subsequently, the Southern Pacific virtually took over the city's land communication. Yet, the final stages of track laying, reducing the distance between the advancing railheads at about eight miles per day, roughly half of the daily rate of travel of an ox team, stimulated flights of fancy. A glorious ending to San Francisco's isolation seemed imminent, through a fusion of the emporium, linked to the harbors of the world, with the railroad bringing new men and opportunities for industrial development. Henry George could think of no other city in the world with equal advantages and considered San Francisco not merely *the* New York of the West, "but *the city,* . . . New York, Boston, Portland, Philadelphia, Richmond and Charleston . . . rolled into one." [33]

The impact of the railroad produced quite different results. Instead of *the* city, San Francisco became *a* city, like most other cities in the United States. Industrialization incorporated San Francisco into the urban network of the national market. In December 1871, the mayor of San Francisco assessed the new situation: "We are successfully rivaling older communities in many articles of home manufacture, and competing with them to supply the wants of the vast populations bordering on the Pacific." [34] Henry George's nostalgia for what was passing and his prophecies of future difficulties proved to be more accurate than his prediction of a unique future for the city. He sensed the closing of San Francisco's existence as instant city but he continued to project the characteristics of that passing phase into the future. However, he recognized that San Francisco as ordinary city would, increasingly, face the dilemma of urbanization without the benefit of constant change obscuring the consequences.

The rails forced San Francisco's pattern of life, the movement of people, and the flow of goods, into direct alignment with the pace-setting centers of economic development in the East. New methods of communication foreshadowed the transformation. The Pony Express and the Overland Telegraph prepared San Franciscans for the altered rhythm of life introduced by the timetable of the transcontinental railroad. Appropriately for a port, the first rider and his pony reached the city in April 1860, on the steamer from Sacramento, not unlike the first locomotives, which had come by sea a decade earlier.[35] From October 1861, telegraph messages went to New York at a rate of about 87 cents per word.[36] The steady ticking of the telegraph, accentuated by the arrival and departure of trains, replaced the gun that had once signaled the arrival of the Panama steamer and shaped the cycle of business transactions.[37]

The message of transformation reached into the hearts of the cities. In 1879, the Denver Postmaster instituted the free delivery of mail by carriers.[38] Newspapers and magazines pumped information into the arteries of San Francisco and Denver. Stimulated by new printing machinery and publishing techniques, they aggressively reached out to touch the man on the street and the woman at home. National scandals and local exposés captured the attention of masses of readers drawn to the new content, changed makeup, and increased size of newspapers. In 1876, the launching of the San Francisco *Wasp*, possibly the first American magazine to use "colored cartoons on an extensive scale over a substantial period of time," demonstrated the cities' movement into a period of "Yellow Journalism." [39] Sensationalism marked the pages of the San Francisco *Examiner*, the San Francisco *Chronicle*, and the Denver *Post*, as well. The popularity of the new press with readers who experienced the transition of their instant cities to ordinary cities was immense.[40]

Industrialization wrought changes in San Francisco and Denver that strongly affected the economy of both cities. Rails and factories brought outside influences to the scenes that replaced gold as the driving force in the society. These forces, however, responded directly to distant influences, minimizing the power of instant cities to control their futures. Industrialization broadened the economic base, providing alternate sources of growth for the city, but at the same time, ended the independence and creativity that have made the instant cities rise.

Real estate speculation reflected the widening opportunities in the city but, as well, added another type of schemer to the groups of men thriving on the cities' development. Industrialization replaced the old-time investors, who bought a lot at market price and held it in anticipation of an increase in value, with a new type of manipulator of the urban environment. These new businessmen ingeniously exploited public projects. Two such projects were the San Francisco City Hall and the Denver Mining and Industrial Exposition of 1882.

By raising $25,000 for the purpose of lobbying in Sacramento in the winter of 1869, these real estate men secured the passage of a bill in the California legislature moving the city hall from its then central location to the outskirts of town. The new site was adjacent to their own land holdings. Quickly, they were caught in the crosscurrents of several other real estate operations stimulated by the coming railroad, and little came of the project. More than twenty years later, the steady expenditure of public funds for construction of the city hall finally brought about its completion.[41] The success which that daring speculation once guaranteed the San Francisco entrepreneur, however, was no longer so sure.

In Denver, the location of the Exposition building three miles south of the city center served the real estate schemes of some of the show's managers. They controlled the Denver Circle Railroad, as well as the *Rocky Mountain News*, and effectively disguised their real interest in the exposition area behind the lively competition for passenger traffic from downtown to the fair. Opponents of the southerly location insinuated that the idea of an exposition was nothing but a land scheme of the Denver Circle Real Estate Company. They suspected that the Circle Railroad would do little more than talk about a rail system encircling the city, and their hunch proved to be correct. The Highland Park Company, which hoped to promote a suburb across the South Platte, offered free space for a fairground northwest of the downtown business district, "within a mile and a quarter from the Tabor block." [42] The Denver Circle Railroad won out, however, and the revenue they received from passenger service was merely a bonus over and above the profits from the sale of real estate adjacent to the exposition.[43]

Because of the fair, real estate values rose in the entire city, but it doubled and trebled in the vicinity of the exposition. "A city has been planted" on the barren prairie between Denver and the exposition grounds, "that will grow with each succeeding day," a reporter predicted, "until the line of demarcation between Denver proper and this appendage has been wholly dissipated." Only a few squatter cabins remained to suggest the days when the haphazard movement of prairie schooners across the plains barely sustained urban life.[44]

The forces of industrialization provided the momentum for San Francisco and Denver to develop long after the urban explosions that produced the instant cities had spent themselves. Now they drew newcomers to the cities and linked old and new residents through an improved technology of communication. Within a few years, the up-to-date Eastern forms of urban transportation appeared in San Francisco and Denver. They quickly replaced the omnibus, a horse-drawn compromise between the long-distance stage and the hackney, which still represented an advance to residents who could not afford to hire horses and carriages from livery stables.[45] In the 1850s, in the cities of the Atlantic seaboard, the omnibus was universally despised because the intolerably narrow roads within the core of these cities discouraged omnibus traffic. But the streets of San Francisco and Denver had always been thronged with people and, consequently, had been laid out more spaciously. The omnibus, however, soon gave way to better means of travel.

The street railway appeared almost simultaneously in San Francisco and the major eastern cities. New York City had experimented with the first horse-drawn streetcars in 1832, but the national streetcar vogue did not occur until the late 1850s. The pioneer lines of Boston began operation in 1856, and those in Philadelphia, Baltimore, Chicago, Cincinnati, Pittsburgh, and St. Louis in 1859 and 1860.[46] In the latter year, similar horse-drawn streetcars also ran in San Francisco, under a franchise granted by the California legislature in 1857.[47] In the 1870s, San Franciscans ranked the "modern horse car" as one of "the most indispensable conditions of modern metropolitan growth," and promoters credited the life style that enabled "laborers and the poorer classes" to live in "sunny suburban homes" to "plenty of horse cars and low fares." [48]

Whereas improved transportation in San Francisco of the 1870s rapidly undermined the physical cohesion the city had achieved and created a new urban interest in the "ultimate limit of suburban growth," the pull of the horse-car in Denver was still to the center.[49] Although Denver's topography did not impede travel, it offered few natural impediments along which vital transport routes could be determined. The operators of street railways shared the dilemma of the real estate speculators who saw infinite possibilities for residential subdivisions but lacked customers attracted to the wide open prairies of buffalo grass. Instead of people in suburban homes, the prairies pastured the cows of the "day herds" taken from, and returned to, their city sheds by "third-rate cowboys" or by a real cowpuncher who wanted a fling at "the delights of the city." [50]

With cows running at large in Denver in the early 1870s, and ample room for newcomers in the city, the horse-car facilitated urbanization more than it promoted urban expansion. In 1873, after the first horse-car line had operated for two years, a second route was built along Fifteenth Street, across the South Platte, to North Denver, but any hope that the service would accelerate the growth of the suburb came to nothing.[51] The horse-cars gave "value to outside property," enabled "men of small means" to live on the outskirts of town, and contributed to the "prosperity of the city," mostly by impressing visitors doubtful of Denver's claim to metropolitan status. With horse-cars, Denver had a genuine right "to a place among cities of the first class, East or West." [52]

The topography of San Francisco and Denver decisively influenced the kinds of new developments each city contributed to the technology of transportation. The hills of San Francisco stimulated experiments with a car pulled by a cable. The vast expanse of the Denver prairies drew the attention of Denverites to the varied uses of electricity. In the early 1880s, Denverites put up three 200-foot frame towers that shed "their beams of light far and wide over the suburbs" from the edge of the business district.[53]

In San Francisco, a city ordinance prohibiting the use of steam dummies to pull passenger cars after 1868 left the railway companies with the horse as the only motor power at a time when the expansion of the city into the hills placed obstacles in the way of horse-drawn streetcars.[54] Witnessing the "difficulty and pain" with which the horses hauled these cars up the hills, Andrew Smith Hallidie was stimulated to perfect the cable car. A manufacturer of wire cable, he had installed tramways in mines to move ore buckets across ravines and up and down steep slopes. In 1873, he operated the Clay Street Hill Railroad Company, but it took nine years for him to overcome widespread national resistance to his cable car system, which was considered a special San Francisco success story, made possible by straight streets, extreme grades, and the mild climate.[55]

Ultimately, national acceptance did come as the only alternative, the horse, was no match for the cable car. Most large cities had banned the dirty and noisy steam dummies; compressed-air and battery cars were limited in range and speed, and the electric car was still rudimentary and untested. By the 1880s, experimentation had improved the cable car so that it could negotiate the unusual right-angle curves of horse-car lines. The Chicago City Railway installed cable car traction on the city's south side and demonstrated that the system could work in a severe climate, with many pull curves and no grade, and that it moved people at about half the cost of horse-cars and double the speed. These results finally assured the general popularity of the cable car.[56]

Denver turned to the cable car only after an electric line proved to be too costly. Their experiments with a conduit electric streetcar during the mid-1880s reflected the city's fascination with electricity and its association of urban greatness with technical ingenuity. The preoccupation dated back to July 1862, when a steam wagon, constructed in New York and assembled in Nebraska City, attempted to cross the Great Plains. The wagon, a combination of locomotive and automobile rolled nine miles in the direction of Denver under its own power before a broken crank scuttled the dream of overland steam wagons on trails.[57]

Denver's electric street car operated on a three-thousand-foot track. Its motor was invented by Sidney H. Short, Professor of Physics at the University of Denver. The car received power through a mid-track slot, instead of an overhead wire.[58] One of the Denverites who crowded the sidewalks on Fifteenth Street in July 1886, considered it "one of the most laughable and . . . thrilling experiences" of his life.[59] Others stretched the facts slightly in favor of their city and boasted of having "the second electric streetcar service in the world." [60]

Although electricity as a source of energy captivated the imagination of Denverites in the 1880s, little came of Short's electric streetcar.[61] Denverites lacked the patience to iron out the technical and legal difficulties and, within a few years, the innovation was abandoned. The residents of the expanding city wanted better transportation immediately, and the cable car, now universally acclaimed, seemed a quick answer to the problem. In December 1888, Denver returned to cable traction and at the end of the decade constructed a two-storey power house, the "largest single street-car cable plant in the world." [62]

Another electrical innovation, the telephone, conquered Denver in 1879, a year before it reached San Francisco.[63] The opening of the first telephone exchange not only brought about an improved system of communication but changed the physical appearance of the city dramatically. During the thirty years of its lifetime the city had taken on a certain look. Many changes had altered this look—the row of shanties had given way to the business block, paved streets had slowly replaced the boarded sidewalk, the open ditch, and the muddy or dusty road and the five-storey Windsor Hotel and the six-storey Tabor Block altered somewhat the city's skyline, but none of these improvements had the overall impact of the sudden addition of the accoutrements of telephone service.

After home owners objected to running lines across the roofs of their buildings, telephone poles and wires invaded downtown streets and alleys. Some poles, with as many as twenty-four cross arms, made "a veritable forest of wires, 240 in number, on the principal streets." [64] Plenty of fine spruce came from nearby mountains, and symmetrical poles could, by splicing, be extended to a length of ninety feet. Telephone men were proud of the imposing appearance of these wired masts, but the poles rising on the sidewalks and the wires extending along and across the downtown streets cut into the inconography of the city. The new setting appeared as distant from

the familiar urban sight as the pole from the live spruce on the slopes
of the mountains.

The maze of wires and the forest of poles, a San Francisco paper
reported in 1882, disfigured the streets.[65] They transformed the
instant cities in a far different way than had the carriages, hacks, and
trains. Omnibuses, horse-cars, and cable cars were all variations of
modes of transportation that in one shape or another had been
present ever since the first ship reached San Francisco's wharves or
the first ox carts Denver's Elephant Corral, the large campsite of
early travelers at Fifteenth and Blake.[66] The telephone apparatus
was completely new to the urban scene. The long poles and the web
of wires stood not only between people and their urban environment
but also between one man and his neighbor. Initially, subscribers
asked for connections by name, but "after much effort" they were
"trained to call by numbers." [67]

Telephone service not only facilitated human contact but also
heightened the anonymity of life in instant cities. It severed the
vestiges of common bonds that had once been necessary for the
common welfare. These links, now often only sentimental bonds, had
endured despite the differences that soon began to separate people.
In the urban centers on the Atlantic seaboard, the introduction of the
telephone with the practice of identifying people by numbers simply
intensified the evolving anonymity of urban life. In the instant cities,
the rapid advances of technology reinforced social dividing lines that
eliminated the treasured appearances of egalitarian days when
miners hailed a Comstock or a Leadville millionaire by his first name.

Despite the consequences, San Franciscans and Denverites were
dependent upon advances in communications and transportation
technology for continued urban development. The railroad and
telegraph brought the cities into the national market. Sensational
newspapers and magazines carried the affairs of the world to every
street corner. New industry intensified the pace of urbanization and
reduced the frontier qualities of San Francisco and Denver by
linking them to manufacturing centers as well as to new markets in
their territories. The steady introduction of innovations stimulated

the flow of people, goods, and ideas. Every step, however, diminished the unique characteristics of the instant cities and made them more and more like cities in general.

The impact of the intensified technology ended the wilderness isolation. The remaining blank spots on the maps of the Far West began to disappear as the residents began trading information flowing in from the surrounding countryside into the cities in exchange for investment capital from the Eastern centers of finance. The forces of industrialism now furnished the momentum initially engendered by gold and the masses of people who spawned the instant cities. Manufacturing produced the legions of steady workers unavailable to early entrepreneurs. Transportation reduced strange cities to familiar points in an urban network. Once cities of drifters and strangers, Denver and San Francisco became cities of rooted men and women, who patterned their actions after the national way of life, because of the impact of technology and communications.[68]

The general process of industrialization now provided the stimulus for gradual growth. The powerful routine of industrial discipline and the painstaking cost accounting of managerial bureaucracy reduced most speculation to plain folly. In 1906, speculative capital, a significant item in the rise of San Francisco, no longer constituted an "important factor in the classification of local capital." [69] Regularity bred uniformity and stripped chance of its power to make and break cities and set the tone for the hectic tempo of life. Thus, the cities of change and chance were transformed into ordinary cities.

Under the impact of improved technology, the cities outgrew their strangeness and became carbon copies of eastern norms. They replaced insecurity, heightened by remoteness and chance, with the regularity of life molded by intensified communication, transportation, and routine. The anonymity of the new industrial society merely intensified the tendency of the residents to divide up among themselves and separate themselves from their urban creations. The technology of communication brought San Franciscans and Denverites closer together only to draw them further apart. It linked them closer to cities, but reduced the intimacy of the contact. The innovations, symbolized by the forest of telephone poles and wires, cut the residents off from the landscape of the cities just when the cities' amorphous contours seemed to have been gaining definition. The street railways facilitated the flight into the suburbs that reduced the cities to factories of work and leisure and asylums of the poor.

Ironically, the transformation wrought by technology allowed San Franciscans and Denverites, now residents of ordinary cities, only a brief respite from living with chance and change. The appearance of the automobile sealed the disintegration of all cities built around social, political, economic, and cultural centers. Neither Denver nor San Francisco escaped the onslaught. A diarist recorded in May 1899, that he ran an "electric carriage on the streets of Denver." [70] Although the president of the Automobile Club of California considered the topography of San Francisco "peculiarly unfavorable to the use of the automobile," and the streets "hilly or poorly paved, or both," the impact of this innovation began to overwhelm that city, too.[71]

The automobile would hasten the urbanization of the countryside and obliterate many distinctions between city and country. More decisively than railroad and streetcar, it reversed the process of urbanization that, within memory of San Franciscans and Denverites, triumphed in the spectacular transformation of wilderness into cities within a generation. The citizens of these two ordinary cities soon faced the need to adjust to a new trend in Western civilization channeling the residents into suburbia. Abrogating a tradition centuries old, the development would undo the process of city-building that just a few years before, almost overnight, produced San Francisco and Denver.

# Epilogue
# A Measure of Man

The transformation of San Francisco and Denver into ordinary cities assured their importance in the chain of instant cities that spans the history of Western man. For more than two thousand years, there have been examples of instant cities, sprouting periodically throughout a protracted development that has slowly concentrated the majority of people in metropolitan centers. The explosive rise and development of these special cities compressed urban realization into one generation. During that short span of years, those features of city life that generally lost contour and color by prolonged exposure to time burned like Roman candles, intense and dynamic, casting light not only on the role of man in what appeared as nature's handiwork but also on the role of chance in the design of man and in the work of nature.

The metamorphoses of San Francisco and Denver capped a phase of urbanization that produced, on a smaller scale, other instant cities on the plains, in the mountains, and along the coast of the Pacific. Yet many a budding settlement that held the promise of becoming another instant city ended up as another ghost town. Most rival cities lacked the ferocious outbursts of energy that marked the California and Colorado gold rushes and the expansion of the economic base that gave permanence to San Francisco and Denver.

The meteoric rise of San Francisco and Denver stood in striking contrast to the measured beat of life in those settlements that dotted the Far West before the momentous changes stimulated by the Mexican War, the Oregon Treaty, and the California Gold Rush prepared the ground for the emergence of instant cities. Their ways were steeped in tradition and custom. The economic town, the colonial outpost, and the market place seemed to be as ancient as mountain, ocean, and valley, the three elements that provided these types of settlements their kinship with nature. Represented by Santa Fe in New Mexico, Monterey in California, and Champoeg in Oregon, they defied innovations and absorbed change that stimulated the frenzied pulse of the instant cities.

The instant cities produced by gold and sustained by commerce and industry also differed sharply from a variant of the type that emerged in the heart of the Western mountains in 1847: Salt Lake City, the temple city. The earthly center of the Church of Jesus Christ of Latter-day Saints rose because of the Mormon Exodus from Illinois. The Mormons' urban experiment gave form to their religious ideal of a city sheltering a temple. The Saints strove to protect Zion in the Mountains from the influence of Babylon with religious sanction, social and political control as well as economic and urban planning. They assured the future of their temple city through a religious zeal that contrasted with the worldly passion that propelled the other instant cities.

San Francisco and Denver lacked purity, but the residents' greed was not the only reason for its absence. Few restraints governed the hectic interplay of social, economic, political, and cultural forces shaping these cities. The intensified technology quickly overcame the limits set by topography and isolation. The ordering hand of government was weak, and the residents did little to strengthen it. The builders of San Francisco and Denver cherished individual freedom and personal dignity more highly than the advantages of planned order. They recognized the ease with which planned order becomes threatened coercion in societies like their own that knew no way to shield the dissident. They avoided inertia by dedicating themselves wholeheartedly to the spirit of the age that equated progress with more inhabitants, taller buildings, faster streetcars, and bigger stores. Their attitude generated the anarchy of urban development that set San Francisco and Denver apart from other instant cities created centuries earlier by mining and commerce, or the Alexandrias of urban history that owed their existence to an emperor's command.

The interaction of human and material influences, generously riddled by accident, accounted for the distinct styles of San Francisco and Denver. They exhibited urbanization in the raw, untouched by the intricate rules and practices of feudal Europe that governed the mining towns and commercial centers of the Late Middle Ages. Time and location were important factors buttressing this uniqueness. But they were not the sole factors propelling those who conquered the Far West, terminated the wilderness isolation, and appropriated the spoils. The instant cities emerged in the United States at a time when Americans knew how to move their civilization across the continent. They were built by people who considered the exploitation of natural resources their divined task, viewed government as a benevolent uncle of the enterprise, and relied on spectacular technological advances to overcome the obstacles provided by man and nature. The urban explosions were triggered by vast deposits of gold and silver that had long been there but were mined only when man and his technology were ready to seize them.

San Francisco and Denver emerged at roughly the same time. Both were cities of the Far West. These links of chronology and geography allowed viewing them as variants of a type without ignoring those elements of each city's identity. San Francisco and Denver, like most cities, differed from one another, but the design of instant cities that employed both cities as a specific form of the type was distinctive enough to protect their individuality.

Many superficial differences separated a seaport linked to the harbors of the world from a landlocked town. They looked different, attracted different people, and developed different industries. They were similar in essence, but unaware of their similarity. Their residents showed little recognition that they lived in cities intimately related to one another. The local scene was powerful, and when they tried to compare their cities with others, San Franciscans selected Melbourne and Sydney and Denverites chose Kansas City and Chicago.

Despite their differences, however, San Francisco and Denver shared sufficient characteristics to make them a distinct variant of that specific class of cities, the instant cities. Both rose within a generation from wilderness to city, unencumbered by legal restrictions, political dictates, or cultural conventions. Gold begot them, and the lure of riches attracted strangers who learned to live with one another and the frantic pace of development that marked their cities. Their style of life served the moment and vanished. Technological advancement crowned their accomplishments, relieved the isolation, and drew them into the circle of ordinary cities, but even in their glory, San Francisco and Denver were cities marked by the sadness of human suffering, paid by many for their cities' greatness.

As instant cities, San Francisco and Denver distilled the problems of urbanization. In the age of the city in the United States, they concentrated a global dilemma into isolated local settings. Their struggle became a measure of man. Their residents, made up of the odds and ends of creation, asserted their common humanity by rising above city, as well as wilderness. They endeavored to solve ageless problems of cities in their own small ways by living, day by day, with change and chance, and in the course of it they endured the strains of accelerated urbanization. Their stamina rivaled the magnitude of the cities they built.

# Sources

There is a tremendous amount of material on nineteenth-century San Francisco and Denver. A great portion of it documents the concept of the instant city, and a meaningful bibliography is therefore difficult to compile. Instead, a few comments on the kind of sources I used frequently may suggest the range of the evidence. Consequently, this is not an exhaustive bibliography, not even a discussion of all items cited in the notes, but an attempt to present groups of documents and to delineate their role in the investigation.

All this suggests that conventional bibliographical listings do not make much sense in my case, and I begin with newspapers, the backbone of the study, rather than manuscripts or public documents. Newspapers mirrored the explosive rise of the cities; they had their ups and downs, too, but they provided a convenient journal of the urban life of the first generation because their moderate size still allowed them to be read. Two covered almost the entire span of time, the San Francisco *Alta California* (1849–91) and the Denver *Rocky Mountain News* (1859–    ). For diverse coverage, as well as for very practical reasons, I delved into other newspapers, too. The *Alta* started its long decline early in the 1860s, and I relied mostly on the San Francisco *Call* (1856–1929) for the 1870s, on the *Call* and the

San Francisco *Chronicle* (1865–   ) for the 1880s, and again on the *Call* for most of the 1890s. I made that last switch because of a good *Call Index* . . . (San Francisco, 1905) that covers the decade between 1894 and 1904. The microfilm of the *News* at my disposal was incomplete, and at times an extremely poor copy of a defective original. I filled gaps with the Denver *Tribune* (1871–1913) and the Denver *Republican* (1876–1913).

The newspapers furnished a wealth of information on San Francisco and Denver life. Four examples will illustrate the range of the reporting which ran the gamut from urban poverty ("Trying Tramping," San Francisco *Daily Evening Post*, Aug. 3, 6, 8, 10, 16, 20, 24, Oct. 12, 1878) to urban wealth (Luke North, "The Richest Man of the World; A Tale of Primitive San Francisco," *Call*, July 23, 1893), from a perceptive self-assessment ("The Ducal Ball," *Rocky Mountain News*, Jan. 19, 1872) to a charitable portrayal of others ("His Crowning Ovation," *Republican*, May 13, 1891).

For the coverage of the 1870s, 1880s, and 1890s weeklies helped to reduce the sheer amount of newsprint. In the case of Denver I did not find a shortcut, although I profited from the *Inter-Ocean* (1880–83), not to be confused with the Chicago publication, and the *Colorado Exchange Journal* (1887–91). For San Francisco I used the *News Letter and California Advertiser* (1856–1928) as an elaborate index to the dailies. The *News Letter* itself offers an inexhaustible supply of information on urban life in the form of commentaries, journals, biographies, and columns on the stage and on architecture. These reams of jottings provide an immediacy that does not come from literary journals. The outstanding example is the *Overland Monthly*, published in San Francisco from 1868 to 1875, as *Californian* from 1880 to 1882, and again under the original title from 1883 to 1935. The San Francisco *Wasp* (1870–1935) is in a league by itself on account of its inspired colored cartoons.

The manuscripts of the 1870 Census and the 1880 Census, of population as well as of industries, provide bench marks for the chaotic life detailed in the dailies. Initially, I read the microfilm of the population census simply to strengthen my contact with the people who made up the cities, very much as a musician reads a score without touching an instrument. Later I went back to resolve questions that came up, such as the specific composition of a ward, but I never played the entire score on that instrument called quantitative analysis because I needed not a greater wealth of details but rather clues to their meaning.

Clues came from five categories of sources: observations, chronicles, commentaries, public documents, and belles-lettres. The vague term, observations, circumscribes the mountain of letters, journals, travelogues, and reminiscences. Frequently this material harbors seemingly unconnected facts. A few travelers buried perceptive utterances in a mass of trivia. They are represented by Ida Pfeiffer, . . . *Journey* . . . (London, 1855), with her California experience reprinted by Joseph A. Sullivan (ed.), . . . *Visit* . . . (Oakland, 1950); Edwin S. Morby (trans. and ed.), *Guillermo Prieto* . . . (San Francisco, 1938); Isabella L. Bird Bishop, *Lady's Life* . . . (Norman, 1960); and the "Diary of Rezin H. Constant," *Colorado Magazine* XII (May 1935): 103–16. Keen observations, or well-rounded scenes, characterized George P. Hammond (ed.), *Larkin Papers* . . . (Berkeley, 1951–68); Bayard Taylor, *El Dorado* . . . (New York, 1850); Peter H. Burnett, *Recollections* . . . (New York, 1880); James D. Hart (ed.), *From Scotland* . . . *By Robert Louis Stevenson* (Cambridge, 1966); and Milo Milton Quaife (ed.), *Uncle Dick Wootton* . . . (Chicago, 1957). Their quality is epitomized by the three classic commentaries on early Denver in LeRoy R. Hafen (ed.), . . . *Pike's Peak* . . . *By Henry Villard* (Princeton, 1932); Horace Greeley, *Overland Journey* . . . (New York, 1860); and Albert D. Richardson, *Beyond the Mississippi* . . . (Hartford, 1867).

An intimate connection to the journalism of the day characterizes the chronicles; they reflect early attempts to come to grips with detail. Frank Soulé, John G. Gihon, and James Nesbit, . . . *Annals* . . . (New York, 1855); John W. Dwinelle (ed.), . . . *Colonial History* . . . (San Francisco, 1863); Junius E. Wharton, . . . *Denver* . . . (Denver, 1866); John S. Hittell, . . . *San Francisco* . . . (San Francisco, 1878); and W. B. Vickers, . . . *Denver* . . . (Chicago,

1880), put facts into order. The text sections of the early city directories detail physical changes. The various editions of Hittell, *Resources* . . . (San Francisco, 1863); Frank Fossett, . . . *Colorado* . . . (New York, 1879); and George A. Crofutt, . . . *Guide of Colorado* . . . (Omaha, 1881); are running commentaries on the hectic development. Other valuable sources, made up of compilations from the daily papers, were such publications as *A "Pile"* . . . (San Francisco, 1851); *Commercial Herald . . . for . . . 1876* (San Francisco, 1877); and *Rocky Mountain News Illustrated Almanac* . . . (Denver, 1882). Among the many guides to the cities, Frank S. Woodbury, . . . *Denver* . . . (Denver, 1882), well depicts Denver's Great Boom.

A variety of documents ranging from titillating exposés to philosophical speculations threw the data into bold relief. Benjamin E. Lloyd, . . . *San Francisco* . . . (San Francisco, 1876), and G. N. Scamehorn, . . . *Denver* . . . (Denver, 1894), painted most things black and white. James Gilroy, . . . *Stock Market* . . . (San Francisco, 1879), and James McCarthy, *Political Portraits* . . . (Colorado Springs, 1888), concentrated well on specifics. On account of the excellence or their scope, the numerous writings of William Gilpin and Henry George dominate similar efforts. A speech by Gilpin, *Notes* . . . (London, 1870), and an article by George, ". . . Railroad . . . ," *Overland Monthly* I (October 1868): 297–306, stress the relationship between people, technology, and environment.

Among the public documents, the annual publication of the San Francisco Board of Supervisors, *Municipal Reports* (1859–1917), stand out. From the assessor to the treasurer, the *Reports* cover the activities of most officials, and their appendices are fonts of such abstruse information as the content of a leaden casket placed into the base of the Benjamin Franklin Fountain, *ibid., 1881*, Appendix, 262. Among the state documents, the reports of the bureaus of labor statistics are useful indices of life, first published as *First Biennial Report . . . 1883–84* (Sacramento, 1884), and *First Biennial Report . . . 1887–1888* (Denver, 1888). In the case of Denver, the hearings on voting frauds, published with the *Joint Session Journal* of the Colorado General Assembly, 15th sess., 1905, as part of the contested gubernatorial election of 1904, document political practices. The entries on both cities in John S. Billings (comp.), . . . *Vital and Social Statistics . . . Part II . . .* (Washington, 1896), 219, 334, contain only the most perfunctory information and enhance the importance of the various federal publications that came out of the census.

Belles-lettres provide well-turned phrases coined by well-known writers. However, sweeping panoramas of the internal conditions of the social milieu are scarce. Frank Norris, *McTeague* . . . (New York, 1899), is one exception. Ambrose Bierce's contribution, his running commentaries on the scene in his column in the *News Letter* (1868–72), the San Francisco *Argonaut* (1877–79), the *Wasp* (1881–86), and the San Francisco *Examiner* (1887–99), seem to tell more about Bierce than about San Francisco. The same goes for Eugene Field's comparatively brief activities in Denver. Literary ambitions were strong, but provided fewer insights than newspaper reports. A few isolated stories in local magazines, such as James F. Watkins, "San Francisco," *Overland Monthly* IV (January 1870): 9–23, and a few novels, such as Mary Hallock Foote's story of Leadville silver mining, *The Led-Horse Claim* (Boston, 1882), touch on aspects of social life. I found a wealth of information in the photographs of the cities and much less in the lithographs and etchings that had first directed my attention to the sites.

There is, finally, one important source I drew from continually: the cities. Walking the downtown streets of the 1960s and 1970s, I detected most where I saw least. In San Francisco, a skyscraper has replaced the asphalt of a parking lot at the site of the Montgomery Block, one of the earliest landmarks and one of the last to fall. In Denver, the corner of Larimer and Eighteenth partly repeated the experience, with the asphalt of another parking lot marking the site of the Windsor Hotel, pride of the nineteenth-century city. In the shadows of the abutments of the Bay Bridge, I still found traces of the South Park that Bret Harte's poem evoked and on the left bank of Cherry Creek, Auraria appeared briefly like the Museum's Model.

Beyond fire and man, the tearing down and building up revealed the fierce energies stimulating the cities' constant changes, and the people enduring all.

The theme of change, in the distance of time and geography, spoke also from medieval fairy tales and chronicles. Articles in *Forschungen zur deutschen Landes- und Volkskunde*, in *Neues Archiv für Sächsische Geschichte und Altertumskunde*, and in *Mitteilungen des Vereins für die Geschichte der Deutschen in Böhmen* sharpened my awareness of what to look for. Two stupendous works were invaluable. Paulus Niavis, *Iudicium Iovis* . . . (Berlin, 1953), translated into German and edited by Paul Krenkel, in a medieval Latin poem spelled out the familiar maxim of San Francisco and Denver, "It takes a mine to run a mine." Georgius Agricola, *De Re Metallica* . . . (New York, 1950), translated into English by Herbert Clark Hoover and Lou Henry Hoover, guided me through some of the mining rushes of the Middle Ages.

The immediate context in which San Francisco and Denver rose gained focus from the comments of journals and travelogues on the temple city (Salt Lake City), the economic town (Santa Fe), the colonial outpost (Monterey), and the marketplace (Champoeg). In particular, John Williams Gunnison, *Mormons* . . . (Philadelphia, 1852); James B. Thayer, *Western Journey* . . . (Boston, 1884); Josiah Quincy, *Figures* . . . (Boston, 1883); Fawn M. Brodie (ed.), *City of the Saints* . . . *By Richard F. Burton* (New York, 1963); and Jules Remy and Julius Brenchley, *Journey* . . . (London, 1861), threw light on the Mormon urban experiments. LeRoy R. Hafen (ed.), *Ruxton* . . . (Norman, 1950); Robert A. Griffen (ed.), *My Life* . . . *By David Meriwether* (Norman, 1965); and William Watts Hart Davis, *El Gringo* . . . (New York, 1857); offered hints for the transformation of Santa Fe. Crucial leads to Monterey's unique role came from Mariano G. Vallejo, *Ecspocisión* . . . (Sonoma, Aug. 17, 1837); George Simpson, *Overland Journey* . . . (Philadelphia, 1847); Harold A. Small (ed.), *Seventy-five Years* . . . *By William Heath Davis* (San Francisco, 1967); and Walter Colton, *Three Years* . . . (New York, 1850). The three series of the *Letters of John McLoughlin* . . .

(Toronto, 1941–44), edited by E. E. Rich, the "Memorial of William A. Slacum," 25 Cong., 2 Sess., *Sen. Ex. Doc. No. 24*, I, 1–31, reprinted in the *Oregon Historical Quarterly* XIII (June 1912): 175–224; Charles Wilkes, *Narrative* . . . (Philadelphia, 1845); F. G. Young (ed.), *Correspondence . . . of . . . Nathaniel J. Wyeth* (Eugene, 1899); and the three installments of the "Diary of . . . Jason Lee," *Oregon Historical Quarterly* XVII (June, September, December, 1916): 116–46, 240–66, 397–430; alerted me to the position of Champoeg in the Oregon Country. Margaret Jewett Bailey, *The Grains* . . . (Portland, 1854), added dimensions to the life of pioneers.

Some of the epics of the wilderness, Washington Irving, *Astoria* . . . (New York, 1836); Josiah Gregg, *Commerce* . . . (New York 1844); and Francis Parkman's *Journals* . . . (New York, 1947), edited by Mason Wade, stimulated a realization of the distinct settings of San Francisco and Denver. Charles M. Clark, *Trip to Pike's Peak* . . . (Chicago, 1861); Ovando J. Hollister, *Mines* . . . (Springfield, 1867); Margaret I. Carrington, *Ab-Sa-Ra-Ka* . . . (Philadelphia, 1868); and the testimony before the military commission investigating the "Sand Creek Massacre," 39 Cong., 2 Sess., *Senate Ex. Doc. No. 26*, 1–228; in various ways revealed the clash between white and Indian civilization along the South Platte. Several collections of documents edited by LeRoy R. Hafen, *Colorado Gold Rush* . . . (Glendale, 1941); *Reports from Colorado* . . . (Glendale, 1961); and Hafen and Ann W. Hafen (eds.), *Relations with the Indians* . . . (Glendale, 1959); provided perspective. A specific Eastern touch came from Libeus Barney, *Letters* . . . (San Jose, 1959), and Agnes Wright Spring (ed.), "Nathaniel P. Hill . . . ," *Colorado Magazine* XXXIII (October 1956): 241–76. My understanding of the attitude of Americans in Mexican California gained from John C. Ewers (ed.), . . . *Zenas Leonard* (Norman, 1959); Edwin Bryant, *What I Saw* . . . (Santa Ana, California, 1936); and Richard Henry Dana, Jr., *Two Years* . . . (New York, 1936). Shrewd observations on conditions in early San Francisco appear in William T. Sherman, *Memoirs* . . . (Bloomington, 1957); John Henry Brown, *Early Days* . . .

(Oakland, 1949); J. L. Ver Mehr, ". . . Argonauts . . . ," *Overland Monthly* X (May, June, 1873): 434–43, 546–64; and James C. Ward, ". . . Diary . . . ," *Argonaut* III (Aug. 3, 10, 17, 24, 31, Sept. 7, 14, 21, 28, Oct. 5, 1878).

Two monuments of scholarship tower over the secondary materials, the pertinent volumes of Hubert Howe Bancroft, *Works* (San Francisco, 1883–91), and Lewis Mumford, *City in History* . . . (New York, 1961). Although I made a different road than the turnpikes laid out by these master builders, the building stones they gathered helped me on many occasions. Jakob Seibert, *Metropolis und Apoikie* . . . (Würzburg, 1963); Victor Tcherikover, *Die Hellenistischen Städtegründungen* . . . (Leipzig, 1927); William Reuben Farmer, *Maccabees* . . . (New York, 1956); Emel Esin, *Mecca* . . . (London, 1963); Norman Cohn, . . . *Millennium* (Fair Lawn, New Jersey, 1957); George Huntston Williams, *Radical Reformation* . . . (Philadelphia, 1962); and Howard Kaminsky, . . . *Hussite Revolution* (Berkeley, 1967); furnished important links for the chain of instant cities and temple cities.

Details for the discussion of the commercial ventures and mining rushes accompanying the Western European expansion into Central Europe came from the magisterial work of Edith Ennen, *Frühgeschichte* . . . (Bonn, 1953); Walter Kuhn, . . . *Ostsiedlung* . . . (Cologne, 1955); and Joachim Herrmann (ed.), *Die Slawen* . . . *Ein Handbuch* (Berlin, 1970). John U. Nef, "Mining . . . ," in the second volume of the *Cambridge Economic History*, and Otto Hue, *Die Bergarbeiter* . . . (Stuttgart, 1910), provided perspective for the mining rushes of the Middle Ages. Although various studies of the *Freiberger Forschungshefte* covered the ground well, Gustav Eduard Benseler, *Geschichte Freibergs* . . . (Freiberg, 1853), and Carl Friedrich Mosch, *Zur Geschichte des Bergbaues* . . . (Liegnitz, 1829), are still rich in detail. Lesley Byrd Simpson, Gordon Griffiths, and Woodrow Borah, "Representative Institutions. . . ," *The Americas* XII (January 1956): 223–57, isolate elements essential in the movement of Spanish cities across the Atlantic. For the English colonies in North America, the works of Carl Bridenbaugh, especially

*Cities in the Wilderness* . . . (New York, 1938), and *Cities in Revolt* . . . (New York, 1955); and for the early national period, Richard C. Wade, *Urban Frontier* . . . (Cambridge, 1959), are milestones of scholarship.

Leads to the relationship between the Mormon urban experiments and the theology of the Church of Jesus Christ of Latter-day Saints become particularly clear in studies on the Mormons in Illinois: Brigham Henry Roberts, . . . *Nauvoo* (Salt Lake City, 1900); Robert Bruce Flanders, *Nauvoo* . . . (Urbana, 1965); and in an issue devoted to the subject by *Dialogue* V (Spring 1970): edited by Stanley B. Kimball. Whitney R. Cross, *Burned-over District* . . . (New York, 1950), establishes the setting in upstate New York; Dale L. Morgan, "The State of Deseret," *Utah Historical Quarterly* VIII (April, July, October, 1940): 65–251, deals with the beginnings of Utah. Fawn M. Brodie, . . . *Life of Joseph Smith* . . . (New York, 2nd ed., 1971), and Leonard Arrington, *Great Basin Kingdom* . . . (Cambridge, 1958), demonstrate the high level of scholarship that various aspects of the subject "Mormons" have produced.

The literature of the American West is enormous, and my efforts to penetrate it were facilitated by the extensive files of many magazines, in particular the *California Historical Quarterly, Colorado Magazine, New Mexico Historical Review, Oregon Historical Review,* and *Utah Historical Quarterly*. Several scholars have made knowledge more accessible through their editorial projects, and the services of LeRoy R. Hafen speak well for their great contributions. Earl Pomeroy, *Pacific Slope* . . . (New York, 1965), and Howard Lamar, *Far Southwest* . . . (New Haven, 1966), are not only excellent studies of their regions but also good guides to the literature. Rodman Paul's work occupies a similar position in the area of a specific activity; significant in particular are his *California Gold* . . . (Cambridge, 1947), and an article, "Colorado . . . in the Mining West," *Journal of American History* XLVII (June 1960): 34–50. Ray Allen Billington, *Westward Expansion* . . . (New York, 4th ed., 1974), provides the best detailed view of the larger story together with a superb bibliography.

San Francisco and Denver, as other cities of the Far West, are the subject of many specific studies, only a few of which can be mentioned. One admirable city history from the turn of the century deserves special attention: Jerome C. Smiley, . . . *Denver* . . . (Denver, 1901). A wealth of detail is compressed into almost one thousand pages, and before an offprint appeared in 1971, with a good index compiled by Robert L. Perkin, Smiley was a research project in itself to get at the information. Perkin, *First Hundred Years* . . . (Garden City, 1959), and Louisa Ward Arps, *Denver in Slices* (Denver, 1959), are fascinatingly informal histories of the city. Clyde Lyndon King, . . . *Government of Denver* . . . (Denver, 1911) is still useful. John P. Young, . . . *San Francisco* . . . (San Francisco, 1912), does not come up to Smiley, but Bernard Moses, *Establishment of Municipal Government* . . . (Baltimore, 1889), and several articles of J. N. Bowman in the *California Historical Quarterly* are seminal accomplishments. Both cities have always stimulated labors of love, and how much that tradition persists is well documented by Nolie Mumey, . . . *Early Settlements of Denver* . . . (Glendale, 1942), and Albert Shumate, . . . *Rincon Hill and South Park* (San Francisco, 1963).

.

# Notes

CHAPTER 1

1. James D. Hart (ed.), *From Scotland to Silverado. By Robert Louis Stevenson* (Cambridge, Mass., 1966), pp. xix–xxii, 123, 127–29. Throughout the text, words in quotation marks and titles appear as found in the original.
2. "The Railroad System," *North American Review* CIV (April 1867): 478, 480.
3. Hart (ed.), *From Scotland to Silverado*, p. 129.
4. After I had been working for some time with the concept of instant city, I noticed that David Lavender used the words, but not the concept, in the title of his article on the Leadville mining rush, "This Wondrous Town; This Instant City," *American West* IV (August 1967): 4. For another descriptive term, see Don Pfeil, "Las Vegas: The Sudden City," *Mankind: The Magazine of Popular History* IV (June 1973): 17, 62–64.
5. Adelbert Baudissin, *Der Ansiedler im Missouri-Staate* (Iserlohn, 1854), pp. 67–68. See also Ralph Gregory, "Count Baudissin on Missouri Towns," *Missouri Historical Society Bulletin* XXVII (January 1971): 111–24.
6. Charles N. Glaab and Lawrence H. Larsen, "Neenah-Menasha in the 1870's: The Development of Flour Milling and Papermaking," *Wisconsin Magazine of History* LII (Autumn 1968): 19–20.
7. "History of the Settlements on Cherry Creek," *Denver City and Auraria, the Commercial Emporium of the Pike's Peak Gold Regions in 1859* (St. Louis, 1860), p. 5.
8. Peter H. Burnett, *Recollections and Opinions of an Old Pioneer* (New York, 1880), p. 306.
9. Meadow Lake *Morning Sun*, June 9, 1866. For an account of the rush to the

Meadow Lake mining district in Nevada County, California, turn to Paul Fatout, *Meadow Lake: Gold Town* (Bloomington, 1969).

10. "The New El Dorado. Leadville, the Great Mining Centre of Colorado," *Frank Leslie's Illustrated Newspaper*, April 12, 1879, p. 86; Ernest Ingersoll, "The Camp of the Carbonates: Ups and Downs in Leadville," *Scribner's Monthly* XVIII (October 1879): 801.

11. A. J. Graham, "The Character of the Evidence," *Colony and Mother City in Ancient Greece* (Manchester, 1964), pp. 8–22; Jakob Seibert, *Metropolis und Apoikie: Historische Beiträge zur Geschichte ihrer gegenseitigen Beziehungen* (Würzburg, 1963), pp. 1–8, 234–35.

12. Graham, *Colony and Mother City*, p. 5.

13. Georg Busolt and Heinrich Swoboda, *Griechische Staatskunde*. 2 vols. (Munich, 3rd rev. ed., 1926), II: 1268.

14. Graham, *Colony and Mother City*, p. 14.

15. Armin von Gerkan, *Griechische Städteanlagen; Untersuchungen zur Entwicklung des Städtebaues im Altertum* (Berlin, 1924), pp. 5–6, 32–33; Alfred Zimmern, *The Greek Commonwealth: Politics and Economics in Fifth-Century Athens* (Oxford, 5th rev. ed., 1931), pp. 252–53; R. E. Wycherley, *How the Greeks Built Cities* (London, 2nd ed., 1962), pp. 4–5, 15.

16. Plato, *Laws*, pp. 735–36; Zimmern, *Greek Commonwealth*, p. 252.

17. Ernest Baker, "Xenophon and Isocrates," "Plato and Aristotle," "The End of the Polis, and Its Political Theory," J. B. Bury, S. A. Cook, and F. E. Adcock (eds.), *The Cambridge Ancient History*, 12 vols. (Cambridge, 1923–39), VI:515–35.

18. W. W. Tarn, "Finance and the New Cities," *The Cambridge Ancient History*, VI: pp. 9–31.

19. W. W. Tarn, "The Conquest of Turkestan," *ibid.*, 391–93.

20. V. Tscherikover [Victor Cherikover], *Die Hellenistischen Städtegründungen von Alexander dem Grossen bis auf die Römerzeit* (Leipzig, 1927), pp. 138–39; M. Rostovtzeff, *The Social and Economic History of the Hellenistic World*, 3 vols. (Oxford, 1941), I: 557, 559, 568.

21. Steven Runciman, *Byzantine Civilization* (London, 1933), pp. 11–14, 27–29; Robert Mayer, *Byzantion, Konstantinopolis, Istanbul: Eine genetische Stadtgeographie* (Vienna, 1943), p. 199; Peter Classen, "Causa Imperii: Probleme Roms in Spätantike und Mittelalter," *Jahrbuch für die Geschichte Mittel- und Ostdeutschlands* I (1952): 230–31.

22. Richard E. Sullivan, *Aix-la-Chapelle in the Age of Charlemagne* (Norman, Oklahoma, 1963), pp. 31–32.

23. Heinrich Sproemberg, "Residenz und Territorium in niederländischen Raum," *Rheinische Vierteljahrsblätter* VI (May 1936): 113–17; Edith Ennen, *Frühgeschichte der Europäischen Stadt* (Bonn, 1953), pp. 96–98; Felix Kreusch, "Kirche, Atrium und Portikus der Aachener Pfalz," Wolfgang Braunfels and Hermann Schnitzler (eds.), *Karolingische Kunst* (Düsseldorf, 1965), p. 463; Gerhard Seeliger, "Charles in Legend and in History," H. M. Gwatkin and J. P. Whitney (eds.), *The Cambridge Medieval History*, 8 vols. (Cambridge, 1911–36), II:628; J. E. Anderson (trans.), *Land and Work in Medieval Europe: Selected Papers by Marc Bloch* (Berkeley, 1967), p. 18.

24. Fritz Gräf, *Die Gründung Alessandrias. Ein Beitrag zur Geschichte des Lombardenbundes* (Dresden, 1887), pp. 5, 16–21, 55.

25. Viola Garvin (trans.), *Peter the Great. By Constantin de Grunwald* (London, 1956), pp. 154–72; Reinhard Wittram, *Peter I, Czar und Kaiser; Zur Geschichte Peter des Grossen in seiner Zeit*, 2 vols. (Göttingen, 1964), II:56, 79.

26. Friedrich von Weech, *Badische Geschichte* (Karlsruhe, 1896), pp. 383–85; I. A. R. Wylie, "South German Towns in General and Karlsruhe in Particular," *The Germans* (Indianapolis, 1911), pp. 10–28.

27. Constance McLoughlin Green, *Washington: Village and Capital, 1800–1878* (Princeton, 1962), pp. vii, 3–4.

28. George Woodcock, *The British in the Far East* (London, 1969), pp. 134–61; Lionel Wigmore, *The Long View: A History of Canberra, Australia's National Capital* (Melbourne, 1963), pp. 59–66; Moisés Gicovate, *Brasília: Uma realização em marcha* (São Paulo, 1959), pp. 87–88.

29. For a discussion of the literature on one aspect of the migration, see Herbert Helbig, "Deutsche Siedlungsforschung im Bereich der mittelalterlichen Ostkolonisation (Forschungsbericht)," *Jahrbuch für die Geschichte Mittel- und Ostdeutschlands* II (1953): 238–345.

30. Hans Walther, "Siedlungsentwicklung und Ortsnamengebung östlich der Saale im Zuge der deutschen Ostexpansion und Ostsiedlung," Hellmut Kretzschmar (ed.), *Vom Mittelalter zur Neuzeit; Zum 65. Geburtstag von Heinrich Sproemberg* (Berlin, 1956), p. 88.

31. Johannes Schulze, "Der Wendenkreuzzug 1147 und die Adelsherrschaften in Prignitz und Rhingebiet," *Jahrbuch für die Geschichte Mittel- und Ostdeutschlands* II (1953): 96.

32. Hermann Aubin, "The Lands East of the Elbe and German Colonization Eastwards," M. M. Postan and H. T. Habakkuk (eds.), *The Cambridge Economic History of Europe*, 5 vols. in 6 (Cambridge, 1941–67), I:364–65.

33. Hubert Ermisch, "Die Anfänge des sächsischen Städtewesens," Robert Wuttke (ed.), *Sächsische Volkskunde* (Dresden, 1900), p. 121.

34. Herbert Helbig, "Das Vorortproblem in der Frühzeit des Städtewesens im Gebiet der deutschen Ostkolonisation," *Jahrbuch für die Geschichte Mittel- und Ostdeutschlands* I (1952): 45.

35. Walter Kuhn, *Geschichte der deutschen Ostsiedlung in der Neuzeit*, 2 vols. (Cologne, 1955–57), I:44, 50.

36. Fritz Rörig, " 'Territorialwirtschaft und Stadtwirtschaft,' " *Historische Zeitschrift* CL (August 1934): 472; Rörig, "Gründungsunternehmerstädte des 12. Jahrhunderts," Paul Kaegbein (ed.), *Fritz Rörig, Wirtschaftskräfte im Mittelalter: Abhandlungen zur Stadt- und Hansegeschichte* (Cologne, 1959), pp. 249, 256, 271–72; Theodor Mayer, *Mittelalterliche Studien: Gesammelte Aufsätze* (Lindau, 1959), pp. 253–57.

37. Walter Kuhn, *Die deutschrechtlichen Städte in Schlesien und Polen in der ersten Hälfte des 13. Jahrhunderts* (Marburg/Lahn, 1968), p. 14.

38. Aubin, "German Colonization," *Cambridge Economic History*, I:452–53; Karl Gruber, "Der niederländische Einfluss in der Baukunst des Deutschordenslandes

Preussen," *Deutsches Archiv für Landes- und Volksforschung* I (August 1937): 715–16; Walter Schlesinger, "Städtische Frühformen zwischen Rhein und Elbe," Konstanz Institut für geschichtliche Landesforschung des Bodenseegebietes, *Studien zu den Anfängen des europäischen Städtewesens, Reichenau-Vorträge, 1955–1956* (Lindau, 1958), 297–362.

39.   Kuhn, *Geschichte der deutschen Ostsiedlung*, I:44, 50.

40.   Rörig, "Gründungsunternehmerstädte," Kaegbein (ed.), *Fritz Rörig*, pp. 250–51; Paul Johansen, "B. Die Städte Hanse," in "Umrisse und Aufgaben der hansischen Siedlungsgeschichte und Kartographie," *Hansische Geschichtsblätter* LXXIII (1955): 78–83; Otto Brunner, "Stadt und Bürgertum in der europäischen Geschichte," *Geschichte in Wissenschaft und Unterricht* IV (September 1953): 532–33.

41.   Aubin, "German Colonization," *Cambridge Economic History*, I:384–85. For an analogy, see the discussion of the relation between peasant and merchant in Heinz Stoob, "Dithmarschen und die Hanse," *Hansische Geschichtsblätter* LXXIII (1955): 117–45.

42.   Herbert Ludat, "Frühformen des Städtewesens in Osteuropa," *Studien zu den Anfängen des europäischen Städtewesens*, 553; Jan Brankačk, "Einige Betrachtungen über Handwerk, Handel und Stadtentwicklung der Westslawen an der Ostseeküste vom 9. zum 12. Jahrhundert," Gerhard Heitz and Manfred Unger (eds.), *Hansische Studien: Heinrich Sproemberg zum 70. Geburtstag* (Berlin, 1961), 32–33.

43.   For a brief description of the state of the debate, see Kuhn, *Die deutschrechtlichen Städte in Schlesien und Polen*, pp. 9–14, and in particular his lengthy quote from Karol Buczek, *Targi i miasta na prawie polskim: okres wczesnośredniowieczny* (Warsaw, 1964), p. 21. See also Helbig, "Deutsche Siedlungsforschung," *Jahrbuch für die Geschichte Mittel- und Ostdeutschlands* II (1953): 319, 345; and "Städtische Siedlungen," specifically the literature on the work of Polish archaeologists in Pomerania, in Hans Branig, "Zur älteren Geschichte Pommerns, 9. bis 12. Jahrhundert. Ein Bericht über die polnische Nachkriegsforschung," *Jahrbuch für die Geschichte Mittel- und Ostdeutschlands* VIII (1959): 378–89; and Richard Koebner, "German Towns and Slav Markets," Sylvia L. Thrupp (ed.), *Change in Medieval Society: Europe North of the Alps, 1050–1500* (New York, 1964), pp. 44–46.

44.   James Westfall Thompson, *Feudal Germany*, 2 vols. (New York, 1928), II:522–27.

45.   Joachim Herrmann (ed.), *Die Slawen in Deutschland; Geschichte und Kultur der slawischen Stämme westlich von Oder und Neisse vom 6. bis 12. Jahrhundert. Ein Handbuch* (Berlin, 1970), p. 474. For the effects of political views on the historiography of the question, note the examples in Horst Jabolonowski, "Die mittelalterliche Ostsiedlung in der östlichen Literatur. Bemerkungen zu einigen Erwiderungen auf Walter Schlesingers Abhandlung über 'Die geschichtliche Stellung der mittelalterlichen deutschen Ostbewegung' [*Historische Zeitschrift* CLXXXIII (Heft 3, 1957), 517–42], *Jahrbuch für die Geschichte Mittel- und Ostdeutschlands* X (1961): 304–10, and Wolfgang F. Fritze, "Slawomanie oder

Germanomanie? Bemerkungen zu W[alther]. Stellers neuer Lehre von der älteren Bevölkerungsgeschichte Ostdeutschlands," *ibid.*, 293–304.

46. For a discussion of one aspect of the problem, see Heinrich Reincke, "Volkszahl und Gewichtigkeit der Städte," in "Bevölkerungsprobleme der Hansestädte," *Hansische Geschichtsblätter* LXX (1951): 1–7.

47. John U. Nef, "Mining and Metallurgy in Medieval Civilisation," *Cambridge Economic History*, II:436–39.

48. H. Quiring, "Die Anfänge des Bergbaus in Deutschland und die Herkunft der 'fränkischen Bergleute,'" *Zeitschrift für das Berg-, Hütten- und Salinenwesen im Preussischen Staate* LXXVII (4. Abhandlungsheft, 1929): 248–51; Franz Rosenhainer, *Die Geschichte des Unterharzer Hüttenwesens von seinen Anfängen bis zur Gründung der Kommunionverwaltung im Jahre 1635* (Goslar, 1968), p. 12.

49. Paul Reinhard Beierlein, "Die Goldsucher von Werda i. V., Beitrag zur Geschichte der 'Wahlen' im Vogtlande," *Neues Archiv für Sächsische Geschichte und Altertumskunde* XLIX (1. Heft, 1928): 7–12; Gabriele Schwarz, "Die Bergbausiedlungen im Mährischen Gesenke," *Petermanns Geographische Mitteilungen* XCIII (3. Quartalsheft, 1949): 98; Heinrich Schurtz, "Der Seifenbergbau im Erzgebirge und die Walensagen," *Forschungen zur deutschen Landes- und Volkskunde* V (Heft 3, 1890): 120–41; Karl Schneider, "Die Walen im Riesengebirge," *Mitteilungen des Vereines für Geschichte der Deutschen in Böhmen* (Prague) LX (1.–4. Heft, 1922): 276–314; Robert Cogho and Will-Erich Peuckert, *Volkssagen aus dem Riesen- und Iser-Gebirge* (Göttingen, 1967), pp. 49–55.

50. Herbert Clark Hoover and Lou Henry Hoover (trans.), *Georgius Agricola, De Re Metallica, Translated from the First Latin Edition of 1556* (New York, 1950), pp. 327–36. For a sketch of the prospector in the mining rushes of the American West, see Otis E. Young, Jr., "The Craft of the Prospector," *Montana Magazine of Western History* XX (Winter 1970): 28–39.

51. Jan Brankačk, "Stadtentwicklung der Westslawen," Heitz und Unger (eds.), *Hansische Studien*, p. 24.

52. Hoover and Hoover (trans.), *Georgius Agricola, De Re Metallica*, pp. 35–36.

53. Gustav Eduard Benseler, *Geschichte Freibergs und seines Bergbaues*, 2 vols. (Freiberg, 1843–53), I:54–60.

54. Nef, "Mining and Metallurgy in Medieval Civilisation," *Cambridge Economic History of Europe*, II:436–39; Klaus Schwarz, *Untersuchungen zur Geschichte der deutschen Bergleute im späteren Mittelalter* (Berlin, 1958), pp. 13–14; Schwarz, "Die Bergbausiedlungen," *Petermanns Geographische Mitteilungen* XCIII (3. Quartalsheft, 1949): 99; Johannes Langer, "Der ostelbische Bergbau im und am Gebiet der Dresdner Heide und der Sächsischen Schweiz," *Neues Archiv für Sächsische Geschichte und Altertumskunde* L (1. Heft, 1929): 2–3; Neda von Relković, "Aus dem Leben der sieben 'niederungarischen Bergstädte' im 14.–17. Jahrhundert," *Ungarische Jahrbücher* VI (1927): 39.

55. "Mitteldeutschland im Zeitalter der mittelalterlichen deutschen Ostsiedlung," Walter Schlesinger, *Kirchengeschichte Sachsens im Mittelalter*, 2 vols. (Cologne, 1962), II:25–29.

248 INSTANT CITIES

56. Manfred Unger, *Stadtgemeinde und Bergwesen Freibergs im Mittelalter* (Weimar, 1963), pp. 3–6.
57. Johannes Langer, "Die Anfänge Freibergs und seines Bergbaues," *Neues Archiv für Sächsische Geschichte und Altertumskunde* LII (1. Heft, 1931): 9, 15.
58. Johannes Langer, "Flurgeographische Untersuchung über die ältesten Freiberger Besiedlungsverhältnisse," *Neues Archiv für Sächsische Geschichte und Altertumskunde* XLVIII (2. Heft, 1927): 189, 225.
59. Hubert Ermisch, *Das sächsische Bergrecht des Mittelalters* (Leipzig, 1887), pp. xiv–xvii.
60. E. O. Schulze, "Verlauf und Formen der Besiedlung des Landes," Wuttke (ed.), *Sächsische Volkskunde*, p. 75; Walther Herrmann, "Der Zeitpunkt der Entdeckung der Freiberger Silbererze," *Bergbau und Kultur: Beiträge zur Geschichte des Freiberger Bergbaus und der Bergakademie* (Berlin, 1953), pp. 7–22; Walter Hoffmann, *Bergakademie Freiberg* (Frankfurt, 1959), pp. 7–11.
61. Ermisch, "Die Anfänge des sächsischen Städtewesens," Wuttke (ed.), *Sächsische Volkskunde*, p. 128.
62. House Ex. Doc. 17, *31 Cong., 1 Sess.*, 707; Thomas J. Green, "Report on Mines and Foreign Miners," *California Senate Journal*, 1 Sess., 1850, Appendix S, 493; San Francisco *Daily Alta California*, March 5, 1852. See also J. S. Holliday, "The California Gold Rush Reconsidered," K. Ross Toole *et al.* (eds.), *Probing the American West* (Santa Fe, 1962), pp. 35–41.
63. Wilhelm Hermann and Hubert Ermisch, "Das Freiberger Bergrecht," *Neues Archiv für Sächsische Geschichte und Altertumskunde* III (1882): 130; Wilhelm Weizsäcker, "Eindringen und Verbreitung der deutschen Stadtrechte in Böhmen und Mähren," *Deutsches Archiv für Landes- und Volksforschung* I (January 1937): 104–5.
64. H. Achenbach, "Die deutschen Bergleute der Vergangenheit," *Zeitschrift für Bergrecht* XII (1871): 81–83.
65. Johann Friedrich August Breithaupt, *Die Bergstadt Freiberg im Königreich Sachsen* (Freiberg, 1825), p. 7. For a detailed survey of the privileges of mining towns, see the chapter, "Die freien Bergstädte," in Carl Friedrich Mosch, *Zur Geschichte des Bergbaues in Deutschland*, 2 vols. (Liegnitz, 1829), II:223–80.
66. James B. Allen, *The Company Town in the American West* (Norman, 1966), p. 7.
67. Georg Wilhelm Sante and A. G. Ploetz-Verlag (eds.), *Geschichte der deutschen Länder*, "*Territorien-Ploetz*," 1. Band: *Die Territorien bis zum Ende des alten Reiches* (Würzburg, 1964), p. 480.
68. Richard Dietrich, "Untersuchungen zum Frühkapitalismus im mitteldeutschen Erzbergbau und Metallhandel," *Jahrbuch für die Geschichte Mittel- und Ostdeutschlands* VII (1958): 144–45.
69. Adolf Laube, "Bergbau, Bergstädte und Landesherrschaft in Sachsen im 15./16. Jh.," *Zeitschrift für Geschichtswissenschaft* XVI (Heft 12, 1968): 1577, 1579, 1580–1583.
70. Ingrid Mittenzwei, *Der Joachimsthaler Aufstand 1525: Seine Ursachen und Folgen* (Berlin, 1968), pp. 7–8.
71. Samuel Johnson, *A Dictionary of the English Language*, 2 vols. (London, 1755), Leaf C-one, verso.

72. Paul Krenkel (trans. and ed.), *Paulus Niavis: Iudicium Iovis oder Das Gericht der Götter über den Bergbau. Ein literarisches Dokument aus der Frühzeit des deutschen Bergbaus* (Berlin, 1953), p. 39.

73. See the detailed discussion about the origin of capital and sources of investment in the Erz Mountains in the fifteenth and sixteenth centuries in Richard Dietrich, "Untersuchungen zum Frühkapitalismus im mitteldeutschen Erzbergbau und Metallhandel," *Jahrbuch für die Geschichte Mittel- und Ostdeutschlands* VIII (1959): 51–119, X (1961): 127–94.

74. Johann Koehler, *Die Keime des Kapitalismus im sächsischen Silberbergbau (1168 bis um 1500)* (Berlin, 1955), pp. 122–23; Mittenzwei, *Der Joachimsthaler Aufstand*, pp. 9, 10–15.

75. Schwarz, *Bergleute im späteren Mittelalter*, pp. 26–28.

76. Manfred Unger, "Die Freiberger Stadtgemeinde im 13. Jahrhundert," Kretzschmar (ed.), *Heinrich Sproemberg*, 72–73.

77. Wilhelm Bornhardt, *Geschichte des Rammelsberger Bergbaues von seiner Aufnahme bis zur Neuzeit* (Berlin, 1931), pp. 28–29. [Preussische Geologische Landesanstalt, *Archiv für Lagerstättenforschung*, Heft 52.]

78. Walter Schlesinger, "Zur Gerichtsverfassung des Markengebiets östlich der Saale im Zeitalter der deutschen Ostsiedlung," *Jahrbuch für die Geschichte Mittel- und Ostdeutschlands* II (1953): 37.

79. Otto Hue, *Die Bergarbeiter: Historische Darstellung der Bergarbeiter-Verhältnisse von der ältesten bis in die neueste Zeit* (Stuttgart, 1910), p. 131.

80. *Ibid.*, pp. 129–43.

81. Herbert Jankuhn, "Die frühmittelalterlichen Seehandelsplätze im Nord- und Ostseeraum," *Studien zu den Anfängen des europäischen Städtewesens*, 451–98. Helmut Roth, "Handel und Gewerbe vom 6. bis 8. Jahrhundert östlich des Rheins," *Vierteljahrschrift für Sozial- und Wirtschaftsgeschichte* LVIII (Heft 3, 1972): 323–24.

82. Ennen, *Frühgeschichte der europäischen Stadt*, pp. 50–69; Karl Lehmann-Hartleben, *Die antiken Hafenanlagen des Mittelmeeres: Beiträge zur Geschichte des Städtebaues im Altertum* (Leipzig, 1923), pp. 26–45; (*Klio*, Beiheft XIV, neue Folge, Heft 1).

83. Paul Johansen, "Novgorod und die Hanse," A. von Brandt and W. Koppe (eds.), *Städtewesen und Bürgertum als geschichtliche Kräfte; Gedächtnisschrift für Fritz Rörig* (Lübeck, 1953), pp. 132–35.

84. Leopoldo Torres Balbas, et al., *Resumen histórico del urbanismo en España* (Madrid, 1954), pp. vii, viii.

85. Woodrow Borah, "The New World," Lesley Byrd Simpson, Gordon Griffiths and Woodrow Borah, "Representative Institutions in the Spanish Empire in the Sixteenth Century," *The Americas* XII (January 1956): 249–50.

86. Anton Blok, "South Italian Agro-Towns," *Comparative Studies in Society and History* XI (April 1969): 121.

87. Robert S. Smith, "Spain," *Cambridge Economic History*, I:345–46.

88. J. A. Pitt-Rivers, *The People of the Sierra* (Chicago, 1961), pp. 39, 46–47.

89. Carl Ortwin Sauer, *The Early Spanish Main* (Berkeley, 1966), p. 151.

90. Borah, "The New World," Simpson, Griffiths and Borah, "Representative Institutions in the Spanish Empire," *The Americas* XII (January 1956): 249–50. See also Mario Góngora, *El estado en el derecho Indiano: Época de fundación (1492–1570)* (Santiago de Chile, 1951), p. 69, and Inge Wolff, *Regierung und Verwaltung der Kolonial-spanischen Städte in Hochperu, 1538–1650* (Cologne, 1970), pp. 4, 5–7.

91. John C. Rainbolt, "The Absence of Towns in Seventeenth-Century Virginia," *Journal of Southern History* XXXV (August 1969): 360.

92. Carl Bridenbaugh, *Cities in the Wilderness: The First Century of Urban Life in America, 1625–1742* (New York, 1960), p. 3.

93. F. M. Stenton, *Anglo-Saxon England* (Oxford, 2nd ed., 1947), p. 463.

94. Carl Stephenson, *Borough and Town: A Study of Urban Origins in England* (Cambridge, Mass., 1933), p. 47–52; S. S. Frere, "The End of Towns in Roman Britain," J. S. Wacher (ed.), *The Civitas Capitals of Roman Britain* (Leicester, 1966), p. 87; James Tait, *The Study of Early Municipal History in England* (London, 1922), pp. 2–3, 4; Sir Walter Savage, *The Making of Our Towns* (London, 1952), pp. 44, 47–48. For a discussion of various outlooks on the Saxon period, turn to Donald A. White, "Changing Views on the *Adventus Saxonum* in Nineteenth and Twentieth Century English Scholarship," *Journal of the History of Ideas* XXXII (October–December, 1971): 585–94.

95. Edith Ennen, "Les différents types de formation des villes européennes," *Le Moyen Age* LXII (No. 4, 1956): 404–5.

96. Christopher Hill, "The Norman Yoke," *Puritanism and Revolution; Studies in Interpretation of the English of the 17th Century* (London, 1958), pp. 54–55.

97. Chester E. Eisinger, "The Freehold Concept in Eighteenth-Century American Letters," *William and Mary Quarterly* IV (January 1947): 42–43; Paul H. Johnstone, "In Praise of Husbandry," *Agricultural History* XI (April 1937): 80–92, 93, 94; Renato Poggioli, "Naboth's Vineyard or the Pastoral View of the Social Order," *Journal of the History of Ideas* XXIV (January–March 1963): 3–24; Perez Zagorin, *The Court and the Country: The Beginning of the English Revolution* (London, 1969), pp. 40–118.

98. Paul H. Johnstone, "Turnips and Romanticism," *Agricultural History* XII (July 1938): 224, 225; Gillian Beer, "Charles Kingsley and the Literary Image of the Countryside," *Victorian Studies* VIII (March 1965): 243; Kenneth MacLean, *Agrarian Age: A Background for Wordsworth* (New Haven, 1950), p. 83.

99. Louis B. Wright (ed.), *The History and Present State of Virginia. By Robert Beverley* (Chapel Hill, 1947), pp. xxi, xxxii, 233.

100. David Lowenthal and Hugh C. Prince, "English Landscape Tastes," *Geographical Review* LV (April 1965), 186–87.

101. Samuel Eliot Morison (ed.), *Of Plymouth Plantation, 1620–1647, by William Bradford, Sometime Governor Thereof* (New York, 1967), pp. 187–88, 333.

102. Bridenbaugh, *Cities in Revolt*, pp. 4, 216–17.

103. A. Whitney Griswold, "The Jeffersonian Ideal," *Farming and Democracy* (New York, 1948), pp. 18–46; MacLean, *Agrarian Age*, p. 83; W. Burlie Brown, "The Cincinnatus Image in Presidential Politics," *Agricultural History* XXXI (January

1957): 23–29; Paul H. Johnstone, "Old Ideals Versus New Ideas in Farm Life," U. S. Department of Agriculture, *Farmers in a Changing World* (Washington, 1940), pp. 116–18; Clifford B. Anderson, "The Metamorphosis of American Agrarian Idealism in the 1920's and 1930's," *Agricultural History* XXXV (October 1961): 183–84; Edward Higbee, *Farms and Farmers in an Urban Age* (New York, 1963), pp. 80–84; John P. White and Norman C. Thomas, "Urban and Rural Representation and State Legislative Apportionment," *Western Political Quarterly* XVII (December 1964): 726; Gilbert C. Fite, "The Agrarian Tradition and Its Meaning For Today," *Minnesota History* XL (Summer 1967): 293–99; William A. Bullough, " 'It Is Better to Be a Country Boy': The Lure of the Country in Urban Education in the Gilded Age," *The Historian* XXXV (February 1973): 183.

104. For a discussion of the Marxian argument and the bibliography, see Walter Markov, "Bemerkungen zur geschichtlichen Stellung der Siedlungskolonie," Kretzschmar (ed.), *Heinrich Sproemberg*, pp. 312–49.

105. See Richard C. Wade, *The Urban Frontier; The Rise of Western Cities, 1790–1830* (Cambridge, Mass., 1959), for a detailed discussion of the operation of the pattern in the Ohio Valley.


CHAPTER 2


1. Initially, I devised the label temple city as an abstract classification to distinguish between such divergent instant cities in the Far West as Salt Lake City and San Francisco as well as Denver. I soon found that the term appeared in print as early as 1852, in John Williams Gunnison, *The Mormons, or, Latter-Day Saints, in the Valley of the Great Salt Lake* (Philadelphia, 1852), p. 33. In the meantime, one of my students pursued the idea further in a thesis, Edwin Gustavus Quattlebaum III, "Salt Lake City as Temple City" (Ph.D. thesis, University of California, 1972), and I have profited from our discussions on the subject. The untimely death of Dale L. Morgan on March 30, 1971, deprived me of a friend in The Bancroft Library who was always ready to share with me his mastery of the history of the Far West and his concern for the history of the Mormons.

2. Salt Lake City Council, *Revised Ordinances and Resolutions of the City Council of Salt Lake City in the Territory of Utah with Congressional and Territorial Laws on Townsites and Great Salt Lake City Charter and Amendments* (Salt Lake City, 1875), p. 17; Brigham Henry Roberts, *A Comprehensive History of the Church of Jesus Christ of Latter-day Saints; Century I*, 6 vols. (Salt Lake City, 1930), III: 281.

3. Gunnison, *The Mormons*, p. 33.

4. Orson Pratt gave a succinct explanation of the doctrine of eternal progression in his famous discourse, "Celestial Marriage," in the Salt Lake City Tabernacle on August 29, 1852. I was not able to locate a separate edition of the sermon and I used the version found on pages 12–38 of an appendix, "Mormonism," to the

American edition of Maria Ward (ed.), *The Husband in Utah; or, Sights and Scenes among the Mormons: With Remarks on Their Moral and Social Economy. By Austin N. Ward* (New York, 1859), pp. 1–30. There it was called "Celestial Marriage, A Discourse Delivered by Elder Orson Pratt, in the Tabernacle, Great Salt Lake City," pp. 12–38. I considered that text in general agreement with the first Danish translation, Orson Pratt, *Det celestiale Ægteskab eller den af Gud aabenbarede Ægteskabsorden for Tig og al Efighed, og Det Nye Jerusalem* (Copenhagen, 1855), pp. 7–30, where the sermon appeared in company different than Mrs. Ward's harangue. See also, "Discourse on Celestial Marriage, Delivered by Elder Orson Pratt, in the New Tabernacle, Salt Lake City, October 7th, 1869," in George A. Smith, *The Rise, Progress and Travels of the Church of Jesus Christ of Latter-day Saints, Being a Series of Answers to Questions, Including the Revelation on Celestial Marriage, and A Brief Account of the Settlement of Salt Lake Valley, with Interesting Statistics* (Salt Lake City, 2nd ed., 1872), pp. 73–76.

5. James B. Thayer, *A Western Journey with Mr. Emerson* (Boston, 1884), p. 39.

6. John Winthrop, "A Model of Christian Charity," Perry Miller (ed.), *The American Puritans: Their Prose and Poetry* (New York, 1956), p. 83.

7. Richard Mather, The Summe of Seventie Lectures Upon the First Chapter of the Second Epistle of Peter (MS, American Antiquarian Society, Worcester), 393. I am indebted to Robert L. Middlekauff for the reference.

8. William Reuben Farmer, *Maccabees, Zealots, and Josephus: An Inquiry into Jewish Nationalism in the Greco-Roman Period* (New York, 1956), pp. 85–87, 98–99, 150–51; S. G. F. Brandon, *Jesus and the Zealots: A Study of the Political Factor in Primitive Christianity* (Manchester, 1967), pp. 48–49, 58–59, 62–63; C. R. Conder, "Jerusalem," James Hastings (ed.), *A Dictionary of the Bible*, 5 vols. (New York, 1902–5), II 586–89.

9. Emil Esin, *Mecca the Blessed, Madinah the Radiant* (London, 1963), pp. 92–93; Gerald de Gaury, *Rulers of Mecca* (London, 1951), p. 52.

10. Lewis Mumford, *The City in History: Its Origins, Its Transformations, and Its Prospects* (New York, 1961), pp. 74–75, 82, 135–37; M. Cary and John Wilson, *A Shorter History of Rome* (London, 1963), p. 355.

11. Bruce Kinney, *Mormonism, the Islam of America* (New York, 1912); Charles Mackay, *The Mormons, or Latter-day Saints, with Memoirs of the Life and Death of Joseph Smith, the "American Mohamet"* (London, 1851); Arnold H. Green and Lawrence P. Goldrup, "Joseph Smith, An American Muhammed? An Essay on the Perils of Historical Analogy," *Dialogue* VI (Spring 1971): 55.

12. Howard Kaminsky, *A History of the Hussite Revolution* (Berkeley, 1967), pp. 278–89, 312–13, 329–36. See also, George Huntston Williams, *The Radical Reformation* (London, 1962), pp. 263, 363, 385; Norman Cohn, *The Pursuit of the Millennium* (Fairlawn, New Jersey, 1957), pp. 8–13, 44–45, 283–306; Herbert Grundmann, *Religiöse Bewegungen im Mittelalter* (Berlin, 1935), pp. 479–80. Initially, William Slottman directed my attention to Tabor.

13. William Mulder, "Mormonism's 'Gathering': An American Doctrine with a Difference," *Church History* XXIII (September 1954): 249; David Brion Davis,

"The New England Origins of Mormonism," *New England Quarterly* XXVI (June 1953): 162.

14. William Mulder, *Homeward to Zion: The Mormon Migration from Scandinavia* (Minneapolis, 1957), p. 21; Richard Lloyd Anderson, "Joseph Smith and the Millenarian Time Table," *Brigham Young University Studies* III (Spring–Summer 1961): 64.

15. *Journal History*, May 18, 1839, quoted from Hyrum L. Andrus, "Joseph Smith and the West," *Brigham Young University Studies* II (Spring–Summer 1960): 133.

16. Thomas Cottam Romney, "The State of Deseret" (Ph.D. thesis, University of California, Berkeley, 1929), pp. 94–95, 101, 111; Andrew Love Neff, "The Mormon Migration to Utah, 1830–1847" (Ph.D. thesis, University of California, Berkeley, 1918), 180–83; T. Edgar Lyon, "This Is the Place," *Utah Historical Quarterly* XXVII (July 1959): 203–7; Nels Anderson, *Desert Saints: The Mormon Frontier in Utah* (Chicago, 1942), p. 67.

17. For a detailed discussion of the location factors, see "Settlement and Other Planning," Chauncy Dennison Harris, *Salt Lake City: A Regional Capital* (Chicago, 1940), pp. 93–106.

18. Romney, "Deseret," pp. 108–11; Neff, "Mormon Migration," p. 189; Roberts, *Comprehensive History*, III:279.

19. Samuel Brannan to Jesse C. Little, September 18, 1847 (quoted in Romney, "Deseret," p. 111); Daniel Tyler, *A Concise History of the Mormon Battalion in the Mexican War. 1846–1847* (Glorieta, New Mexico, 1964), p. 315; Reva Scott, *San Francisco's Forgotten Jason: Samuel Brannan and the Golden Fleece, a Biography* (New York, 1944), pp. 161–79; Paul Bailey, *Sam Brannan and the California Mormons* (Los Angeles, 1953), pp. 101–7; Louis J. Stellman, *Sam Brannan: Builder of San Francisco* (New York, 1953), pp. 81–86.

20. Jesse D. Hunter to Brigham Young, February 20, 1848, A. Lathrop to Brigham Young, May 18, 1848, Frank Alfred Golder (ed.), *The March of the Mormon Battalion from Council Bluffs to California. Taken from the Journal of Henry Standage* (New York, 1928), pp. 248–49, 271–73; Erwin G. Gudde (ed.), *Bigler's Chronicle of the West: The Conquest of California, Discovery of Gold, and Mormon Settlement as Reflected in Henry William Bigler's Diaries* (Berkeley, 1962), 75–77; Eugene E. Campbell, "Authority Conflicts in the Mormon Battalion," *Brigham Young University Studies* VIII (Winter 1968): 137–38.

21. Romney, "Deseret," 112–14; Neff, "Mormon Migration," 189–90; Roberts, *Comprehensive History*, III:279–81.

22. Edward W. Tullidge, *History of Salt Lake City* (Salt Lake City, 1886), 44, 47.

23. Nelson, *Mormon Village*, 25–53.

24. Romney, "Deseret," 115; Neff, "Mormon Migration," 194; Roberts, *Comprehensive History of the Church*, I:310–12, III:280–81; Nelson Lowry, *The Mormon Village: A Pattern and Technique of Land Settlement* (Salt Lake City, 1952), pp. 25–26; Charles L. Sellers, "Early Mormon Community Planning," *Journal of the American Institute of Planners* XXVIII (February 1962): 24–30; Orson Pratt (ed.), *The Doctrine and Covenants of the Church of Jesus Christ of Latter-day Saints, Containing the Revelations Given to Joseph Smith, Jun., the Prophet, for*

*the Building Up of the Kingdom of God in the Last Days* (Salt Lake City, 1901), p. 215 (Sec. LVII); John W. Reps, *The Making of Urban America: A History of City Planning in the United States* (Princeton, 1965), pp. 466–72; Joel Edward Ricks, *Forms and Methods of Early Mormon Settlement in Utah and the Surrounding Region, 1847–1877* (Logan, Utah, 1964), pp. 6, 16.

25.  Andrew Jenson, "Kirtland," *Historical Record* V (May 1886): 66; Robert Kent Fielding, "The Mormon Economy in Kirtland, Ohio," *Utah Historical Quarterly* XXVII (October 1959): 331, 333, 340; Dean A. Dudley, "Bank Born of Revelation: The Kirtland Safety Society Anti-Banking Company," *Journal of Economic History* XXX (December 1970): 848–53; Richard L. Bushman, "Mormon Persecutions in Missouri, 1833," *Brigham Young University Studies* III (Autumn 1960): 11–20; Andrew Jenson, "Caldwell County, Missouri," *Historical Record* VIII (January 1889), pp. 691, 719–22; Andrew Jenson, "Davies County, Missouri," *Historical Record*, 730–32; Warren A. Jennings, "The Expulsion of the Mormons from Jackson County, Missouri," *Missouri Historical Review* LXIV (October 1969): 41–63; Warren A. Jennings, "Importuning for Redress," *Missouri Historical Society Bulletin* XXVII (October 1970): 15–29; Brigham Henry Roberts, *The Missouri Persecutions* (Salt Lake City, 1900), pp. 69–110, 168–83, 187–91, 196–251, 261–64; Ricks, *Early Mormon Settlement*, pp. 5–6.

26.  Hancock County, Illinois, Board of Supervisors, *History of Hancock County, Illinois, Illinois Sesquicentennial Edition* (Carthage, 1968), between pp. 84 and 85.

27.  James L. Kimball, Jr., "The Nauvoo Charter: A Reinterpretation," *Journal of the Illinois State Historical Society* LXIV (Spring 1971): 67, 73; Roberts, *Nauvoo*, pp. 128–30, 134–40; Flanders, *Nauvoo*, pp. 188–89, 307–8. For details of the Mormon-Gentile conflict, see Kenneth W. Godfrey, "The Road to Carthage Led West," *Brigham Young University Studies* VIII (Winter 1968): 204–15; Robert Bruce Flanders, "The Kingdom of God in Illinois: Politics in Utopia," *Dialogue* V (Spring 1970): 26–36; and Douglas L. Wilson and Rodney O. Davis (eds.), "Mormons in Hancock County: A Reminiscence. By Eudocia Baldwin Marsh," *Journal of the Illinois State Historical Society* LXIV (Spring 1971): 22–65.

28.  Josiah Quincy, *Figures of the Past* (Boston, 1883), p. 389; Brigham Henry Roberts, *The Rise and Fall of Nauvoo* (Salt Lake City, 1900), pp. 17–20, 162; Robert Bruce Flanders, *Nauvoo: Kingdom on the Mississippi* (Urbana, 1965), pp. v, 41, 47–48, 56. The studies by Roberts and Flanders, in their respective ways, are milestones in an understanding of Nauvoo. For succinct introductions into the literature and significance, see Richard L. Bushman, "The Historian and Mormon Nauvoo," *Dialogue: A Journal of Mormon Thought* V (Spring 1970): 51–61; and Stanley B. Kimball, "The Mormons in Illinois, 1838–1846; A Special Introduction," *Journal of the Illinois State Historical Society* LXIV (Spring 1971): 5–21. The entire issue of *Dialogue* V (Spring 1970), edited by Kimball, is called "The Mormons in Early Illinois."

29.  R. Kent Fielding, "Historical Perspectives for a Liberal Mormonism," *Western Humanities Review* XIV (Winter 1960): 76.

30.  Flanders, *Nauvoo*, pp. 209, 242–77; Roberts, *Nauvoo*, pp. 92–93, 112–27,

163–217; James E. Talmage, *The House of the Lord: A Study of Holy Sanctuaries, Ancient and Modern* (Salt Lake City, 1912), pp. 89–109; Duncan M. McAllister, *A Description of the Great Temple, Salt Lake City, and a Statement Concerning the Purposes for Which It Has Been Built* (Salt Lake City, 2nd ed., 1909); McAllister, *Temples of the Church of Jesus Christ of Latter-day Saints and the Sacred Purposes to Which They Are Dedicated* (Salt Lake City, 1956); Thomas F. O'Dea, *The Mormons* (Chicago, 1957), pp. 56–61; Stanley S. Ivins, "Notes on Mormon Polygamy," *Utah Historical Quarterly* XXXV (Fall 1967): 311. Besides these official, or brief, accounts, the restraint Mormons showed in talking about the nature of ordinances has stimulated considerable curiosity and contributed to the appearance of many exposés. Relatively sensible is the section in Stuart Martin, *The Mystery of Mormonism* (London, 1920), pp. 244–65. See also William E. Berrett, *The Restored Church: A Brief History of the Growth and Doctrines of the Church of Jesus Christ of Latter-day Saints* (Salt Lake City, 12th ed., 1964), pp. 361–68, 456–58; "Efficacy and Sacredness of Temple Ordinances," N. B. Lundwall (comp.), *Temples of the Most High* (Salt Lake City, 1968), pp. 273–85; David S. Andrew and Laurel B. Blank, "The Four Mormon Temples in Utah," *Journal of the Society of Architectural Historians* XXX (March 1971): 63–64.

31. Fawn M. Brodie, *No Man Knows My History: The Life of Joseph Smith, the Mormon Prophet* (New York, 2nd ed., 1971), p. 282.

32. Kenneth W. Godfrey, "Joseph Smith and the Masons," *Journal of the Illinois State Historical Society* LXIV (Spring 1971): 90; Brodie, *No Man Knows My History*, pp. 367–95. Some of the documents were published as a paperback by Keith Huntress (comp.), *Murder of an American Prophet: Events and Prejudices Surrounding the Killing of Joseph and Hyrum Smith; Carthage, Illinois, June 27, 1844* (San Francisco, 1963).

33. The text of the "Official Declaration," the so-called Manifesto of 1890, can be conveniently found in William Mulder and A. Russell Mortensen (eds.), *Among the Mormons: Historic Accounts by Contemporary Observers* (New York, 1958), pp. 416–17.

34. *Times and Seasons* V (Apr. 15, 1844): 510.

35. Flanders, *Nauvoo*, pp. 188–89, 307.

36. Roberts, *Nauvoo*, p. 136; Flanders, *Nauvoo*, pp. 246–47; Arthur Rulon Jones, "A Historical Survey of Representative Recreation Activities Among the Mormons in Nauvoo" (Ph.D. thesis, Southern Illinois University, Carbondale, 1970), quoted in Kimball, "Mormons in Illinois," *Journal of the Illinois State Historical Society* LXIV (Spring 1971): 13; Leonard J. Arrington, "An Economic Interpretation of the 'Word of Wisdom,'" *Brigham Young University Studies* I (Winter 1959): 40.

37. For the complexities of the rural world of upstate New York, see Whitney R. Cross, *The Burned-over District: The Social and Intellectual History of Enthusiastic Religion in Western New York, 1800–1850* (New York, 1950), particularly pp. 138–50. No biography may ever fathom the Prophet; however, Brodie, *No Man Knows My History*, comes closest to accomplishing the task. See specifically Joseph Smith to Emma Smith, October 13, 1832, *ibid.*, p. 123.

38. Brigham Henry Roberts (ed.), *History of the Church of Jesus Christ of Latter-day Saints. Period I. History of Joseph Smith, the Prophet, by Himself. Period II. From the Manuscript History of Brigham Young and Other Original Documents.* 7 vols. and Index (Salt Lake City, 1902–70), V:8.

39. Dean D. McBrien, "The Economic Content of Early Mormon Doctrine," *Southwestern Political and Social Science Quarterly* VI (September 1925): 180.

40. Flanders, *Nauvoo*, pp. 115–21, 126–27, 140–41.

41. Dudley, "The Kirtland Safety Society Anti-Banking Company," *Journal of Economic History* XXX (December 1970): 853; Fielding, "Mormon Economy in Kirtland, Ohio," *Utah Historical Quarterly* XXVII (October 1959): 341, 344–55.

42. Flanders, *Nauvoo*, pp. 117–19.

43. Brigham Robert Young, *The Rise and Fall of Nauvoo* (Salt Lake City, 1900), p. 12. See also Joseph Earl Arrington, "Destruction of the Mormon Temple at Nauvoo," *Journal of the Illinois State Historical Society* XL (December 1947): 414–25. For a survey of the subsequent development of Nauvoo as a place, apart from the *History of Hancock County* and the studies by Roberts and Flanders, see Sister M. Stephen Ring, "Communal Life in Nauvoo," *American Benedictine Review* XIII (December 1962): 523–35; and T. Edgar Lyon, "The Current Restoration in Nauvoo, Illinois," *Dialogue* V (Spring 1970): 13–25.

44. Dale L. Morgan, "The State of Deseret," *Utah Historical Quarterly* VIII (April, July, October, 1940): 107.

45. Flanders, *Nauvoo*, p. 209.

46. Leonard J. Arrington and Jon Haupt, "The Missouri and Illinois Mormons in Ante-bellum Fiction," *Dialogue* V (Spring 1970): 49.

47. William Mulder, "The Mormons in American History," *Utah Historical Quarterly* XXVII (January 1959): 60–62.

48. Robert Flanders, "To Transform History: Early Mormon Culture and the Concept of Time and Space," *Church History* XL (March 1971): 117.

49. Andrew Dickson White, *Autobiography*, 2 vols. (New York, 1906), II:87.

50. Flanders, *Nauvoo*, p. 58.

51. Andrew Jenson, "The Nauvoo Temple," *Historical Record* VIII (June 1889): 872; Arrington, "Mormon Temple," *Journal of the Illinois State Historical Society* XL (December 1947): 414.

52. McAllister, *Description of the Great Temple*, 1–13, 18–19; Wallace Alan Raynor, *The Everlasting Spires: A Story of the Salt Lake Temple* (Salt Lake City, 1965), pp. 153–59.

53. Nauvoo *Neighbor*, Oct. 29, 1845.

54. Leonard J. Arrington, *Great Basin Kingdom: An Economic History of the Latter-day Saints, 1830–1900* (Cambridge, Mass., 1958), pp. 26–27. This study is a valuable guide to an understanding of the economic setting.

55. "The Promised Land," Mulder and Mortensen (eds.), *Among the Mormons*, p. 225.

56. N. B. Lundwall (comp.), *Exodus of Modern Israel by Orson Pratt and Others. Being the daily diary of Orson Pratt on the Exodus of the Latter-day Saints from Nauvoo to the Rocky Mountains. Also detailed information on plans instituted by*

the Prophet Joseph Smith for this Exodus, as related by Anson Call, Wilford Woodruff, Brigham Young, Historian Edward W. Tullidge, Samuel W. Richards, Helen Mar Whitney and by Joseph the Prophet himself. (Salt Lake City, 1947), pp. 76, 83.

57. Herbert E. Bolton (trans. and ed.), *Pageant in the Wilderness: The Story of the Escalante Expedition to the Interior Basin, 1776; Including the Diary and Itinerary of Father Escalante* (Salt Lake City, 1950), pp. 70–73, 184–97.

58. Erwin G. and Elisabeth K. Gudde (trans. and eds.), *From St. Louis to Sutter's Fort, 1846. By Heinrich Lienhard* (Norman, 1961), p. 103; William James Snow, "The Great Basin Before the Coming of the Mormons" (Ph.D. thesis, University of California, Berkeley, 1923), 22–182; Dale L. Morgan, "Utah Before the Mormons," *Utah Historical Quarterly* XXXVI (Winter 1968): 3–23.

59. John Bidwell, *In California Before the Gold Rush* (Los Angeles, 1948), pp. 29–44.

60. Snow, "Great Basin," 182–94; Morgan, "Utah Before the Mormons," *Utah Historical Quarterly* XXXVI (Winter, 1968): 22–23.

61. T. Edgar Lyon, "Religious Activities and Development in Utah, 1847–1910," *Utah Historical Quarterly* XXXV (Fall 1967): 293.

62. Franklin Dewey Richards, Narrative (MS, Bancroft Library), 87; Andrew Love Neff, *History of Utah, 1847 to 1869* (Salt Lake City, 1940), p. 109.

63. Romney, "Deseret," 103–4; Roberts, *Comprehensive History*, III: 269.

64. George Q. Cannon, "History of the Church. Early Life in the Valley!" *Juvenile Instructor* IX (Jan. 31, 1874): 34. See also Dale L. Morgan, "The Changing Face of Salt Lake City," *Utah Historical Quarterly* XXVII (July 1959): 215.

65. Dale L. Morgan, "The State of Deseret," *Utah Historical Quarterly* VIII (April, July, October, 1940): 87.

66. Leonard J. Arrington, "Women as a Force in the History of Utah," *ibid.* XXXVIII (Winter 1970): 3–4. See also his comments, "The Male Bias," in "The Search for Truth and Meaning in Mormon History," *Dialogue* III (Summer 1968): 56–65.

67. Arrington, *Great Basin Kingdom*, pp. 47–48, 50–52, 64–65; Thomas F. O'Dea, *The Mormons* (Chicago, 1957), pp. 82–83.

68. Arrington, *Great Basin Kingdom*, pp. 58–62, 64–71.

69. "Why the Mormons Did Not Go to California. Brigham Young's Speech to the Mormon Battalion on October 1, 1848," Golder (ed.), *Journal of Henry Standage*, 246; Eugene Edward Campbell, "The Mormon Gold Mining Missions of 1849," *Brigham Young University Studies* I–II (Autumn 1959–Winter 1960): 19–20.

70. Salt Lake City *Deseret News*, Apr. 13, 1854.

71. Tullidge, *Salt Lake City*, p. 56; Roberts, *Comprehensive History*, I:310.

72. Neff, *History of Utah*, p. 110; Berrett, *Restored Church*, pp. 268–70.

73. Tullidge, *Salt Lake City*, pp. 56–58; "Mormon Theocracy," Neff, *History of Utah*, pp. 107–12; "Ordinances of the High Council," Morgan; "The State of Deseret," *Utah Historical Quarterly* VIII (April, July, October, 1940): 234–35; Klaus J. Hansen, *Quest for Empire: The Political Kingdom of God and the Council of Fifty in Mormon History* (East Lansing, 1967), pp. 123–32; J. Keith Melville, "Theory and Practice of Church and State During the Brigham Young Era," *Brigham Young University Studies* III (Autumn 1960): 34–36.

74. Morgan, "The State of Deseret," *Utah Historical Quarterly* VIII (April, July, October, 1940): 70.
75. Ricks, *Early Mormon Settlement*, pp. 19–21, 23–25, 29–30; Leonard J. Arrington, "Religion and Economics in Mormon History," *Brigham Young University Studies* III (Spring–Summer 1961): 22.
76. Hansen, *Quest for Empire*, pp. 133, 134, 136.
77. D. W. Meinig, "The Mormon Culture Region: Strategies and Pattern in the Geography of the American West, 1847–1964," *Annals of the Association of American Geographers* LV (June 1965): 200.
78. Everett L. Cooley, "Report of an Expedition to Locate Utah's First Capitol," *Utah Historical Quarterly* XXIII (October 1955): 329–38; Cooley, "Utah's Capitols," *ibid.*, XXVII (July 1959): 260–61.
79. Fawn M. Brodie (ed.), *The City of the Saints and Across the Rocky Mountains to California. By Richard F. Burton* (New York, 1963), p. 223. See also Fawn M. Brodie, "Sir Richard F. Burton: Exceptional Observer of the Mormon Scene," *Utah Historical Quarterly* XXXVIII (Fall 1970): 295–311.
80. Dale L. Morgan, "Salt Lake City, City of the Saints," Ray B. West, Jr. (ed.), *Rocky Mountain Cities* (New York, 1949), p. 179.
81. Thomas Adams, *Outline of Town and City Planning: A Review of Past Efforts and Modern Aims* (New York, 1936), p. 173.
82. Leonard J. Arrington and Jon Haupt, "Intolerable Zion: The Image of Mormonism in Nineteenth Century American Literature," *Western Humanities Review* XXII (Summer 1968): 247.
83. Jules Remy and Julius Brenchley, *A Journey to Great-Salt-Lake City; With a Sketch of the History, Religion, and Customs of the Mormons, and an Introduction on the Religious Movement in the United States*, 2 vols. (London, 1861), II:55.

CHAPTER 3

1. John P. Bloom, "Notes on the Population of New Mexico, 1846–1849," *New Mexico Historical Review* XXXIV (July 1959): 200.
2. Ralph Emerson Twitchell, *Old Santa Fe: The Story of New Mexico's Ancient Capital* (Santa Fe, 1925), pp. 162–63.
3. Max L. Moorhead, *New Mexico's Royal Road: Trade and Travel on the Chihuahua Trail* (Norman, 1958), p. 102.
4. Howard Roberts Lamar, *The Far Southwest, 1846–1912: A Territorial History* (New Haven, 1966), pp. 88–92, 102–3.
5. James Madison Cutts, *The Conquest of California and New Mexico, by the Forces of the United States, in the Years 1846 & 1847* (Philadelphia, 1847), p. 60.
6. Ralph P. Bieber (ed.), *Marching with the Army of the West, 1846–1848, by Abraham Robinson Johnston, Marcellus Ball Edwards, Philip Gooch Ferguson* (Glendale, 1936), p. 159; James M. Lacy, "New Mexican Women in Early

American Writings," *New Mexico Historical Review* XXXIV (January 1959), pp. 48–51.

7. L. Bradford Prince, *Old Fort Marcy, Santa Fe, New Mexico: Historical Sketch and Panoramic View of Santa Fe and Its Vicinity* (Santa Fe, 1912), pp. 3, 6.

8. W. H. H. Allison (comp.), "Santa Fe in 1846 [Recollections of Col. Francisco Perea]," *Old Santa Fe* II (April 1915): 396.

9. Chris Emmett, *Fort Union and the Winning of the Southwest* (Norman, 1965), p. 47.

10. LeRoy R. Hafen (ed.), *Ruxton of the Rockies, Collected by Clyde and Mae Reed Porter* (Norman, 1950), p. 188.

11. *Ibid.*, 180.

12. Beverly Trulio, "Anglo-American Attitudes Toward New Mexican Women," *Journal of the West* XII (April 1973): 229, 239.

13. Hafen (ed.), *Ruxton of the Rockies*, pp. 180, 188.

14. John P. Bloom, "New Mexico Viewed by Anglo-Americans, 1846–1849," *New Mexico Historical Review* XXXIV (July 1959): 197–98.

15. Daniel Tyler, "Gringo Views of Governor Manuel Armijo," *New Mexico Historical Review* XLV (January 1970): 23–46; Lawrence R. Murphy, "The United States Army in Taos, 1847–1852," *ibid.*, XLVII (January 1972): 33–35.

16. *Congressional Globe*, 32 Cong., 2 Sess., Jan. 10, 1853, Appendix, 104.

17. Lamar, *Far Southwest*, 96.

18. Emmett, *Fort Union*, 12.

19. William Wallace Long, "A Biography of Major General Edwin Vose Sumner, U.S.A., 1797–1863" (Ph.D. thesis, University of New Mexico, 1971), 79. For the effect of the attitude on another town, Taos, turn to Lawrence R. Murphy, "Cantonment Burgwin, New Mexico, 1852–1860," *Arizona and the West* XV (Spring 1973): 5–26.

20. Emmett, *Fort Union*, 3, 9–12; Earl C. Kubicek, "Soldiers and Sinners at Loma Parda," *Smithsonian Journal of History* II (Spring 1967): 43.

21. Emmett, *Fort Union*, 137, 141–43, 153; Ralph E. Twitchell (ed.), "Historical Sketch of Governor William Carr Lane, Together with Diary of His Journey from St. Louis, Mo. to Santa Fe, N.M. July 31st, to September 9th, 1852," Historical Society of New Mexico, *Publications*, No. 20 (Nov. 1, 1917): 52.

22. Emmett, *Fort Union*, p. 181.

23. Robert A. Griffen (ed.), *My Life in the Mountains and on the Plains. The Newly Discovered Autobiography by David Meriwether* (Norman, 1965), pp. 155–63.

24. *Ibid.*, 82–103; Hiram Martin Chittenden, *The American Fur Trade of the Far West*, 3 vols. (New York, 1902), II:500; R. L. Duffus, *The Santa Fe Trail* (London, 1930), pp. 65–66; Twitchell, *Old Santa Fe*, pp. 58, 173, 331; Calvin Horn, "Trouble Shooter from Kentucky," *New Mexico Magazine* XXXVI (April 1958): 26.

25. William Watts Hart Davis, *El Gringo; or, New Mexico and Her People* (New York, 1857), p. 246.

26. New Mexico (Territory), *Laws of the Territory of New Mexico, Passed by the Second Legislative Assembly in the City of Santa Fe, at a Session Begun on the Sixth Day of December, 1852* (Santa Fe, 1853), p. 97.

27. New Mexico (Territory), *Laws of the Territory of New Mexico, Passed by the Third Legislative Assembly in the City of Santa Fe, at a Session Begun on the Fifth Day of December, A.D. 1853* (Santa Fe, 1854), pp. 10–12.

28. John Hammond Moore (ed.), "Letters from a Santa Fe Army Clerk, 1855–1856, by Charles E. Whilden," *New Mexico Historical Review* XL (April 1965): 162.

29. William J. Parish, *The Charles Ilfield Company: A Study of the Rise and Decline of Mercantile Capitalism in New Mexico* (Cambridge, 1961), pp. 3–8.

30. Moorhead, *New Mexico's Royal Road*, pp. 64–65. For the different practices of merchants located in Missouri, see Lewis E. Atherton, "Business Techniques in the Santa Fe Trade," *Missouri Historical Review* XXXIV (April 1940): 335–41.

31. Lansing Bloom, "Ledgers of a Santa Fe Trader," *El Palacio* XIV (May 1, 1923): 133–36.

32. Barry E. Supple, "A Business Elite: German-Jewish Financiers in Nineteenth-Century New York," *Business History Review* XXXI (Summer 1957): 149–54.

33. William J. Parish, "The German Jew and the Commercial Revolution in Territorial New Mexico, 1850–1900," *New Mexico Historical Review* XXXV (January 1960): 1–23, (April 1960), 129–50. See also, Floyd S. Fierman, *Some Early Jewish Settlers on the Southwestern Frontier* (El Paso, 1960), and his comments on Jewish merchants in Santa Fe in his article, "The Impact of the Frontier on a Jewish Family: The Bibos," *American Jewish Historical Quarterly* LIX (June 1970): 461–63.

34. New Mexico Bureau of Immigration, *The Resources of New Mexico* (Santa Fe, 1881), p. 21; Twitchell, *Old Santa Fe*, pp. 476–77; Floyd S. Fierman, *The Spiegelbergs of New Mexico: Merchants and Bankers, 1844–1893* (El Paso, 1964), 11–12, 15.

35. Centennial Celebration, Santa Fe, New Mexico, July 4, 1876, *Centennial Historical Oration by Ex-Governor W. F. M. Arny, "Santa Fé, New Mexico—The Oldest City in North America"* (Santa Fe, 1876), pp. 6, 7.

36. Hubert Howe Bancroft, *History of California*, 7 vols. (San Francisco, 1884–90), III:117; IV:206.

37. Sir George Simpson to Sir John H. Pelly, March 10, 1842, Joseph Schafer (ed.), "Letters of Sir George Simpson, 1841–1843," *American Historical Review* XIV (October 1908): 88–89; Harold A. Small (ed.), *Seventy-five Years in California: Recollections and Remarks by One Who Visited These Shores in 1831, and Again in 1833, and Except When Absent on Business Was a Resident from 1838 Until the End of a Long Life in 1909. By William Heath Davis* (San Francisco, 1967), pp. 34, 79, 80.

38. Bancroft, *History of California*, IV: 628, 639, 650; J. Gregg Layne, "Annals of Los Angeles, Part I, From the Founding of the Pueblo to the American Occupation," *California Historical Quarterly* XIII (September 1934): 221; "Annals of Los Angeles, Part II, From the American Conquest to the Civil War," *ibid.*, XIII (December 1934): 310; Maurice H. Newmark and Marco R. Newmark, *Census of the City and County of Los Angeles, California, for the Year 1850; Together with an Analysis and an Appendix* (Los Angeles, 1929), 23, 115; Fred B. Rogers, *Bear Flag Lieutenant: The Life Story of Henry L. Ford*

(1822–1860) *Together with Some Reproductions of Related and Contemporary Paintings by Alexander Edouart* (San Francisco, 1951), p. 4.

39. Bancroft, *History of California*, I: 134, 137, 170; Theodore E. Treutlein, "The Portolá Expedition of 1769–1770," *California Historical Quarterly* XLVII (December 1968): 291, 307.

40. Bancroft, *History of California*, II: 676.

41. George Simpson, *An Overland Journey Round the World, During the Years 1841 and 1842.* 2 parts (Philadelphia, 1847), Part I, p. 190.

42. Bancroft, *History of California*, IV: 677–79; Mariano Vallejo to Bautista Alvarado, July 27, 1841, Clarence John Du Four (ed.), "The Russian Withdrawal from California," *California Historical Quarterly* XII (September 1933): 255; George Tays, "Mariano Guadalupe Vallejo and Sonoma, A Biography and a History," *ibid.*, XVII (June 1938): 145–51, 164; Erwin G. Gudde, *Sutter's Own Story: The Life of General John Augustus Sutter and the History of New Helvetia in the Sacramento Valley* (New York, 1936), pp. 66–70; James Peter Zollinger, *Sutter: The Man and His Empire* (New York, 1939), pp. 116–18.

43. Simpson, *Overland Journey*, Part I, 190; Jeanne Van Nostrand, *History of Monterey* (San Francisco, 1968): pp. 23, 39.

44. Simpson, *Overland Journey*, Part I, p. 191. Mariano G. Vallejo, in his suggestions for commercial reforms in California, also discussed the crucial role of the custom house, *Ecsposición que hace el Comdanante General de la Alta California al Gobernador de la misma* (Sonoma, August 17, 1837).

45. Adele Ogden, "Alfred Robinson, New England Merchant in Mexican California," *California Historical Quarterly* XXIII (September 1944): 195–97; Leon G. Campbell, "The First Californios: Presidial Society in Spanish California, 1769–1822," *Journal of the West* XI (October 1972): 593; Daniel Garr, "Planning, Politics and Plunder: The Missions and Indian Pueblos of Hispanic California," *Southern California Quarterly* LIV (Winter 1972): 300–306; Leonard Pitt, *The Decline of the Californios: A Social History of the Spanish-Speaking Californians, 1846–1890* (Berkeley, 1966), p. 11.

46. Bancroft, *History of California*, III: 628.

47. Warren A. Beck and Ynez D. Haase, *Historical Atlas of New Mexico* (Norman, 1969), pp. 17, 20.

48. Thomas Savage (comp.), "Life of a Rancher. By Don José del Carmen Lugo," *Southern California Quarterly* XXXII (September 1950): 236.

49. Robert M. Fogelson, *The Fragmented Metropolis: Los Angeles, 1850–1930* (Cambridge, 1967), p. 10.

50. Small (ed.), *Seventy-five Years in California. By William Heath Davis*, pp. 78–83, 190–93.

51. Thomas Oliver Larkin, "Notes on Personal Character of the Principal Men," George P. Hammond (ed.), *The Larkin Papers: Personal, Business, and Official Correspondence of Thomas Oliver Larkin, Merchant and United States Consul in California.* 10 vols. and Index (Berkeley, 1951–68), IV:322–34; Walter Colton, *Three Years in California* (New York, 1850), p. 92.

52. Tirey L. Ford, *Dawn and the Dons: The Romance of Monterey* (San Francisco, 1926), p. 216.

53. Thomas Oliver Larkin to Moses Yale Beach, May 31, 1840, Hammond (ed.), *Larkin Papers*, III: 219.

54. William H. Meyers, Journal (MS, Bancroft Library), May 28, 1843.

55. Erwin Gustav Gudde (trans.), "Edward Vischer's First Visit to California," *California Historical Quarterly* XIX (September 1940): 196.

56. Edwin Bryant, *What I Saw in California: Being the Journal of a Tour by the Emigrant Route and South Pass of the Rocky Mountains, Across the Continent of North America, the Great Desert Basin, and Through California, in the Years 1846, 1847* (Santa Ana, California, 1936), p. 367.

57. Robert J. Parker, "Building the Larkin House," *California Historical Quarterly* XVI (December 1937): 321–335; Oscar Lewis, *Here Lived the Californians* (New York, 1957), pp. 76–81; Harold Kirker, *California's Architectural Frontier: Style and Tradition in the Nineteenth Century* (San Marino, 1960), pp. 16–22.

58. Thomas Oliver Larkin to Samuel J. Hastings, November 16, 1846, Hammond (ed.), *Larkin Papers* V: 279.

59. "The Centennial Celebration of the Settlement of Monterey, Cal., June 3, 1870," *Historical Magazine and Notes and Queries Concerning the Antiquities, History and Biography of America* IX (Second Series, February 1871): 90, 97, 98.

60. T. C. Elliott (ed.), "The Peter Skene Ogden Journals," *Oregon Historical Quarterly* X (December 1909): 364–65.

61. John McLoughlin to Governor, Deputy Governor, and Committee, November 20, 1840, E. E. Rich (ed.), *The Letters of John McLoughlin from Fort Vancouver to the Governor and Committee, Second Series, 1839–44* (Toronto, 1943), p. 18; Kate Ball Powers, Flora Ball Hopkins, and Lucy Ball (comps.), *Autobiography of John Ball* (Grand Rapids, Michigan, 1925), pp. 94–95; W. Kaye Lamb, "Introduction," Rich (ed.), *Letters of John McLoughlin, First Series*, pp. cxxiii–cxxiv; John S. Galbraith, "The Early History of the Puget's Sound Agricultural Company, 1838–43," *Oregon Historical Quarterly* LV (September 1954): 244–45.

62. James Douglas to the Governor, Deputy Governor, and Committee, October 18, 1838, E. E. Rich (ed.), *The Letters of John McLoughlin from Fort Vancouver to the Governor and Committee, First Series, 1825–38* (Toronto, 1941), p. 241.

63. *Ibid.*, p. 242.

64. Lamb, "Introduction," Rich (ed.), *Letters of John McLoughlin, First Series*, pp. xiv–xv.

65. John McLoughlin, Private Papers, 1825–1856 [An Account of His Relations With Americans, 1825–1845] (MS, Bancroft Library), 4–5, 7; Joseph Jarvay *et al.* to the Bishop of Juliopolis, March 22, 1836 (typed transcript, Bancroft Library); Francis Norbert Blanchet, *Historical Sketches of the Catholic Church in Oregon, During the Past Forty Years* (Portland, 1878), pp. 7–9, 22–29; *Autobiography of John Ball*, p. 95: Charles L. Camp (ed.), *James Clyman, Frontiersman: The Adventures of a Trapper and Covered-Wagon Emigrants as Told in His Own Reminiscences and Diaries* (Portland, 1960), pp. 118–19, 141.

66. "Russian Agreement," Edmund Henry Oliver (ed.), *The Canadian North-West: Its Early Development and Legislative Records*; 2 vols. (Ottawa, 1914), pp. 791–96; Rich (ed.), *Letters of John McLoughlin, Second Series*, pp. 25–26.

NOTES 263

67. George B. Roberts, Recollections (MS, Bancroft Library), 107.
68. Minto, "Champoeg," *Oregon Historical Quarterly* XV (December 1914): 283.
69. John A. Hussey, *Champoeg: Place of Transition. A Disputed History* (Portland, 1967), pp. 57–58, 109–12. This book is very useful for details of the Champoeg scene.
70. Francis W. Pettygrove, Oregon in 1843 (MS, Bancroft Library), 20–21.
71. John McLoughlin to Governor, Deputy Governor, and Committee, November 20, 1844, E. E. Rich (ed.), *The Letters of John McLoughlin From Fort Vancouver to the Governor and Committee, Third Series, 1844–46* (Toronto, 1944), p. 33.
72. H. S. Lyman (comp.), "Reminiscences of F. X. Matthieu," *Oregon Historical Quarterly* I (March 1900): 90; Charles B. Moores, "Memorial Address Commemorating Life, Character and Services of Francis Xavier Matthieu," *ibid.* XV (June 1914): 73, 74; John Minto, "Champoeg, Marion County, the First Grain Market in Oregon," *ibid.* XV (December 1914): 283–84.
73. George B. Roberts to Frances Fuller Victor, November 28, 1878, "The Round Hand of George B. Roberts; The Cowlitz Farm Journal, 1847–51," *ibid.* LXIII (June-September, 1962): 182.
74. Ewing Young and Lawrence Carmichael to Oregon Temperance Society, January 13, 1837, Appendix D, "Slacum's Report on Oregon, 1836–7," *Oregon Historical Quarterly* XIII (June 1912): 213; "The Mission Record Book of the Methodist Episcopal Church, Willamette Station, Oregon Territory, North America, Commenced 1834," *ibid.* XXIII (September 1922): 248–51; F. G. Young (ed.), "Ewing Young and His Estate," *ibid.* XXI (September 1920): 183. Kenneth L. Holmes, *Ewing Young, Master Trapper* (Portland, 1967), pp. 116–22.
75. "Articles of Agreement Made and Entered into this 13th Day of January, in the Year of Our Lord One Thousand Eight Hundred and Thirty-Seven," Appendix A, "Slacum's Report on Oregon," *Oregon Historical Quarterly* XIII (June 1912): 211–14. Hubert Howe Bancroft, *History of Oregon*, 2 vols. (San Francisco, 1886–88), I:141; Cornelius J. Brosnan, *Jason Lee: Prophet of the New Oregon* (New York, 1932), p. 84.
76. "Memorial of William A. Slacum," *Sen. Ex. Doc.* 24, 25 Cong., 2 Sess., I, 1–31. The references are to a conveniently located reprint of the account, "Slacum's Report on Oregon, 1836–7," *Oregon Historical Quarterly* XIII (June 1912): 191–92, 200–202. For early Indian-white contact, see "The First Inhabitants," Hussey, *Champoeg*, pp. 8–19.
77. Elsie Frances Dennis, "Indian Slavery in the Pacific Northwest," *Oregon Historical Quarterly* XXXI (June 1930): 194–95.
78. "Slacum's Report on Oregon," *ibid.* XIII (June 1912): 197.
79. F. G. Young (ed.), *The Correspondence and Journals of Captain Nathaniel J. Wyeth, 1831–6* (Eugene, Oregon, 1899), p. 233; Joseph Schafer, "Nathaniel Jarvis Wyeth," *DAB* XX: 576–77.
80. "Diary of Reverend Jason Lee—I," *Oregon Historical Quarterly* XVII (June 1916), 137–46; "Diary of Reverend Jason Lee—II," *ibid.* (September 1916): 240–66; "Diary of Reverend Jason Lee—III," *ibid.* (December 1916): 401–3, 410–12; Cornelius James Brosnan, "Jason Lee, A Missionary's Part in the

Founding of the Commonwealth of Oregon" (Ph.D. dissertation, University of California, Berkeley, 1929), pp. 237–38, 250–53; W. J. Ghent, "Jason Lee," *DAB* XI:112; R. J. Loewenberg, "Elijah White vs. Jason Lee: A Tale of Hard Times," *Journal of the West* XI (October 1972): 636–62; D. Lee and J. H. Frost, *Ten Years in Oregon* (New York, 1844), pp. 129–35, 139–51, 166–74, 192–94, 256–64, 303–4; Loewenberg, " 'Not . . . by feeble means': Daniel Lee's Plan to Save Oregon," *Oregon Historical Quarterly* LXXIV (March 1973): 71–78; Gustavus Hines, *Life on the Plains of the Pacific. Oregon: Its History, Conditions and Prospects* (Buffalo, 1851), pp. 10–37, 235–43; "Reverend David Leslie," Caroline C. Dobbs, *Men of Champoeg: A Record of the Lives of the Pioneers Who Founded the Oregon Government* (Portland, 1932), p. 60; John Kirk Townsend, *Narrative of a Journey Across the Rocky Mountains, to the Columbia River, and a Visit to the Sandwich Islands, Chili, &. With a Scientific Appendix* (Philadelphia, 1839), p. 219.

81.  Cornelius James Brosnan, "The Oregon Memorial of 1838 and Its Signers," George P. Hammond (ed.), *New Spain and the Anglo-American West; Historical Contributions Presented to Herbert Eugene Bolton*, 2 vols. (Los Angeles, 1932), II: 49–53, 67–70; C. F. Pike, "Petitions of Oregon Settlers, 1838–48," *Oregon Historical Quarterly* XXXIV (September 1933): 218–21.

82.  Wade Crawford Barclay, *History of Methodist Missions, Part One, Early American Methodism, 1769–1844, Vol. II, To Reform the Nation* (New York, 1950), p. 232.

83.  Elisabeth Walton, "Jason Lee's Home on the Willamette," *Pacific Historian* XIV (Winter 1970): 68–71.

84.  Margaret Jewett Bailey, *The Grains, or, Passages in the Life of Ruth Rover, With Occasional Pictures of Oregon, Natural and Moral* (Portland, 1854), pp. 91, 115; Bailey, "French Prairie Farm, 1839–1850," *Marion County History* V (June 1959): 42–43; Charles Wilkes, *Narrative of the United States Exploring Expedition. During the Years 1838, 1839, 1840, 1841, 1842*, 5 vols. (Philadelphia, 1845), IV: 387; Herbert B. Nelson, "First True Confession Story Pictures Oregon 'Moral,' " *Oregon Historical Quarterly* XLV (June 1944): 168–69; Nelson, "Ruth Rover's Cup of Sorrow," *Pacific Northwest Quarterly* L (July 1959): 97–98; O. W. Frost, "Margaret J. Bailey: Oregon Pioneer Author," *Marion County History* V (June 1959): 64–70; Janice K. Duncan, " 'Ruth Rover'—Vindictive Falsehood or Historical Truth?" *Journal of the West* XII (April 1973): 248–49; Nelson, *The Literary Impulse in Pioneer Oregon* (Portland, 1949), pp. 36–41.

85.  Hussey, *Champoeg*, pp. 192–98.

86.  "Petition to U.S. Senate, March 25, 1843," David C. Duniway and Neil R. Riggs (eds.), "The Oregon Archives, 1841–1843," *Oregon Historical Quarterly* LX (June 1959): 228–33.

87.  Sidney W. Moss, Pictures of Pioneer Times at Oregon City (MS, Bancroft Library), 28–31; John M. Bacon, Mercantile Life at Oregon City (MS, Bancroft Library), 7–8; Ninevah Ford, The Pioneer Road Makers (MS, Bancroft Library), 21–23; Jesse Applegate, Views of Oregon History (MS, Bancroft Library), 6–7; F. G. Young (ed.), *Journal of Medorem Crawford* (Eugene, Oregon, 1897), p. 23.

For a detailed analysis of the population movement to Oregon, turn to William
Adrian Bowen, "Migration and Settlement on a Far Western Frontier: Oregon to
1850" (Ph.D. thesis, University of California, Berkeley, 1972).

88. Bancroft, *History of Oregon*, I: 292–314; Walter C. Winslow, "Contests over the
Capital of Oregon," *Oregon Historical Quarterly* IX (June 1908): 173; Robert
Carlton Clark, "How British and American Subjects Unite in a Common
Government for Oregon Territory in 1844," *ibid.* XIII (June 1912): 140–59. Most
recently the political details have been assessed by Kent D. Richards, "The
Methodists and the Formation of the Oregon Provisional Government," *Pacific
Northwest Quarterly* LXI (April 1970): 87–93.

89. For a discussion of the "Champoeg Legend," see Hussey, *Champoeg*, pp. 316–37.

90. Lamb, "Introduction," *Letters of John McLoughlin, Third Series*, pp. xl–xliii.

91. Lyman (comp.), "Reminiscences of F. X. Matthieu," *Oregon Historical Quarterly*
I (March 1900), 104; Henry E. Reed, "William Johnson," *ibid.* XXXIV
(December 1933): 314, 316–19; Leslie M. Scott, "Beginnings of East Portland,"
*ibid.* III (December 1902): 425–26; R. C. Clark, "Asa Lawrence Lovejoy," *DAB*
XI: 433–34.

92. New York *Herald*, Dec. 28, 1844, quoted from "Letters of Peter H. Burnett,"
*Oregon Historical Quarterly* III (December 1902): 425–26; Peter H. Burnett,
*Recollections and Opinions of an Old Pioneer* (New York, 1880), pp. 137–38, 177;
Thomas W. Prosch, *McCarver and Tacoma* (Seattle, 1906), pp. 30–31.

93. Leslie M. Scott, "First Taxes in Oregon, 1844," *Oregon Historical Quarterly*
XXXI (March 1930): 2, 3, 8, 9; Scott, "Oregon Tax Roll," *ibid.* 12–24.

94. "Letters of Peter H. Burnett," *ibid.* III (December 1902): 425; Joseph Schafer,
"Jesse Applegate; Pioneer and State Builder," *University of Oregon Bulletin* IX
(February 1912): 10; Work Progress Administration, Writers' Program, *Oregon:
End of the Trail* (Portland, 1940), pp. 150–52.

95. J. V. Huntington (trans. and ed.), *Narrative of a Voyage to the Northwest Coast of
America in the Years 1811, 1812, 1813, and 1814, or the First American
Settlement on the Pacific. By Gabriel Franchère* (New York, 1854), pp. 163,
168–69, 170; Hoyt C. Franchère (trans. and ed.), *Adventure at Astoria,
1810–1814. By Gabriel Franchère* (Norman, 1967), pp. 73, 75, 76; Fred S.
Perrine, "Early Days on the Willamette," *Oregon Historical Quarterly* XXV
(December 1924): 304.

96. Clarence B. Bagley (ed.), "Letter by Daniel H. Lownsdale to Samuel R.
Thurston, First Territorial Delegate from Oregon to Congress," *Oregon Histori-
cal Quarterly* XIV (September 1913): 215–16; Lewis A. McArthur, *Oregon
Geographic Names* (Portland, 3rd. rev. ed., 1952), pp. 83, 97–98, 407–8, 528–29.

97. Scott, "First Taxes in Oregon, 1844," *Oregon Historical Quarterly* XXXI (March
1930): 2.

CHAPTER 4

1. "List of Trading Posts," Hiram Martin Chittenden, *The American Fur Trade of
the Far West*, 3 vols. (New York, 1902), III:947–74; Edmond S. Meany, "The

Towns of the Pacific Northwest Were Not Founded on the Fur Trade," *Annual Report of the American Historical Association for the Year 1909* (Washington, 1911), pp. 165–72.

2. Marvin Meyers, *The Jacksonian Persuasion* (New York, 1960), p. 34; Richard Hofstaedter, *The American Political Tradition* (New York, 1954), p. 57; William H. Goetzmann, "The Mountain Man as Jacksonian Man," *American Quarterly* XV (Fall 1963): 404–6, 413.

3. Washington Irving, *Astoria*, 2 vols. (Philadelphia, 1961), I:117–18; R. Halliburton, Jr., "John Colter's Run for Life," *Great Plains Journal* III (Fall 1963), 32–33; Reuben G. Thwaites (ed.), *Original Journals of the Lewis and Clark Expedition*, 8 vols. (New York, 1904–5), V: 335, 341.

4. Gouverneur K. Warren, "Memoir to Accompany the Map of the Territory of the United States from the Mississippi River to the Pacific Ocean," *Reports of Explorations and Surveys to Ascertain the Most Practicable and Economical Route for a Railroad from the Mississippi River to the Pacific Ocean*, 33 Cong., 2 Sess., *Senate Ex. Doc.* No. 78, XI; Herman R. Friis, "The Image of the American West at Mid-Century (1840–60); A Product of Scientific Geographical Exploration by the United States Government," John Francis McDermott (ed.), *The Frontier Re-examined* (Urbana, 1967), pp. 55–59.

5. John W. Dwinelle, "Sir Francis Drake's Bay," P. J. Thomas (comp.), *Our Centennial Memoir. Founding of the Missions. San Francisco de Assis in Its Hundredth Year. The Celebration of Its Foundation. Historical Reminiscences of the Missions of California* (San Francisco, 1877), p. 191; John W. Caughey (ed.), *Six Months in the Gold Mines: From a Journal of Three Years' Residence in Upper and Lower California, 1847–8–9, by E. Gould Buffum* (Los Angeles, 1959), pp. 3–4.

6. Sherburne Friend Cook, *The Conflict between the California Indian and White Civilization*, 4 vols. (Berkeley, 1943), I:8–9, 51; III:3–4.

7. George Simpson, *An Overland Journey Round the World, During the Years 1841 and 1842*. 2 parts (Philadelphia, 1847), Part I, p. 184.

8. Theodore H. Hittell, *History of California*, 4 vols. (San Francisco, 1885–97), II:208–10; Zephyrin Engelhardt, *San Francisco or Mission Dolores* (Chicago, 1924), pp. 242–44.

9. Hubert Howe Bancroft, *History of California*, 7 vols. (San Francisco, 1884–90), V:660.

10. *Ibid.*

11. Edwin Bryant, *What I Saw in California: Being the Journal of a Tour by the Emigrant Route and South Pass of the Rocky Mountains, Across the Continent of North America, the Great Desert Basin and Through California in the Years 1846, 1847* (Santa Ana, California, 1936), p. 300.

12. Charles Edward Pickett to William Heath Davis, December 18, 1846, Lawrence Clark Powell, *Philosopher Pickett* (Berkeley, 1942), p. 137.

13. J. L. Ver Mehr, "One of the Argonauts of '49," *Overland Monthly* X (June 1873): 547.

14. Fred Blackburn Rogers (ed.), *Filings from an Old Saw: Reminiscences of San Francisco and California's Conquest by "Filings"—Joseph T. Downey* (San Francisco, 1956), p. 9.

15. 30 Cong., 2 Sess., *House Ex. Doc. No. 1*, pp. 1018–19; William D. Phelps, *Fore and Aft; or, Leaves from the Life of an Old Sailor. By "Webfoot"* (Boston, 1871), pp. 252–53; Douglas S. Watson, "San Francisco's Ancient Cannon: An Inquiry Into Their History and Origin Together with Some Notes on the Castillo de San Joaquin," *California Historical Quarterly* XV (March 1936): 60, 61.

16. Fred Blackburn Rogers (ed.), *A Navy Surgeon in California, 1846–1847: The Journal of Marius Duvall* (San Francisco, 1957), p. 38.

17. George H. Elliot, "The Presidio of San Francisco," *Overland Monthly* IV (April 1870):338.

18. Jessie D. Francis, "An Economic and Social History of Mexican California (1822–1846)," one volume in two parts (Ph.D. thesis, University of California, Berkeley, 1935), Part 2, 366–67.

19. Bancroft, *History of California*, II:422; Francis, "Mexican California," Part 2, 354–55.

20. George Tays, "Mariano Guadalupe Vallejo and Sonoma: A Biography and a History," *California Historical Quarterly* XVI (June 1937): 109; Clarence John Du Four, "The Russian Withdrawal from California," *ibid.* XII (September 1933): 240–76; E. O. Essig, "The Russian Settlement at Ross," *ibid.* 191–209; Adele Ogden, "Russian Sea-Otter and Seal Hunting on the California Coast, 1803–1841," *ibid.* 217–39; Bancroft, *History of California*, IV:98; Francis, "Mexican California," Part 2, 369.

21. Benjamin Morrell, *A Narrative of Four Voyages to the South Sea, North and South Pacific Ocean, Chinese Sea, Ethiopic and Southern Atlantic Ocean, Indian and Antarctic Ocean. From the Year 1822 to 1831* (New York, 1832), p. 211.

22. Bernard Moses, *The Establishment of Municipal Government in San Francisco* (Baltimore, 1889), p. 21.

23. J. N. Bowman, "Determination of the Birthdays of Urban Communities," *California Historical Quarterly* XXVII (March 1948): 58, 59.

24. Albert D. Richardson, *Beyond the Mississippi* (Hartford, 1867), pp. 157–58; Calvin W. Gower, "Kansas 'Border Town' Newspapers and the Pike's Peak Gold Rush," *Journalism Quarterly* XLIV (Summer 1967): 281–82; Gower, "Gold Fever in Kansas Territory: Migration to the Pike's Peak Gold Fields, 1858–1860," *Kansas Historical Quarterly* XXXIX (Spring 1973): 58; Raymond Calhoun, "The Naming of Pikes Peak," *Colorado Magazine* XXXI (April 1954): 104.

25. Daniel Blue, *Thrilling Narrative of the Adventures, Sufferings and Starvation of Pike's Peak Gold Seekers on the Plains of the West, in the Winter and Spring of 1859. By One of the Survivors* (Fairfield, Washington, 1968), p. 11.

26. Libeus Barney, *Letters of the Pike's Peak Gold Rush, or Early Day Letters from Auraria, Reprinted from the Bennington Banner, Vermont, 1859–1860* (San Jose, 1959), pp. 25, 27, 76, 85.

27. Alfred L. Kroeber, "The Arapaho," *Bulletin of the American Museum of Natural History* XVIII (1907): 405; Lillian B. Shields, "Relations with the Cheyennes and

Arapahoes in Colorado to 1861," *Colorado Magazine* IV (August 1927): 147; Jerome C. Smiley, *History of Denver; With Outlines of the Earlier History of the Rocky Mountain Country* (Denver, 1901), pp. 69–70; Kroeber, *Cultural and Natural Areas of Native North America* (Berkeley, 1963), pp. 80, 82; Symmes C. Oliver, *Ecology and Natural Continuity as Factors in the Social Organization of the Plains Indians* (Berkeley, 1962), pp. 35–36; Robert H. Lowie, *Indians of the Plains* (Garden City, New York, 1963), p. 39. Details about the encounter between Arapaho and whites can be located conveniently in Virginia Cole Trenholm, *The Arapahoes, Our People* (Norman, 1970).

28.  Mason Wade (ed.), *The Journals of Francis Parkman*, 2 vols. (New York, 1947), II:472; J. Neilson Barry (ed.), "Journal of E. Willard Smith While With the Fur Traders, Vasquez and Sublette, in the Rocky Mountain Region, 1839–1840," *Oregon Historical Quarterly* XIV (September 1913): 261, reprinted by LeRoy R. Hafen (ed.), "With Fur Traders in Colorado, 1839–40; The Journal of E. Willard Smith," *Colorado Magazine* XXVII (July 1950): 171–72; Hafen, "The Early Fur Trade Posts on the South Platte," *Journal of American History* XII (December 1925): 334–41; Hafen, "Fort Vasquez," *Colorado Magazine* XLI (Summer 1964): 199–210; W. James Judge, "The Archaeology of Fort Vasquez," *ibid.* XLVIII (Summer 1971): 181–203; Hafen, "Fort St. Vrain," *ibid.* XXIX (October 1952): 241–57; Hafen, "Old Fort Lupton and Its Founder," *ibid.* VI (November 1929): 220–26; Hafen, "Fort Jackson and the Early Fur Trade on the South Platte," *ibid.* V (February 1928): 9–17; Hafen, "Mountain Men—Louis Vasquez," *ibid.* X (January 1933): 18–19; Hafen, "Mountain Men—Andrew W. Sublette," *ibid.* (September 1933): 181–82; Hafen, "Map of Early Trails, Forts and Battlefields of Colorado," *Denver Municipal Facts* VIII (March-April 1925): 17–18.

29.  Robert Morris Peck, "Recollections of Early Times in Kansas Territory," *Transactions of the Kansas State Historical Society, 1903–1904* VIII: 491–92.

30.  Chittenden, *Fur Trade*, II:543; George Bent to George Hyde, February 26, 1906 (Denver Public Library) cited in Janet Lecompte, "Charles Autobees," *Colorado Magazine* XXXV (January 1958): 56; *ibid.* (April 1958): 143; Lecompte, "Gantt's Fort and Bent's Picket Post," *ibid.* XLI (Spring 1964): 111–25; LeRoy R. Hafen, "When Was Bent's Fort Built?" *ibid.* XXXI (April 1954): 105–9.

31.  LeRoy R. Hafen, "The Fort Pueblo Massacre and the Punitive Expedition Against the Utes," *Colorado Magazine* XXXV (January 1958): 49–51; Lecompte, "Charles Autobees," *ibid.* XXXV (January 1958): 65–66.

32.  LeRoy R. Hafen and Frank M. Young, "The Mormon Settlement at Pueblo, Colorado, During the Mexican War," *ibid.* IX (July 1932): 121–36; Lecompte, "Charles Autobees," *ibid.* XXXV (January 1958): 66–69.

33.  Joseph Jablow, *The Cheyenne in Plains Indian Trade Relations, 1795–1840* (New York, 1950), pp. 65, 72–77.

34.  Cheetham, "Early Settlements," *Colorado Magazine* V (February 1928): 3–4. See also Michael D. Heaston, "Whiskey Regulation and Indian Land Titles in New Mexico Territory, 1851–1861," *Journal of the West* X (July 1971): 474–83.

35.  Andrew Drips to Thomas H. Harvey, Superintendent of Indian Affairs, April 11, 1845, Chittenden, *Fur Trade*, I:369.

36. "Report of Thomas Fitzpatrick," Appendix to the Report of the Commissioner of Indian Affairs, 30 Cong., 1 Sess., *Senate Ex. Doc. No. 1*, p. 754.

37. Josiah Gregg, *Commerce of the Prairies*, 2 vols. (New York, 1844), II:54; Charles L. Kenner, *A History of New Mexican Plains Indian Relations* (Norman, 1969), pp. 87, 88, 91.

38. LeRoy R. Hafen, "Mexican Land Grants in Colorado," *Colorado Magazine* IV (May 1927): 85, 86–88; Ralph Carr, "Private Land Claims in Colorado," *ibid.* XXIV (January 1948): 10, 19–20; Francis T. Cheetham, "The Early Settlements of Southern Colorado," *ibid.* V (February 1928): 5–7.

39. Lecompte, "Hardscrabble," *Colorado Magazine* XXXI (April 1954): 95–96.

40. Helen G. Gill, "The Establishment of Counties in Kansas," *Transactions of the Kansas State Historical Society* VIII (1903–4): 449–52; Frank W. Blackmar (ed.), *Kansas: A Cyclopedia of State History, Embracing Events, Institutions, Industries, Counties, Cities, Towns, Prominent Persons, Etc.*, 2 vols. (Chicago, 1912), I:459–61, 646–66.

41. Peck, "Recollections," *Transactions of the Kansas State Historical Society* VIII:487.

42. Barney, *Letters*, 40.

43. Douglas S. Watson, "An Hour's Walk Through Yerba Buena Which Later Became San Francisco," *California Historical Quarterly* XVII (December 1938): 291.

44. J. N. Bowman, "The Spanish Anchorage in San Francisco Bay," *ibid.* XXV (December 1946): 323.

45. List of the foreigners established in the sixth section of San Francisco de Asís, May 10, 1840, California Land Grant Case, No. 427, N.D. (MS, Bancroft Library), Exhibit Hopkins No. 10, pp. 1–5; "Letter of Francisco de Haro to the Five Merchants of Yerba Buena," *California Historical Quarterly* XIV (June 1935): 121.

46. Richard Henry Dana, Jr., *Two Years Before the Mast: A Personal Narrative of Life at Sea* (New York, 1936), p. 251; Bowman, "Urban Communities," *California Historical Quarterly* XXVII (March 1948): 60; John Bernard McGloin, S. J., "William A. Richardson, Founder and First Resident of Yerba Buena," *Journal of the West* V (October 1966): 493–503.

47. Watson, "Hour's Walk," *California Historical Quarterly* XVII (December 1938): 292.

48. "William Glen Rae," E. E. Rich (ed.), *The Letters of John McLoughlin From Fort Vancouver to the Governor and Committee, First Series, 1825–38* (Toronto, 1941), pp. 353–55; McLoughlin to Governor, Deputy Governor, and Committee, May 24, 1841, Aug. 19, 1842, Nov. 15, 1843, July 4, 1844; Rich (ed.), *The Letters of John McLoughlin From Fort Vancouver to the Governor and Committee, Second Series, 1838–44* (Toronto, 1943), pp. 35, 62–63, 123, 194–95.

49. Simpson, *Overland Journey*, Part I, p. 161.

50. Sir George Simpson to John McLoughlin, March 3, 1842, Rich (ed.), *Letters of John McLoughlin, Second Series*, p. 277.

51. James H. Wilkins (ed.), "The Days of the Dons: Reminiscences of California's

Oldest Native Son. By 'Steve' Richardson," San Francisco *Bulletin*, Apr. 26, 1918.

52.  William Glen Rae to William Smith, August 27, 1843, Anson S. Blake (ed.), "The Hudson's Bay Company in San Francisco," *California Historical Quarterly* XXVIII (September 1949): 251; Harold A. Small (ed.), *Seventy-five Years in California. Recollections and Remarks by One Who Visited These Shores in 1831, and Again in 1833, and Except When Absent on Business Was a Resident from 1838 Until the End of a Long Life in 1909. By William Heath Davis* (San Francisco, 1967), p. 70; Bancroft, *History of California* IV:593–94; W. Kaye Lamb, "Introduction," Rich (ed.), *Letters of John McLoughlin, Third Series*, p. xxvii; Alice B. Maloney, "Hudson's Bay Company in California," *Oregon Historical Quarterly* XXXVII (March 1936): 21–23.

53.  San Francisco *Call*, March 11, 1877; Small (ed.), *Seventy-five Years in California. By William Heath Davis*, pp. 288–92.

54.  California Land Grant Case, No. 427, N.D., 600–606; John W. Dwinelle, (ed.), *The Colonial History of San Francisco* (San Francisco, 1863), Addenda, LV.

55.  California Land Grant Case, No. 427, N. D., 11. For details of the American Conquest of Yerba Buena turn to John S. Hittell, *A History of the City of San Francisco and Incidentally of the State of California* (San Francisco, 1878), p. 86; Joeth Skinner Eldredge, *The Beginnings of San Francisco*, 2 vols. (San Francisco, 1912) II:539–45; Bancroft, *History of California* V:238–39, 295; Hittell, *History of California* II:467–68.

56.  Washington A. Bartlett to Jasper O'Farrell, November 26, 1846, Douglas S. Watson, "The Great Express Extra of the *California Star* of April 1, 1848; The Forerunner of California Promotion Literature," *California Historical Quarterly* XI (June 1932): 134; Hittell, *History of San Francisco*, p. 86.

57.  San Francisco *California Star*, January 23, 30, 1847; John Henry Brown, *Early Days of San Francisco, California* (Oakland, 1949), pp. 26, 37; Fred Blackburn Rogers, *Montgomery and the Portsmouth* (San Francisco, 1958), p. 75.

58.  Bancroft, *History of California* II:416–17; IV:296–97; Rodman W. Paul, *California Gold: The Beginning of Mining in the Far West* (Cambridge, Mass., 1947), pp. 36–39.

59.  Bruno Fritzsche, "San Francisco 1846–1848: The Coming of the Land Speculator," *California Historical Quarterly* LI (Spring 1972): 17, 32.

60.  Richardson, *Beyond the Mississippi*, p. 177.

61.  Smiley, *History of Denver*, pp. 293, 314, 320, 331, 333, 339–50. Some accounts of life in the diggings can be found in LeRoy R. Hafen (ed.), *Colorado Gold Rush: Contemporary Letters and Reports, 1858–1859* (Glendale, 1941), pp. 137–386. For a vivid picture turn to Stanley M. Zamonski and Teddy Keller, *The '59ers: Roaring Denver in the Gold Rush Days* (2nd ed., Denver, 1967).

62.  Robert L. Stearns, "Who Have the Power?" *Colorado Magazine* XVI (January 1939): 11.

63.  Henry Villard, "To the Pike's Peak Country in 1859 and Cannibalism on the Smoky Hill Route," *Colorado Magazine* VIII (November 1931): 236. For the site of Denver as a favorite Arapaho campground, see also Trenholm, *The Arapahoes*, pp. 152–56.

64. John C. Frémont, *The Exploring Expedition to the Rocky Mountains, Oregon and California* (Buffalo, 1852), pp. 133–34; Frank Hall, *History of the State of Colorado*, 4 vols. (Chicago, 1889–95), I:120.

65. Smiley, *History of Denver*, p. 70.

66. Charles J. Kappler (comp.), *Indian Affairs: Laws and Treaties*, 5 vols. (Washington, 1904–41), II:594–96; "The Great Fort Laramie Treaty Council, 1851," LeRoy R. Hafen and Francis Marion Young, *Fort Laramie and the Pageant of the West, 1834–1890* (Glendale, 1938), pp. 177–96. For the fact that the amended treaty was referred to the Indians, see also Lillian B. Shields, "Relations with the Cheyennes and Arapahoes in Colorado to 1861," *Colorado Magazine* IV (August 1927): 149; James C. Murphy, "The Place of the Northern Arapahoes in the Relations Between the United States and the Indians of the Plains, 1851–1879," *Annals of Wyoming* XLI (October 1969): 203–4.

67. 33 Cong., 1 Sess., *United States Statutes at Large* X:284.

68. Stearns, "Who Have the Power?" *Colorado Magazine* XVI (January 1939): 11.

69. "The Fort Wise Treaty," LeRoy R. and Ann W. Hafen (eds.), *Relations with the Indians of the Plains, 1857–1861: A Documentary Account of the Military Campaigns, and Negotiations of Indian Agents—With Reports and Journals of P. G. Lowe, R. M. Peck, J. E. B. Stuart, S. D. Sturgis, and Other Official Papers* (Glendale, 1959), pp. 283–99; Shields, "Relations with the Cheyennes and Arapahoes," *Colorado Magazine* IV (August 1927): 153–54; Morris F. Taylor, "Fort Wise," *ibid.* XLVI (Spring 1969): 105–7.

70. 37 Cong., 1 Sess., *United States Statutes at Large* XII:1166–67.

71. Denver *Rocky Mountain News*, Dec. 1, 1859; Richardson, *Beyond the Mississippi*, p. 299.

72. LeRoy R. Hafen, "The Last Years of James P. Beckwourth," *Colorado Magazine* V (August 1928): 135–37.

73. *Rocky Mountain News*, Apr. 4, 1860.

74. *Ibid.*

75. Nolie Mumey, *James Pierson Beckwourth, 1856–1866, An Enigmatic Figure of the West: A History of the Latter Years of His Life* (Denver, 1957), pp. 149–59.

76. Margaret I. Carrington, *Ab-Sa-Ra-Ka, Home of the Crows: Being the Experience of an Officer's Wife on the Plains* (Philadelphia, 1868), p. 131.

77. *Rocky Mountain News*, Feb. 5, 1867; Thomas D. Bonner, *The Life and Adventures of James P. Beckwourth, Mountaineer, Scout, and Pioneer, and Chief of the Crow Nation of Indians* (New York, 1856), p. 13; Incomplete Abstract of *Life* by T. D. Bonner, in the handwriting of Walter M. Fisher (Photostat of missing original, Bancroft Library), p. 1; William N. Byers, *Encyclopedia of Biography of Colorado* (Chicago, 1901), pp. 20–21; "Sand Creek Massacre," 39 Cong., 2 Sess., *Senate Ex. Doc. No. 26*, pp. 68–76. Mumey, *Beckwourth*, pp. 121–45, transcribed Beckwourth's testimony before the military commission investigating the campaign. See also Hafen, "Last Years of Beckwourth," *Colorado Magazine* V (August 1928): 139; Delmont R. Oswald, "James P. Beckwourth," Hafen (ed.), *Mountain Men and Fur Trade* VI:37–38; Elinor Wilson, *Jim Beckwourth, Black Mountain Man and War Chief of the Crows* (Norman, 1972), pp. 18–19.

272                                                                    INSTANT CITIES

78. Bonner, *Life of Beckwourth*, p. 371; "Sand Creek Massacre," 39 Cong., 2 Sess., *Senate Ex. Doc. No. 26*, p. 76.
79. "Templeton Diary," Mumey, *Beckwourth*, p. 173.
80. *Rocky Mountain News*, Apr. 18, 1860. See also "Justice for Indians," Mumey, *Beckwourth*, pp. 149–59; Hafen, "Last Years of Beckwourth," *Colorado Magazine* V (August 1928): 135–37.
81. *Rocky Mountain News*, Apr. 18, 1860.
82. Denver *Bulletin* (Supplement to *Rocky Mountain News*), May 2, 1860.
83. Smiley, *History of Denver*, pp. 69, 228, 304, 402.
84. Charles M. Clark, *A Trip to Pike's Peak and Notes by the Way, With Numerous Illustrations: Being Descriptive of Incidents and Accidents that Attended the Pilgrimage; of the Country through Kansas and Nebraska, Rocky Mountains, Mining Regions, Mining Operations, Etc., Etc.* (Chicago, 1861), pp. 71–72.
85. Bancroft, *History of California* VI:83; Hittell, *History of San Francisco*, pp. 127–28; Paul, *California Gold*, p. 21.
86. *California Star*, Apr. 1, 1848; Frank Soulé, John H. Gihon, and James Nesbit, *The Annals of San Francisco* (New York, 1855), p. 200.
87. Helen Harding Bretnor (ed.), *A History of California Newspapers, 1846–1858, by Edward C. Kemble. Reprinted from the Supplement to the Sacramento Union of December 25, 1858* (Los Gatos, 1962), p. 78; Fred Blackburn Rogers (ed.), *A Kemble Reader; Stories of California, 1846–1848. By Edward Cleveland Kemble, Early California Journalist* (San Francisco, 1963), pp. 130–39; Bancroft, *History of California* VI:56; Reva Scott, *San Francisco's Forgotten Jason; Samuel Brannan and the Golden Fleece; A Biography* (New York, 1944), pp. 221–22.
88. Soulé, *Annals*, p. 204.
89. Bancroft, *History of California*, VI:95, 357.
90. Sherman, *Memoirs*, p. 66.
91. Frederick J. Teggart (ed.), *Around the Horn to the Sandwich Islands and California, 1845–1850: Being a Personal Record Kept by Chester S. Lyman* (New Haven, 1924), p. 283; John A. Hussey (ed.), *A Trip to the Gold Mines of California in 1848. By John A. Swan* (San Francisco, 1960), p. 13; Brown, *Early Days*, 83–85; James C. Ward, "Extracts from My Diary. By An Early Californian," *Argonaut* III (August 24, 1878): 10; Hittell, *History of San Francisco*, pp. 128–29.
92. Caughey (ed.), *Six Months in the Gold Mines by E. Gould Buffum*, p. 4.
93. Ver Mehr, "Argonauts," *Overland Monthly* X (June 1873): 546.
94. John Sedgwick to Emily Sedgwick Welch, November 30, December 10, 1860, Jan. 16, 1861, *Correspondence of John Sedgwick, Major-General*, 2 vols. (New York, 1902–3) II:28, 29, 31.
95. Billie Barnes Jensen, "Confederate Sentiment in Colorado," Denver Westerners, *1957 Brand Book* (Boulder, 1958), pp. 85–117.
96. Milo Milton Quaife (ed.), *Uncle Dick Wootton: The Pioneer Frontiersman of the Rocky Mountain Region. By Howard Louis Conard* (Chicago, 1957), pp. 361–64.
97. John Sedgwick to Emily Sedgwick Welch, Sept. 25, 1860, *Correspondence of John Sedgwick* I:24.

98. Agnes Wright Spring (ed.), "Nathaniel P. Hill Inspects Colorado," *Colorado Magazine* XXXIII (October 1956): 246.

99. "Letter from the Regular Correspondent of the [St. Louis] *Missouri Democrat*," June 4, 1859, LeRoy R. and Ann W. Hafen (eds.), *Reports from Colorado. The Wildman Letters, 1859–1865, With Other Related Letters and Newspaper Reports, 1859* (Glendale, 1961), p. 91; *Rocky Mountain News*, June 18, July 9, 1859; LeRoy R. Hafen, "Supplies and Market Prices in Pioneer Denver," *Colorado Magazine* IV (August 1927): 136–42; Agnes Wright Spring, "Food Facts of 1859," *ibid.* XXII (May 1945): 113–16; Mumey, *Early Settlements of Denver*, pp. 139–40.

100. "Major John Sedgwick's Report on the Building of Fort Wise, October 22, 1860," Hafen and Hafen (eds.), *Relations with the Indians*, pp. 273–74; Smiley, *History of Denver*, p. 404; Nolie Mumey, "John Milton Chivington, the Misunderstood Man," Denver Westerners, *1956 Brand Book* (Denver, 1957), 134–35.

101. Susan Riley Ashley, "Reminiscences of Colorado in the Early 'Sixties," *Colorado Magazine* XIII (November 1936): 223.

102. Spring (ed.), "Hill Inspects Colorado," *ibid.* XXXIV (January 1957): 24–25; Smiley, *History of Denver*, pp. 404–10.

103. Richardson, *Beyond the Mississippi*, p. 300; Spring (ed.), "Hill Inspects Colorado," *Colorado Magazine* XXXIV (January 1957): 24, 34, 36, 45; Alice Polk Hill, *Colorado Pioneers in Picture and Story* (Denver, 1915), pp. 202, 203, 207–12; Edith Parker Low, "History of the Twenty-Mile House on Cherry Creek," *Colorado Magazine* XII (July 1935): 142–43; James Harvey (ed.), "The Twelve Mile House; Recollections by Mrs. Jane Melvin," *ibid.* (September 1935): 177–78; LeRoy R. Hafen, "Gerry Elbridge, Colorado Pioneer," *ibid.* XXIX (April 1952): 144. On the warfare of the 1860s, see also, " 'They Must Go,' " Trenholm, The *Arapahoes*, pp. 158–96.

104. *Rocky Mountain News*, Dec. 22, 1864; Denver *Times*, Sept. 13, 1883; Denver *Republican*, Sept. 14, 1883; Quaife (ed.), *Uncle Dick Wootton*, pp. 388–92; Lynn I. Perigo, "Major Hal Sayr's Diary of the Sand Creek Campaign," *Colorado Magazine* XV (March 1938): 56–57.

105. *Rocky Mountain News*, Dec. 7, 8, 1864.

106. Central City *Daily Miners' Register*, Jan. 25, 1865; "Sand Creek Massacre," 39 Cong., 2 Sess., *Senate Ex. Doc. No. 26*; Smiley, *History of Denver*, pp. 409–10. For a discussion of the Sand Creek literature turn to Michael A. Sievers, "Sands of Sand Creek Historiography," *Colorado Magazine* XLIX (Spring 1972): 118–42.

107. Manuscript report of the annual meeting of Colorado Pioneers in Denver, September 13, 1883, State Historical Society of Colorado Library, Denver.

108. Manuscript copy of John M. Chivington's address of September 13, 1883, State Historical Society of Colorado, Denver.

109. Smiley, *History of Denver*, p. 410; Harry Kelsey, "Background to Sand Creek," *Colorado Magazine* XLV (Fall 1968): 293, 300.

110. Ovando J. Hollister, *The Mines of Colorado* (Springfield, 1867), p. 429.

111. Smiley, *History of Denver*, pp. 410–12; Mumey, "Chivington," *1956 Brand Book*, pp. 125–48.
112. *Rocky Mountain News*, July 15, 16, 1874; James W. Covington, "Ute Scalp Dance in Denver," *Colorado Magazine* XXX (April 1953): 119–24; Wilson Rockwell, *The Utes: A Forgotten People* (Denver, 1956), pp. 93–94.
113. *Denver City and Auraria, The Commercial Emporium of the Pike's Peak Regions, in 1859* (Denver, 1859).
114. Quoted from Roderick Nash, *Wilderness and the American Mind* (New Haven, 1967), p. 23.
115. Smiley, *History of Denver*, p. 161.
116. Quaife (ed.), *Uncle Dick Wootton*, pp. 369–70.
117. "How They Were Christened; Denver's Original Streets and How They Got Their Titles," Denver *Republican*, July 8, 1888; Smiley, *History of Denver*, 182, 188, 191–92, 198, 199, 208, 221–22, 448; Hafen, "Colorado Mountain Men," *Colorado Magazine* XXX (January 1953): 21–22; J. Nevin Carson, "Naming Denver's Streets," Denver Westerners, *1964 Brand Book* (Denver, 1965), pp. 13–14.

CHAPTER 5

1. "Denver, Colorado," *St. Louis Illustrated Magazine* XXI (October 1881): 382.
2. For the hotels, see Richard A. Van Orman, "San Francisco: Hotel City of the West," John Alexander Carroll (ed.), *Reflections of Western Historians* (Tucson, 1969), pp. 14–15; Oscar Lewis and Carroll D. Hall, *Bonanza Inn: America's First Luxury Hotel* (New York, 1939), p. 40; "The Denver Mansions Company," Denver *Times*, December 3, 1879; "The Windsor," *Colorado Exchange Journal* (October 1889), 30; Joseph Emerson Smith, "Personal Recollections of Early Denver," *Colorado Magazine* XX (March 1943): 57, 68; John W. and Doris G. Buchanan, *A Story of the Fabulous Windsor Hotel* (Denver, 2nd ed., 1956), p. 9; Caroline Bancroft, "Debut of the Windsor," Denver Westerners, *1951 Brand Book* (Denver, 1952), p. 292.
3. For general discussions of the populations of California and Colorado, turn to Doris Marion Wright, "The Making of Cosmopolitan California; An Analysis of Immigration, 1848–1870," *California Historical Quarterly* XIX (December 1940): 323–43; XX (March 1941): 65–79; Marion Clawson, "What It Means To Be a Californian," *ibid.* XXIV (June 1945): 139–61; John Burton Phillips, "The Population of Colorado," *University of Colorado Studies* V (June 1908): 197–219; Colin B. Goodykoontz, "The People of Colorado," *Colorado Magazine* XXIII (November 1946): 241–55; Goodykoontz, "The People of Colorado," LeRoy R. Hafen (ed.), *Colorado and Its People: A Narrative and Topical History of the Centennial State*, 4 vols. (New York, 1948), II:77–120.
4. Ernest Ingersoll, *The Crest of the Continent: A Record of a Summer's Ramble in the Rocky Mountains and Beyond* (Chicago, 1885) p. 22.
5. "The Movements of Population," San Francisco *News Letter and California Advertiser*, July 26, 1879, p. 5.

6. James Philip MacCarthy, "Denver—An Impressional Sketch. By Fitz-Mac [pseud.] and Others—Mainly Others," *Colorado Magazine* I (July 1893): 285, 288, 292. For the appearance of Denver in 1860, turn to Edgar C. McMechen, "The Model of Auraria-Denver of 1860," *Colorado Magazine* XII (July 1935): 121–26. See also "How Denver Is Growing. Impressions of One Who Has Been Absent. How a Return to Denver Makes the Building Very Noticeable—New Structures Going Up on All Sides," Denver *Times*, Nov. 2, 1886.

7. "Report of Don Pedro de Alberni, July 1, 1796," John W. Dwinelle (ed.), *Colonial History of the City of San Francisco* (San Francisco, 1863), Addenda No. IX, 18; Josiah Dwight Whitney, *Geological Survey of California*, 2 vols. (Philadelphia, 1865–82) I:77–79; William Gilpin, *The Cosmopolitan Railway, Compacting and Fusing Together All the World's Continents* (San Francisco, 1890), pp. 217–18, 226–27.

8. Thomas W. Norris (publ.), *A Letter of Captain J. L. Folsom Reporting on Conditions in California in 1848* (Livermore, California, 1944); "To the Public," San Francisco *Daily Alta California*, May 17, 1849; E. Gould Buffum, *Six Months in the Gold Mines* (Philadelphia, 1850), p. 150; William T. Sherman, *Memoirs*, 2 vols. in one (Bloomington, 1957), pp. 73–74; Frank Soulé, John H. Gihon, and James Nisbet, *The Annals of San Francisco* (New York, 1855), p. 756; John Adam Hussey, "Identification of the Author of 'The Farthest West' Letters from California, 1846," *California Historical Quarterly* XVI (September 1937): 209–15; Robert Ernest Cowan, "The Leidesdorff-Folsom Estate: A Forgotten Chapter in the Romantic History of Early San Francisco," *ibid.* VII (June 1928): 105–11; Ernest A. Wiltsee, "The City of New York of the Pacific," *ibid.* XII (March 1933): 30–32; Brooke Nihart, "A New York Regiment in California, 1846–1848," *Military Collector & Historian* XXI (Spring 1969): 11.

9. Zoe Green Radcliffe, "Robert Baylor Semple, Pioneer," *California Historical Quarterly* VI (June 1927): 130–58; Hubert Howe Bancroft, *History of California*, 7 vols. (San Francisco, 1884–90), V:670–74. Part of the extensive correspondence of Thomas O. Larkin about Benicia can conveniently be found in George P. Hammond (ed.), *The Larkin Papers: Personal, Business, and Official Correspondence of Thomas Oliver Larkin, Merchant and United States Consul in California.* 10 vols. and Index (Berkeley, 1951–68), in volumes VI, VII, and VIII. For histories of Benicia, see Jacqueline McCart Woodruff, *Benicia: The Promise of California* (Vallejo, 1947), and Peter T. Conmy, *Benicia, Intended Metropolis* (San Francisco, 1958).

10. Bayard Taylor, *El Dorado, or, Adventures in the Path of Empire*, 2 vols. (New York, 1850), I: 217.

11. Sherman, *Memoirs*, 55–56.

12. Hubert Howe Bancroft, *California Pastoral. 1769–1848* (San Francisco, 1888), p. 732.

13. Junius E. Wharton, *History of the City of Denver from Its Earliest Settlement to the Present Time, To Which Is Added a Full and Complete Business Directory of the City. By D. O. Wilhelm* (Denver, 1866), pp. 3, 6, 9. For Wharton, see Douglas C. McMurtrie and Albert H. Allen, *Early Printing in Colorado: With a*

*Bibliography of the Issues of the Press, 1859 to 1876, Inclusive, and a Record and Bibliography of Colorado Territorial Newspapers* (Denver, 1935), pp. 45, 91, 92, 95–96, 227, 241, 269.

14. LeRoy R. Hafen (ed.), *Overland Routes to the Gold Fields, 1859. From Contemporary Diaries* (Glendale, 1942), p. 323; LeRoy R. Hafen, "Map of Early Trails, Forts and Battlefields of Colorado," *Denver Municipal Facts* VIII (March–April 1925): between pp. 17 and 18; James Truslow Adams (ed.), *Atlas of American History* (New York, 1943), pp. 118–19, 120; Nolie Mumey, *History of the Early Settlements of Denver (1599–1860)* (Glendale, 1942), pp. 24–25, 48–49. Detailed stories of the earliest days are Jerome C. Smiley, *History of Denver: With Outlines of the Earlier History of the Rocky Mountain Country* (Denver, 1901), pp. 184–97, and Charles W. Henderson, *Mining in Colorado: A History of Discovery, Development, and Production* (Washington, 1926), pp. 1–7.

15. Samuel S. Curtis to Henry Curtis, November 2, 1858, LeRoy R. Hafen (ed.), *Colorado Gold Rush: Contemporary Letters and Reports, 1858–1859* (Glendale, 1941), p. 147; Hafen (ed.), *Pike's Peak Gold Rush Guidebooks of 1859* (Glendale, 1941), pp. 45, 51, 55, 56–60, 77, 98, 121, 132, 161, 270, 297, 298, 302, 305; Smiley, *History of Denver*, p. 225; Wilbur Fisk Stone, *History of Colorado*, 4 vols. (Chicago, 1918–19), I: 134–35; Mumey, *Early Settlements of Denver*, pp. 54–59, 81–86; Hafen, "Elbridge Gerry, Colorado Pioneer," *Colorado Magazine* XXIX (April 1952): 141.

16. Richard E. Whitsitt to Daniel Witter, May 11, 1859, "Mr. Whitsitt's Letter to Daniel Witter," *Colorado Magazine* I (July 1893): 283–85; J. Thoe Parkinson to J. Jewett Wilcox, April 20, 1859, John Scudder to the St. Louis *Missouri Republican*, January 16, 1859; Hafen (ed.), *Colorado Gold Rush*, pp. 215–17, 338–39; Horace Greeley, *An Overland Journey, From New York to San Francisco, in the Summer of 1859* (New York, 1860), p. 159; Libeus Barney, *Letters of the Pike's Peak Gold Rush, or Early Day Letters from Auraria, Reprinted from the Bennington Banner, Vermont, 1859–1860* (San Jose, 1959), pp. 59, 79; Smiley, *History of Denver*, p. 632; Frank Hall, *History of the State of Colorado*, 4 vols. (Chicago, 1889–95) I: 217; Agnes Wright Spring, "Rush to the Rockies, 1859; Colorado's Gold Rush of 1859," *Colorado Magazine* XXXVI (April 1959): 86–96, 119; LeRoy R. Hafen, "Historical Introduction," Hafen (ed.), *Pike's Peak Gold Rush*, pp. 73–78; Clyde Lyndon King, *The History of the Government of Denver with Special Reference to Its Relations with Public Service Corporations* (Denver, 1911), pp. 13, 23.

17. Milo Milton Quaife (ed.), *Uncle Dick Wootton: The Pioneer Frontiersman of the Rocky Mountain Region. By Howard Louis Conard* (Chicago, 1957), pp. 369–70; Dwight L. Smith (ed.), *John D. Young and the Colorado Gold Rush* (Chicago, 1969), p. 43; Hafen (ed.), *Pike's Peak Gold Rush*, pp. 27, 78, 216; Hafen (ed.), *Colorado Gold Rush*, pp. 167, 173, 184, 203, 204, 210, 212, 224, 226, 230, 236, 239, 241, 243, 337; Hafen (ed.), *Overland Routes*, pp. 162, 169, 175; Hubert Howe Bancroft, *History of Nevada, Colorado, and Wyoming, 1540–1888* (San Francisco, 1890), pp. 376–84; Benjamin Franklin Gilbert, "Pike's Peak or Bust: A Summary of the Colorado Mining Rushes," *Journal of the West* IV (January 1965): 22–23.

18. *News Letter*, July 17, 1880, p. 10, June 28, 1890, p. 26, July 19, 1890, p. 11; Hittell, *Resources of California*, p. 359; Louisa Ward Arps (ed.), "Dean Hart Pre-Views His Wilderness; Excerpts from the 1872 Diary of H. Martyn Hart," *Colorado Magazine* XXXVI (January 1959): 32; W. B. Vickers, *History of the City of Denver* (Chicago, 1880), p. 230; "The Population of Denver," Charles H. Reynolds (comp.), *Sixth Annual Report of the Denver Chamber of Commerce for 1888* (Denver, 1889), p. 32; Smiley, *History of Denver*, pp. 648–49, 936–38.

19. "Population of Cities Having 25,000 Inhabitants or More in 1900, at Each Census: 1790 to 1900," United States, Bureau of the Census, *Twelfth Census*, (Washington, 1901), I:430, 432. Julian Ralph, "Colorado and Its Capital," *Harper's New Monthly Magazine* LXXXVI (May 1893): 940, described Denver's increase between 1870 and 1890 as more than 2000 per cent.

20. Carroll D. Wright, *Outline of Practical Sociology. With Special Reference to American Conditions* (New York, 1899), pp. 8, 11–16; Adna F. Weber, *The Growth of Cities in the Nineteenth Century: A Study in Statistics* (New York, 1899), pp. 476–78. See also, James Leiby, *Carroll Wright and Labor Reform: The Origin of Labor Statistics* (Cambridge, Mass., 1960), pp. 98–100.

21. F. Bret Harte, "San Francisco. From the Sea," *Overland Monthly* I (July 1868): 63; Phil Robinson, *Sinners and Saints: A Tour Across the States, and Round Them; With Three Months Among the Mormons* (Boston, 1883), p. 58; Rudyard Kipling, *American Notes* (New York, 1891), p. 5.

22. Arps (ed.), "Dean Hart Pre-Views His Wilderness," *Colorado Magazine* XXXVI (January 1959): 32.

23. For a meteorological discussion of the subject, see Harold Gilliam, *Weather of the San Francisco Bay Region* (Berkeley, 1962). See also, James E. Vance, Jr., "The Influence of the Fog," *Geography and Urban Evolution in the San Francisco Bay Area* (Berkeley, 1964), pp. 28–32.

24. *News Letter*, Mar. 30, 1867, p. 8, Sept. 16, 1871, p. 8; Hittell, *Resources of California*, pp. 22–24; D. L. Phillips, "Peculiarities of the Climate," *Letters from California* (Springfield, 1877), p. 12.

25. James F. Watkins, "San Francisco," *Overland Monthly* IV (January 1870): 9, 11.

26. Alexander McAdie, *The Clouds and Fogs of San Francisco* (San Francisco, 1912).

27. *Harper's Weekly* XXVI (May 27, 1882), p. 334; Denver *Rocky Mountain News*, Sept. 20, Oct. 10, 1882.

28. Smith (ed.), *John D. Young*, p. 43.

29. Isabella L. Bird Bishop, *A Lady's Life in the Rocky Mountains* (London, 1879), pp. 159–60.

30. Ernest Ingersoll, "The Metropolis of the Rocky Mountains," *Scribner's Monthly* XX (July 1880): 459; Jules Leclercq, *Un été en Amérique de l'Atlantique aux Montagnes Rocheuses* (Paris, 1877), pp. 248–49.

31. "Early Morning in Denver," *Times*, Apr. 30, 1874; *Rocky Mountain News*, Aug. 15, 19, 24, 1882.

32. *Rocky Mountain News*, Aug. 15, 1882.

33. Charles Denison, *Rocky Mountain Health Resorts: An Analytical Study of High Altitudes in Relation to the Arrest of Chronic Pulmonary Disease* (Boston, 1880),

pp. 48–49. Ten years earlier, Fitz Hugh Ludlow, *The Heart of the Continent: A Record of Travel Across the Plains and in Oregon, With an Examination of the Mormon Principle* (New York, 1870), p. 131, also spoke about a revelation. See also, "Denver Through Eastern Spectacles," *Times*, Jan. 10, 1882.

34.  Sara Jane (Clarke) Lippincott, *New Life in New Lands: Notes of Travel. By Grace Greenwood* [pseud.] (New York, 1873), p. 117.

35.  "When Uncle Sam Moves to Denver," *Trail* II (October 1909): 12–13.

36.  Paul de Rousiers, *La vie américaine. Ranches, fermes et usines: L'Éducation et la Société*, 2 vols. (Paris, 1889–1900), I:233; Phillips, "Population of Colorado," *University of Colorado Studies* V (June 1908): 218; Denver Board of Trade, *The Manufacturing and Commercial Industries of Denver, Colorado, Together with the Mineral Statistics of the State* (Denver, 1882), p. 9; Smiley, *History of Denver*, p. 871; John P. Young, *San Francisco: A History of the Pacific Coast Metropolis*, 2 vols. (San Francisco, 1912), I:321; II:509, 511, 674.

37.  Carl I. Wheat, "The Rocky-Bar Mining Company: An Episode in Early Western Promotion and Finance," *California Historical Quarterly* XII (March 1933): 65–66.

38.  San Francisco *Evening Post*, April 13, 1875; John Franklin Swift, *Robert Greathouse: An American Novel* (New York, 1870); Robert Upton Collins, *John Halsey, the Anti-Monopolist: A Novel* (San Francisco, 1881).

39.  Letter of Joseph P. Machebeuf, Bishop of Denver, February 1879, published in W. J. Howlett, *Life of the Right Reverend Joseph P. Machebeuf* (Pueblo, 1908), pp. 387–88; Frank Fossett, *Colorado: Its Gold and Silver Mines, Farms and Stock Ranges, and Health and Pleasure Resorts. Tourist's Guide to the Rocky Mountains* (New York, 2nd ed., 1880), p. 157; John Franklin Graff, *"Graybeard's" Colorado; or, Notes on the Centennial State. Describing a Trip from Philadelphia to Denver and Back, in the Autumn and Winter of 1881–82* (Philadelphia, 1882), p. 69; Robinson, *Sinners and Saints*, pp. 43–46; Rodman W. Paul (ed.), *A Victorian Gentlewoman in the Far West: The Reminiscences of Mary Hallock Foote* (San Marino, 1972), pp. 200–201; Don L. and Jean Harvey Griswold, *The Carbonate Camp Called Leadville* (Denver, 1951), p. 125; Gunther Barth, "Metropolism and Urban Elites in the Far West," Frederic C. Jaher (ed.), *The Age of Industrialism in America; Essays in Social Structure and Cultural Values* (New York, 1968), pp. 173–74.

40.  Rodman W. Paul, "Colorado as a Pioneer of Science in the Mining West," *Journal of American History* XLVII (June 1960): 38–42, 48–49.

41.  LeRoy R. Hafen (ed.), *The Past and Present of the Pike's Peak Gold Regions by Henry Villard* (Princeton, 1932), p. 144; Barney, *Letters*, pp. 26, 27, 29, 33–35, 40–43, 50, 55, 57, 89; Abner E. Sprague, "My First Trip to Denver," *Colorado Magazine* XV (November 1938): 221; Carrie Scott Ellis, "The Diary of a Pioneer Woman. By Mollie E. Dorsey Sanford," Denver Westerners, *1954 Brand Book* (Denver, 1955), pp. 313, 315–17, 319–22, 325, 327–29; "Population of Cities," *Twelfth Census*, I:430; Will C. Ferril (ed.), *Sketches of Colorado* (Denver, 1911), p. 37; S. D. Mock, "Effects of the 'Boom' Decade, 1870–1880, Upon Colorado Population," *Colorado Magazine* XI (January 1934): 27; Smiley, *History of Denver*, p. 558. A quick impression of the ups and downs of early Denver can be

gained conveniently from two sections of Levette Jay Davidson and Prudence
Bostwick (eds.), *The Literature of the Rocky Mountain West, 1803–1903*
(Caldwell, Idaho, 1939), pp. 277–96, excerpts from Alice Polk Hill, *Tales of the
Colorado Pioneers* (Denver, 1884), pp. 54, 79–84, 221–28, and Howard Louis
Conard, *"Uncle Dick" Wootton, The Pioneer Frontiersman of the Rocky
Mountain Region: An Account of the Adventures and Thrilling Experiences of the
Most Noted American Hunter, Trapper, Guide, and Indian Fighter Now Living*
(Chicago, 1890), pp. 371–84.

42. Smiley, *History of Denver*, pp. 552, 812, 876; Albert E. Seep, "History of The
Mine and Smelter Supply Company," *Colorado Magazine* XXIII (May 1946):
128–29.

43. Ralph E. Blodgett, "The Colorado Territorial Board of Immigration," *Colorado
Magazine* XLVI (Summer 1969): 245.

44. Lewis Cass Gandy, *The Tabors: A Footnote of Western History* (New York,
1934), pp. 120, 148, 151, 156, 184–85, 187–90.

45. Denver *Mining Industry*, March 2, April 13, 20, May 4, 11, October 19,
December 7, 1888; Denver *Republican*, January 1, 1890, January 1, 1891; T. S.
McMurray, "History and Report of the Denver Real Estate and Stock
Exchange," Denver Real Estate and Stock Exchange, *Annual Report, 1890–91*
(Denver, 1891), pp. 3–4; John E. Leet, *Outside Denver Real Estate* (Leaflet of
articles from Denver newspapers, reprinted in 1893, Library, State Historical
Society of Colorado); Robert Lee Harper, *Colorado Mines* (Denver, 1891), pp.
11–15; "Scraps from My Note Books," Hall, *History of the State of Colorado* IV:
52; Smiley, *History of Denver*, p. 576. H. L. Thayer, *Thayer's Map of Denver*
(Denver, 1882), provides a glimpse at the variety of real estate projects.

46. Samuel Bowles, *Our New West* (Hartford, 1869), p. 89; Ralph, "Colorado and Its
Capital," *Harper's New Monthly Magazine* LXXXVI (May 1893): 937; Barth,
"Metropolitan and Urban Elites," Jaher (ed.), *Age of Industrialism*, pp. 166–69.

47. "Denver and the Mining Industry," *Denver Journal of Commerce* VIII (April 12,
1888): 6; "Denver Real Estate," Denver Chamber of Commerce and Board of
Trade, *Ninth Annual Report, For the Year Ending December 31st, 1891* (Denver,
1892), pp. 65–69; Henry Dudley Teetor, "A Chapter of Denver's History. H. B.
Chamberlin's Visit in Search of Health and What Came Of It," *Magazine of
Western History* X (1889): 150–51: Alvin T. Steinel, *History of Agriculture in
Colorado: A Chronological Record of Progress in the Development of General
Farming, Livestock Production and Agricultural Education and Investigation, on
the Western Border of the Great Plains and in the Mountains of Colorado, 1858 to
1926* (Fort Collins, 1926), pp. 108–11, 113, 117–25, 141–42.

48. *Mining Industry*, May 11, 1888.

49. Smiley, *History of Denver*, pp. 574, 576; Franklin Lawton, "History of the San
Francisco Stock and Exchange Board," *Stock Buyers Manual and Hand Book of
Reference* (San Francisco, 1875), pp. 5–9; Joseph L. King, *History of the San
Francisco Stock and Exchange Board* (San Francisco, 1910), pp. 1–16; Charles A.
Fracchia, "The Founding of the San Francisco Mining Exchange," *California
Historical Quarterly* XLVIII (March 1969): 3–18.

50. King, *History of the San Francisco Stock and Exchange Board*, pp. 73–83, 101–13.
51. Anson S. Blake, "A San Francisco Boyhood, 1874–1884," *California Historical Quarterly* XXXVII (September 1958): 218–19. See also "The Ruling Passion," *News Letter*, June 17, 1876, p. 8.
52. "The Sharks of the Street," *News Letter*, July 15, 1876, p. 8.
53. *Commercial Herald and Market Review: A Review of the Commercial, Financial and Mining Interests of the State of California . . . for the Year 1876* (San Francisco, 1877), p. 29; *United States Annual Mining Review and Stock Ledger* (San Francisco, 1879), p. 19; Squire P. Dewey, *The Bonanza Mines and the Bonanza Kings of California: Their 5 Year Reign: 1875–1879* (San Francisco, 1879), Preface; United States Bureau of the Census, *Wealth and Industry of the United States . . . at the Ninth Census* (Washington, 1872), p. 496; John S. Hittell, *A History of the City of San Francisco and Incidentally of the State of California* (San Francisco, 1878), pp. 489–92.
54. J. F. Clark, *The Society in Search of Truth; or Stock Gambling in San Francisco* (Oakland, 1878). For the interaction between mine managers and speculators, see Eliot Lord, *Comstock Mining and Miners* (Washington, 1883), pp. 316–19; Oscar Lewis, *Silver Kings: The Lives and Times of Mackay, Fair, Flood, and O'Brien, Lords of the Nevada Comstock Lode* (New York, 1947), pp. 222–26, 235–48.
55. James Gilroy, *The Mining Stock Market; or, "How They Do It." An Inside and Outside View of the "Manipulation" of the Entire Stock System. How Men Get Rich and Poor* (San Francisco, 1879), p. 3.
56. *United States Annual Mining Stock Ledger* (San Francisco, 1879), p. 19.
57. *Rocky Mountain News Illustrated Almanac* (Denver, 1882), p. 44.
58. San Francisco *Chronicle*, Apr. 14, 1878.
59. The paragraph benefited from observations on gambling by Fray Angélico Chávez, "Doña Tules, Her Fame and Her Funeral," *El Palacio* LVII (August 1950): 230–31.
60. B. E. Lloyd, *Lights and Shades in San Francisco* (San Francisco, 1876), p. 204; G. N. Scamehorn, *Behind the Scenes, or Denver by Gas Light* (Denver, 1894), p. 29.
61. Frank Roney, Diary, April 1875–March 1876 (MS, Bancroft Library), Jan. 15, 29, Feb. 14, 1876. Neil Larry Shumsky directed me to the diary.
62. *Ibid.*, February, March, 1876; Gunther Barth, *Bitter Strength: A History of the Chinese in the United States, 1850–1870* (Cambridge, Mass., 1964), pp. 126–27.
63. United States, Bureau of the Census, *Tenth Census of the United States. Social Statistics of Cities, Part 2* (Washington, 1887), pp. 769, 800.
64. Forbes Parkhill, "He Drove the Wild West Wild," Denver Westerners, *1958 Brand Book* (Boulder, 1959), 71–87; Lloyd Lewis and Henry Justin Smith, *Oscar Wilde Discovers America* (New York, 1936), p. 302.
65. "There Be No Honest Men," *Chronicle*, Dec. 8, 1872.
66. Bruce A. Woodard, *Diamonds in the Salt* (Boulder, Colorado, 1967), pp. 91–94.
67. Clarence King to General A. A. Humphreys, Nov. 26, 1872, "Report of the Chief of Engineers," 43 Cong., 1 Sess., *House Ex. Doc. No. 1* II:1208–10; Peter

Farquhar, "Site of the Diamond Swindle of 1872," *California Historical Quarterly* XLII (March 1963): 49–53; Richard A. Bartlett, "The Diamond Hoax," *Great Surveys of the American West* (Norman, 1962), pp. 187–205.

68. Emma Hardinge Britten, *Modern American Spiritualism: A Twenty Years' Record of the Communion Between Earth and the World of Spirits* (New York, 1870), p. 439.

69. *San Francisco City Directory, 1867*, pp. 153, 201; *1868*, p. 224; *1869*, p. 245; "Radicalism in San Francisco," *Chronicle*, Mar. 19, 1876.

70. "Mark Twain on the New Wild Cat Religion," San Francisco *Golden Era*, Mar. 4, 1866, p. 5; Franklin Walker (ed.), *The Washoe Giant in San Francisco; Being Heretofore Uncollected Sketches by Mark Twain Published in the Golden Era in the Sixties* (San Francisco, 1938), pp. 119–37.

71. *San Francisco City Directory, 1873*, p. 693, *1880*, p. 994, *1890*, p. 1466: William Hepworth Dixon, *New America*, 2 vols. (London, 3rd ed., 1867), I:126–29.

72. *Times*, Feb. 25, Mar. 8, 1875, Sept. 19, 1876; Salt Lake City *Herald*, Sept. 14, 1876.

73. Bishop, *A Lady's Life in the Rocky Mountains*, p. 162.

74. Lloyd, *Lights and Shades*, p. 180.

75. *Ibid.*, pp. 182–85; Hubert Howe Bancroft, *California Inter Pocula* (San Francisco, 1888), pp. 673, 674–75; Kipling, *American Notes*, pp. 10–11.

76. Gordon C. Roadarmel (comp.), "Some California Dates of 1860," *California Historical Quarterly* XXXVIII (December 1959): 329, 336; Gilman M. Ostrander, *The Prohibition Movement in California, 1848–1933* (Berkeley, 1957), pp. 9, 20, 32–33.

77. William Elliot West, "Dry Crusade: The Prohibition Movement in Colorado, 1858–1933" (Ph.D. thesis, University of Colorado, 1971), pp. 60, 63; Smiley, *History of Denver*, p. 463.

78. Lloyd, *Lights and Shades*, 181.

79. San Francisco Board of Supervisors, *San Francisco Municipal Reports, 1879–80* (San Francisco, 1880), p. 110; *Denver City Directory, 1880*, pp. 211–13; *1890*, pp. 223–25.

80. Bancroft, *History of California* VII: 68–75; Frank E. Shepard, "Industrial Development in Colorado," James H. Baker (ed.), *History of Colorado*, 5 vols. (Denver, 1927), II: 697–705. One of my students probed the transition of San Francisco from a commercial city to an industrial city in a thesis—Neil Larry Shumsky, "Tar Flat and Nob Hill: A Social History of Industrial San Francisco During the 1870's" (Ph.D. thesis, University of California, 1972), and I have benefited from our discussions of the subject.

81. George Tucker, *Progress of the United States in Population and Wealth in Fifty Years, As Exhibited by the Decennial Census* (New York, 1843), p. 127.

82. Denver *Tribune*, July 9, Aug. 3, 1870, Aug. 21, 31, Sept. 1, 10, 1871, Mar. 8, 28, May 28, 1879; *Rocky Mountain News*, July 7, Aug. 30, 1871, May 14, July 20, 1881; *Times*, Jan. 11, 1877, May 14, 1881, Aug. 3, 1887; New York *Daily Graphic*, Nov. 29, 1878; Henry George, "The Kearney Agitation in California," *Popular Science Monthly* XVII (August 1880): 436–37, 452–53; Mary Roberts

Coolidge, *Chinese Immigration* (New York, 1909), 67, 115–19; Hall, *History of Colorado* II: 465; Elmer Clarence Sandmeyer, *The Anti-Chinese Movement in California* (Urbana, 1939), pp. 57–67; Gerald E. Rudolph, "The Chinese in Colorado, 1869–1911" (M.A. thesis, University of Denver, 1964), 107–21; Roy T. Wortman, "Denver's Anti-Chinese Riot, 1880," *Colorado Magazine* XLII (Fall 1965): 275–91.

83. For evidence of a re-examination of the stereotypes of society in the East or in the West, see Mary Hallock Foote, "The Last Assembly Ball: A Pseudo-Romance of the Far West," *Century Magazine* XXXVII (March 1889): 773. Mary Lou Benn, "Mary Hallock Foote; Early Leadville Writer," *Colorado Magazine* XXXIII (April 1956): 103, provided a lead.

84. San Francisco *Call*, Nov. 20, 1884; Irving McKee, "The Shooting of Charles de Young," *Pacific Historical Review* XVI (August 1947): 271–84.

85. "Homicidal Tendencies," San Francisco *Daily Alta California*, Nov. 23, 1884.

86. Lloyd, *Lights and Shades*, p. 350.

87. Robert Louis Stevenson and Lloyd Osbourne, *The Wrecker* (New York, 1892), pp. 131–32. For Joshua A. Norton, see Robert Ernest Cowan, "Norton I, Emperor of the United States and Protector of Mexico (Joshua A. Norton, 1819–1880)," *California Historical Quarterly* II (October 1923): 237–45.

CHAPTER 6

1. J. P. Mayer (ed.) and George Lawrence (trans.), *Democracy in America. By Alexis de Tocqueville* (Garden City, New York, 1969), p. 517.

2. Bradford Franklin Luckingham, "Associational Life on the Urban Frontier: San Francisco, 1848–1856" (Ph.D. thesis, University of California, Davis, 1968), provides an understanding about the variety of associations in early San Francisco.

3. Brooke Nihart, "A New York Regiment in California, 1846–1848," *Military Collector & Historian* XXI (Spring 1969): 11; San Francisco *Daily Alta California*, Sept. 1, Oct. 31, 1850, July 7, 1852; Frank Soulé, John H. Gihon, and James Nisbet, *The Annals of San Francisco* (New York, 1855), pp. 97, 192, 787–89; W. F. Swasey, *The Early Days and Men of California* (Oakland, 1891), pp. 218–19; Ernest A. Wiltsee, "The City of New York of the Pacific," *California Historical Quarterly* XII (March 1933): 30–32.

4. "Panama Pioneer Passengers," San Francisco *Call*, June 6, 1874; "The Panama's Anniversary," San Francisco *News Letter and California Advertiser*, June 3, 1893, p. 28; Ernest A. Wiltsee, *Gold Rush Steamers of the Pacific* (San Francisco, 1938), pp. 15, 17–18.

5. Nolie Mumey, *History of the Early Settlements of Denver (1599–1860)* (Glendale, 1942), pp. 45–49, 53–64; Jerome C. Smiley, *History of Denver: With Outlines of the Earlier History of the Rocky Mountain Country* (Denver, 1901), pp. 183–223; O. J. Goldrick, "The First School in Denver," *Colorado Magazine* VI (March 1929): 73.

6. Edward Ring, "Denver Clubs of the Past," *Colorado Magazine* XIX (July 1942): 140. For the Colorado hunts of Windham Thomas Wyndham-Quin, 4th Earl of Dunraven and Mountearl in the Irish peerage in the 1870s and 1880s, see the Thomas F. Dawson Scrapbooks (Library, State Historical Society of Colorado, Denver), LXVI.

7. Robert E. Park and Herbert A. Miller, *Old World Traits Transplanted* (New York, 1921), presented an early treatment of the subject.

8. Ida Pfeiffer, *A Lady's Second Journey Round the World: From London to the Cape of Good Hope, Borneo, Java, Sumatra, Celebes, Ceram, the Moluccas, etc., California, Panama, Peru, Ecuador, and the United States*, 2 vols. (London, 1855), II:43, 52, 53. Her account of California has been reprinted from the 1856 New York edition by Joseph A. Sullivan (ed.), *A Lady's Visit to California, 1853* (Oakland, 1950), pp. 3, 11, 12.

9. *Denver City and Auraria: The Commercial Emporium of the Pike's Peak Gold Regions in 1859* (St. Louis, 1860), Preface.

10. *Annals of San Francisco*, p. 202.

11. *Ibid.*, pp. 42, 225, 423, 425–26, 687–717.

12. Denver *Tribune*, Jan. 26, 1881. For a reprint of the address, see Frederick J. Stanton, "The Founders of Denver and Their Doings," *Trail* XIV (May 1922): 3–12.

13. Albert D. Richardson, *Beyond the Mississippi* (Hartford, 1867), p. 177.

14. Adelbert Baudissin, *Der Ansiedler im Missouri-Staate* (Iserlohn, 1854), p. 70; Ernst zu Erbach-Erbach, *Reisebriefe aus Amerika* (Heidelberg, 1873), p. 321.

15. Rosemary Lick, *The Generous Miser: The Story of James Lick of California* (Los Angeles, 1967), pp. 32, 33–35, 38–39, 43–44, 56–57, 65–85.

16. "The Life of James Lick," *Quarterly of the Society of California Pioneers* I (No. 2, June 30, 1924): 36–37, 52, 61. Samuel Clemens, "The Lick House Ball," San Francisco *Golden Era*, Sept. 27, 1863, p. 4. For a reprint, see Franklin Walker (ed.), *The Washoe Giant in San Francisco: Being Heretofore Uncollected Sketches by Mark Twain, Published in the Golden Era in the Sixties* (San Francisco, 1938), pp. 33–38.

17. Quoted from Mumey, *Early Settlements of Denver*, 157.

18. *Ibid.*, 158, 159; Robert L. Perkin, *The First Hundred Years: An Informal History of Denver and the Rocky Mountain News* (Garden City, New York, 1959), pp. 31, 34.

19. Bernard Moses, *The Establishment of Municipal Government in San Francisco* (Baltimore, 1889), p. 38; Smiley, *History of Denver*, p. 336.

20. 31 Cong., 1 Sess., *House Ex. Doc. No. 17*, pp. 288, 289; William Henry Ellison, *A Self-governing Dominion: California, 1849–60* (Berkeley, 1950), pp. 68–72.

21. Zoeth Skinner Eldredge, *The Beginnings of San Francisco*, 2 vols. (San Francisco, 1912), II:604; San Francisco *California Star*, June 19, 1847; 31 Cong., 1 Sess., *House Ex. Doc. 17*, p. 773; *Annals of San Francisco*, p. 135; Moses, *Municipal Government in San Francisco*, p. 46; Joseph Ellison, "The Struggle for Civil Government in California, 1846–1850," *California Historical Quarterly* X (June 1931): 143.

22. *Alta*, Feb. 15, Mar. 15, 29, Apr. 26, June 2, 1849; Peter H. Burnett, *Recollections and Opinions of an Old Pioneer* (New York, 1880), pp. 306–16.

23. *Annals of San Francisco*, p. 229.

24. *Ibid.*, pp. 230, 231.

25. *Alta*, June 14, July 12, 19, 26, Aug. 9, 1849; Burnett, *Recollections*, pp. 319–34; William Henry Ellison (ed.), "Memoirs of Hon. William M. Gwin," *California Historical Quarterly* XIX (March 1940): 14; Bayard Taylor, *El Dorado, or, Adventures in the Path of Empire*, 2 vols. (New York, 1850), I: 147; *Annals of San Francisco*, p. 272; Moses, *Municipal Government in San Francisco*, p. 55; Samuel H. Willey, *The Transition Period of California, From a Province of Mexico in 1846 to a State of the American Union in 1850* (San Francisco, 1901), p. 87; Cardinal Goodwin, *The Establishment of State Government in California, 1846–1850* (New York, 1914), pp. 80–81; Ellison, "Struggle for Civil Government," *California Historical Quarterly* X (June 1931): 138, 143–45.

26. For the Spanish-Mexican office of *alcalde* which was brought to the Colorado diggings by California miners, see James Grafton Rogers, "The Beginnings of Law in Colorado," *Dicta* XXXVI (March–April 1959): 118–19.

27. Kansas (Territory), *The Statutes of the Territory of Kansas. General Laws* (St. Louis, 1855), chapters XXXVII and XXXVIII.

28. Denver *Rocky Mountain News*, Apr. 23, 1859.

29. Junius E. Wharton, *History of the City of Denver from Its Earliest Settlement to the Present Time, To Which Is Added a Full and Complete Business Directory of the City. By D. O. Wilhelm* (Denver, 1866), p. 69; Frank Hall, *History of the State of Colorado*, 4 vols. (Chicago, 1889–95), I:217; Smiley, *History of Denver*, p. 632; Agnes Wright Spring, "Rush to the Rockies, 1859; Colorado's Gold Rush of 1859," *Colorado Magazine* XXXVI (April 1959): 86–96, 119; LeRoy R. Hafen, "Historical Introduction," Hafen (ed.), *Pike's Peak Gold Rush Guidebooks of 1859* (Glendale, 1941), pp. 73–78; Clyde Lyndon King, *The History of the Government of Denver with Special Reference to Its Relations with Public Service Corporations* (Denver, 1911), p. 13.

30. *Rocky Mountain News*, Nov. 7, 1859.

31. LeRoy R. Hafen (ed.), *The Past and Present of the Pike's Peak Gold Regions. By Henry Villard. Reprinted from the Edition of 1860* (Princeton, 1932), pp. 127–28.

32. LeRoy R. Hafen, "Steps to Statehood in Colorado," *Colorado Magazine* III (August 1926): 97–106.

33. Colorado (Territory), *Colorado Laws, 1861, Special Acts* (Denver, 1861), part 4, chapter I, article 1, pp. 267–68; Smiley, *History of Denver*, p. 325; King, *Government of Denver*, pp. 24–25.

34. There are many descriptions of "lawless" Denver. For an early example, see Wharton, *History of the City of Denver*, pp. 43–51, 178–80. For a recent one, see Stanley W. Zamonski and Teddy Keller, *The '59ers: Roaring Denver in the Gold Rush Days* (Denver, 2nd ed., 1967).

35. Hall, *History of Colorado*, I:236.

36. Hafen (ed.), *Pike's Peak Gold Region. By Henry Villard*, pp. 128–29; Richardson, *Beyond the Mississippi*, pp. 177, 186.

37. Horace Greeley, *An Overland Journey from New York to San Francisco in the Summer of 1859* (New York, 1860), p. 159; Mrs. Elmo Scott Watson, "Horace Greeley, the Man Who Took His Own Advice," Denver Westerners, *1962 Brand Book* (Denver, 1963), pp. 336–40, 343.

38. B. Richard Burg, "Vigilantes in Lawless Denver: The City of the Plains," *Great Plains Journal* VI (Spring 1967): 68–84.

39. William T. Sherman to Henry Smith Turner, July 2, 1856, Dwight L. Clarke, *William Tecumseh Sherman: Gold Rush Banker* (San Francisco, 1969), pp. 224, 225. The letter was published earlier in part, "Sherman and the San Francisco Vigilantes. Unpublished Letters of General W. T. Sherman," *Century Magazine* XLIII (December 1891): 306–8. For Mammon and Gammon, see Hubert Howe Bancroft, *Popular Tribunals*, 2 vols. (San Francisco, 1887), II:332.

40. *Denver Republican*, Dec. 21, 1895.

41. Sherman L. Richards and George M. Blackburn, "The Sydney Ducks: A Demographic Analysis," *Pacific Historical Review* XLII (February 1973): 30–31; George R. Stewart, *Committee of Vigilance: Revolution in San Francisco, 1851. An Account of the Hundred Days When Certain Citizens Undertook the Suppression of the Criminal Activities of the Sydney Ducks* (Boston, 1964), p. 2.

42. Edward McGowan, *Narrative of Edward McGowan, Including a Full Account of the Author's Adventures and Perils, While Persecuted by the San Francisco Vigilance Committee of 1856* (San Francisco, 1857), p. 43. Most recently, the account has been reprinted, *McGowan vs. California Vigilantes* (Oakland, 1946). For a biographical sketch of McGowan turn to Carl I. Wheat, "Ned, the Ubiquitous, Soldier of Fortune par Excellence, Being the Further Narrative of Edward McGowan," *California Historical Quarterly* VI (March 1927): 3–36. See also, Judge Harvey S. Brown, *Early Days of California* (MS, Bancroft Library), a strong statement against the Vigilance Committee of 1851.

43. Sherman to Turner, July 2, 1856, Clarke, *William Tecumseh Sherman*, p. 225.

44. Smiley, *History of Denver*, p. 348; Franklin Tuthill, *The History of California* (San Francisco, 1866), p. 465.

45. "Grand Parade and Review of the Military Forces of the Vigilance Committee, Under Command of Brig. General James N. Olney, August 18, 1856," (Oversize lithograph, Bancroft Library). For details of the parade turn to the San Francisco newspapers and *Judges and Criminals: Shadows of the Past. History of the Vigilance Committee of San Francisco, Cal. With the Names of Its Officers* (San Francisco, 1858), pp. 92–94. See also, "A Portfolio of Letter Sheets on the Vigilance Committee of 1856," Doyce B. Nunis, Jr. (ed.), *The San Francisco Vigilance Committee of 1856. Three Views: 1. William T. Coleman, 2. William T. Sherman, 3. James O'Meara* (Los Angeles, 1971), pp. 127–47. The membership certificate of Hiram S. Wheeler, designed by Charles Nahl and lithographed by Britton & Rey, is in the Bancroft Library.

46. Cooke & LeCount, Booksellers (comp.), *A "Pile," or a Glance at the Wealth of the Monied Men of San Francisco and Sacramento City. Also, An Accurate List of the Lawyers, Their Former Places of Residence, and Date of Their Arrival in San Francisco* (San Francisco, 1851). Reprinted in *Magazine of History* XLVIII (Extra number 190, 1933): 89–107.

47. For biographies of these four men, see Cecil G. Tilton, *William Chapman Ralston, Courageous Builder* (Boston, 1935); Norman E. Tutorow, *Leland Stanford: Man of Many Careers* (Menlo Park, 1971); Harry E. Kelsey, Jr., *Frontier Capitalist, The Life of John Evans* (Denver, 1969); Lewis Cass Gandy, *The Tabors: A Footnote of Western History* (New York, 1934).

48. *Call*, Aug. 6, 1871; Cooke & LeCount, Booksellers (comp.), *A "Pile,"* pp. 7, 8.

49. "Rich Men Abroad and at Home," San Francisco *Bulletin*, July 21, 1877 (quoting Frankfurt-on-the Main *Gazette*).

50. Denver *Tribune*, Aug. 27, 1872.

51. *Ibid.*, Oct. 23, 24, 1883.

52. W. H. Kistler Stationary Co., *Who's Who in Denver Society, 1908* (Denver, 1908).

53. Ward McAllister, *Society As I Have Found It* (New York, 1890), pp. 23–25, 123–24.

54. William H. Chambliss, *Chambliss' Diary; or, Society as It Really Is* (New York, 1895), pp. 39–40. For the Southern tone of San Francisco Society during the 1850s turn to Floride Green (ed.), *Some Personal Recollections of Lillie Hitchcock Coit* (San Francisco, 1935), p. 2; Doyce B. Nunis, Jr. (ed.), *The California Diary of Faxon Dean Atherton, 1836–1839* (San Francisco, 1964), pp. xiv-xxxii; Douglas S. Watson, "The San Francisco McAllisters," *California Historical Quarterly* XI (June 1932): 124–28; Albert Shumate, *A Visit to Rincon Hill and South Park* (San Francisco, 1963), pp. 8–9.

55. *News Letter*, July 14, 1888, p. 14.

56. *Tribune*, Feb. 4, 1881. For a biographical sketch of Margaret Gray Evans, see her obituary in the Denver *Rocky Mountain News*, September 8, 1906, p. 7, and Helen Cannon, "First Ladies of Colorado—Margaret Gray Evans (Governor John Evans—1862–1865)," *Colorado Magazine* XXXIX (January 1962): 19–28.

57. San Francisco and Denver newspapers competed to report each ball and social gathering in meticulous detail. Samuel Clemens' satire, " 'Mark Twain'—The Pioneers' Ball," *Golden Era* (San Francisco Correspondence, Virginia City *Territorial Enterprise*), Nov. 26, 1865, p. 5, and Eugene Field's hoax, "Senator Tabor's Frills," *Tribune*, Feb. 15, 1883, were smothered by the waves of deadly serious reports. For a reprint of Mark Twain's story, see Bernard Taper (ed.). *Mark Twain's San Francisco* (New York, 1963), pp. 139–41; for Field, see Willard S. Morse (comp.), *Clippings from Denver Tribune, Written by Eugene Field, 1881–1883* (New York, 1909), p. 23.

58. *News Letter*, Feb. 16, 1889, p. 6.

59. For similar observations on two mining towns in the foothills of the Sierra Nevada, see Ralph Mann, "The Decade After the Gold Rush: Social Structure in Grass Valley and Nevada City, California, 1850–1860," *Pacific Historical Review* XLI (November 1972): 498.

60. *Tribune*, Jan. 26, 1881; "Our Colored Citizens; The Most Prosperous Negro Community in the North Found in Denver," *Republican*, March 17, 1890. Forbes Parkhill, *Mister Barney Ford: A Portrait in Bistre* (Denver, 1963), pp. 96, 185, states that Barney Ford, a black who came to Denver in May 1860, and his

wife Julia, "were the first members of their race ever to attend" the annual banquet of the Colorado Association of Pioneers in January 1882.

61. "How a Man Gets in With the 'Upper Crust,' " A. E. D. De Rupert, *Californians and Mormons* (New York, 1881), pp. 95, 96.

62. "Californians at the Play," *News Letter*, July 19, 1879, p. 2. For the lithograph and key, see *ibid.*, pp. 14–15. The lithograph was published again in the fortieth anniversary number of the *News Letter*, July 18, 1896, pp. 48–49.

63. Rudyard Kipling, *American Notes* (New York, 1891), pp. 15, 29, 31; Benjamin E. Lloyd, *Lights and Shades in San Francisco* (San Francisco, 1876), pp. 488–89.

64. "Residences," *Denver Illustrated* (Denver, 1887), 51.

65. "San Francisco Has No Regular Negro Quarter, But She Has a Peculiar Negro Colony," San Francisco *Chronicle*, Feb. 7, 1904, p. 7. My work on blacks in San Francisco has benefited from conversations with one of my students, Douglas Daniels, who is on the point of completing a Ph.D. thesis on Negroes in San Francisco between 1860 and 1930. My clue for Denver came from Judge Frank Thomas Johnson, *Autobiography of a Centenarian* (Denver, 1961), p. 60. The 985 black residents of Denver, located in the Manuscript of the 1880 Census, "Schedule 1.—Inhabitants in Denver" (microfilm, Bancroft Library) were distributed in the following wards: 1 (74), 2 (85), 3 (74), 4 (420), 5 (326), 6 (6). In 1880, the location of the three "African Churches" given in Vickers, *History of Denver*, pp. 282–83, reflected the dispersal of the black people through the city. This spatial distribution continued into the twentieth century; in 1910 the city's 5,426 Negroes lived in every ward, with many of them again in wards 4 (1,098) and 5 (940), U.S. Census Bureau, *Negro Population, 1790–1915* (Washington, D.C., 1918), table 13, p. 105.

66. United States, Bureau of the Census, *Population of the United States at the Tenth Census* (Washington, 1883), p. 649; Warren S. Thompson, *Growth and Changes in California's Population* (Los Angeles, 1955), p. 337.

67. See the advertisements in the San Francisco *Matrimonial News*, Dec. 20, 1873, Jan. 24, 1874; Lloyd, *Lights and Shades in San Francisco*, pp. 380–83.

68. "Leaves from a Lady's Diary," *New Letter*, Mar. 23, 1872, p. 4. The installments of the journal began on Jan. 6, p. 4, ran through the entire year, and spilled over into 1873.

69. San Francisco *Examiner*, Mar. 15, 1888. See also, Lillian Ruth Matthews, *Women in Trade Unions in San Francisco* (Berkeley, 1913), p. 4.

70. *Woman's Herald of Industry and Social Science Cooperator* I (September 1881): 1 (July 1882): 1 (August 1882): 1, 4. For a biographical sketch of Marietta Lois Beers Stow, Mrs. Joseph W. Stow, turn to "The Story of Oakland's Junior Republic," *Call*, February 24, 1901, p. 5; Theodora Selk, "Early Fighter for Women's Rights," Oakland *Montclarion*, Jan. 5, 1972, pp. 1, 8.

71. *Golden Dawn*, I (November 1874): 4.

72. "Their Women," Walter M. Fisher, *The Californians* (London, 1876), pp. 84–105.

73. A few references will indicate the range of the large literature. For Ah Toy and Bella Cora, see Curt Gentry, *The Madams of San Francisco: An Irreverent*

*History of the City by the Golden Gate* (New York, 1964), pp. 57–59, 76–136. Laura D. Fair is the subject of Franklin Walker, "An Influence from San Francisco on Mark Twain's *The Gilded Age*," *American Literature* VIII (March 1936): 63–66; Robert O'Brien, "Wolves in the Fold," Joseph Henry Jackson (ed.), *San Francisco Murders* (New York, 1947), pp. 17–47; Kenneth Lamott, *Who Killed Mr. Crittenden? Being a True Account of the Notorious Murder That Stunned San Francisco–The Laura D. Fair Case* (New York, 1963). For Sarah Althea Hill Terry, see Robert H. Kroninger, *Sarah and the Senator* (Berkeley, 1964). Max Miller, *Holladay Street* (New York, 1962), focuses his Denver story on Mattie Silks. For Jennie Rogers, see Caroline Bancroft, *Six Racy Madams of Colorado* (Boulder, 1956), pp. 5–31. Elizabeth McCourt Doe Tabor is portrayed by Caroline Bancroft, *Silver Queen: The Fabulous Story of Baby Doe Tabor* (Boulder, 1965). For Lilian B. Abbott Daniels, see Forbes Parkhill, *Donna Madixxa Goes West: The Biography of a Witch* (Boulder, 1968).

74. Forbes Parkhill, "Scarlet Sister Mattie," Denver Westerners, *1948 Brand Book* (Denver, 1949), p. 26.

75. Elizabeth Cady Stanton, Susan B. Anthony, and Matilda Joslyn Gage (eds.), *History of Woman Suffrage*, 4 vols. (Rochester, 1887), III: 717–18; Helen Cannon, "First Ladies of Colorado—Mary Thompson McCook (Governor Edward Moody McCook—1869–1873; 1874–1875)," *Colorado Magazine* XXXIX (July 1962): 183–84; Vickers, *History of Denver*, p. 233. For the women suffrage movement in Colorado in the 1870s and 1890s, see Billie Barnes Jensen, "Colorado Woman Suffrage Campaigns of the 1870s," *Journal of the West* XII (April 1973): 254–71, and "Let the Women Vote," *Colorado Magazine* XLI (Winter 1964): 13. William B. Faherty, "Regional Minorities and the Woman Suffrage Struggle," *ibid.* XXXIII (July 1956): 212–17, showed that the Mexican vote had little if any effect on the outcome of the 1877 woman suffrage campaign in Colorado.

76. *Rocky Mountain News*, Aug. 20, Sept. 21, 1882.

77. *Ibid.*, Aug. 4, Sept. 25, 1882.

78. *Ibid.*, Sept. 17, 1882.

79. *Ibid.*, Sept. 14, 17, 19, 20, 24, 25, 28, 1882.

80. John Bernard McGloin, S.J., *California's First Archbishop: The Life of Joseph Sadoc Alemany, O.P., 1814–1888* (New York, 1966), p. 244; William J. Scanlon (ed. and comp.), *One-hundredth Anniversary: St. Boniface Parish, San Francisco, California, 1860–1960* (San Francisco, 1960), pp. 4, 26, 35, 36, 91.

81. For a brief discussion of a theoretical model of several functions of the classic political machine as outlined by Robert K. Merton, *Social Theory and Social Structure* (Glencoe, Illinois, 1949), pp. 71–81, see Eric L. McKitrick, "The Study of Corruption," *Political Science Quarterly* LXXII (December 1957): 502–14.

82. *Plan for the Reorganization of the Democracy of the City and County of San Francisco* (San Francisco, 1882); San Francisco *Examiner*, Apr. 15, 1882, 1, 3; "How I Came to Be a Boss Against My Will—Only True Story of Incident," James H. Wilkins (ed.), "The Reminiscences of Christopher A. Buckley," San Francisco *Bulletin*, Dec. 28, 1918, p. 7, "George Marye From Nob Hill Makes Hit With South of Market Club," *ibid.* Jan. 25, 1919, p. 9.

83. F. I. Vassault, "Why the Political 'Boss' Is a Power," *Overland Monthly* XVII (April 1891): 362.

84. For a short review of San Francisco bosses, see "The Bossology of San Francisco. Brief Outline of the Political Potentates That Ruled the City During the Last Century," James H. Wilkins (ed.), "Martin Kelley's Story; Former San Francisco Boss Discloses Political Methods," *Bulletin*, Sept. 5, 1917, p. 8. There is nothing as succinct in the Denver material; for a few hints, see James MacCarthy, *Political Portraits. By Fitz-Mac* [pseud.] (Colorado Springs, 1888), and R. G. Dill, *The Political Campaigns of Colorado, With Complete Tabulated Statements of the Official Vote* (Denver, 1895).

85. Abraham Ruef, "The Road I Traveled. An Autobiographic Account of My Career from University to Prison. With an Intimate Recital of the Corrupt Alliance Between Big Business and Politics in San Francisco," *Bulletin*, May 23, 1912, p. 12.

86. *Ibid.*, May 21, 1912, p. 12; Ben B. Lindsey and Harvey J. O'Higgins, *The Beast* (New York, 1910), pp. 281, 287, 290, 307; J. Paul Mitchell, "Boss Speer and the City Functional; Boosters and Businessmen Versus Commission Government in Denver," *Pacific Northwest Quarterly* LXIII (October 1972): 155–64; Lyle Dorsett, "The City Boss and the Reformer; A Reappraisal," *ibid.*, 150–54. For the two bosses, see Walton Bean, *Boss Ruef's San Francisco. The Story of the Union Labor Party, Big Business, and the Graft Prosecution* (Berkeley, 1952); Edgar C. McMechen (ed.), *Robert Speer: A City Builder* (Denver, 1919); Charles A. Johnson, *Denver's Mayor Speer. The Forgotten Story of Robert W. Speer, the Political Boss With a Rather Unsavory Machine Who Transformed Denver Into One of the World's Most Beautiful Cities* (Denver, 1969).

87. *Rocky Mountain News*, Mar. 20, 21, 22, 23, 25–31, Apr. 6, 1890.

88. Dill, *Political Campaigns of Colorado*, p. 141.

89. *Rocky Mountain News*, Sept. 14, 1890.

CHAPTER 7

1. Richard Henry Dana, Jr., *Two Years Before the Mast; A Personal Narrative of Life at Sea* (New York, 1936), pp. 434–35.

2. Sigfried Giedion, *Space, Time and Architecture: The Growth of a New Tradition* (Cambridge, 5th rev. and enl. ed., 1967), 249–52. For a study of the building, see C. R. Fay, *Palace of Industry, 1851: A Study of the Great Exhibition and Its Fruits* (Cambridge, England, 1951).

3. William Dean Howells, "A Sennight of the Centennial," *Atlantic Monthly* XXXVIII (July 1876): 92–107.

4. F. Reuleaux, *Briefe aus Philadelphia* (Braunschweig, 1877), p. 21.

5. Montgomery Schuyler, "Last Words About the World's Fair," *Architectural Record* III (January–March, 1894): 291–301.

6. Herman S. Davis (ed.), *Reminiscences of General William Larimer and of His*

*Son, William H. H. Larimer: Two of the Founders of Denver City* (Lancaster, Pa., 1918), pp. 168–69.

7. For a picture of Apollo Hall, see Jerome C. Smiley, *History of Denver: With Outlines of the Earlier History of the Rocky Mountain Country* (Denver, 1901), p. 339. The first performance is discussed by Lillian De La Torre, "The Theatre Comes to Denver," *Colorado Magazine* XXXVII (October 1960): 285–93.

8. Libeus Barney, *Letters of the Pike's Peak Gold Rush: Early-Day Letters by Libeus Barney, Reprinted from the Bennington Banner, Vermont, 1859–1860* (San Jose, 1959), p. 50.

9. Smiley, *History of Denver*, p. 303. For comments on "Cibolla Hall," see Hugh R. Steele, "Old Landmarks," *The Trail* II (November 1909): 12.

10. "Denver Architecture," Denver *Inter-Ocean* V (July 29, 1882): 533.

11. "Queen Anne Hodge-Podge," *California Architect and Building News* V (November 1884): 205. For some of the varieties of style, see Joseph A. Baird, Jr., *Time's Wondrous Changes, San Francisco Architecture, 1776–1915* (San Francisco, 1962); Wesley D. Vail, *Victorians: An Account of Domestic Architecture in Victorian San Francisco, 1870–1890* (San Francisco, 1964); Harold Kirker, *California's Architectural Frontier: Style and Tradition in the Nineteenth Century* (San Marino, 1960); Edith Eudora Kohl, *Denver's Historic Mansions: Citadels to the Empire Builders* (Denver, 1957); Sally Davis and Betty Baldwin, *Denver Dwellings and Descendants* (Denver, 1963).

12. For Willoughby J. Edbrooke, see "Death of W. J. Edbrooke," Denver *Republican*, March 26, 1896, *Frank E. Edbrooke* (Denver, 1918), pp. 39, 40, 56. F. P. Burnham, who helped with the design, had participated in the rebuilding of Chicago after the Fire of 1871; *Rocky Mountain News*, Apr. 9, 1882; *Republican*, Aug. 2, 1882.

13. Denver *Republican*, Aug. 2, 1882; Denver *Rocky Mountain News*, Oct. 10, 1882; "The Main Building," *Catalogue of the Third Annual Exhibition of the National Mining and Industrial Exposition at Denver. Will Open Sept. 1 and Close Oct. 4* (Denver, 1884), pp. 9–14; "The Main Building," James D. McCabe, *The Illustrated History of the Centennial Exhibition Held in Commemoration of the One Hundredth Anniversary of American Independence* (Philadelphia, 1876), pp. 337–49; "No. 1. The Main Exhibition Building," United States Centennial Commission, *International Exhibition, 1876. Official Catalogue*, 3 vols. (Philadelphia, 2nd rev. ed., 1876), I:23–26. For pictures of the Denver building, see *Republican*, Aug. 2, 1882; Gunnison *Daily Review*, Mar. 13, 1882; *Rocky Mountain News*, Jan. 1, 1884; *Harper's Weekly* XXVI (May 27, 1882): 333; W. H. Jackson and Co., *The National Mining and Industrial Exposition, Denver* (Denver, 1882); "The National Mining and Industrial Exposition," H. S. Reed & Co., *The Leading Industries of the West. Denver. The "Magic City of the Plains."* (Chicago, 1883), p. 22.

14. *Republican*, Aug. 2, 1882.

15. Marcus Whiffen, *American Architecture Since 1780: A Guide to Styles* (Cambridge, Mass., 1969), p. 79.

16. Oakland *Times*, June 9, 1879; Oakland *Press*, June 14, 1879; Bureau of News,

Southern Pacific Company, *Historical Outline of the Southern Pacific Company* (San Francisco, 1933), pp. 28–29; Works Progress Administration, Edgar J. Hinkel and William E. McCann, *Oakland, 1852–1938: Some Phases of the Social, Political and Economic History of Oakland, California*, 2 vols. (Oakland, 1939), I:87.

17. *Times*, Jan. 16, 1882; Oakland *Tribune*, Jan. 13, 17, 18, 20, 23, 1882.

18. Benjamin Parke Avery, Growth of Architectural Forms (MS, Bancroft Library), 65. The essay, written about 1872, was never published. For a biographical sketch of Avery, see *DAB* I:443–44.

19. Wilson O. Clough (trans.), *The Rocky Mountain West in 1867 by Louis L. Simonin* (Lincoln, 1966), p. 33: Charles A. Renouard, "Recollections of Early Denver and the First Embalming School Here," *Colorado Magazine* XXVII (July 1950): 216. For a biographical sketch of Frederick J. Charpiot, see Vickers, *History of Denver*, pp. 380–81.

20. The first volume of Renate Wagner-Rieger (ed.), *Die Wiener Ringstrasse—Bild einer Epoche. Die Erweiterung der Inneren Stadt Wien unter Kaiser Franz Joseph*, 8 vols. (Vienna, 1969–72), contains numerous photos of buildings which could have inspired the "indescribable massiveness" of the Palace Hotel. *San Francisco City Directory, 1875*, p. 30; Oscar Lewis and Carroll D. Hall, *Bonanza Inn; America's First Luxury Hotel* (New York, 1939), p. 19; John W. and Doris G. Buchanan, *A Story of the Fabulous Windsor Hotel* (Denver, 2nd. ed., 1956), p. 7; Caroline Bancroft, "Debut of the Windsor," Denver Westerners, *Brand Book 1951* (Denver, 1952), pp. 313–15; Bancroft, *Silver Queen: The Fabulous Story of Baby Doe Tabor* (Boulder, 1965), pp. 73–78.

21. "Daily Life in Denver. Street Scenes Unknown to Any Other City on the Continent," New York *Daily Graphic*, Nov. 29, 1878.

22. *Official History of the California Midwinter International Exposition* (San Francisco, 1894), pp. 15, 29, 31, 126, 194. See also, Gunther Barth, *California Midwinter International Exposition*, pamphlet number two in a collection of pamphlets by Samuel Stark (ed.), *West Coast Expositions and Galas* (San Francisco, 1970), [3].

23. San Francisco *Call*, July 2, 8, 15, Aug. 3, 17, 1893; "The Midwinter Fair," *Argonaut*, Jan. 8, 1894, p. 15; "California's Mid-Winter Fair," *The Great Divide* II (January 1894): 6; C. B. Turrill, "California Midwinter Fair," *Traveler* III (February 1894): 14.

24. See the lithographs by Charles Graham, Director of Color of the Midwinter Fair, published as San Francisco *Examiner Art Supplement*, in the Sunday editions of the *Examiner* during the exposition.

25. *Official History of the California Midwinter International Exposition*, pp. 15, 20–21, 130–31.

26. *Rocky Mountain News*, Sept. 9, 1882. For a biographical sketch of Constant Mayer, see *DAB* XII:449–50, for one of Thomas Hood, *DNB* IX:1164–66.

27. J. C. Reid, *Thomas Hood* (London, 1963), p. 208; John Clubbe, *Victorian Forerunner: The Later Career of Thomas Hood* (Durham, 1968), pp. 154–55.

28. Graham Reynolds, *Painters of the Victorian Scene* (London, 1953), p. 10.

29. *Republican*, Aug. 2, 1882.

30. *Examiner*, Jan. 13, 14, 17, 20, 1894.

31. *In Remembrance of the Midwinter International Exposition, San Francisco, California, 1894* (San Francisco, 1894), [8].

32. For examples, see Mary Bornemann, *Madame Jane Junk and Joe: A Novel. By Oraquill* [pseud.] (San Francisco, 1876); Horra Zon-Tell [D. L. Tracy], *"Parallelograms" from Market Street to Capitol Hill* (Denver, 1899); Rachel Wild Peterson, *The Long-lost Rachel Wild, or, Seeking Diamonds in the Rough* (Denver, 1905); Kate M. Bishop, "A Shepherd at Court," *Overland Monthly* II (October 1883): 359–67, (November 1883): 472–86, (December 1883): 561–74; III (January 1884): 6–16, (February 1884): 113–27, (March 1884): 263–75, (April 1884): 344–56, (May 1884): 461–76, (June 1884): 598–616; IV (July 1884): 59–75; and an illustrated poem, "Denver," by Mary G. Crocker in *The Great Divide* I (January 1894): 21.

33. Biographical sketches are available in the cases of de Young, *DAB* V:283–84, and Bonfils and Tammen, *ibid.* XXI:93–96. The *DAB* has not yet reached Hearst, who died in 1951. For a biography, see W. A. Swanberg, *Citizen Hearst: A Biography of William Randolph Hearst* (New York, 1961).

34. San Francisco *Daily Alta California*, Apr. 29, 1876.

35. "Denver Architecture," Denver *Colorado Exchange Journal* II (October 1889): 25.

36. For an example, see the opening editorial in the first number of a new Denver magazine, *The Great Divide* I (March 1889): 6.

37. *Rocky Mountain News*, Aug. 22, 23, 24, 1882.

38. *Rocky Mountain News*, Aug. 28, 30, 31, Sept. 3, 4, 7, 8, 9, 10, 14, 17, 1882. For similar debates during the San Francisco Midwinter Fair, see *Examiner*, Jan. 4, 5, 6, 7, 8, 9, 11, 12, 13, 14, 1894; San Francisco *Chronicle*, Jan. 27, 28, 29, 30, 31, February 1, 2, 3, 4, 5, 6, 1894. Marlene Keller directed my attention to the incident in San Francisco.

39. San Francisco *Call*, June 4, 11, 20, 1893. For a biographical sketch of Clara Shortridge Foltz, see Edward T. James (ed.), *Notable American Women, 1607–1950: A Biographical Dictionary*, 3 vols. (Cambridge, Mass., 1971) I:641–43.

40. *Call*, June 11, 1893.

41. *Ibid.*, June 21, 22, 1893, Jan. 28, 1894.

42. *Ibid.*, Aug. 25, 1893.

43. "Denver Architecture," Denver *Times*, Apr. 15, 1873.

44. Smiley, *History of Denver*, pp. 465, 965.

45. John S. Hittell, "Art Beginnings in San Francisco," *Pacific Monthly* X (July 1863): 101–2; Benjamin P. Avery, "Art Beginnings on the Pacific," *Overland Monthly* I (July 1868): 30, (August 1868): 113–19; "Famous Pictures Owned on the West Coast," *ibid.* XXII (January 1893): 2–3, (February 1893): 144–45, (March 1893): 286–87, (April 1893): 400–402, (May 1893): 504–5, (June 1893): 600–601, (July 1893): 78–80, (August 1893): 135–37, (September 1893): 239–41, (October 1893): 360–61 (November 1893): 496–97, (December 1893): 634–35; XXIII (January 1894): 84–85, (February 1894): 174–75; Genevieve L. Browne, "Masterpieces of the Pacific Coast," *Californian Illustrated Magazine* III (April 1893): 600–8.

46. Thomas F. Dawson, "Colorado's First Woman School Teacher," *Colorado Magazine* VI (July 1929): 130; William Newton Byers, "Bierstadt's Visit to Colorado," *Magazine of Western History*, XI (January 1890): 237–40.

47. "Early 'Frisco Reminiscences.—LI," San Francisco *News Letter and Daily Advertiser*, July 20, 1889, p. 12.

48. *Republican*, Dec. 31, 1881.

49. *Harper's Weekly*, May 27, 1882, pp. 333–34.

50. Flora Ellice Stevens, "Molecules from the Denver Mining Exposition," *Kansas City Review of Science and Industry* VI (August 1882): 249. See also, Rossiter W. Raymond, "A National Mining Exposition," *Engineering and Mining Journal* XXXI (Apr. 16, 1881): 263.

51. *Republican*, August 2, 1882. Actually, the Exposition Building was torn down within a few years. After its great moment in 1882, the following two years brought attempts to repeat the success, but the Exposition of 1884 had to resort to a "Great Dog Show Feature," races, and parades to avoid outright fiasco. *Rocky Mountain News*, Sept. 4, 1884.

52. *Daily Alta California*, May 25, 1860.

53. Hubert Howe Bancroft, *Literary Industries* (San Francisco, 1890), p. 17.

54. Charles Harrington, *Summering in Colorado* (Denver, 1874), p. 13.

55. Junius, "Atlanta's Exposition," *Republican*, Jan. 20, 1882. For the Atlanta fair, see "The Cotton Exposition of 1881," in Walter G. Cooper, *Official History of Fulton County* (Atlanta, 1934), pp. 301–4.

56. *Republican*, Dec. 31, 1881, Jan. 25, 1882; Ivan D. Steen, "America's First World's Fair; The Exhibition of the Industry of All Nations at New York's Crystal Palace, 1853–1854," *New York Historical Society Quarterly* XLVII (July 1963): 258, 261.

57. *Republican*, Jan. 5, 1882.

58. *Call*, June 3, 6, 10, 11, 1893; *Chronicle*, June 7, 8, 1893.

59. Gunther Barth, "Metropolism and Urban Elites in the Far West," in Frederic C. Jaher (ed.), *The Age of Industrialism in America: Essays in Social Structure and Cultural Values* (New York, 1968), pp. 159–60.

60. Ann W. Hafen and LeRoy R. Hafen, "The Beginnings of Denver University," *Colorado Magazine* XXIV (March 1947): 58. For a biographical sketch, see *DAB* VI:204–5.

61. M. H. de Young, "The Columbia World's Fair," *Cosmopolitan* XII (March 1892): 599–611; de Young, "Benefits of the Midwinter Exposition," *Californian Illustrated Magazine* V (March 1894): 393–95; "Our World's Fair," *News Letter*, June 3, 1893, p. 3.

62. Edgar C. McMechen, "Literature and the Arts," James H. Barker (ed.), *History of Colorado*, 5 vols. (Denver, 1927), III: 1258; Robert L. Perkin, *The First Hundred Years: An Informal History of Denver and the Rocky Mountain News* (Garden City, 1959), p. 357. "Tabor and the Painting of Shakespeare's Profile," an appendix in Elmer S. Crowley, "The History of the Tabor Grand Opera House, Denver, Colorado, 1881–1891" (M.A. thesis, University of Denver, 1940), pp. 244–45, explodes the fallacious story.

63. Charles Hirschfeld, "America on Exhibition: The New York Crystal Palace," *American Quarterly* IX (Summer 1957): 102.

64. *Republican*, January 19, 29, Feb. 1, 8, 1882.

65. *Rocky Mountain News*, May 3, Aug. 4, 13, 1882.

66. Lewis Cass Gandy, *The Tabors: A Footnote of Western History* (New York, 1934), pp. 215–18. For some of the most vitriolic comments against de Young turn to *Arthur McEwen's Letter*, Feb. 17, 1894, pp. 2–4; Mar. 3, 1894, p. 2; Mar. 10, 1894, pp. 3–4; Mar. 24, 1894, p. 4; Oct. 20, 1894, p. 1; Nov. 3, 1894, p. 2; Jan. 5, 1895, pp. 2–3; Jan. 12, 1895, pp. 1–2; Jan. 26, 1895, pp. 1–2.

67. *Midwinter Steal*, May 25, 1894, pp. 1–4; San Francisco *Wave*, Oct. 21, 1893, cover (portrait of de Young as Napoleon); Jan. 6, 1894, p. 4, Jan. 13, 1894, p. 7; "De Young and the Fair," *News Letter*, Aug. 5, 1893, p. 3; Frederick Beecher Perkins, *Mike* (San Francisco, 1891).

68. *Rocky Mountain News*, Aug. 9, 1882.

69. *Ibid.*, Aug. 4, 9, 13, 14, 15, 16, 17, 18, 23, 26, 28, Sept. 1, 23, Oct. 1, 1882; *Republican*, July 22, Aug. 2, 1882.

70. *Republican*, July 22, Aug. 2, Oct. 2, 1882; *Rocky Mountain News*, Aug. 4, 13, 20, 23, 28, Sept. 1, 8, 9, 1882.

71. Benjamin E. Lloyd, *Lights and Shades in San Francisco* (San Francisco, 1876), p. 31; Ernest C. Peixotto, "Architecture in San Francisco," *Overland Monthly* XXI (May 1893): 460–61.

72. "Colorado as Seen by a Visitor of 1880. Diary of Rezin H. Constant," *Colorado Magazine* XII (May 1935): 108, 109; Smiley, *History of Denver*, p. 427; Louisa Ward Arps, *Denver in Slices* (Denver, 1959), p. 17.

73. Views of these mansions can be found frequently, but the glass negatives of photographs of the outside *and* inside of Leland Stanford's residence in San Francisco, taken by Eadweard Muybridge in the 1870s, are something special. They are in the Stanford Museum; copy negatives of nine are in the University Archives of the Stanford University Libraries. Prints of them were generously placed at my disposal by the University Archivist, Ralph W. Hansen.

74. J. B. Burr and Hyde (publ.), *The Great Industries of the United States: Being an Historical Summary of the Origin, Growth, and Perfection of the Chief Industrial Arts of this Country* (Hartford, 1873), pp. 515–20.

75. Frederick Law Olmsted, "Public Parks and the Enlargement of Towns," *Journal of Social Science* III (1871): 1.

76. *Overland Monthly* IV (June 1870): 576; Socrates Hyacinth, "A Flock of Wool," *ibid.* (February 1870): 143.

77. Olmsted, Vaux & Co., *Preliminary Report in Regard to a Plan of Public Pleasure Grounds for the City of San Francisco* (New York, 1866), p. 17.

78. Smiley, *History of Denver*, p. 645.

79. *Rocky Mountain News*, Sept. 20, Oct. 10, 1882; *Harper's Weekly*, May 27, 1882, p. 334.

80. *News Letter*, Aug. 29, 1874, p. 8; San Francisco *Evening Post*, August 22, 1879; Olmsted, Vaux & Co., *Public Pleasure Grounds for San Francisco*.

81. Caroline Lawrence Dier, *The Lady of the Gardens: Mary Elitch Long* (Hollywood, 1932), p. 24; Smiley, *History of Denver*, p. 908.

82. Santa Rosa *Democrat*, quoted in Works Progress Administration, Writers'
Program, *San Francisco: The Bay and Its Cities* (New York, 2nd ed., 1947),
p. 329.

83. *Call*, July 10, 15, 17, Aug. 17, 25, 1893.

84. W. C. Bartlett, "A Breeze from the Woods," *Overland Monthly* I (July 1868): 9.

85. "Etc.," *ibid.* I (August 1868): 190.

86. Seth B. Bradley, "The Origin of the Denver Mountain Parks System," *Colorado
Magazine* IX (January 1932): 26–29.

87. "Daily Life in Denver," *Daily Graphic*, Nov. 29, 1878; *Rocky Mountain News*,
Sept. 13, 23, 26, 1882.

88. *Rocky Mountain News*, Aug. 16, 1882.

89. *Ibid.*, Sept. 26, 1882.

90. *Ibid.*, Sept. 29, 30, 1882.

91. *Rocky Mountain News*, Sept. 23, 24, 1882. Few facts about John Taylor seem to
have been preserved. For a reference to him as a participant in the White River
Canyon Fight of 1884, see Wilson Rockwell, *The Utes: A Forgotten People*
(Denver, 1956), p. 227.

92. Margaret I. Carrington, *Ab-Sa-Ra-Ka, Home of the Crows: Being the Experience
of an Officer's Wife on the Plains* (Philadelphia, 1868), p. 131. For details on
James P. Beckwourth see above, Chapter IV: 115–17.

93. James Mooney, "The Ghost-Dance Religion and the Sioux Outbreak of 1890,"
*Fourteenth Annual Report of the Bureau of Ethnology to the Secretary of the
Smithsonian Institution, 1892–93* (Washington, 1896), pp. 767, 927. See also,
the abridged reprint, Mooney, *The Ghost-Dance Religion and the Sioux
Outbreak of 1890* (Chicago, 1965), p. 200. For Wovoka, see Grace Dangberg,
"Wovoka," *Nevada Historical Society Quarterly* XI (Summer 1968): 5–53.

94. *Official Guide to the California Midwinter International Exposition* (San
Francisco, 1893), p. 13.

95. *The San Francisco Midwinter Appeal and Journal of Forty-nine* was published
from January 7, 1894, to June 30, 1894. The Henry E. Huntington Library and
Art Gallery, San Marino, California, graciously allowed me to make a copy of
their complete file.

96. Samuel Clemens, "In the Metropolis," San Francisco *Golden Era*, June 26,
1864, p. 4. For a reprint, see Bernard Taper (ed.), *Mark Twain's San Francisco*
(New York, 1963), pp. 41–43; *News Letter*, Nov. 5, 1870, p. 16.

97. *Official History of the California Midwinter International Exposition*, p. 152.

98. *Call*, May 5, 1893. For a biographical sketch of Pio Pico, see Zoeth Skinner
Eldredge, *The Beginnings of San Francisco*, 2 vols. (San Francisco, 1912), I:
358–64.

99. John S. Hittell, *A History of the City of San Francisco and Incidentally of the
State of California* (San Francisco, 1878), p. 5.

100. O. L. Baskin & Co., "Preface," in Vickers, *History of the City of Denver*, p. iii.

101. *Call*, Nov. 23, Dec. 9, 1893. Colonel J. D. Stevenson, another "old San
Franciscan," died on February 14, 1894. *Ibid.*, Feb. 15, 1895.

102. James A. B. Scherer, *"The Lion of the Vigilantes": William T. Coleman and the*

*Life of Old San Francisco* (New York, 1939), pp. 95–127; John Myers Myers, *San Francisco's Reign of Terror* (Garden City, New York, 1966), pp. 270–83; John Walton Caughey, *Hubert Howe Bancroft: Historian of the West* (Berkeley, 1946), pp. 182–200.

103.   William T. Coleman, "San Francisco Vigilance Committees. By the Chairman of the Committees of 1851, 1856, and 1877," *Century Magazine* XLIII (November 1891): 133–50; "Sherman and the San Francisco Vigilantes. Unpublished Letters of General W. T. Sherman," *ibid.* XLIII (December 1891): 296–309.

104.   *Rocky Mountain News*, Aug. 2, Oct. 1, 1882.

105.   *Republican*, Aug. 28, 30, 1882; *Rocky Mountain News*, Aug. 28, 30, 1882; Smiley, *History of Denver*, pp. 216–18. For a biographical sketch of James W. Denver, see *DAB* V:242–44.

106.   For biographies of William Gilpin, see Hubert Howe Bancroft, *History of the Life of William Gilpin: A Character Study* (San Francisco, 1889), practically identical with the major portion of Hubert Howe Bancroft, *Chronicles of the Builders of the Commonwealth*, 7 vols. and Index (San Francisco, 1891), I: chapter VIII; Thomas L. Karnes, *William Gilpin: Western Nationalist* (Austin, 1970); *DAB* VII:316–17. Several essays discuss specific aspects of Gilpin; as politician, Maurice O. Georges, "A Suggested Revision of the Role of a Pioneer Political Scientist," *Reed College Bulletin* XXV (April 1947): 67–83; J. Christopher Schnell, "William Gilpin: Advocate of Expansion," *Montana Magazine of Western History* XIX (Summer 1969): 30–37; as territorial governor, "Sheldon Stanley Zweig, William Gilpin: First Territorial Governor of Colorado" (M.A. thesis, University of Colorado, 1950); Zweig, "The Civil Administration of Governor William Gilpin," *Colorado Magazine* XXXI (July 1954): 179–93; as promoter, James C. Malin, "William Gilpin," *The Grassland of North America: Prolegomena to Its History* (Lawrence, Kansas, 1947), pp. 173–92; Charles N. Glaab, "Visions of Metropolis: William Gilpin and Theories of City Growth in the American West," *Wisconsin Magazine of History* XLV (Autumn 1961): 21–31; Schnell, "William Gilpin and the Destruction of the Desert Myth," *Colorado Magazine* XLVI (Spring 1969): 131–44; as iconoclast, Kenneth W. Porter, "William Gilpin: Sinophile and Eccentric," *ibid.* XXXVII (October 1960): 245–53.

107.   *Rocky Mountain News*, Sept. 17, 1882.

108.   William Gilpin, *Notes on Colorado; and Its Inscription in the Physical Geography of the North American Continent* (London, 1870), p. 32; Gilpin, *The Cosmopolitan Railway: Compacting and Fusing Together All the World's Continents* (San Francisco, 1890), pp. 235, 285. Clarence S. Jackson, "My Recollections of William Gilpin," *Colorado Magazine* XXVI (July 1949): 237.

109.   *Rocky Mountain News*, Sept. 17, 1882; Helen Cannon, "First Ladies of Colorado—Julia Pratte Gilpin (Governor William Gilpin, 1861–1862)," *Colorado Magazine* XXXVIII (October 1961): 271–74; Karnes, *Gilpin*, p. 332.

110.   "Fine Arts in Denver," Denver *Times*, Oct. 15, 1872.

111.   For links between the Denver Exposition of 1882 and the land schemes of the Circle Railroad Company, see *Republican*, Feb. 9, Aug. 2, 1882.

112. *Daily Alta California*, Nov. 23, 1884.
113. For photos of Selby's Shot Tower, see "Telegraph Hill—From First Street, Rincon Hill," Picture Drawer (Bancroft Library), No. 15185, Hills Collection of Photos of San Francisco (Bancroft Library), No. 7031, Wyland Stanley Collection of San Francisco Photos (Bancroft Library), No. 5278 (18); for Denver's Old Mint, see Smiley, *History of Denver*, p. 560.

CHAPTER 8

1. "Etc.," *Overland Monthly* VIII (May 1872): 474. For details, see Martyn J. Bowden, "The Dynamics of City Growth: An Historical Geography of the San Francisco Central District, 1850–1931" (Ph.D. thesis, University of California, Berkeley, 1967); Mellier G. Scott, *The San Francisco Bay Area: A Metropolis in Perspective* (Berkeley, 1959); and Jerome C. Smiley, *History of Denver: With Outlines of the Earlier History of the Rocky Mountain Country* (Denver, 1901).
2. "Wages. The Rewards of Labor in San Francisco. A Glance into Our Manufactories and Work-Shops," San Francisco *Call*, May 4, 1873; Andrew S. Hallidie, "Manufacturing in San Francisco," *Overland Monthly* XI (June 1888): 636–37; W. B. Vickers, *History of the City of Denver, Arapahoe County, and Colorado* (Chicago, 1880), pp. 180, 219, 221.
3. San Francisco *Examiner*, July 20, 1888. For a history of the *Charleston* project turn to Ruth Teiser, "The Charleston: an Industrial Milestone," *California Historical Quarterly* XXV (March 1946): 39–53. Denver *Colorado Exchange Journal* II (October 1889): 14. A list of Colorado smelters with their year of incorporation can be found in Richard A. Ronzio, "Colorado Smelting and Reduction Works," Denver Westerners, *1966 Brand Book* (Denver, 1967), pp. 117–43.
4. Frank Soulé, John H. Gihon, and James Nisbet, *Annals of San Francisco* (New York, 1855), pp. 291–93, 359.
5. William T. Sherman, *Memoirs*, 2 vols. in one (Bloomington, 1957), p. 56.
6. *Annals of San Francisco*, p. 293.
7. Ida Pfeiffer, *A Lady's Second Journey Round the World: From London to the Cape of Good Hope, Borneo, Java, Sumatra, Celebes, Ceram, the Moluccas, etc., California, Panama, Peru, Ecuador, and the United States*, 2 vols. (London, 1855), II, 51–52; also available as Joseph A. Sullivan (ed.), *A Lady's Visit to California, 1853* (Oakland, 1950), p. 11.
8. Bruno Fritzsche, "San Francisco 1846–1848: The Coming of the Land Speculator," *California Historical Quarterly* LI (Spring 1972): 25.
9. San Francisco *Bulletin*, May 1, 1860; Lamberta Margarette Voget, "The Waterfront of San Francisco: 1863–1930; A History of Its Administration by the State of California" (Ph.D. thesis, University of California, Berkeley, 1943), 10–21. For a colorful account, see William Martin Camp, *San Francisco, Port of Gold* (Garden City, New York, 1948), pp. 104–21.

10. I have benefited from the comments on the gridiron system by Montgomery Schuyler, "The Art of City-Making," *Architectural Record* XII (May 1902): 1–4. For the survey of San Francisco in 1847 by Jasper O'Farrell, see Geoffrey P. Mawn, "Framework for Destiny: San Francisco, 1847," *California Historical Quarterly* LI (Summer 1972): 165–78.

11. James D. Hart (ed.), *From Scotland to Silverado. By Robert Louis Stevenson* (Cambridge, 1966), p. 146; Olmstead, Vaux, & Co., *Preliminary Report in Regard to a Plan of Public Pleasure Grounds for the City of San Francisco* (New York, 1866), pp. 30–31; Samuel Bowles, *Our New West. Records of Travel between the Mississippi and the Pacific Ocean* (Hartford, 1869), pp. 335–36; Lewis Mumford, "The Sky Line: Not Yet Too Late," *New Yorker* XXXIX (Dec. 7, 1963): 147.

12. Smiley, *History of Denver*, pp. 368, 371–73; George D. Wakely, "Denver's Cherry Creek on a Rampage," U.S. Library of Congress, *Image of America: Early Photography, 1839–1900; A Catalog* (Washington, 1957), pp. 34–35. The most grandiose account of the flood of 1864 came from the versatile pen of O. J. Goldrick. It appeared originally in the Denver *Commonwealth*, May 24, 1864, and has been reprinted in Junius E. Wharton, *History of the City of Denver, From Its Earliest Settlement to the Present Time* (Denver, 1866), pp. 121–43, and in Levette Jay Davidson and Prudence Bostwick (eds.), *The Literature of the Rocky Mountain West, 1803–1903* (Caldwell, Idaho, 1939), pp. 337–42.

13. William Gilpin, *The Central Gold Region: The Grain, Pastoral, and Gold Regions of North America with Some New Views of Its Physical Geography; and Observations on the Pacific Railroad* (Philadelphia 1860), pp. 115–17, 127, 143; William Gilpin to William Seward, Jan. 28, 1862, 37 Cong., 2 Sess., *House Ex. Doc. No. 56*, p. 1; Gilpin, *Notes on Colorado; And Its Inscription in the Physical Geography of the North American Continent* (London, 1870), pp. 33, 45, 47.

14. Denver *Rocky Mountain News*, May 17, 1862.

15. Carol Gendler, "Territorial Omaha as a Staging and Freighting Center," *Nebraska History* XLIX (Summer 1968): 108–10; LeRoy R. Hafen, *The Overland Mail, 1849–1869: Promoter of Settlement, Precursor of Railroads* (Cleveland, 1926), pp. 159–60; James Vincent Frederick, *Ben Holladay: The Stage Coach King: A Chapter in the Development of Transcontinental Transportation* (Glendale, California, 1940), p. 140.

16. Hafen, *Overland Mail*, p. 327.

17. Gendler, "Omaha as Freighting Center," *Nebraska History* XLIX (Summer 1968), 115–16; H. T. Clarke, "Freighting—Denver and Black Hills," *Proceedings and Collections of the Nebraska State Historical Society, Second Series* V (1902): 300; Oscar Osburn Winther, *The Transportation Frontier: Trans-Mississippi West, 1865–1890* (New York, 1964), pp. 25–28.

18. Ferdinand Vandiveer Hayden, *Seventh Annual Report of the United States Geological and Geographical Survey of the Territories, Embracing Colorado, Being a Report of Progress of the Exploration for the Year 1873* (Washington, 1874), p. 85.

19. Alan H. Grey, "Denver and the Locating of the Union Pacific Railroad, 1862–1866," *Rocky Mountain Social Science Journal* VI (October 1969): 59.

20. Denver *Rocky Mountain Herald*, April 23, June 18, 1869; A. J. Flynn, "The Moffat Tunnel," *Colorado Magazine* I (November 1923): 40–41; S. D. Mock, "The Financing of Early Colorado Railroads," *ibid.* XVIII (November 1941): 201–9; Thomas J. Noel, "All Hail the Denver Pacific: Denver's First Railroad," *ibid.* L (Spring 1973): 91–116; Smiley, *History of Denver*, pp. 442, 596; Edgar C. McMechen, *Life of Governor Evans, Second Territorial Governor of Colorado* (Denver, 1924), pp. 163–74; Harry E. Kelsey, Jr., *Frontier Capitalist: The Life of John Evans* (Denver, 1969), pp. 169–80; E. O. Davis, *The First Five Years of the Railroad Era in Colorado* (Denver, 1948), pp. 89–91; George L. Anderson, *Kansas West* (San Marino, California, 1963), p. 63; Robert G. Athearn, *Rebel of the Rockies: A History of the Denver and Rio Grande Western Railroad* (New Haven, 1962), pp. 5, 251–52.

21. Howard Roberts Lamar, *The Far Southwest, 1846–1912: A Territorial History* (New Haven, 1966), pp. 252, 301.

22. Richard C. Overton, *Gulf to Rockies: The Heritage of the Fort Worth and Denver-Colorado and Southern Railways, 1861–1898* (Austin, 1953), p. 14.

23. Denver Board of Trade, *The Manufacturing and Commercial Industries of Denver, Colorado, Together with the Mineral Statistics of the State* (Denver, 1882), p. 10.

24. Overton, *Gulf to the Rockies*, pp. 14–24; Herbert O. Brayer, "History of Colorado Railroads," in LeRoy R. Hafen (ed.), *Colorado and Its People: A Narrative and Topical History of the Centennial State*, 4 vols. (New York, 1948), II:635–77.

25. Denver Dry Goods Co., "Denver as a Manufacturing Centre," *Denver by Pen and Picture* (Denver, 1899), p. 8; Smiley, *History of Denver*, p. 480; Robert L. Perkin, *The First Hundred Years: An Informal History of Denver and the Rocky Mountain News* (Garden City, 1959), pp. 358–59; Alvin T. Steindel, *History of Agriculture in Colorado* (Fort Collins, 1926), p. 322.

26. Frank Hall, *History of the State of Colorado*, 4 vols. (Chicago, 1889–95), II:449–51; *Rocky Mountain News*, Feb. 1, 12, 16, 1878; Smiley, *History of Denver*, pp. 551–54; Carroll D. Wright, *A Report on Labor Disturbances in the State of Colorado from 1880–1904* (Washington, 1905), pp. 73–74; Frank E. Shephard, "Industrial Development in Colorado," in James H. Baker (ed.), *History of Colorado*, 5 vols. (Denver, 1927), II: 701–4; Jesse D. Hale, "The First Successful Smelter in Colorado," *Colorado Magazine* XIII (September 1936): 161–67; Don L. Griswold and Jean Harvey Griswold, *The Carbonate Camp Called Leadville* (Denver, 1951), pp. 63–66, 69, 178–99, 240.

27. H. S. Reed & Co., *The Leading Industries of the West: Denver, the "Magic City of the Plains"* (Chicago, 1883), pp. 10, 26.

28. San Francisco *News Letter and California Advertiser*, Mar. 23, 1867, p. 9; Apr. 6, 1867, p. 4; Apr. 13, 1867, p. 4; May 18, 1867, p. 4; Jan. 11, 1868, p. 8; Feb. 8, 1868, p. 8; Mar. 7, 1868, p. 8; Apr. 4, 1868, p. 8; Apr. 18, 1868, p. 8; *San Francisco Real Estate Circular* I (October 1867): 4; II (February 1868): 3; (May 1868): 1; (June 1868): 4; (July, 1868): 1; (October 1868): 1; III (November 1868): 3; (May 1869): 4; Bret Harte, "Etc.," *Overland Monthly* I (July 1868): 99–100.

29. *San Francisco Real Estate Circular* I (December 1866): 4; "Table Showing the Total Sale of Real Estate Made in all Sections of the City and County during the year 1870; also the Total Sales made during the years 1869, 1868, 1867, and 1866," *ibid.* V (December 1870): 2; *News Letter*, Sept. 11, 1869, p. 4; Louis Richard Miller, "The History of the San Francisco and San Jose Railroad" (M.A. thesis, University of California, Berkeley, 1947), 68; Stuart Daggett, *Chapters on the History of the Southern Pacific* (New York 1922), pp. 94–100.

30. San Francisco *Call*, May 5, 23, June 7, Dec. 7, 1869.

31. Gunther Barth, "Metropolism and Urban Elites in the Far West," in Frederic C. Jaher (ed.), *The Age of Industrialism in America: Essays in Social Structure and Cultural Values* (New York, 1968), pp. 164–66. My work on Rincon Hill gained from Albert Shumate's insights into the history of San Francisco and his *Visit to Rincon Hill and South Park* (San Francisco, 1963). Dr. Shumate also owns Fortunato Arriola's painting, *Howard Street by Night*, which has captured the spirit of the early center of urban life; a reproduction of the painting can be found in Lucius Beebe and Charles Clegg, *San Francisco's Golden Era: A Picture Story of San Francisco Before the Fire* (Berkeley, 1960), p. 121.

32. *News Letter*, Mar. 23, 1867, p. 9; Apr. 6, 1867, p. 4; July 27, 1867, p. 5; Dec. 7, 1867, p. 6; Feb. 8, 1868, p. 8; Mar. 7, 1868, p. 8; Aug. 15, 1868, p. 16; Oct. 31, 1868, p. 9; Jan. 16, 1869, p. 8; Aug. 7, 1869, p. 18.

33. Henry George, "What the Railroad Will Bring Us," *Overland Monthly* I (October 1868): 298, 300.

34. *San Francisco Municipal Reports, 1871–72*, p. 616.

35. San Francisco *Daily Alta California*, Mar. 2, Apr. 8, 16, 1851; Gordon C. Roadarmel (comp.), "Some California Dates of 1860," *California Historical Quarterly* XXXVIII (December 1959): 333; Gerald M. Best, "San Francisco Locomotives," *Western Railroader* XXXIII (June 1970): 3; John H. White, Jr., "The Railroad Reaches California: Men, Machines, and Cultural Migration," *California Historical Quarterly* LII (Summer 1973): 136.

36. *Bulletin*, Oct. 25, 1861; Robert Luther Thompson, *Wiring a Continent: The History of the Telegraph Industry in the United States, 1832–1866* (Princeton, 1947), p. 370.

37. George, "Railroad," *Overland Monthly* I (October 1868): 299; Benjamin E. Lloyd, "Steamer-Day," *Lights and Shades in San Francisco* (San Francisco, 1876), pp. 519–23.

38. Smiley, *History of Denver*, p. 465.

39. Kenneth M. Johnson, *The Sting of the Wasp: Political & Satirical Cartoons from the Truculent Early San Francisco Weekly* (San Francisco, 1967), p. 4.

40. For the San Francisco press, see Ella Sterling Mighels, *The Story of the Files: A Review of Californian Writers and Literature* (San Francisco, 1893); John P. Young, *Journalism in California* (San Francisco, 1915; Federal Writers Project, Works Progress Administration, *History of Journalism in San Francisco*, 20 vols. (San Francisco, 1940). For Denver, see Douglas C. McMurtrie and Albert H. Allen, *Early Printing in Colorado* (Denver, 1935); Gene Fowler, *Timber Line: A Story of Bonfils and Tammen* (Garden City, 1933); and Perkin, *First Hundred*

*Years.* An early scholarly discussion of the new journalism is W. I. Thomas, "The Psychology of the Yellow Journal," *American Magazine* LXV (March 1908): 491–97; a good recent monograph, George Juergens, *Joseph Pulitzer and the New York World* (Princeton, 1966).

41. *Daily Alta California,* Mar. 11, 18, 25, 31, Apr. 5, 1870; San Francisco *Chronicle,* Mar. 25, 1870; *Call,* Mar. 30, 1870; Sacramento *Union,* Mar. 31, Apr. 2, 1870; *San Francisco Real Estate Circular* V (May 1871): 3. A discussion of some of the real estate schemes can be found in Asbury Harpending, *The Great Diamond Hoax and Other Stirring Incidents in the Life of Asbury Harpending* (San Francisco, 1913), pp. 146–58; Bowden, "Dynamics of City Growth," 275–333. For the old city hall, see "Old City Hall Building," *San Francisco Municipal Reports, 1894–95,* pp. 318–27; for the new city hall the weekly illustration of the *News Letter,* September 26, 1896, and "The Completed Rotunda," *ibid.,* July 10, 1897, pp. 20–21; "A Grand Dedication," *ibid.,* July 17, 1897, p. 5.

42. Denver *Republican,* Feb. 1, 1882.

43. *Republican,* Feb. 1, 8, 9, Aug. 1, 2, 1882; *Rocky Mountain News,* Aug. 16, 1882; Smiley, *History of Denver,* p. 615; Perkin, *First Hundred Years,* p. 337.

44. *Republican,* Aug. 2, 1882.

45. "Review of Transit Development in San Francisco," in Bion J. Arnold, *Report on the Improvement and Development of the Transportation Facilities in San Francisco* (San Francisco, 1913), pp. 411–12, 414.

46. George Rogers Taylor, "The Beginning of Mass Transportation in Urban America, Part II," *Smithsonian Journal of History* I (Fall 1966): 36, 39, 43, 49.

47. "Transit Development," in Arnold, *Report on Transportation Facilities,* pp. 411–12.

48. "Street Railroads," in *San Francisco City Directory 1875,* p. 20.

49. *Ibid.*

50. W. T. Bergtold, "Denver Fifty Years Ago," *Colorado Magazine* VIII (March 1931): 70.

51. John Rolfe Burroughs, "As It Was in the Beginning," *ibid.* XLVI (Summer 1969): 188; Smiley, *History of Denver,* p. 854.

52. Smiley, *History of Denver,* pp. 854–55. See also, "Beginning of Denver's Street Car System," Denver *Sun,* Dec. 27, 1891.

53. F. S. Woodbury, "The Electric Light," *Tourists' Guide Book to Denver, 1882* (Denver, 1882), p. 47.

54. "Transit Development," in Arnold, *Report on Transportation Facilities,* pp. 412, 414.

55. Edgar Myron Kahn, "Andrew Smith Hallidie," *California Historical Quarterly* XIX (June 1940): 148–50. For a biography of Hallidie, see *DAB* VIII:156.

56. George W. Hilton, "Denver's Cable Railways," *Colorado Magazine* XLIV (Winter 1967): 36.

57. LeRoy R. Hafen, "The Coming of the Automobile and Improved Roads to Colorado," *ibid.* VIII (January 1931): 1–2.

58. For a biography of Sidney H. Short, see *DAB* XVII:128; for Frank J. Sprague, see *ibid.* XXI:669–70.

59. Joseph Emerson Smith, "Personal Recollections of Early Denver," *Colorado Magazine* XX (March 1943): 66.

60. Bergtold, "Denver," *ibid.* VIII (March 1931): 70. See also "Electric Street Railway," in Frank Hall (comp.), *Fourth Annual Report of the Denver Chamber of Commerce and Board of Trade, Denver Colorado. For the Year Ended December 31st, 1886* (Denver, 1887), pp. 25–26. For illustrations, see William C. Jones, F. Hol Wagner, Jr., and Gene C. McKeever, *Mile-high Trolleys: A Nostalgic Look at Denver in the Era of the Streetcars* (Denver, 1965), p. 12. Frank J. Sprague, "The Electric Railway. First Paper: A Resume of the Early Experiments," *Century Magazine* LXX (July 1905): 434–51, and "The Electric Railway. Second Paper: Later Experiments and Present State of the Art," *ibid.* (August 1905): 512–27, provide perspective.

61. Woodbury, "The Electric Light," *Tourists' Guide Book to Denver, 1882,* pp. 46–47.

62. Smiley, *History of Denver,* pp. 856–61.

63. Howard T. Vaille, "Early Years of the Telephone in Colorado," *Colorado Magazine* V (August 1928): 123; John P. Young, *San Francisco: A History of the Pacific Coast Metropolis,* 2 vols. (San Francisco, 1913), II:583.

64. Vaille, "Telephone," *Colorado Magazine* V (August 1928): 129.

65. "A Bare-faced Swindle," *News Letter,* Jan. 7, 1882, p. 3.

66. Belle Cassidy, "Recollections of Early Denver," *Colorado Magazine* XXIX (January 1952): 56.

67. Vaille, "Telephone," *ibid.* V (August 1928): 129.

68. "Annual Address, at the Opening of the San Francisco Mechanics' Institute Fair, Delivered by James A. Banks," in *Report of the Second Industrial Exhibition of the Mechanics' Institute of the City of San Francisco, Held at the Pavillion of the Institute, From the 2nd to the 26th September, A.D. 1858* (San Francisco, 1859), p. 9; John Burton Phillips, "Freight Rates and Manufactures in Colorado: A Chapter in Economic History," *University of Colorado Studies* VII (December 1909): 12–13.

69. Edward F. Adams, "Financial San Francisco; Its Status as a Center of Banking and Investment," San Francisco *Chronicle,* Dec. 20, 1906, p. 7. My understanding of San Francisco in the first decade of the twentieth century has benefited from conversations with one of my students, Judd Kahn, who probed the decade in his dissertation, "Imperial San Francisco: History of a Vision" (Ph.D. thesis, University of California, Berkeley, 1971).

70. Hafen, "Automobile," *Colorado Magazine* VIII (January 1931): 2–3.

71. F. A. Hyde, "Automobile Club of California," *Overland Monthly* XL (August 1902): 100.

# Index